Invasion USA

ALSO FROM DAVID J. HOGAN

Edited by David J. Hogan. *Science Fiction America: Essays of SF Cinema* (McFarland, 2006; paperback 2011)

Dark Romance: Sexuality in the Horror Film (McFarland, 1986; paperback 1997)

Invasion USA

*Essays on Anti-Communist Movies
of the 1950s and 1960s*

Edited by David J. Hogan

McFarland & Company, Inc., Publishers
Jefferson, North Carolina

LIBRARY OF CONGRESS CATALOGUING-IN-PUBLICATION DATA

Names: Hogan, David J., 1953– editor.
Title: Invasion USA : essays on anti-communist movies of the 1950s and 1960s / edited by David J. Hogan.
Description: Jefferson, North Carolina : McFarland & Company, Inc., Publishers, 2017 | Includes bibliographical references and index.
Identifiers: LCCN 2017032819 | ISBN 9780786499045 (softcover : acid free paper) ∞
Subjects: LCSH: Motion pictures—Political aspects—United States—History—20th century. | Motion picture industry—Political aspects—United States—History—20th century. | Communism and motion pictures—United States—History. | Anti-communist movements—United States—History—20th century. *?*
Classification: LCC PN1995.9.P6 I68 2017 | DDC 791.43/6581—dc23
LC record available at https://lccn.loc.gov/2017032819

BRITISH LIBRARY CATALOGUING DATA ARE AVAILABLE

ISBN (print) 978-0-7864-9904-5
ISBN (ebook) 978-1-4766-3010-6

© 2017 David J. Hogan. All rights reserved

No part of this book may be reproduced or transmitted in any form or by any means, electronic or mechanical, including photocopying or recording, or by any information storage and retrieval system, without permission in writing from the publisher.

Front cover: Artwork by Anselmo Ballester from the one-sheet poster for the Italian release of the 1952 film *Invasion USA* (author's collection)

Printed in the United States of America

McFarland & Company, Inc., Publishers
Box 611, Jefferson, North Carolina 28640
www.mcfarlandpub.com

For Peggie Castle

In this rarely seen 1952 publicity photo, *Invasion USA* co-star Peggie Castle inspects a miniature Manhattan skyscraper featured in the film's startling atomic-bomb sequence.

Acknowledgments

My gratitude to DTA Collectibles, Florida,
for special image assistance;
Ted Okuda, for facts, useful visuals, and all-around encouragement;
Gary Svehla and Susan Svehla, Midnight Marquee Press,
for editorial help;
Mike Stein, editor-publisher of *Filmfax*, for generosity;
… and the Columbus, Ohio, gang, just for being the best.

Special thanks to this book's contributing writers;
they really care about this stuff, and it shows.

Preliminary work on this collection began some years ago.
The book had to be put aside when other projects demanded my attention; despite that, the contributors were faithful about getting essays to me, and mulling over suggestions I offered after looking
at first drafts. They also have been preternaturally patient during
the long period I needed for the project's final assembly.

My only regret about *Invasion USA* is that one contributor,
Mark A. Miller, passed away before the book's completion.
Mark wasn't simply my best friend, but the best friend of many writers
represented in these pages. We respect Mark's expansive
grasp of film history, and his devotion to conscientious scholarship. His
knowledge and wit enliven *Invasion USA*, and numerous
other books, as well, including two of his own.

Cheers, pal.

Table of Contents

Acknowledgments — vi

Introduction: Communism, Movies and the Big Dance Party — 1
  DAVID J. HOGAN

PART 1: SPACE INVADERS — 11

Target Earth: Politicians from Venus — 13
  JOHN T. SOISTER

Not of This Earth: Myth, Brooks Brothers and Subversion — 21
  DAVID J. HOGAN

The Cold Hands of Strangers: The Politics of Disaster in Eight Invasion Thrillers of the 1950s — 38
  STEVEN THORNTON

PART 2: RED MISCHIEF HERE, THERE AND EVERYWHERE — 59

Happy Trails in Cold War Valley: *Bells of Coronado* and *Spoilers of the Plains* — 61
  TED OKUDA

The Flying Saucer: Top Secret Travelogue — 72
  DAVID J. HOGAN

The Whip Hand: Accidental Template for Fear and Paranoia — 76
  MARK A. MILLER

Artists and Models: The Day the Slobs Saved Democracy — 89
  ERMINE DEGRAFFENRIED

The Girl in the Kremlin: Can a Monster Change Its Face? — 99
  ZSÓFIA BODNÁR-HAMILTON

Atomic Thrillers and the Danger at Home — 106
  ARTHUR JOSEPH LUNDQUIST

Memo to the State Department: Seven Overlooked Cold War Films — 118
  CHASE WINSTEAD

PART 3: DUPES, VICTIMS AND CRUSADERS — 141

Big Brains and Betrayal: *Walk a Crooked Mile* — 143
   BRUCE DETTMAN

Cvetic Takes One for the Team: *I Was a Communist for the F.B.I.* — 149
   BRUCE DETTMAN

American Virtue and *Big Jim McLain* — 157
   GAYE WINSTON LARDNER

Trial: Love in a Time of Communism — 168
   ANTHONY AMBROGIO

The Tears of a Clown: Chaplin's *A King in New York* — 178
   MARK CLARK

Riddle of the Pinks: Did *The Fearmakers* Have *The Whip Hand*? — 187
   REYNOLD HUMPHRIES

PART 4: TOTAL WAR — 201

The End of Civilization and Its Discontents: *Five* and *The World, the Flesh and the Devil*, Two Films of Massive Post-Nuclear Depopulation — 203
   LYNDON W. JOSLIN

Dream of Tyranny: *Invasion USA* — 214
   BRUCE DETTMAN

PART 5: ROT AND RESPONSE — 223

God vs. the Commies: *Red Planet Mars* — 225
   BRYAN SENN

Violent Saturday: The Danger Within Us — 233
   DAVID J. HOGAN

Panic in Year Zero! It's the End of the World as We Know It (and I Feel Fine) — 241
   MARK CLARK

About the Contributors — 251

Index — 253

Introduction
Communism, Movies and the Big Dance Party

DAVID J. HOGAN

Movies are marvelous bellwethers of contemporaneous thinking, so it cannot be a surprise that Hollywood produced a wealth of films during the 1950s and early 1960s that deal with the initial phase of the Cold War, that tensely adversarial geopolitical relationship linking two main players, the United States and the USSR, and both nations' multitudinous allies and satellites. Oh dear, how did *that* happen? Well, the strictly pragmatic wartime alliance of the two became inconvenient at the close of World War II in 1945. Hitler's Germany had been defeated due largely to the efforts of the Red Army, an inexorable force that pummeled Hitler's troops on Soviet soil and then drove all the way to Berlin. But the cost to the USSR was enormous: some twenty million service members and civilians killed, and countless others injured and orphaned, made insensible and homeless. Great swaths of Russian territory—including cities, rail lines and other infrastructure, farmland, and industrial capacity—had been mashed flat, and an entire generation of Soviet men destroyed. Because of the breadth and depth of damage levied by Germany against Russia, and because of the geographical closeness of Western Europe to the Soviet Union and the rest of Eastern Europe, the Soviets became ferociously preoccupied with their security. It is partly from this enhanced—and understandable—Soviet desire for physical safety that the Cold War sprang.

Others reasons had to do with ideology: the West's stated dedication to freedom of movement, thought and expression, free-market economics, and religion lay in opposition to Soviet-style communism that practiced state control not just of markets and economies but of people's minds. Officially atheistic and grounded in the cult of Stalin, postwar Russia, and cat's-paws in its Eastern European satellites, maintained a grip on all aspects of political activity and daily life. To casual observers in the West, day-to-day Soviet existence appeared perpetually gray. To Soviet eyes, the United States and the other Western democracies were sunk in decadent materialism bred by capitalism. Although each side exaggerated the failings of the other, the Soviet Union had good cause to fret about its citizens' exposure to images and artifacts of Western commercial culture, particularly clothing and household goods (one's people must be kept happy at home, and free of envy); and such idea-driven media as books, magazines, radio, and motion pictures. Given that the Soviet economy had been crushed by war, Communist fears of Western prosperity grew particularly acute because the United States emerged from the conflict economically stronger than when it had entered the fight. Further, the USA had ended the Asian war with an atomic bomb, an intimidating new weapon that was (for the short term) an American exclusive.

The Spy Game

Many details of the bomb had come to Russia via espionage carried out in the States by longtime moles, and by "ordinary" citizens (Julius Rosenberg is the most famed early postwar example) who, for reasons ranging from the idealistic to the cynical, allowed themselves to be coaxed into betraying America's security interests. Alger Hiss, a State Department functionary who loudly proclaimed his loyalty, almost surely was a Communist. The trials of Rosenberg and his wife Ethel, Ethel's brother David Greenglass, Klaus Fuchs, Harry Gold and others alarmed Americans and brought out ugly, animalistic anger in many.

The Rosenbergs died in the electric chair—a frankly pitiless punishment that was encouraged by public sentiment. As the Rosenbergs awaited their sentencings, in fact, American servicemen and civilians happily drove through New York City, Washington, D.C., and elsewhere, displaying crudely hand-lettered signs that said "God hates the Rosenbergs" and "Sizzle 'em!" If much of the Cold War sprouted from Soviet concerns about security, another root cause is the fear-driven ugliness (and inevitable anti–Semitism) of the American spirit that drove those amateur sign-makers, and that inspired young Richard Nixon and other cheaply opportunistic "Red bashing" politicians. Highly publicized Red-hunting activities of the House Un-American Activities Committee (HUAC) exploited and heightened American unease, and culminated in that apotheosis of meanness, cruelty, and naked ambition—the drunken junior senator from Wisconsin, Joseph McCarthy.

The Broad Reach of Bad Behavior

Very soon after 1945, America and the USSR hurried to establish their respective spheres of influence. The North Atlantic Treaty Organization (NATO), devised in 1949 by the United States as a guarantor of the safety of its Western European allies (and American interests), frightened Stalin and his successors, who responded with the Warsaw Pact of 1955, which welded Russia and its Eastern European satellites into a formal, military-economic bond. For forty-five years after World War II, the Soviet Union kept a boot on the necks of its own citizens, and on the necks of millions trapped behind what Churchill termed "the Iron Curtain."

In August 1961 the Soviets insisted that German Communist authorities in East Berlin construct a wall separating the Soviet-ruled part of the city from Allied-controlled West Berlin, not to *protect* its citizens in the eastern sector, *but to prevent them from running away*. Not long before, the Soviets had brazenly disregarded the Free World's protests by smashing the Hungarian Revolution of 1956, but the Berlin Wall, a physical verification of the abject failure and moral bankruptcy of communism, especially startled the world and disgusted anyone with a conscience.

In the interests of historical truth, we must note that the USA was not an innocent player in the Cold War drama. To the contrary, America's illegal depredations abroad (or *extralegal*, as some will have it) during the 1940s, '50s, and '60s were brazen and many: manipulation of elections in Italy (1947–48); active support of cold-blooded rightist factions in Greece (1947–49) and South Korea (1945–53); attempts, in concert with Great Britain, to turn Communist Albania to Fascism (1949–53); and the CIA overthrow of a democratically elected government in Guatemala (1953). The U.S. and Britain set in motion the Iranian coup that removed democratically elected nationalist Prime Minister Mossadegh (1953) and returned the autocratic but America-friendly Shah to power. Washington also laid the heavy hand of intimidation on Jordan, Lebanon, and Egypt (1956–58), and tried to foment civil war and assassination in Indonesia (1957–58). Cambodia, British Guiana, and Vietnam also fell prey to American violence and other meddling during the 1950s.

The 1960s brought a considerable expansion of America's intrusion into Vietnam's civil war, and the politics of the rest of Southeast Asia, as well as in Greece (again), Cuba, the Dominican Republic, the Congo, Brazil, Chile, and Indonesia (again). Although outside the time period that is the focus of this book, we will add that from the 1970s until the end of the Cold War in 1991, the United States interfered illegally in the governance of nations in the Middle East, Eastern Europe, the Caribbean, and Central America.

Naturally enough, none of this pleased the Soviets.

Anyone who wanted to dance in those Cold War years needed a partner. The USSR was an ideologically debased criminal regime that killed millions and crushed the spirit of generations. The United States, preoccupied with its global influence and motivated more fiercely by commerce than democracy, employed violence and trickery to shape the world landscape to suit its own interests.

The USSR and the United States: dance partners, glued together, snarling and furious, 1945–91.

The Threat Was Real (No, Really, It Was)

Fully aware of their respective sins, and absorbed with expansionist agendas, campaigns of propaganda, and quick-step development of new weapons systems, the USA and USSR painted each other as evil, unprincipled, avaricious, underhanded, decadent— you name it. Some of the rivalry amounted to mere bluster, as when Soviet Premier Nikita Khrushchev purportedly banged his shoe on his desk at the United Nations in 1960.[1] At other times, though, events and tensions built to unbearable levels. In 1961, U.S. and Soviet tanks came close to firing on each other in contested East Berlin, and a year after that, shortly after American intelligence discovered Soviet missiles in Cuba, the world nearly ended. Yes: *ended*.

At about that same time, I traded with another kid for a ten-year-old paperback called *How to Survive an Atomic Bomb*. I had already seen the movies *Invasion USA* and *Day the World Ended* on television, and so it seemed to me that just about *no one* was going to survive an atomic war, but I wanted the book because I liked science fiction and related things, and because the subtitle intrigued me. It read, "Complete easy-to-read guide for every home, office, and factory." I wondered if the book said anything about schools. Mine was six miles away, on a two-lane highway surrounded by country roads. I wondered how much warning time the teachers would need. And if the warning came,

After more than fifteen years of frayed U.S.–Soviet relations, this purposely shocking compilation of film clips and still photographs tracing a hundred years of communism opened in New York City on October 24, 1962—even as the nearly apocalyptic Cuban Missile Crisis was still unfolding. (Timing is everything.) Few everyday Americans that saw this lurid documentary were inclined to take it lightly.

what would happen next? When an older boy in my neighborhood had been in grade school, he and all his classmates wore dog tags, so that the school could identify everybody after an atomic attack. I wondered whether I needed dog tags.

The dad of a pal who lived one house over told me he'd like to read my copy of *How to Survive an Atomic Bomb*. They never did build a bomb shelter next door, and the only food hoarding I noticed over there involved endless stores of Creamsicles and Charles Chips. When the father returned the book to me, I couldn't tell if he'd taken it seriously, or if he just thought it was funny.

Let us be clear that although this book's main title may suggest a playful tone, not every American holding profound apprehension about communism was on the wrong track. The Communist system, particularly Soviet communism, was inimical to everything America claimed to represent. The Soviets actively worked toward the diminishment or ruin of the United States. The Communist Party USA, bulging first with immigrants and later with members of the intelligentsia, was no idle diversion for hobbyists (though it did attract its share of dilettantes); rather, it was a reasonably focused organization that took funding and direction from Moscow. The Party dedicated itself to the overthrow of the United States government via espionage, subversion, and—if things progressed as some Party members dreamed they might—force. The CPUSA became skilled at managing a layer of high-visibility stooges and functionaries that allowed American authorities to carry out news-making arrests, while the Party effectively shielded its true homegrown leaders.

CPUSA activities naturally roused the interest of the FBI, and although that agency put a damper on a great deal of potentially harmful Party activity in the States, its director, J. Edgar Hoover, pursued many of the Bureau's Communist-related investigations for political reasons, to embarrass rivals and settle old scores, and so that Hoover could claim that communism, and not a Mafia that he insisted was fictional, presented the number-one threat to American law and security.

HUAC Spooks Hollywood

American popular culture, which is perpetually aiming for broad and essentially undiscriminating audiences, reduced American-Soviet antagonism to its simplest elements, represented by pat melodrama, stock characters, and, occasionally, burlesque (recall *The Bullwinkle Show*'s Boris Badenov, or the "I Was a Spy for the F.O.B." episode of *The Many Loves of Dobie Gillis*, in which a beautiful Red agent chases after beatnik Maynard G. Krebs because she's mistaken him for a rocket scientist). Vis-à-vis feature films, much of Hollywood's anti–Communist tone arose as a defense mechanism: spurred by voter anxiety about the Soviet threat, HUAC began to investigate the film industry's Communist faction in 1947, and then returned in 1951 to conduct further snooping. Highly publicized hearings (calculated by committee members to get themselves in the newspapers, newsreels, and on television, thus ensuring re-election and more time at the public teat) caused even the likes of studio chief Jack Warner to sweat while giving testimony. (Warner, for example, was unable to defend his studio's Soviet-friendly 1943 feature, *Mission to Moscow*, because he had made the picture at the request of President Roosevelt, and acceded to FDR's demand that White House involvement never be revealed.)

Committee members reserved special vitriol for smaller fish, particularly leaders of unions with ties to the film industry, and for a wealth of actors, writers, directors, and others suspected of being Communists, or ex–Communists, or of knowing Communists. As has been exhaustively documented in general histories and in memoirs, many Hollywood careers were ruined and lives turned upside down. (Recall, for instance, the unhappy fates of Edward Dmytryk and Dalton Trumbo, as well as the miserable behavior of frightened industry figures who ratted out friends and co-workers.)

Motivated by fear of depleted box office, and egged on by *Red Channels* and other reactionary publications that claimed to "out" industry Communists, Hollywood inaugurated an employment blacklist that inhibited or ended the careers of more than three hundred people. For some, inclusion on the blacklist became a point of pride many years after the fact, but while it was going on, many victims struggled with house payments, groceries, and other elements of everyday life. Threats against the blacklisted were not uncommon. It is from this miasma that the "golden age" of anti–Communist Hollywood films emerged.

The free expression that is a hallmark of American life was only barely at play in early Cold War Hollywood. Bullied by the first foray of HUAC, and then sent reeling by the 1948 U.S. Supreme Court divestiture decision that forced studios to remove themselves from the exhibition business, industry moguls were not eager to anger anybody else. Early postwar labor strife and unemployment were calming, and the studios reasoned that American moviegoers were not likely to tolerate films critical of the U.S. Too, television was sucking people from movie theaters, forcing studios and exhibitors to put out millions to pay for CinemaScope, stereophonic sound, big-budget spectaculars, 3-D, and other innovations calculated to keep the industry in the black. So: how to appease HUAC and attract audiences? You play along. You produce anti–Communist films, in a variety of genres and budgets; with big stars and non-stars; with seriousness or with (very occasionally) tongue in cheek; and with this as the takeaway: America is good, communism is awful.

Sometimes, as in *Target Earth* and *I Married a Monster from Outer Space,* the anti–Communist message is hidden beneath standard-seeming seeming science fiction. *Violent Saturday*, a straight drama ostensibly concerned with a small-town bank robbery, looks at communism obliquely, through the strengths and weaknesses of the townies. Other times, the movies are Roy Rogers B-westerns with anti–Communist messages that zip over the heads of kids but that are plain enough to grownups. Some of the dramas and melodramas—like *I Was a Communist for the F.B.I., Trial,* and *Big Jim McLain*—are blatantly political. The Soviet menace even inspired the Three Stooges and Martin & Lewis to tussle with Reds. In all, Hollywood's anti–Communist movies comprise a kind of variety pack in which the message is always, roughly, the same. The variety is seen in genre and execution.

What to Look for in These Pages

Invasion USA (this book) is the work of sixteen writers represented in twenty-one essays. Within those essays, about forty discrete films are examined. Some are "major" pictures; others were designed for quick play-offs at the bottoms of double bills. For more than thirty-five years, in my introductions to one book after another, I have noted that popular cinema is priceless archaeology. I know I've been repeating myself about that, but it's important because all movies (and *every* creative work, for that matter) are inestimably valuable indicators of culture. If you wish to discover the nature of local societies and the world during a particular period of the past 120 years, look at the movies. And if you hope for a better grasp of what's happening now, go see and then think about films that opened last week. Whatever your period of interest, you'll discern a wealth of cultural messages, spoken and unspoken, big and seemingly small, and all of them consequential.

Contributors to this book were encouraged to select films that intrigue them, films that deserve fresh treatment, or movies that have rarely, if ever, been discussed seriously in any way, let alone in a relevant Cold War context. Variety is almost always good for mental stimulation, so the essays consider works by auteurs as varied as Roger Corman and Charles Chaplin, Arch Oboler and Robert Wise, Frank Tashlin and Robert Aldrich. Big stars are in these pages, too—including Victor Mature, Glenn Ford, George Raft, and John Wayne—along with less-famous personalities—such as Richard Denning, Frank Lovejoy, Peggie Castle, John Agar, Lori Nelson—known mainly to nostalgia buffs and cultists. Like those cultural messages mentioned earlier, every one of these people matters.

Essays are arranged according to general themes noted in the Table of Contents, such as "Red Mischief Here, There and Everywhere," "Dupes, Victims and Crusaders," and "Total War." I briefly considered a straight chronological arrangement, but that's unimaginative, and besides, it adds very little to our understanding of the films or of broader themes that tend to recur.

Each essay concludes with a filmography noting cast, credits, release date, and other information. Filmographies in essays discussing more than one movie appear periodically within the essay, immediately following discussion of discrete films. Authors have also provided source notes.

Stills and advertisement art, many pieces never before published in book form, appear throughout.

Looking Back and Looking Forward

A quarter-century after the 1991 collapse of the Soviet Union, the event remains one of the 20th century's most remarkable developments. Such a circumstance was mightily wished for in the West during the 1950s and 1960s, and yet seemed an impossibility. Even Red China, bellicose and suffering the spasms of Cultural Revolution by the mid–'60s, seemed a far less dangerous adversary than the USSR. For anyone who came of age during the first forty-five years after World War II, the dissolution of the Soviet Union had no peer for pure astonishment value. Not until the 2001 terrorist attacks against the U.S. was there an event that seemed as improbable and surreal.

On the broadest level, the termination of the USSR forced political realignments across the globe. Nations in Eastern Europe lost their sponsor-oppressor, and Russia lost convenient access to those nations' workers, goods, raw materials, transport, and other resources. The United States and other Western nations no longer had an intimidating adversary in Europe; the USSR's disappearance almost seemed anticlimactic. We thought, *Now what?*

8   Introduction

At this writing, Russia's president, former KGB operative Vladimir Putin, presents his nuclear-armed nation as a principal player on the international stage. But the price of oil dropped through the floor after the middle of 2014, and Russia's 2016 Gross Domestic Product landed in twelfth place among all nations, far behind the USA, China, Japan, and Germany, and behind even India, Italy, Brazil, and South Korea. Arizona Senator John McCain's 2014 assessment of Russia as "a gas station masquerading as a country" is glib and unwisely dismissive, but it has a grain of truth.

Despite Russian bluster and its barefaced hack of America's 2016 election machinery, and despite the personality cult surrounding Putin, today's Russia—though potentially dangerous—is a mere shadow of the USSR that so concerned America and the world two generations ago.

Here at home, the Communist Party USA advocates democratic capitalism as a useful step on a presumed road to socialism. Although the group claims between 2,000 and 3,000 members, the true figure is probably considerably smaller.[2] CPUSA has not bothered to field candidates for president and vice president since 1988 (Gus Hall and Angela Davis, respectively), and soldiers on as an irrelevant curiosity. Russia and the United States still trade acts of espionage, of course (long-term professional moles are fielded by each nation), but the kind of domestic Communist threat that informed so many of the movies discussed in these pages no longer exists. We are preoccupied today with religious-based terrorism rather than with Communist ideology and infiltration. We have passed into a new age of strife.

America never was truly innocent—its origins and expansionist history are too steeped in blood and conquest for that—but the Cold War did tire America, teaching us hard lessons about the costs of victory and defeat, and turning American against American, encouraging anti-intellectualism and class-based resentment, and an inexplicable disdain for social safety nets and workers' rights. The figurative fallout of those days led us also to a healthy skepticism about politicians … and a foolish and misplaced distrust of newspapers and other legitimate media. Made tribal by an angry Right and a strident Left, Americans no longer care to hear each other. Our new president has publicly expressed his desire to inaugurate a fresh arms race with Russia, even as he hopes to be a pal to the bloodless leader of that much-diminished but ambitious nation.

All of this intranational and international conflict, the culture wars and political events, will inspire movies, and in thirty or forty years we'll read interesting essays about those films. For now, though, look back at Hollywood's response to America's *first* great postwar challenge.

NOTES

1. No genuine photograph of Khrushchev brandishing a shoe exists; a widely circulated image of the premier gripping his footwear is a fifty-five-year-old fake that inserts a shoe into his upraised fist. Numerous witnesses to the event insist that Khrushchev did bang his shoe, though there is disagreement as to whether Nikita removed the shoe specifically to rap his desk, or if he had taken off both shoes earlier, for comfort, and then, when angered, simply grabbed one out of convenience.
2. Communist Party USA membership peaked at 75,000–85,000, during 1941–45.

WORKS CITED

Books

Hardt, Tom Engel. *The End of Victory Culture: Cold War America and the Disillusioning of a Generation*. New York: BasicBooks, 1995.
Hogan, David J., ed. *The Fifties Chronicle*. Lincolnwood, IL: Legacy Publishing, 2006.

Inglis, Fred. *The Cruel Peace: Everyday Life and the Cold War*. New York: BasicBooks, 1991.
Isaacs, Jeremy, and Taylor Downing. *Cold War: An Illustrated History, 1945–1991*. Boston: Little, Brown, 1998.
Mishler, Paul C. *Raising Reds: The Young Pioneers, Radical Summer Camps, and Communist Political Culture in the United States*. New York: Columbia University Press, 1999.

Web

statisticstimes.com/economy
worldbank.org

Part 1

Space Invaders

"I occasionally think how quickly our differences worldwide would vanish if we were facing an alien threat from outside this world."
—Ronald Reagan

"At first glance, everything looked the same. It wasn't. Something evil had taken possession of the town."
—Dr. Miles Bennell (Kevin McCarthy);
Invasion of the Body Snatchers (1956)

Target Earth
Politicians from Venus
John T. Soister

Time was when the refrain "they hunt him here, they hunt him there" referred to the French, the Reign of Terror in Paris, and that "damned, elusive Pimpernel," the creation of the Baroness Orczy. The government, such as it was during Robespierre's ascension to power, was frantic to track down the insidious phantom, whose ideology diametrically opposed everything the Révolution stood for and whose alter-ego—Sir Percival Blakeney—was a noble (and an Englishman) to boot. Another Englishman—unlike Sir Percy, possessed of real flesh and blood—writing about a half century before le baroness and a half-century after the beheading of Louis XVI, opened his second historical novel by exulting in freedom from tyranny while deploring the tyranny that may result from freedom. "It was the best of times, it was the worst of times," wrote Charles Dickens in 1859, and his European readership doubtless agreed.

Not quite a century later, for many Americans the "worst of times" made an appearance. Although the Allied forces had defeated the combined might of Germany and Japan in 1945, the decade that followed V-J Day was marked by the almost preternatural presence of *another* insidious phantom whose ideology, this time 'round, ran counter to "American values." It was during Wisconsin senator Joseph McCarthy's ascension to power that the chase was on once again: "They hunt him here, they hunt him there"— the almost-antiphonal anthem of frustration mouthed by the omniscient narrator in Baroness Orczy's memorable fiction—now reflected the ramped-up paranoia of the Cold War U.S. Congress, which sought to track down and slay what it had perceived to be the real-life archenemy of the Land of the Free: the American Communist.

In 1953, at the very height of the political paranoia that had come to be termed "McCarthyism," playwright Arthur Miller—one of many of the suspect "artistic intelligentsia" to be blacklisted—wrote *The Crucible*. One didn't need a literature degree to perceive the parallels between Miller's fictionalization of the 1692 Salem witch trials and the Senate hearings that were going on at that very moment. The play, regarded by many theatergoers as a classic almost as worthy as Miller's earlier *Death of a Salesman*, is still studied and appreciated for its focus on the social injustices that marred America in two disparate centuries.

In nineteen fifty-three, the year *The Crucible* opened at New York's Martin Beck Theatre, Paul W. Fairman penned the short story, "Deadly City." Fairman's gritty, noirish tale concerns a group of average Americans who find themselves being stalked in a mysteriously deserted Chicago. A year later, Hollywood scenarist William Raynor—aiming to transfer Fairman's pulp fiction tale to a favorite 1950s-vintage movie genre, science fiction—added robots to the mix, and Allied Artists released *Target Earth* (1954) to modest box-office revenues and tepid critical commentary. While Fairman's original was not written as an intentional rebuke of the then-current persecution of some of America's citizenry by the more paranoid element in their own government, *Target Earth*'s simple plot can be perceived as a parable thematically similar to Miller's *Crucible*.

Thus, a question that is germane to the discussion at hand: when considering a work of art—whether a musical composition, a painting, a drama, a piece of literature—is there a validity to extrapolated meanings that the artist had *not* intended? What if the artist's position is either no longer extant or simply not clear? Do any of the multiple viewpoints about da Vinci's *Mona Lisa*, for example, have merit when we remember that the Master purposefully left vague his own take on the painting? Given the unlikelihood that producer Herman Cohen intended the *Target Earth* invasion-survival screenplay he had commissioned to operate on any level beyond "What you see is what you get," is a viewer's awareness of parallels between the movie story and real-life American political feeling of the day anything more than projection? Because intentionality is as much a factor in art's "What if?" dimension as it is part of the essence of the science fiction genre itself, the question demands debate that moves beyond the parameters of this essay and this book. Thus, while *Target Earth* may not have been shot and released with an eye to commenting upon (or cashing in on) disaffected American progressives or pro–McCarthy superpatriots, the existence of a persuasive argument for its being skewed to reflect—however inadvertently—the political morass in which the country then found itself is undeniable.

Without a jot of *The Crucible*'s portent or prestige—and, of course, with none of the stage drama's dual historicity or clarity of purpose—*Target Earth*, these six decades on, barely registers with anyone save the most devoted fans of Hollywood SF of the 1950s. Once a mainstay of Saturday-afternoon, local-TV programming (due both to the presence of its tin man and its microscopic rental fees), the picture has lately all but vanished from sight. Weak sales led to the discontinuation of the *Target Earth* DVD soon after VCI Video offered it in 2003 (though factory copies of that disc sell today for between forty and sixty dollars). The picture's minuscule budget, set-bound nature, and threadbare look excited no one but those hardcore fans we mentioned earlier, and VCI pulled the plug. (A 1997 Roan Group laserdisc is also long out of print.)

* * *

As for plot: Venusian robots have successfully invaded Earth, and events focus on the aliens' mop-up exercises following the contraptions' occupation of an unnamed American city. (Source author Paul Fairman set his tale in the Windy City, and the picture was shot in Los Angeles, but the scenario stubbornly refuses to identify the metropolis under attack.) We discover at the outset that just about everyone has been evacuated. Only a handful of stragglers wander the streets, seeking shelter in deserted hotel rooms and sustenance in hastily abandoned night clubs and bars. *Target Earth* is, essentially, the story of their finding said necessities—and each other—while evading the mass of mechanical men directed to eradicate any remaining human life. In the end, the most photogenic of the principal cast are saved by the army and a jerry-rigged device that emits the pitch-perfect sound waves needed to disable the robots.

Each of the folks left behind is portrayed as a bit of a loser (harsh but apt), a person who was drunk, unconscious, or otherwise oblivious to the evacuation and subsequent takeover of a great city. This cast of character types includes Frank Brooks, an in-transit businessman who missed high-tailing it with everybody else because he was out cold, having been sapped and robbed in a saloon. Played by the wholesome—if slightly ferret-like—Richard Denning, Frank is a limitless font of wisdom and counsel who spouts off knowledgeably (and incessantly) while admitting that he occasionally fails to practice what he preaches ("I should have known better than to flash a big roll of bills in a bar"). Moments after he's forced to chase down a panicky Nora King (Kathleen Crowley) and slap some calmness back into her, his pontificating engine chugs back to life:

> FRANK: There's been an evacuation of some kind.
> NORA: The H Bomb?
> FRANK: The enemy wouldn't give us advance warning of that.
> NORA: Our radar system?
> FRANK: Four or five hours warning, at best. It's taken at least twice that long to evacuate the city...

In ictu oculi, Nora—a would-be suicidal widow who took one too few sleeping pills—finds herself conflicted. Should she continue to dwell on the dim, unfulfilled past and her dead husband, or ponder the dim, unforeseeable future and the faceless enemy? Or is it better to concentrate on the dim, terrifying present and the know-it-all traveling salesman who won't shut up? Before Nora is driven to try to kill herself again—or maybe to kill Frank—the pair discover Vicki and Jim.

Vicki Harris (Virginia Grey) is a good-time gal, the kind who reliably forgets the guy who brought her to the dance because of some other guy, or the booze, or the music, or the lights, or anything, really, and who has resigned herself to always being the bridesmaid. For the past ten years, though, she has been the exclusive squeeze of Jim Wilson (Richard Reeves), an unsophisticated hulk who occasionally forgets his own strength and who struggles to complete his sentences (and thoughts), but who nonetheless has a rudimentary moral code with roots in the Jurassic Age. Although Vicki is prone to toss sharply sarcastic barbs at the big oaf, and Jim is given to shaking his girlfriend in momentary fits of anger or frustration, the sight of the two of them making up encourages us to understand that this relationship is the Real Thing.

The two remaining principals are Charles Otis (Mort Marshall), a dumpy *schlimazel* who has "victim" written all over him, and No-First-Name Davis (Robert Roark), a gun-happy sociopath with a plan for getting himself out of there alive, even if it kills everyone else.

The major dramatis personae, then, are a cadre of 1950s stock dramatic types: reasonably capable male with leadership qualities; attractive breeder-female with identity issues; less savvy/serious/sophisticated secondary couple needed to provide counterpoint to the alpha pair; ineffective and expendable nebbish to demonstrate consequences of failure; and unhinged/unpredictable wild card to threaten success of otherwise logical actions.

Of minor but special interest is that the principals' surnames—Brooks, King, Harris, Wilson—are the essence of WASPiness; the happenstance of these people gathering together reflects the segregated, Eurocentric society that was the United States during the Eisenhower Era. (After the Civil Rights Movement of the 1960s, the Token Black would be added to the mix. Token nerds, fat folk, and gays would follow suit as the succeeding decades unfolded.)

The other characters in the film are no less types than the principals, but they—the "scientists" and the "army"—are removed from ordinary society; the action cuts away to them as they do whatever it is scientists and army men do in the seclusion of their laboratories and their headquarters. It's intriguing to note that the third "branch" of 1950s extra-societal authority—the (usually Christian) clergy—is missing from the scene. Like the guys in the lab coats and the camouflage gear, the bible-carrying men in the black suits usually brought their unique slant on life, death, and morality to the table even when (as evidenced famously in 1953's *The War of the Worlds*) their own safety was compromised as they left the protection of the church office or the sanctuary. The dearth of spiritual types in *Target Earth* may have been inadvertent, or it may well have exemplified the less-than-charitable sentiments of some churchgoers who believed that those among their fellows who are prone to drunkenness, suicide, the fast life, intractable ignorance, and/or murderous tendencies aren't deserving of salvation in the first place.

Neither, of course, are robots, so, on the face of it, for *Target Earth* to have included a minister among those left behind would have been, at best, dramatically superfluous; audience assumption may have been that men of the cloth assisted in the city's orderly evacuation and then lammed it with the few who had also stayed behind.

Thankfully, the nation's top scientists—intellectually superior docents who do not easily rub elbows with hoi polloi—are ever at the ready to utilize their microscopes, telescopes, test tubes, periodic table ... *whatever* it takes to solve the myriad problems that confront contemporary America. Watching over all (most effectively from secret bases and undisclosed locations) is the "army," the catch-all tag for the military might of the United States, the country's staunchest line of defense. The brass are unimpeachable in their loyalty, unequaled in their patriotism, and undeterred by setbacks: witness how quickly Arthur Space shakes off the devastating news of the total annihilation of dozens of aircraft. Just as there is no doubt that America's common clay is resilient and tenacious enough to hang in there in the face of surprise attack (in 1954, most moviegoers were old enough to remember Pearl Harbor), the nation's elite intellectuals and warrior chiefs, too, will come through in the clutch to defeat the forces of darkness, whether those forces have arrived from across the ocean or from across the solar system.

But ... the crux of the matter lay in the fact that Joe McCarthy's Venusians were insidious; one couldn't spot them lumbering awkwardly up the steps or clanking their way along the rooftops. The perceived reality was that they were *everywhere*; not merely lurking in stairwells, ready to pounce, but seated one desk over, reading the same newspaper as you, sipping coffee from the same pot ... and ready to pounce. Nor were they as bizarrely accoutered (and thus readily recognizable) as Herman Cohen's tin men. They dressed like Americans, played like Americans, sounded like Americans. In fact, they *were* Americans, in all ways save one: their allegiance was to the Soviet Union.

They were the children of Marx and Uncle Joe Stalin, fanatics looking to abolish the country's moneyed classes (that is, everyone middle class and above) and establish the communal ownership of property. Instead of death rays emanating from faceplates, the flesh-and-blood aliens emitted subversive ideas from their collective intellect. This, unfortunately, meant that many of America's brightest lights—the country's intelligentsia—were automatically suspect. Suddenly, a good number of American philosophers, writers, politicians, businessmen, artists, and scientists felt themselves under intense scrutiny, the objects of uncertainty and mistrust. And was there not a proportional relationship between higher levels of education and agnosticism? Perhaps no clergyman

Target Earth (1954) suggested a massive invasion by Venusian robots, though only one at a time is ever seen on screen—because one was all the production could afford to build. Regardless, the picture has a certain eerie quality, particularly during the opening minutes, when random survivors of the attack wander deserted city streets.

waves his bible or crucifix in the faceplates of the other-worlders in *this* '50s science fiction film because it is only for human beings that conversion and redemption are possible.

    Target Earth is as illogically skewed as the real-life Communist witch hunt was insensitive. Frank's spot-on knowledge of relevant data—a variation on the cinematic convention whereby the scholar in search of crucial (but arcane) information providentially opens just the right volume to just the right page in the nick of time—does allow a couple of the ever-shrinking band of survivors to make it past the climax. Inasmuch as Frank and Nora are the presumptive Adam and Eve of the New Order, though, it is only the decade's dramatic convention that assures that the race (human/white) will survive beyond the end credits. Mere awareness of the invidious workings of the Red Menace will not snatch victory from defeat's jaws. (Conventional weaponry may also prove as powerless against Red infiltration as is Davis's pistol against the mechanical invaders.)

Questionable, too, is the wisdom of civil defense workers removing automobiles' distributor caps during mass evacuations. This woefully pointless ritual assumes either that there will be no stragglers in need of a quick means of escape from the occupied area, or that the invading hordes will opt to utilize abandoned cars—rather than the presumably armored vehicles in which they arrived—to continue with their occupation. (Frank again suffers from synapse misfire when he and Nora find a portable radio, but no batteries, and so elect to leave the radio behind!)

It may well be, of course, that *Target Earth* deserved relegation to its lowly status in the pantheon of fifties' cinematic science fiction. The picture is blatantly and achingly cheap: producer Herman Cohen's ordering that only one (1) Venusian robot be constructed for the project and his insisting that the crack in the mechanism's "face plate"— seen in an expository sequence set in a sparsely appointed "lab"—be *painted on* to spare the expense of a second piece of glass is not the stuff of urban legend. Then, too, despite the paucity of alien invaders, nearly every dramatic moment in the body of the film turns on the appearance of the robot(s), which, like the evil Egyptian high priest in the old

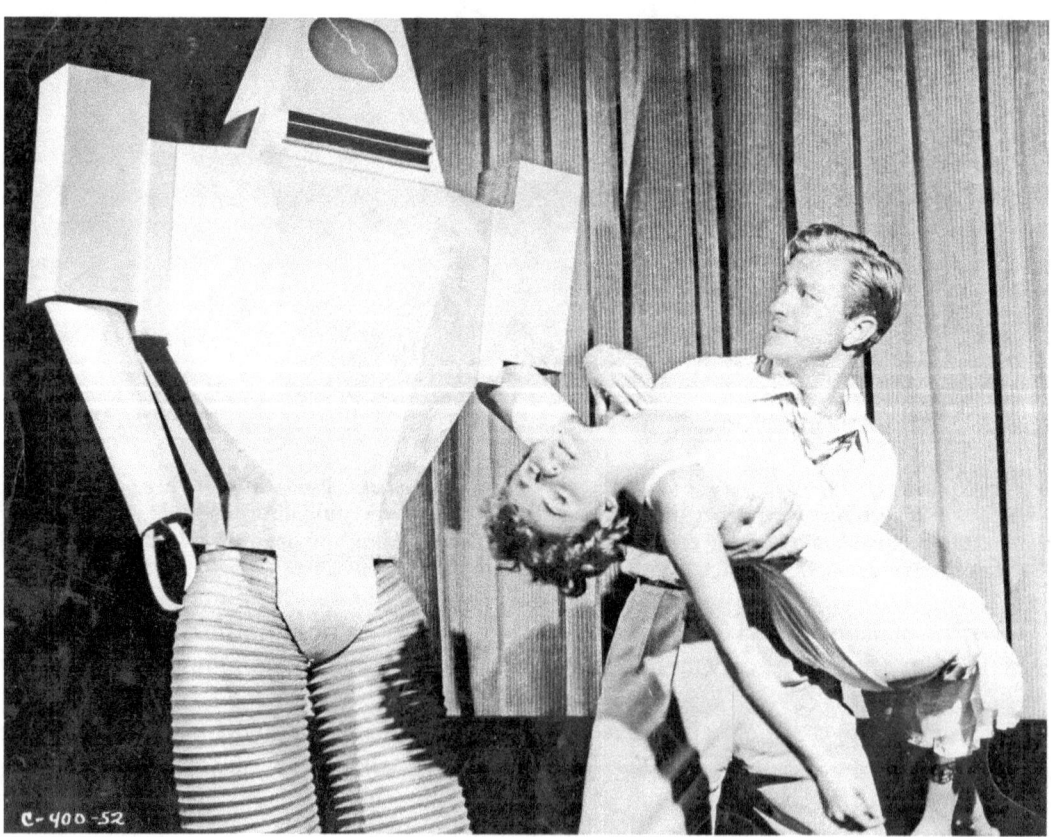

Lumbering and faceless, the robots are humanlike only in barest outline. Here, Frank (Richard Denning) and Nora (Kathleen Crowley) try to defend themselves, but the invaders—like the godless Communist hordes—may be impossible to resist.

Universal mummy series of the 1940s, show up in the damnedest places at precisely the right moments. This supposed ubiquity becomes not just inevitable but predictable. Were it not for the musical brasses that dramatically rattle the soundtrack, the robots' arrivals would be comic. The mechanical heavies come perilously close to *deus ex machina* status, as their gift for repeatedly entering the scene at the exact instant things are coming to a head invites the viewer to conclude that the storytelling device was the only way for the scenarist to resolve most of the tale's human conflict.

* * *

It's also true that the picture is an imperfect mirror of the intentionally McCarthy-oriented screed in *The Crucible*. Miller's witchcraft drama was targeted at the community of playgoers (naturally enough), an arguably more intellectual and politically savvy substratum of the population than were fans of the decade's science fiction movies. Then, too, the film's sundry departures from the McCarthy "norm" are nowhere more evident than in the fact that William Raynor's screenplay portrays government and its adjuncts as the heart of the solution, rather than as the crux of the problem. And although the dispassionate disquisition on the robot-killing oscillator during the picture's closing moments cannot not come close to the cathartic, real-life drama of Joseph Welch's denunciation of Senator McCarthy ("Have you no sense of decency, sir, at long last? Have you left no sense of decency?"), both statements are effective codas to the crises that inspired them.

For all that, in *Target Earth* the "other-worldly" faction may well be seen to represent those suspect governmental forces, whose every approach, aspect, and attitude were touted by Joseph McCarthy as being as alien to the security of the United States as the awkwardly shuffling Venusian robots to big city rooftops. The humans in the picture—Americans all—are little more than prey to the annihilators from beyond. As individuals, they are far from successful and less than admirable; they approach each other warily, squabble endlessly, and kill each other out of fear and rage. They are no match for this foreign menace. As a group—even while on the run from their soulless pursuers—they are united by instinct if still divided by ideology. They are the dregs of a society that has abandoned them; they are the victims of circumstances that have cut them off from their city, their fellow citizens, and their way of life. Is there any strength to be found in their numbers? Is there any courage to be found in their convictions? Or will everything be for naught if the insidious foreign element cannot be exposed for what it is and rendered impotent once and for all?

It is impossible to say whether the typical moviegoer of 1954 would have connected the dots and drawn the political parallels without prompting. Still, average ticket-buyers would have drawn on human nature, the American tendency to pull for the underdog, and the inevitabilities of cinematic convention—along with a shared paranoia about the Atomic Age—to root for the home team. Come hell or high water, nothing spelled xenophobia back then more than Venusian robots from Congress.

FILMOGRAPHY

Target Earth—Abtcon Pictures/Allied Artists; Released November 7, 1954; Black and white; 75 min.

Credits: Producer: Herman Cohen; Director: Sherman Rose; Screenplay: Bill Raynor, b/o an original screenplay by James H. Nicholson and Wyatt Ordung, and the short story "The Deadly City" by Paul W. Fairman (pseudonym of Ivor Jorgensen); Director of photography: Guy Roe;

Editor: Sherman Rose; Music: Paul Dunlap; Art director: James W. Sullivan; Robot design and fabrication: David Koehler; Special effects: Howard A. Anderson Co.

Cast: Richard Denning: Frank Brooks; Kathleen Crowley: Nora King; Virginia Grey: Vicki Harris; Richard Reeves: Jim Wilson; Mort Marshall: Charles Otis; Robert Roark: Davis; Arthur Space: Lt. General Wood; Whit Bissell: Scientist; Steve Calvert: Venusian robot

WORKS CITED

DVD/Video
Target Earth. The Roan Group. 1997
Target Earth. VCI Entertainment. 2008

Not of This Earth
Myth, Brooks Brothers and Subversion

David J. Hogan

"The lamp of the body is the eye. If, then, your eye is simple, your whole body will be bright; but if your eye is wicked, your whole body will be dark. If in reality the light that is in you is darkness, how great that darkness is!"

—Matthew 6:22–23

The Visitor

He's an imposing man of indeterminate middle age, not tall but solid and blocky. His powerful and inelegant physique suggests the stolidity of the prototypical Slav or other Eastern European. His heavy black Cadillac—a new '57 Fleetwood, the long limousine model—announces him with considerable presence. The man alternately drives the big car himself or is chauffeured in it by a uniformed driver. If he's not an influential person, he's clearly a wealthy one.

Wealth, though, doesn't necessarily suggest extravagant personal tastes. Indeed, the sense of sobriety brought by the dark car is heightened by the man's unvarying uniform: dark Brooks Brothers suit, snap brim hat, dark shoes and tie, and white dress shirt adorned with heavy cufflinks. When the man is out and about on errands, a compact and businesslike Samsonite aluminum briefcase is invariably at his side.

The man speaks in a naturally deep voice overlaid with a peculiar, halting dialect. His English is perfect, but you surmise it's not his first language. He could be an immigrant who made it big in business.

He lives in a nicely appointed rented mansion, so Los Angeles apparently isn't his permanent home. Perhaps he's merely visiting on business, and will be happy to leave when that business is concluded.

Partly because the pitch and faintly ponderous cadence of his voice are unchanging, he exudes a quietly intimidating authority. He's accustomed to being obeyed. His manner suggests that his everyday concerns are large and grave. He drives confidently but badly, and what you may have thought was a general indifference to traffic seems more likely to be willful ignorance, a visible symptom of a larger disinclination to grasp everyday American courtesies and protocols.

The man is no proselytizer but there's something intensely focused and political about him. He is impatient with what strikes him as the obtuseness of others. He's not simply humorless; the very nature of humor seems to elude him.

And then there are the man's sunglasses: heavy and very dark, and configured to cover the entirety of the eye orbits, with a subtle wraparound that prevents the eyes from being glimpsed from the sides. The man wears the glasses in sunlight and at night. He even wears them inside his home. If you assumed that he's sensitive to light, you'd be mistaken, but he does have an absolute intolerance for sudden, loud noises.

Were you to observe him from afar you'd note that he comes and goes at all hours, the briefcase always at hand. He spends considerable time in the basement of his home, where he keeps things he wants no one to see.

The man takes a few guests into his home, and most of them never them come out again.

The fabulous L.A. weather seems to interest the man not at all. It is ridiculous and impossible to imagine him in, say, shorts and a Hawaiian shirt. He finds no novelty or special pleasure in what the city offers, and appears to be, in fact, a complete ascetic. His sober, conservative appearance seems to define him.

You're suspicious. You've been scrutinizing this puzzle, and when you disassemble it and look at the pieces, things are clearer. Everything about this dark-suited man with the beige name—"Mr. Johnson"—suggests a foreigner's clumsy attempt at anonymity. Because he works at being invisible, you notice him.

After rendezvousing at a sidewalk newsstand with a young woman who wears dark glasses identical to his, the pair walks off together. Not a word passes between them, but their unspoken mission seems clear to them both.

And then you're sure: This peculiar man and his female cohort are here to do harm—to the city and perhaps to all of America. It's obvious now, isn't it? Mr. Johnson is a Communist agent.

Metaphoric Narrative

As the title of *Not of This Earth* (1957) suggests, Mr. Johnson (Paul Birch) is *not* a Communist. In fact, he wants to crowd Communists into massive pens and take their blood. He wants to do the same to Democrats and Republicans, African herdsmen, shopkeepers in Edinburgh—everybody. Mr. Johnson has come to Earth from a dying planet called Davanna, with a mission: complete "subjugation and pasturing of the Earth sub-humans."

For generations, Davanna has been wracked by atomic war. The planet's atmosphere is toxic and its children are dying. Every Davannan, Johnson included, suffers a hyperanemia that can be mitigated only by frequent transfusions of healthy blood. The "conquered enemies" indigenous to Davanna are dwindling in number, and blood is running short. Worse, internecine warfare threatens to destroy Johnson's faction from within before the blood problem can be resolved.

Like Earth, Davanna is an aggressive, highly political place. Its conquerors' instinct has led it to limited, badly compromised military victories at home, but now the Davannans have had to bring their colonial, expansionist instinct to the fore. There is rich, healthy blood on Earth. Hence the arrival on our planet of Mr. Johnson, a soulless fiend who mesmerizes and kills with the (apparently) electrical force of his iris-free, milky white eyes.

From the den of his mansion, Johnson keeps in touch with a superior via a teleportation device that doubles as an audio-visual communicator. In a moment that's as unnerving as it is usefully expository, the superior reiterates Johnson's role, which is part scout and part subversive. If Johnson determines that Earth blood is as compatible with Davannan blood as is hoped, he is to send sample humans "through the beam" to Davanna, so that their blood can be drawn and inspected. Those results, coupled with a recommendation from Johnson, will lead to full-scale invasion of Earth. (So compelling is this exposition that a slightly abridged version opens TV prints of *Not of This Earth*, functioning as an effective teaser, but primarily to pad out the 67-minute running time in order to make the film long enough for inclusion in syndicated TV packages.)

But if the human blood is not compatible, or if Johnson discovers other insuperable problems here on Earth, he is to conclude his mission by destroying our planet. This is "scorched earth" cum "scorched Earth," and a strategy that, from our perspective, is the end of everything.

Because Johnson is medically ill, he hypnotizes (or brainwashes, if you prefer) a Los Angeles physician, Dr. Rochelle (William Roerick), and arranges for in-home care provided by Rochelle's office nurse, Nadine Storey (Beverly Garland). (In an unintended comment on the vagaries of inflation, Johnson offers Nadine $200 a week, which causes Nadine to laugh: "Mr. Johnson, no nurse would *dream* of getting $200 a week. Why, it's ridiculous!")

The mesmerized Rochelle encourages Nadine to take the private-duty job. Shortly, she's living in Johnson's mansion, transfusing him and interacting with his wiseass chauffer, Jeremy (Jonathan Haze), a young punk who makes *$300* a week for hauling Johnson to and from the library, and driving home with random people whom Johnson has invited as dinner guests—even a trio of winos.

Like Jeremy, Nadine wonders about Johnson's sunglasses, the peculiar dialect, and his chilly intellect.

Johnson brazenly abducts a random male pedestrian (who is beamed to Davanna), the three drunks, a door-to-door salesman, and—in the film's very effective opening sequence—a sprightly teenage girl who's just said goodbye to her boyfriend after a late date. (It is here that the purpose of the Samsonite briefcase becomes clear: It holds a fiendish IV and suction pump that deliver a victim's blood to a neatly arrayed brace of tubes and beakers.)

Eventually, Jeremy confides to Nadine that "the three bums came in but they never came out," and the two of them puzzle over Johnson's daily ingestion of a foul liquid food supplement instead of the traditional toast and eggs Jeremy prepares for him.

The woman with whom Johnson rendezvous complains of anemia, so in Dr. Rochelle's shadowed office Johnson carelessly transfuses the woman with blood Rochelle has been testing—the blood of a rabid dog. Johnson and his companion separate, and the woman is shortly in mortal distress.

At the mansion, Nadine and Jeremy discover the hidden teleporter-communicator and the invisible wall that protects it. Jeremy gives the force field a tentative rap: "You couldn't bust through that with a twenty-pound sledge…. What *is* this thing?"

Nadine responds without hesitation: "I don't know but no one on this world ever built it."

Johnson returns and dispatches Jeremy with his killing gaze. After a chase through a park, he mesmerizes Nadine and instructs her to return to the house and step into the

The blank-eyed humanoid that calls himself Mr. Johnson (Paul Birch) regards his live-in nurse Nadine (Beverly Garland), and everyone else here on Earth, as living sources of blood suited only for "pasturing" on his dying planet, Davanna. In the chilly and pitiless Johnson, *Not of This Earth* (1957) provides a perfect analogue for the dogged Communist bureaucrats performing tasks that killed thousands, even millions.

device for teleportation to Davanna. She obediently treks home and steps into the device; she's saved when her boyfriend, motorcycle cop Harry Sherbourne (Morgan Jones), turns on his siren while pursuing Johnson. The sound pierces the alien's head and causes him to crash the Cadillac. He dies in the flaming wreckage, those awful eyes open and staring.

In a coda that's at once amusing and unnerving, Nadine and Harry visit Johnson's grave. The obelisk marker, which is shot from below so that it dominates the frame, reads: "HERE LIES A MAN WHO IS NOT OF THIS EARTH." Sherbourne—the peace officer charged with our protection—admits sympathy for this visitor who traveled so far from everything he knew. But "everyday citizen" Nadine isn't buying it: "He was a foreign thing, come here to destroy us."

When the couple moves off a distant figure catches our eye. It's a man who walks steadily, stolidly, toward the marker and toward us. He looks like a middle-aged business executive: suit, hat, Samsonite briefcase, and sunglasses. Finally, his implacable face fills the screen

Davanna isn't giving up.

Oppression and Resistance

Not of This Earth was produced and directed by prolific B-movie specialist Roger Corman, and written by Charles B. Griffith and Mark Hanna. As they prepared the film, this is what was happening in the Soviet bloc that is pertinent to the movie's subtexts: In February 1956, three years after the 1953 death of Stalin, First Secretary Nikita Khrushchev delivered the so-called Secret Speech at the 20th Party Congress, attacking the late leader's policies and pouring scorn on Stalin's failings as a man. Khrushchev had grown sick of the Stalin cult, and understood that intolerable levels of government brutality were disastrous in the long term. Transcripts of the speech shortly made their way to Soviet satellite nations, stirring protest. By the middle of 1956 (as Khrushchev successfully labored to hang on to and grow his power), the Party felt that Khrushchev's conception of a softer image was no longer wise, or sustainable, bringing risks to Soviet security. So it was that in the Communist world of 1956–57, modest relaxations of totalitarian control were reversed.

Romania, bent beneath the Poltiburo-friendly dictatorship of Nicolae Ceausescu, had fallen into line, but an abortive student revolt in Czechoslovakia in April-May 1956 (inspired in part by 1952 show trials of Jewish-Czech intellectuals who had been accused of espionage) was a portent of more Eastern European unrest to come, and an indicator of the Politburo's increasingly weak grasp on its client states.[1]

Modest 1956 conflict in Bulgaria amounted to little, but workers in Poland, encouraged by a Soviet amnesty granted to 28,000 Polish political prisoners in February 1956,[2] and undoubtedly well aware of the Czech students' uprising, mounted a massive strike in Poznan in June. The local police station and the headquarters of the secret police were stormed and overwhelmed, and the strikers beat back a counterattack mounted by the Polish army. But on June 29, the second day of the strike, 10,000 troops and 400 tanks overwhelmed the workers. The situation grew increasingly tense. Khrushchev flew into Poland on October 19, and Soviet warships anchored themselves off Gdansk. The strikers' situation was not good, but their reformist leader, Wladyslaw Gomulka, promised Moscow that worker demands would not put the Soviet system at risk. Khrushchev acquiesced.[3]

And then there was Hungary.

Crushing the Populace

As with many popular, nationalist uprisings, the Hungarian revolution began as a student movement, a phenomenon that is rightly feared by totalitarians, for from the noisy activities of students who protest the boot heel on the neck it can be but a small, brisk step to a sympathetic and motivated larger population. That is how events developed in Hungary, and in barely more than a week following an October 23 student march against the Parliament building in Budapest, a whole panoply of Hungarian citizens was energized, focused, and in the streets.

In an angry symbolic gesture of October 23 that infuriated Moscow, Budapest students turned a blowtorch on the knees of the Stalin monument in Budapest Park, and pulled the statue from its base. The same day, students massed at Budapest's radio station and demanded a public reading of their grievances. They wanted Soviet troops out of their nation and they wanted free elections.

A Soviet armored division of eighty tanks and artillery entered Budapest on October 24. On the 25th, Hungary's pro–Soviet leader, Erno Gero, surrendered power to Imre Nagy, a reformer with paradoxically pro-nationalist and pro–Moscow sentiments. Nagy was far from radical—he merely wanted Hungary to establish its own form of communism, independent of Moscow and divorced from the Warsaw Pact—but his vision was sufficient to energize the people of Budapest. Ferocious, partisan-style fighting raged in the streets until October 31, when Soviet forces withdrew. A few days passed in relative quiet.

On November 4, 200,000 Soviet troops and 2,500 tanks overwhelmed the city. Some 7,000 Soviet soldiers died in the brief but vicious fighting that followed, and between 25,000 and 50,000 Hungarians lost their lives. Imre Nagy was driven from power and subsequently executed. The revolution had been squashed and what passed for "order" returned. Peter Fryer, in his book *Hungarian Tragedy*, starkly explained, "Hungary was Stalinism incarnate. Here in one, small tormented country was the picture, complete in every detail: the abandonment of humanism, the attachment of primary importance not to living, breathing, suffering, hoping human beings but to machines, targets, statistics, tractors, steel mills, plan fulfillment figures … and, of course, tanks."[4]

Marxist writer Jean-Paul Sartre criticized Moscow for its ham-handed domination of Hungary, noting that the invasion "was made possible by twelve years of terror and imbecility" that had emanated from Moscow.

Davanna Strikes

The brutal, invasive Soviet response of November 4 encourages the identification of a reversed pattern—this time of pre-emption rather than of reaction—in *Not of This Earth*.

Davanna is dying. Years of atomic warfare have poisoned the blood of its inhabitants, and the numbers of captured enemy—kept alive in pens for blood harvest—are dwindling. Political strife racks both sides of the larger conflict, and authority is breaking down. If imbecility is not a factor in this mess, terror certainly looms large. Mr. Johnson (Paul Birch) is bureaucrat, advance scout, and decision maker. He represents what remains of the Davannan ruling elite.

In what was almost certainly an unconscious decision by screenwriters Griffith and Hanna, and director Corman, the first of Mr. Johnson's victims whose death we witness (we learn later that Johnson has already dispatched close to a dozen innocents) is a teenage girl—a student—who is accosted on her own walkway after her boyfriend drops her off at the end of a late date.[5] Youth, in Southern California as in Hungary, is energetic, reckless, brave out of all proportion to reality, and dangerously unpredictable. The young must be dealt with promptly and harshly.

Johnson thinks and acts like an overlord, so although he gives employment to Nadine and Jeremy—a pair of useful but non-complicit young adults—Johnson remains keenly aware of the pair's youthful vitality, and thus their potential threat to his scheme. The visitor watches them closely.

Youth continues to have its (brief) day: An aggressive hipster (Dick Miller) who sells vacuum cleaners door to door shows up on Johnson's front stoop, and it's immediately apparent that Johnson doesn't dig the guy's cool-kitty patter. "When you see this little baby in action you're gonna do flip flops," the hipster promises. Johnson stares back from behind the heavy, dark glasses. "No flip flops," he slowly pronounces. But when the hipster promises a terrific demonstration "in your own basement," Johnson becomes receptive and opens the door wider.

"Crazy," the salesman says.

In the basement, Johnson removes the sunglasses and fries the salesman's brain with a pointed gaze of his milky orbs. After the deft insertion of a needle he efficiently pumps his victim's blood into a neat row of flasks.

With youth under careful scrutiny or eliminated altogether, Johnson begins to move among the broader population. He meets a Chinese man on the sidewalk, mesmerizes him, and sends him to Davanna via teleportation beam. (Although Griffith, Hanna and Corman made the character Chinese to demonstrate Johnson's ability to speak telepathically in a variety of Earth languages, the selection has a certain political piquancy, given the already dodgy state of Sino-Soviet relations.)

As we'll see, Johnson's campaign of victimization shortly progresses from easy prey to the educated class and finally to the police. It's an inverted progression of totalitarian aggression, bottom to top, and made particularly threatening because of Johnson's special powers.

Unearthly Abilities

So great was American alarm about the Red menace that Communists, and particularly perfidious Communist agents, were imbued by the popular imagination with uncanny powers of deception, guile, and subterfuge. *They could be living next door*, and you'd never know. Why wouldn't you know? Because the Reds are godless and highly motivated, and they're sneakier than you, that's why. Communists are bogeymen. And what psychological advantage does a bogeyman possess if he's reticent, clumsy, or easy to identify? Ultimately, the superhuman cleverness—or lack of it—of Communist agents in the United States was almost beside the point. What mattered was the American *acceptance* of the idea of Red competence.

In the popular American imagination of the day, Communists were somehow less than human—or at least possessed of less than normal capacity for human emotion. Certainly, Communist desires and actions were sufficiently base to put these people in a class barely above animals. On the other hand, fear encouraged many Americans to endow the prototypical Communist with devious, superhuman abilities. Broad political agendas are pursued in steps: unceasing verbal attacks on legislators, shameless appeals to public fears of joblessness and poverty, a stir of the pot of ethnic hatred and xenophobia. If we are to justify our receptiveness to base politicking, the villains must possess those special powers noted here.

Successful quests for power, whether town-council trivial or scarifyingly global, must ultimately be narratives, for without an understandable "story," groups and institutions that seek power are unable to persuade masses of people to acquiesce (that is, to passively roll over) or offer active (if ill-informed) support. *Realpolitik* is little more than convoluted, highly sophisticated drama, a real-life exercise in various fictions. It relies on a stage-managed tale that must contain specific elements: establishment of a threat, narrative examples of the brewing danger, calamitous "what if?" scenarios, and a course of pre-emptive action. In a perverse way, political narrative is a variant of classical storytelling, with villains sufficiently terrifying to justify, and make acceptable to millions, the bad behavior of political institutions and ruthless politicians (and what is a dictator but a politician with a free hand?). This is why Odysseus is challenged by sirens and the Cyclops, and not by quick-change rug merchants or bands of rowdy sailors. The more intimidating the adversary, the more "real" is the carefully crafted fiction that allows governments and other storytellers to move with free hands.

"The light of the body is the eye."

The sirens of *The Odyssey* sing sweet songs of disaster, and Johnson is similarly deceptive. He can communicate telepathically and he has a teleporter and some other nasty gadgets, too, but his real power—a facility to take away our capacity to resist, to reason, and that can take our very lives—is his irresistible gaze.

The killing gaze, familiar in myth and fable, is typically an attribute of the female. Medusa, the chthonic Gorgon of Greek mythology, is the most familiar wielder of the deadly gaze, and any who stare into her eyes are turned to stone. Medusa and her similarly deadly sisters, Euryale and Stheno, are mirrored in *Not of This Earth* by Johnson and his two accomplices—the Davannan woman who joins him only to unwittingly initiate the unraveling of his plan, and the Johnson-twin who strides toward us in the film's final moment. (That the female alien is beautiful jibes with literary descriptions and artworks depicting Medusa that began to appear in the fifth century, by which time the Gorgon was frequently described and depicted as being comely as well as dangerous.)

Ovid's *Metamorphosis* (and other sources) relates the tale of Actaeon, a hunter who stumbles into a secluded glade where the nude goddess Diana, attended by her nymphs, bathes. (The moment of Actaeon's embarrassed discovery is captured in Titian's monumental 1559 painting, *Diana and Actaeon*.[6]) The nymphs are mortified by the intrusion but Diana is mainly incensed. For having gazed upon her, and having received her furious stare in return, Actaeon is transformed into a stag and torn apart by his own hounds as he races through the trees in a hopeless attempt at escape.[7]

Myth does not suggest that the remorseless and irresistible killing gaze is a gift restricted to females. *Metamorphosis* describes the beautiful mortal Semele, who is chosen as a concubine by Jupiter, the king of the gods in Roman myth. So pleased is Jupiter by his conquest that he promises to grant Semele whatever she wishes. In an unwise moment, Semele blurts that she wants to see Jupiter in all his glory, that is, the "real" Jupiter that exists quite separate from the mortal form he adopts for his earthly dalliances. Jupiter agrees, aware (with a god's essential unconcern about the fate of mortals) that Semele will not survive her sight of him. Indeed, she's blown to bits. Her lover's utter lack of concern for her well-being is fatal to her.

A familiar proverb—"the eyes are the window to the soul"—cannot be attributed with certainty, but may have roots in the biblical quote that appears at the head of this essay. Matthew's sentiment is reiterated in Luke 11:34, which says, "The light of the body is the eye." Mr. Johnson's blank orbs suggest a lack of a soul, but his unwavering concern for his planet does suggest concern for his own kind. And like Jupiter and other gods, he has disdain for the "second-stage sub-humans" that the gods referred to simply as "mortals."

The female alien also exhibits attributes that, if not precisely suggestive of a soul, do indicate an animating feature that confirms a sharp self-awareness. With only the barest hint of apology, she tells Johnson that she has escaped Davanna to save herself (and, only incidentally, to inform Johnson of what's happening back home). Later, as she feels the befouled dog blood coursing through her body, she collapses on the steps of a hospital with a plaintive cry of "Davanna!"

Debate about the existence of the Davannan soul might be vigorous, but such discussions are almost certainly irresolvable. More profitable, then, to ponder yet another ancient myth, "the evil eye," a manifestation of schizophrenia that prompts the sufferer to believe that ill will and even physical harm can be conveyed by a glance. In some cases, the sufferer claims to have the evil-eye power himself. In the ancient world, before any thought was given to schizophrenia, the evil eye was described as *oculus fascinus*: a subject of fascination.[8] And a dread fascination it was, for the eye was considered "the privileged weapon of the fascinator."[9] For the hopelessly fascinated (i.e., the victim), escape is impossible.

As levied by Mr. Johnson, the evil eye is a hypnotic device that renders the victim mentally and physically helpless. The power can be modulated, as well, existing at its most powerful as the (literally) crackling gaze that fells the teenage girl and the vacuum cleaner salesman, or kept in partial check when Johnson keeps the sunglasses in place and merely paralyzes his victim (as when Jeremy is discovered snooping in the basement) or subverts the victim's will (as with the pliable Chinese).

The Gaze Is Not Infallible

In Communist Europe and Asia, the totalitarian gaze was omnipresent. Across Russia, the faces of Stalin, Lenin and other, lesser lights glared at the citizenry from enormous rally banners, from wall posters that were as prolific as dandelions, from textbooks and other government-mandated literature, and from coins, currency, and postage stamps.

Satellite states promulgated the watchful visages of Enver Hoxha (Albania, a satellite of Red China after 1959), Nicolae Couceasceau (Romania), Georgi Dimitrov (Bulgaria), Wladyslaw Gomulka (Poland), and Matyas Rákosi (Hungary).

In Red China, the alternately implacable and (dubiously) avuncular face of Mao literally looked down on the populace to reinforce the Mao cult of personality. Similar idolatry went on in Communist North Korea, where the tin pot but dangerous dictator Kim il-Sung successfully promoted himself as a demi-god who controlled, among other things, the weather.

And in George Orwell's 1949 novel *Nineteen Eighty-Four*, of course, the wielder of the killing gaze is the system personified, Big Brother, whose "dark eyes looked deep" into the eyes of the beleaguered citizenry.

Some thirty-five years after the 1957 release of *Not of This Earth*, the West witnessed the spectacle of the Soviet Union imploding because of the regime's inherent weaknesses: profligate spending, denial of a Western style of consumerism to its citizens, a cocksure assumption that the populace would never dare mount a meaningful resistance, and heedlessness about reformist functionaries active in satellite states and even from within. Similarly, Johnson's power isn't infallible. The alien has two innate weaknesses: a thorough contempt for Earthlings ("weak and full of fright" as he describes them to his superior) and a heightened sensitivity to sound. Late in the film, when he attempts to mesmerize a parking lot attendant, his concentration is broken (and the intended victim temporarily regains his senses) when Johnson's ears are assaulted by the impatient bleat of a car horn.

But before all of that, Johnson makes terrifyingly effective use of his physical and mental powers, exercising nothing short of total control through mental suggestion—brainwashing.

Lifton and the Mind

American professor of psychiatry Robert Jay Lifton is well known today for his psychological enquiries into the nature of "apocalyptic violence" and its perpetrators, such as his investigation of the sarin gas attack mounted against Tokyo subways in 1995 by Aum Shinrikyo, an extremist Japanese religious cult. Lifton's interest in emotional fervor and suggestibility date from 1951 to 1953, when Lifton was an Air Force psychiatrist posted to the United States, Japan, and Korea. His service encompassed the Korean War (1950–53), and caused Lifton to become interested in the so-called "brainwashing" techniques used by North Koreans and Chinese against American prisoners of war.

The number of incidents of cooperation of American POWs with their North Korean and Chinese captors alarmed the U.S. military and civilians alike. In some quarters, the situation was viewed as a kind of moral rot that had become endemic in America's post–World War II consumer culture. Cooler heads regarded the issue as proof of the fragility of the suggestible human mind.

Once returned to American hands, "brainwashed" GIs were treated with neither kindness nor understanding, and became unhappy emblems of a national problem that didn't exist in the first place.

The evil eye leads to brainwashing. Johnson's eyes don't simply kill—they also can place a victim in a state of high suggestibility. *Do this, go there*, the brainwasher commands, and the victim obeys. The hypnotic influence continues even when the subject is physically far removed from the mesmerizer.

Brainwashing and the Chain of Command

Significantly, for all of his superhuman abilities, Johnson is clearly just a cog in a large machine, and it is this that makes him at once less and more threatening. Unlike many other SF-film invaders that arrive to act against Earth apparently of their own accord (such as the silent, inexorable *Blob*; and *The Brain from Planet Arous*, who is *so* independent that he's followed to Earth by a policeman-brain), Johnson reports to a superior (the disembodied head in Johnson's transport chamber). The superior, in turn, answers to what we would regard as a government agency, a concentration of power where final decisions are made. Johnson has been allowed tremendous leeway to use his judgment—he is, after all, the person who will decide whether our planet will be subjugated or simply destroyed—but he must keep to an ever-dwindling timetable. In short, he's accountable, and if he determines that subjugation is infeasible, and that Earth will

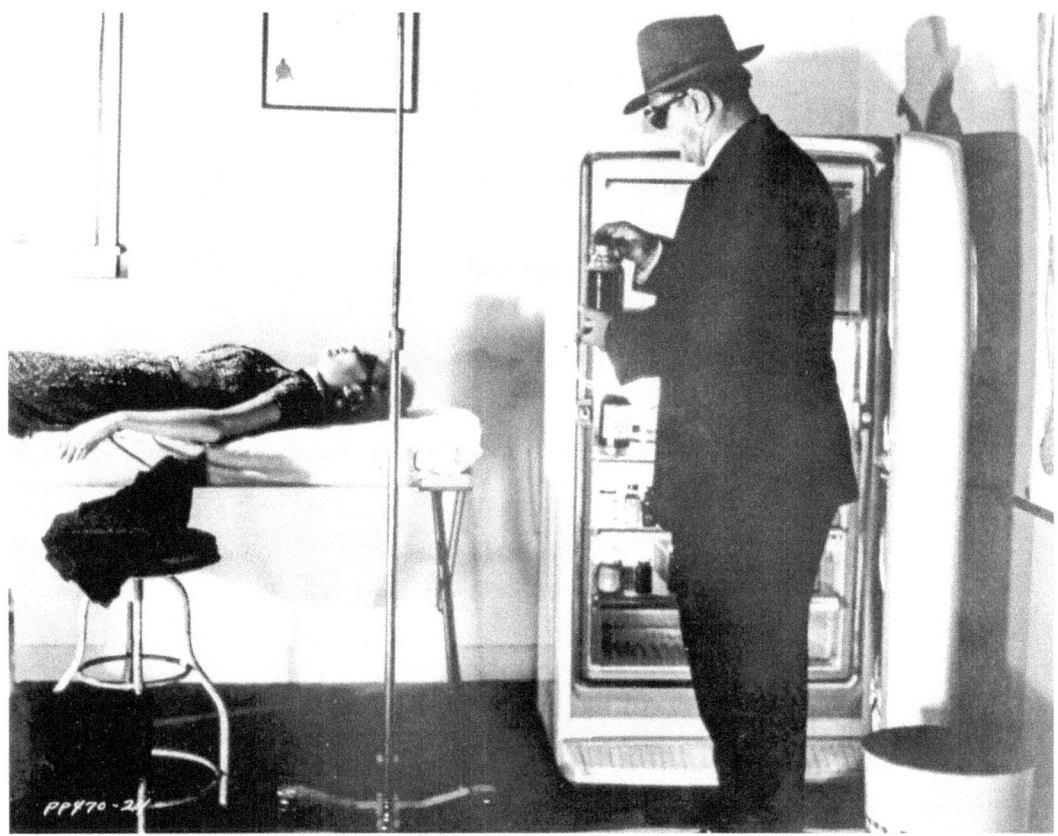

Although clever, Johnson moves in a strange land, and remains unfamiliar with the details of human existence. His undoing begins when he unknowingly transfuses a dying Davannan woman (Anne Carroll) with blood from a rabid dog.

be destroyed, then he will destroy himself along with it (by a method that is left to us to uneasily imagine).

Johnson has agents of his own: the unwitting Jeremy (who prides himself on his independent spirit, and represents every naïf ever taken in by totalitarian lies or misdirection), as well as the coerced Dr. Rochelle (who, in a situation deliberately patterned after the brainwashing model, has no idea he's a slave).

A phone-call sequence from late in the film is perfect parable of mind control and the potential for apocalypse that characterized the Soviet state. Accordingly, the sequence is worth revisiting here. In it, Dr. Rochelle has finished his examination of the dead Davannan woman and describes his findings over the phone to Nadine, who speaks from an upstairs phone in Johnson's house. During the exchange, Corman and editor Charles Gross cut back and forth between Nadine and Rochelle as they speak, creating an uncomfortable contrast between Rochelle's apparently professional interest and Nadine's growing sense of danger:

> ROCHELLE: She has a fantastic blood disease in which the agglutinen [sic] is disintegrating.
> NADINE: Disintegrating? Is that what killed her?
> ROCHELLE: No. She died of rabies.
> NADINE: What?

ROCHELLE: I think I know the cause and the treatment of her disease.
NADINE: You do?
ROCHELLE: Yes. Apparently the victim has lived in an area that's been constantly charged with radioactive material. It was this atmosphere that affected the blood.
NADINE (puzzled): Where would such an atmosphere be found?
ROCHELLE: In a place where continuous nuclear detonations had taken place over a period of years. An area of all-out nuclear warfare.
NADINE: But there is no such place.
ROCHELLE: Yes, I know, my dear. There's no doubt in my mind that this woman is something other than human. She's an alien.
NADINE (slowly): I see. What would be your treatment?
ROCHELLE: First, removal from the toxic atmosphere and then a complete change of blood.
NADINE: Would this cure Mr. Johnson?
ROCHELLE (agitated): I'm not speaking of Johnson.
NADINE: But he fits your description!
ROCHELLE: Nadine, please.
NADINE: Dr. Rochelle, does this man have some kind of power over you? Has he threatened your life or something?
ROCHELLE: Nadine, I, I really must hang up. I have a great deal of work to do.
NADINE: Look, Dr. Rochelle—
JOHNSON (on downstairs phone): The doctor is no longer in contact, Miss Storey.
NADINE (frightened): Mr. Johnson!

Johnson is intimidating, and he has a wee helper, too, a chirping, levitating horror that waits folded in a glass vial until Johnson uncorks the top and brings the creature to corporeality. Silent but with deadly focus and no obvious will of its own, this "umbrella bat" that is so like the presumably faceless Red Army that had ground the Nazi war machine to dust just a dozen years before, finds Rochelle's office, silently enters through the window at the doctor's back, and settles upon the victim's head, destroying not just Rochelle's brain but his individuality, too; the blood that pools across Rochelle's desk after the doctor's head falls upon it suggests a crushing or pulping effect that will leave Rochelle not merely dead but mutilated. Literally faceless, he joins the numberless anonymous victims of Soviet pogroms, purges, and starvation politics.

The Innate American Advantage

If Johnson is a dark parody of the determinedly focused aspect of the Communist attitude, then Nadine and Jeremy epitomize Americanism worn easily and casually, like an off-the-rack windbreaker. Where Johnson is maddeningly stiff, the nurse and the chauffeur are cheeky and colloquial. Jeremy begins to flirt with Nadine the moment he sees her, and because Nadine is a beautiful American girl who's deflected a lot of wolves in her time, she's tolerant of Jeremy's juvenile come-ons. The two of them—the petty thug and the bright, highly trained nurse—suggest America's democratic partnership; amusingly complementary, they function together as the "can-do" American patriot.

Jeremy tells Nadine that Johnson's wealth comes from gems that Jeremy turns into cash. Because the brainwashed Rochelle is no use at all when specifics about Johnson are needed, it's Jeremy who explains to our plucky heroine that Johnson never touches his breakfast ("I think he opens a window and lives on the smog," Jeremy sourly notes).

It's Jeremy, too, who spills the beans about houseguests who come in but never go out again.

The pair's investigative skills suggest American canniness, curiosity, and skepticism. But positive aspects of class issues are at work here, too. Nadine and Jeremy are "working stiffs" who aspire to the bourgeoisie, but who would be labeled proletarian by the uncharitable. One gets the impression that these two live from paycheck to paycheck—and that they don't mind. Work—and life—is what it is. You go along, do your job, take the punches and accept the small rewards. And while you may be committed to your work (as Nadine) or eager to take the system for whatever it offers (as Jeremy), you're a pragmatist who expects neither more nor less than your capabilities will allow.

That Jeremy takes a three-hundred-dollars weekly salary may seem like a lucky fluke, but the fact is that he possesses the useful American qualities of self-reliance, confidence, and cocky aggressiveness that are, paradoxically, part and parcel of the American (and larger human) spirit that Johnson simultaneously exploits and wishes to destroy.

With the exception of Dr. Rochelle, every human character in *Not of This Earth* is a prole. To Johnson's mind, they are powerless as individuals but valuable en masse, as a blood source (or, from the perspective of communism, as a natural resource from which to draw labor and soldiers). What he fails to understand is that, en masse, those proles comprise a formidable obstacle to his plans.

The film's exploration of extraordinary challenges forced upon ordinary people is pointed, and no accident. Nadine is a nurse in a day when that profession, though reasonably well respected, was underpaid and frankly subservient. Nadine's boyfriend, Harry Sherbourne, is a motorcycle cop who, like Nadine, is compelled to "help people." Jeremy is a budding career criminal. Given the realities of the day, we may assume that the "Chinaman" (Jeremy's term) who is abducted by Johnson for transport to Davanna is a gardener, groceryman, or other small businessman. Joe Piper, who brings jive talk to his gig as a vacuum cleaner salesman (a job undoubtedly forced upon him by the need for bread to buy coffee and reefer), exists at the low end of subcontracted labor.

Other characters include a parking lot attendant, a waitress, more cops, the lovestruck teenage girl, her hot-rodder boyfriend, and those potato-nosed winos. These are people apt to be regarded by a mid-level bureaucrat (if they're to be regarded at all) as mere tools. The irony is that, whether by a failure to satisfy his plans (as when the Chinese man arrives on Davanna crushed and useless) or by active resistance, these "tools" will be Johnson's undoing.

America Had Trouble but Moscow's Were Worse

The cop Harry Sherbourne is a particularly important symbol of the times. When *Not of This Earth* was shot and prepared for release in 1956–57, the most visible police chief in America was Thomas A. Parker, who headed the LAPD. Parker was a focused, ramrod-straight reformer who nevertheless allowed (or neglected to adequately control) vigilante uniformed cops, and thuggish plainclothesmen assigned to virtually autonomous vengeance and intimidation squads, in which form they acted against the underworld (and sometimes against other officers) with virtual impunity. All of this is admittedly a bad indicator of the state of American justice, and of the limited perceptiveness of the establishment, which honored Parker in Los Angeles, and from coast to coast. No firestorm of imagination is required to see that the LAPD, like any other institution, including communism, existed not to accomplish its stated goals, but merely to perpetuate itself.

But Parker was a skilled self-deceiver. Besides being a peace officer who countenanced brutality if (in his opinion) it served the larger interests of the city, the chief developed and vigorously propounded a simplistic professional ideology that cast police officers as a vital bastion against communism. Parker was deeply suspicious of intellectuals, civil liberties groups, "sob sisters" that protested LAPD tactics, and others that Parker was happy to lump together in the "Red" category.[10]

Parker was both right and wrong about the Soviet menace. Communism was a serious threat, and the Communist Party USA (CPUSA) received funds, and an agenda, from Moscow. That fact was revealed in the 1990s, when the "new" Russia temporarily fell into a confused sort of transparency and opened the Stalin archives to Western scholars.[11] On the other hand, the CPUSA, although looming large in the public imagination, was a small, poorly organized body that enjoyed few victories, and many of those of the Pyrrhic variety: the perpetrators and their mischief were frequently found out (as with the bumbling, doomed players in the Rosenberg case) and invited additional local and federal scrutiny of Party activities.

The Kremlin's designs on America were real enough, but Moscow lacked committed and competent Party members on the ground. Too many American Communist operatives were idealists instead of pragmatists. Postwar disclosures of the horrors of Stalinism disillusioned many Party members and fellow travelers, and those that remained were obsessed ideologues with limited espionage skills, rather than cool-headed thinkers with gifts for subterfuge.

Police Chief Parker was a closet alcoholic who became impassioned and voluble at the numberless dinners where he was the featured speaker. He made no secret of his belief in his police force, and in the crucial nature of L.A.'s thin blue line—the police officers who, as Parker saw it, protected the city from the anarchy that could resolve itself in a Communist takeover.[12] In this regard, Officer Sherburne's marching orders are clear. He is equipped, and ready, to preserve the American way of life.

Brutality and Godlessness

In the meantime, though, Johnson manages easy victories against individual adversaries. The nature of his triumphs is irredeemably harsh and ugly. The first victim whose fate we witness, the sprightly teenage girl, dies horribly, unfairly. She is a metaphor for all the women, all the weak and innocent, who had been trampled by communism. Later, after the brain of the vacuum cleaner shill is fried in Johnson's basement, Johnson slides the body into the blazing house furnace, an ugly (if reasonably utilitarian) act that's an evocative metaphor of the brutality displayed by the Soviets in Hungary and elsewhere, as well as an unavoidably piquant reminder of specific horrors of another recent dictatorship, Nazi Germany.

A mandated absence of religion always was at the core of Soviet-style communism. There was no God; the state was all. Johnson's personality begins and ends with the needs of Davanna. Although not completely autonomous, Johnson gives the impression of being a high mid-level functionary. He answers to the disembodied head in the closet communicator, but has achieved a level of influence sufficient to determine for himself whether the subjugation of Earth is a workable proposition. He's a monster but, more significantly, he's a bureaucrat absorbed in facts, probabilities, obstacles, and possible outcomes. He's the soulless functionary noted in writer Peter Fryer's remarks about brutalized Hungary.

Johnson also is purely empirical, and his single mention of a higher power comes in the form of ill-disguised sarcasm, during a conversation with the hypnotized Dr. Rochelle, who is bothered by the potential for disaster in Johnson's diseased blood. "God forbid such a dreadful new plague should strike the earth," the doctor muses.

"Yes," Johnson answers flatly. "God forbid."

From the Scarifying to the Ridiculous

By the time of Roger Corman's 1988 remake of *Not of This Earth* (which Corman produced but did not direct), political history and America's liberalized cultural climate had deprived Mr. Johnson of his sub-textual menace. The Soviet Union still existed but its power, particularly over its satellites, had waned. Elsewhere in the world, some African leaders (notably Libya's strongman, Muammar Gaddafi) had been acting badly, and North Korea's Kim Jong-il continued his late father's paranoid, uber–Stalinist course, but Americans of the day did not consider such people threats to what President George W. Bush later dubbed (with calculated emotional freight) "the homeland."

Movies had become infinitely more sexualized by 1988, particularly in the B-movie segment still commanded by Roger Corman, and that disgorged the remake of *Not of This Earth*. Film had grown considerably more juvenile, as well, and notions of subtext at this level of modern moviemaking seem absurd. So, by 1988, what did the controlling Mr. Johnson symbolize? Libertarians? Scientologists? Humorless parents? The answer is that he was simply a faintly novel menace who, by virtue of the stunt casting of retired pornographic actress Traci Lords as his nurse, threatened the all–American integrity of lubricious sex. Johnson has the ability to remove Traci-Nadine from the screen, and thus deprive us of further glimpses of the woman's flesh. This Johnson *is* a frowning parent—and one with a Calvinist streak, at that.

Although the '88 version utilizes the Griffith-Hanna screenplay virtually word for word, it brings forth none of the original's subtext. Director Jim Wynorski, who shot the remake with competence but a complete lack of texture and appropriate mood, didn't help at all—nor did the frequently naked Lords, whose thesping doesn't compare well at all to her concupiscent body. Allegedly cheeky tweaks to the original—such as the replacement of Corman's "Chinaman" with a topless "Happy Birthday" girl; and the winos swapped out for a trio of giggling hookers who disrobe in Johnson's basement—trivialize and make pointless whatever small sense of menace Wynorski might have managed to cobble together.

The story was remade a second time under Corman's auspices for a 1995 release. As Mr. Johnson, Michael York was an improvement over the flat Arthur Roberts of '88. Less noticeably exploitative than the 1988 film, this one used the original Griffith-Hanna screenplay as a template only, elaborating on Johnson's nature and, indeed, presenting him as a rebel fed up with the politics of his planet, and distressed to have to kill humans. All of that introduced some glib humanity, but completely upended the original notion of Johnson as a soulless functionary.

Davanna's Failure

The Mr. Johnson of 1957 played a good game but his inner and external resources were more limited than he knew. His Brooks Brothers suit identifies a company man, a team player, a metronomic and nameless bureaucrat ("Johnson" is, after all, a nom de plume, and a bland one, at that) who stoically pursues the agenda of his superiors and makes it his own. He believes in his cause, but he also goes along to get along.

Davanna is persistent but not particularly competent. Johnson's replacement will cause the police and others some headaches but he'll be undone by the blaring horn of a bus or by the revolt of the rootless but clever kid he hires to be his gofer. Neither he nor Davanna is equipped to prevail. Without soul, without vision beyond survival until tomorrow, Davanna is unable to adequately look after its own.

Historian Peter Fryer: "There is another tragedy, too.... It is the long-term tragedy of the absolute failure of the Hungarian Communist Party, after eight years in complete control of their country, to give the people either happiness or security, either freedom from want or freedom from fear."[13]

The self-perpetuated myth of Davanna will go to dust.

FILMOGRAPHY

Not of This Earth—Allied Artists; Released February 10, 1957; Black and white; 67 min.

Credits: Producer: Roger Corman; Director: Roger Corman; Screenplay: Charles B. Griffith, Mark Hanna; Director of photography: John Mescall; Editor: Charles Gross; Music: Ronald Stein; Art director: Karl Brainard; Special makeup: Curly Batson; Special effects: Paul and Jackie Blaisdell, Bob Burns.

Cast: Paul Birch: Mr. Johnson; Beverly Garland: Nadine Storey; William Roerick: Dr. Rochelle; Morgan Jones: Officer Harry Sherbourne; Jonathan Haze: Jeremy Perrin; Dick Miller: Joe Piper; Anne Carroll: Davannan woman; Roy Engel: Desk sergeant

NOTES

1. Matthews, John P.C. "Majales: The Abortive Student Revolt in Czechoslovakia in 1956." Working Paper No. 24, Woodrow Wilson International Center for Scholars. Washington, D.C.: 1998.
2. This date corresponds with Khrushchev's remarkable "secret speech" in the Great Hall at the Kremlin, in which he repudiated Stalin and Stalinist policy before members of the 20th Party Congress of the Communist Party of the Soviet Union.
3. socialistworker.org.
4. Fryer, Peter. *Hungarian Tragedy*. London: Dobson, 1956.
5. So late, in fact, that the girl wryly tells her fella, "If my father dug the scene he'd put small round holes in your head." Damaged heads figure prominently in *Not of This Earth*.
6. Wethey, Harold E. *The Paintings of Titian, Vol. 3: The Mythological and Historical Paintings*. London: Phaedon, 1975.
7. Tourney, Garfield, and Dean J. Plazak. "Evil Eye in Myth and Schizophrenia." *Psychiatric Quarterly* Volume 28, Number 1, January 1954.
8. Adamson, Joseph, and Hilary Anne Clark. *Scenes of Shame: Psychoanalysis, Shame, and Writing*. Albany: State University of New York Press, 1998.
9. Tourney, *ibid.*
10. Buntin, John. *L.A. Noir: The Struggle for the Soul of America's Most Seductive City*. New York: Crown, 2009.
11. Brent, Jonathan. *Inside the Stalin Archives: Discovering the New Russia*. New York: Atlas & Co., 1998.
12. Buntin, *ibid.*
13. Fryer, *ibid.*

WORKS CITED

Books
Adamson, Joseph, and Hilary Anne Clark. *Scenes of Shame: Psychoanalysis, Shame, and Writing*. Albany: State University of New York Press, 1998.
Brent, Jonathan. *Inside the Stalin Archives: Discovering the New Russia*. New York: Atlas & Co, 1998.
Buntin, John. *L.A. Noir: The Struggle for the Soul of America's Most Seductive City*. New York: Crown, 2009.
Fryer, Peter. *Hungarian Tragedy*. London: Dobson, 1956.
Howe, Irving, and Lewis Coser. *The American Communist Party: A Critical History (1919–1957)*. Boston: Beacon Press, 1957.
Wethey, Harold E. *The Paintings of Titian, Vol. 3: The Mythological and Historical Paintings*. London: Phaedon, 1975.

Journals and Papers
Matthews, John P.C. "Majales: The Abortive Student Revolt in Czechoslovakia in 1956." Working Paper No. 24, Woodrow Wilson International Center for Scholars. Washington, D.C.: 1988.
Tourney, Garfield, and Dean J. Plazak. "Evil Eye in Myth and Schizophrenia." *Psychiatric Quarterly* Volume 28, Number 1. January 1954.

Web
socialistworker.org

DVD
Not of This Earth (1988). Shout! Factory. 2010.
Not of This Earth (1995). New Concorde. 2003.
Roger Corman's Cult Classics Triple Feature: Attack of the Crab Monsters, War of the Satellites, Not of This Earth (1957). Shout! Factory. 2011.

The Cold Hands of Strangers
*The Politics of Disaster in Eight
Invasion Thrillers of the 1950s*

STEVEN THORNTON

The world nearly came to an end in the 1950s. Several times, in fact. The combined forces of flood, fire, alien invasion, and nuclear holocaust nearly obliterated all that was deemed good and orderly on this planet of ours. And all of it was depicted in glorious detail on movie screens across the nation.

In retrospect, it's perhaps not surprising that so much apocalyptic anxiety found expression through the eyes of the cinema. The afterglow of military triumph by the later-named Greatest Generation quickly became tarnished by the political realities of the Cold War and the massive societal changes that accompanied it. Beneath the surface of what is remembered as a peaceful and prosperous decade, fear hung in the air, often wearing a Red disguise and hiding behind an Iron Curtain. While America would eventually emerge as the victor from this chilliest of international conflicts, the changes wrought by the struggle would transform us, in some ways for better, in some ways for worse. But in all ways, the world would no longer be the same as it was before.

The films of this era often reflected the fear of cataclysmic change. Science fiction, with its innate ability to deal with Big Ideas, proved especially adept at giving light to our dark fears in a world fraught with uncertainty. At face value, the innocence of these films makes it easy to overlook their value as social barometers. Movies that depict impending disaster can easily be written off as stimuli for a Saturday matinee crowd and nothing more. But dig a little deeper and you find the common denominators of paranoia, heroism, a determination to overcome an all-powerful (and often unseen) adversary, and the importance of standing up for personal beliefs in times of trial. When one acknowledges where the American psyche was at in the 1950s, the traits shared by these movie suggest that something larger was at work.

Despite their sometimes formulaic nature, the science fiction films of this era depict a range of disasters that is remarkable in its scope and diversity. In some films, our world is besieged by brute forces beyond our comprehension. In others, the danger lies in things little seen and little suspected. Damage is inflicted on a global scale in the most epic storylines while in the more modestly budgeted affairs the threat is on a more intimate level. Deeply held values are also up for grabs in movies that challenged our beliefs concerning fate, the relationships between men and women, and the will of God. In the final reel, all ends well; the conventions of traditional filmmaking allowed viewers to walk home unscathed after witnessing such traumatic events, all social norms having been restored. But for many, this reassurance was one that the real world could not offer.

Politics of Utter Destruction

The end of the world comes with an interstellar bang in 1951's *When Worlds Collide*. Bolstered by elaborate special effects that depict the destruction of major metropolitan areas, the film has long been a favorite of cinema science fiction fans. And although the cause of the catastrophe is celestial rather than earthbound, the parallels to the worst-case political realities of the day are too close for comfort, even when viewed from a distance of several decades.

The plot of *When Worlds Collide* reads like pulp fiction of the hoariest kind. Astronomers at a remote observatory have discovered a star, Bellus, with an orbiting planet that is rushing headlong toward the earth. When the future path of these uninvited galactic guests is plotted, it is discovered that disaster is imminent—our world will initially experience floods, earthquakes, and other calamities, capped off by a head-on collision nineteen days later. The one slim hope for humankind lies in building a modern day Noah's Ark, a rocket ship that can ferry a limited group of survivors to Zyra, the companion planet of the invading star. It's a race against time as scientists and workmen labor to complete humanity's lifeboat before doomsday arrives.

Onscreen reactions to the fateful news say much about the cultural mindset of the 1950s. When insiders first receive confirmation of the coming events, they put forward their bravest faces. Dave Randall (Richard Derr), the everyman who becomes the hero of the film, sets dollar bills on fire as an expression of his newfound "live for today" mindset. Another principal character, Dr. Tony Drake (Peter Hansen), is motivated by the bad news to propose marriage to his reluctant fiancée, presumably because that is the natural order of things. Other scientists react stoically but remain committed to achieving a solution.

At first, the world at large voices skepticism about the scientific death sentence. "Star-Gazers Predict Doomsday," scoff the news headlines while words like "hoax" and "crackpot" are spoken in polite company. But as the fateful day approaches, people are more than happy to line up in orderly fashion and follow the lead of local and regional authorities. More notably, the world's races and creeds unite in a global demonstration of prayer, repentance, and atonement. Whether the world might have actually reacted in such a fashion is another matter, of course, but this depiction speaks volumes about how people viewed themselves in that long ago era. They wanted to belong, and so they obeyed.

To balance out this optimistic worldview, the dark side of humanity is represented by multi-millionaire Stanton (John Hoyt), who provides principal funding for the rocket project. This wheelchair-bound benefactor is no humanitarian—his only concern is to save his cynical hide. The script, seeking added melodrama, ratchets Stanton's nastiness to an almost cartoonish level. He attempts to dictate the passenger list, commandeers a secret cache of weapons ("Provisions," he promises, "for when the panic starts,") and chides the scientists for maximizing the human cargo. Impaired both physically and emotionally, Stanton even gets into an armed altercation with his toadying assistant, who attempts to procure one of the lottery tokens needed to gain access to the salvation ship. At a surface level, *When Worlds Collide* goes light on the politics of the day, although the depiction of uber-capitalist Stanton adds an interesting level of class warfare to the film (and presages today's widespread anger over wealth disparity). One can almost sense the audience cheering when the giant rocket ship comes to life a moment too soon for Stanton to gain entry, leaving the disbelieving tycoon stranded on the launch pad. (Postwar America venerated the new middle class but, as in years past, had little sympathy for the rich and powerful.)

As the title promises, the film does not cheat in its presentation of a world poised on the brink of disaster. The time is 1:00 p.m., the hour of doom, on the day of Bellus's close encounter with Earth. The principals brace themselves for the inevitable and then … silence. "All you scientists are crackpots," mocks Stanton, "nothing is going to happen." Suddenly: an audible rumble. The building shakes and the lights darken. Across the landscape, nature goes mad as a surge of gravity rips across our defenseless planet. Volcanoes, wildfires, icebergs, and cascading rocks all take turns inflicting their own special kind of hell on the bruised and battered terrain. Hurricane winds spread even more havoc as houses are swept away and massive trees are uprooted. In the most memorable destruction sequence, a tidal wave sweeps through a major city (probably intended to be New York), submerging once-busy streets—and any hapless city dwellers—beneath an ocean of water. Even given the technical limitations of the day, the parade of mass destruction is impressive, bolstered by top-notch model work, convincing sound effects, and first-rate editing—all of it a tribute to Hollywood ingenuity and old-school special effects.

Producer George Pal made a number of high profile SF thrillers for Paramount, and *When Worlds Collide* is remembered as one of the best. The movie is not without its weaknesses, especially when seen from today's perspective. To a man, the scientists are so altruistic they become 20th-century versions of plaster saints. A lengthy mid-film sequence depicting the discovery and rescue of a young boy is overly cloying in its "do the right thing" earnestness. Religious references, most notably the inclusion of a Holy Bible among the books that must be taken to the new planet, seem naïve and heavy handed today, though they certainly reflected the feelings of many in the vast middle-class audience.

Technically, the film closes on a real sour note: the scenic panorama depicting the landscape of Zyra is a poorly executed matte painting, described afterward by the artist, Chesley Bonestell, as a mere study that ended up being used because of time and budget. The image is a major letdown contrasted with the superb special effects work seen earlier. Regardless, the film remains a science fiction milestone, for its general ambition and amazing sequence of mass destruction. For viewers that lived in the shadow of the Bomb and the fear of Soviet domination, the significance of this moment likely worked on a subconscious level far beyond anything that is stated in the film. It's an instance of images taking on a life of their own, and *When Worlds Collide* is all the better for it.

FILMOGRAPHY

When Worlds Collide—Paramount; Released November 22, 1951; Technicolor; 83 min.

Credits: Producer: George Pal; Director: Rudolph Maté; Screenplay: Sydney Boehm, b/o the novel *When Worlds Collide* by Edwin Balmer and Philip Wylie; Directors of photography: John F. Seitz, W. Howard Greene; Editor: Arthur Schmidt; Music: Leith Stevens; Art directors: Hal Pereira, Albert Nozaki; Special effects: Gordon Jennings, Henry Barndollar.

Cast: Richard Derr: David Randall; Barbara Rush: Joyce Hendron; Peter Hanson: Dr. Tony Drake; John Hoyt: Sydney Stanton; Larry Keating: Dr. Cole Hendron; Frank Cady: Harold Ferris

A Message and a Warning

The Day the Earth Stood Still (1951) stands tall on any list of great science fiction films. A critical favorite upon its initial release and a cult favorite today, the film tells the story of Klaatu, a space emissary who travels to earth to warn us about the danger of our predilection for aggression in the age of the atom. Various writers have analyzed aspects of the movie's thought-provoking plot, from its veiled religious symbolism (Klaatu calls himself "Carpenter," and is resurrected after being killed), to its now-popular nuclear disarmament subtext. But few reviewers have bothered to notice that, behind his seemingly reasonable spaceman exterior, Klaatu carries a mighty big stick.

Klaatu (Michael Rennie) gets a lesson in Cold War politics soon after he arrives on our planet. Transported to Walter Reed Military Hospital after being wounded by a trigger-happy soldier, he is interviewed by Presidential Secretary Harley (Frank Conroy), who is anxious to learn the motivation behind the space caller's surprise visit. Klaatu's goal is seemingly simple—to address representatives from all the nations on a matter that concerns the existence "of every last creature on earth." But no matter how flexibly he voices his request, the doors of bureaucracy and political inertia remain slammed in his face. "Our world at the moment is full of tensions and suspicions," explains Harley after vetoing each and every suggestion. "Such a meeting would be quite impossible." Harley then ups the ante by voicing the standard lament over the "evil forces" that are to blame for "the trouble in our world." Such intractable positions were well known even to casual observers of world affairs in the 1950s and were easily defended given the political realities of the day. But to an outsider like Klaatu, these attitudes become a smokescreen that threatens to hinder the success of his mission.

This cynical view of our world's situation is soon reinforced by Klaatu's experiences with the common folk. After escaping from his hospitalization/imprisonment, he takes up residence in a boarding house to learn more about the people of this planet. The clues from the culture are not encouraging. A full-page display in a local newspaper screams the provocative question "Are We Long For This World?" accompanied by lurid graphics that would be right at home in a pulp magazine. A commentator on a Sunday-morning radio broadcast slants his coverage to emphasize the sensational, fear-inducing aspects of the space alien's visit. And the boarders themselves react to the latest news with a mixture of curiosity and paranoia. The zinger to this sequence is provided by Mrs. Barley (Frances Bavier), who opines that "he comes from right here on earth ... and you know where I mean!" Hearing Bavier (recalled as sweet-natured Aunt Bea on television's long-running *The Andy Griffith Show*) voice such politically charged dialogue is an amusing shock, and suggests that the meek of this world were no less invested in hardnosed Cold War attitudes than the privileged and the powerful.

Spurred on by the Einstein-like Professor Barnhardt (Sam Jaffe), Klaatu devises a novel plan to capture the world's attention. By means never fully disclosed, he arranges to have electricity neutralized across our planet for a brief period of time. All the machinery to which modern society has become accustomed grinds to an abrupt halt, bringing about a literal representation of the film's title. The result is a mild form of chaos—cars

The Day the Earth Stood Still **(1951). Gort (Lock Martin) stands by as Klaatu (Michael Rennie) explains to Helen (Patricia Neal) the well-intentioned but iron-fisted plan to ensure a peaceful Earth. In this graceful and high-minded SF drama, the arms race seems not only unappetizing but profitless.**

stall, motorcycles refuse to start, assembly lines shut down, and drawbridges are frozen in place. As world disasters go, it's a modest affair; there are no reported injuries as a result of this intergalactic party trick, and exceptions were somehow granted for such essential services as hospitals and airplanes in flight. But the impact of Klaatu's actions brings about the desired result, leaving people the world over in a state of panic.

More importantly, Klaatu keeps yet another ace up his sleeve—the death card. Although he never chooses to use it, he makes it abundantly clear that he also holds the power to destroy this planet and all who live here. He drops subtle hints of this in his encounter with Harley and other government officials. Later, when he and Barnhardt discuss strategy options, Klaatu wonders aloud if a violent course of action, such as leveling New York City or sinking the Rock of Gibraltar, is needed. And in his farewell speech, delivered just prior to his return to the great beyond, he paints a picture of Armageddon-like devastation should we choose to continue on our present course. "It is no concern of ours how you run your own planet," he states bluntly. "But if you threaten to extend your violence, this earth of yours will be reduced to a burned-out cinder." Little violence is actually shown in the film but this threat hangs in the air from beginning to end, leaving us with no doubt that Klaatu is indeed a spaceman of his word.

The Day the Earth Stood Still remains a cultural favorite for countless reasons. The script by Edmund H. North (adapted from a story by Harry Bates) deftly merges political realities into a believable SF scenario. Director Robert Wise keeps the action and the exposition moving at a pleasing pace. Memorable performances, especially from Michael Rennie and Patricia Neal, engage us on emotional as well as intellectual levels. Gort, the menacing robot that accompanies Klaatu on his interplanetary mission, remains one of the iconic images of 1950s cinema, an anthropomorphized representation of the barely controllable atomic might of the day. And behind it all is the fear that a real-life global stalemate of world politics might bring us to the edge of oblivion. It's a heady proposition that makes us wonder this: What would Klaatu's judgment have been if he had paid us a return visit?

FILMOGRAPHY

The Day the Earth Stood Still—20th Century-Fox; Released September 18, 1951 (New York City); September 28, 1951 (Los Angeles); Black and white; 92 min.

Credits: Producer: Julian Blaustein; Director: Robert Wise; Screenplay: Edmund H. North, based on the short story "Farewell to the Master" by Harry Bates (pseudonym of Hiram Gilmore Bates III); Director of photography: Leo Tover; Editor: William Reynolds; Music: Bernard Herrmann; Art directors: Addison Hehr, Lyle Wheeler; Special effects (robot): Melbourne A. Arnold; Visual effects: L. B. Abbott, Fred Sersen, Ray Kellogg.

Cast: Michael Rennie: Klaatu; Patricia Neal: Helen Benson; Hugh Marlowe: Tom Stevens; Sam Jaffe: Prof. Jacob Barnhardt; Billy Gray: Bobby Benson; Lock Martin: Gort

Planet of War

The specter of worldwide devastation—the consequence of a Martian invasion—is vividly, almost lovingly depicted in 1953's *The War of the Worlds*. Yet another George Pal production for Paramount, this film ups the ante of mass destruction seen in earlier SF efforts and then some. Given the widespread fears associated with life in the age of atomic weapons, it isn't difficult to connect the dots between the film's images of major world cities in flames and the direst predictions from nuclear critics during the early years of the Cold War era.

Armed conflict characterizes much of this thriller, and right from the film's earliest moments. A gripping pre-credits sequence sets the stage by summarizing the major military conflicts of the 20th century, each one with a higher death toll than the last. The mood shifts briefly in the opening reel when the initial Martian landing ship, mistaken for a meteor, crashes and lies dormant in a remote rural area. But by the twenty-minute mark, the invaders and their weapons have sprung to life and a trio of dimwit watchmen lies vaporized. More ships fall from the sky, and as the nature of the alien threat becomes clear, the military is called into action. The weapons of man are no match, however, for the superior Martian technology and soon the region, like all other landing sites, has been laid waste by the heat ray atop the interplanetary landing crafts. At times, the depiction of wanton destruction is so explicit that the film begins to look more like a wartime newsreel than an SF fantasy.

The Cold War parallels grow stronger when the decision is made to deploy an atomic bomb against the invading Martian army. But the deployment of this fearful weaponry, "ten times more powerful" than anything previously used, proves futile against the Martians' superior capabilities. The chronology is off a bit (the far more destructive hydrogen

In a key moment from *The War of the Worlds* (1953), Dr. Forrester (Gene Barry) severs a Martian electronic eye from its stalk, an act that will lead him to a partial understanding of Martian physiognomy. His companion, Sylvia (Ann Robinson), has reservations about Forrester's brazenness.

bomb was first tested in November 1952, a good nine months prior to the film's general release) but the idea still resonates—the fear of the outsider whose technological capabilities far outstrip our own. Although the West overestimated Stalin's military might during the 1950s, the Soviet expansionist appetites were real, and their impressive achievements in both the arms and (later) the space race demonstrated that they were committed to spreading their influence, and their ideology, by means peaceful and otherwise. As a consequence, *The War of the Worlds* is an illustration of the ultimate Cold War fear: that the hopes of freedom-loving people everywhere may be dashed by an unbending force that cannot be vanquished by conventional means.

The Martian indifference to religion has Cold War resonance too. Pastor Collins (Lewis Martin), uncle of heroine Sylvia Van Buren (Ann Robinson), is the lone voice arguing that some attempt should be made to communicate with the interplanetary intruders. "If they're more advanced than us, they should be nearer the Creator for that reason," he confides to Sylvia. Alas, his optimism proves groundless—moments later, the pastor is turned to ashes as he approaches the Martian landing craft, the words of Psalm 40 ringing from his lips. Later, a concerned scientist calculates that the civilized world may fall under Martian subjugation in as little as six days, a parallel to Genesis that is not lost on the film's characters.

The film's finale brings the religious references full circle. Dr. Clayton Forrester (Gene Barry) searches for Sylvia in the ruins of Los Angeles. As the Martian death machines close in, the pair is reunited in a church, where a handful of other believers have turned for solace. They embrace as the church is attacked. Suddenly, and unexpectedly, all is quiet. The Martians, all-powerful and seemingly invincible, begin to succumb to airborne bacteria. "After all that men could do had failed, the Martians were destroyed and humanity was saved by the littlest things which God in his wisdom had put upon this earth," intones narrator Sir Cedric Hardwicke. Contemporary reviews tend to get snarky at the heavy-handedness of this scene, but at a time when the Soviet bear proudly trumpeted atheism as the official religion of the state, Western audiences likely viewed such a hopeful denouement as a welcome affirmation of their traditional beliefs.

H.G. Wells's original 1897 text was regarded as a cautionary tale against the evils of colonialism. George Pal's version of the story updates the political context by drawing connections between the Red Planet and the Red menace, a connection that inspired numerous filmmakers later in the decade. The use of an oversaturated color palette is especially noteworthy in this regard, a visual metaphor that strengthens the link between the combative Red-planet aliens and America's chief rival on the world stage. Despite the obligatory happy ending, a sense of desperation hangs over the film. The survival of the world, the story suggests, is by no means guaranteed. Victory may be achieved, *The War of the Worlds* assures its Cold War audience, but, as in the real world, the price of defending life and liberty is likely to be great.

FILMOGRAPHY

The War of the Worlds—Paramount; Released February 20, 1953 (Los Angeles); July 29, 1953 (Atlantic City); August 13, 1953 (New York City); August 26, 1953 (general); Technicolor; black and white (pre-credits historical montage); 85 min.

Credits: Producer: George Pal; Director: Byron Haskin; Screenplay: Barré Lyndon, b/o the novel *The War of the Worlds* by H.G. Wells; Director of photography: George Barnes; Editor: Everett Douglas; Music: Leith Stevens; Art directors: Hal Pereira, Albert Nozaki; Special effects: Chester Pate, Bob Springfield, A. Edward Sutherland, Barney Wolff; Visual effects: Gordon Jennings, Jan Domela (matte paintings), Farciot Edouart (process photography), Marcel Delgado (miniatures), Ivyl Burks; Martian design: Charles Gemora; Astronomical art: Chesley Bonestell; Sound: Harry Lindgren, Gene Garvin.

Cast: Gene Barry: Dr. Clayton Forrester; Ann Robinson: Sylvia Van Buren; Les Tremayne: Major General Mann; Bob (Robert) Cornthwaite: Dr. Pryor; Sandra Giglio: Dr. Bilderbeck; Lewis Martin: Pastor Matthew Collins; Bill (William) Phipps: Wash Perry (man #1 at saucer pit); Jack Kruschen: Salvatore (man #2 at saucer pit); Paul Birch: Alonzo Hogue (man #3 at saucer pit); Martian: Charles Gemora; Paul Frees: pre-credits narrator; radio reporter at saucer pit; Sir Cedric Hardwicke: narrator

Zero Hour

By the middle of the 1950s, disaster themes had begun to permeate low-budget movie making. *Day the World Ended*, released by American Releasing Corporation (later to become American International Pictures) in 1955, displays flaws that were typical of the lower end of Hollywood's production chain. But despite its modest pedigree, the film taps into some interesting implications concerning the day after doomsday.

Day the World Ended eschews invading aliens and natural disasters to focus instead on the nuclear elephant in the world's living room. The pre-title sequence tells us that the story begins with "The End" as an atomic explosion morphs into a deceptively serene cloudscape. "From this hour forward," the God-like narrator informs us, "the world as we know it no longer exists." Against this doom-laden scenario, we meet Jim Maddison (Paul Birch), a survivalist who foresaw the end, and his daughter, Louise (Lori Nelson). Unexpectedly, a handful of others who somehow managed to survive the deluge arrive at Jim's mountain hideaway: geologist Rick (Richard Denning), small-time hood Tony Lamont (Mike "Touch" Connors), girlfriend/stripper Ruby (Adele Jergens), grizzled prospector Pete (Raymond Hatton), and Radek (Paul Dubov), a victim of severe radiation exposure. This mismatched group struggles with interpersonal conflicts and atomic mutations as the future of the human race hangs in the balance.

The dread of nuclear disaster hangs over the film like a mushroom cloud. There is talk of food rationing, of using water in sealed jars, of Geiger counters and roentgens, of an atomic haze that hangs over the hills, and of rain water saturated with radioactive death. Worst of all, Jim hints at the misshapen creatures he once observed at ground zero of a nuclear test site. "Some lived through it," Jim explains to Rick as he thumbs through a ghoulish art gallery of sketches that he made from memory. The images depict various small mammals with multiple limbs and skin with the appearance of armor, the horrific byproducts of evolution given a push in the wrong direction. And when the badly burned Radek begins to eschew food and disappears into the night for hours on end, the more knowledgeable members of the group begin to suspect that something terrible is afoot … and so it is, in the form of a hideous, scaly humanoid (designed and built by Paul and Jackie Blaisdell) with a peculiar attraction to Louise.

Given that the picture was designed to thrill audiences comprised of kids, the late-in-the-day monster angle should come as no surprise. Still, the somber mood and thoughtful attention to detail (the film could almost be subtitled "How to Survive A Nuclear Strike") make for interesting viewing.

While other melodramas in this survey promise the hope of mankind's eventual salvation, *Day the World Ended* delivers the unrelenting fatalism of a book from the Old Testament. The action is confined to Jim's house and the surrounding valley because of lingering radiation, which shrouds the rest of the world like a Biblical curse. As confirmed by the endless static on the shortwave radio, the cast of seven appears to be the only people left alive. As in ancient legend, the characters, and their dominant traits, are drawn in the broadest of strokes. Especially noticeable in this regard is the pairing of good guy Rick and virtuous Louise, functioning as a counterbalance to hot-tempered Tony and goodtime girl Ruby. Talk eventually turns to the propagation of the species, with Jim strongly hinting that Rick and Louise owe it to the world to give the human race a second chance. Not unexpectedly, Tony has other ideas, and his wandering eye soon becomes fixed on Louise. Emotions run high on all sides as the principals face off to determine who will become the new Adam and the new Eve. The "clean" rain that falls near the end of the film is like a healing balm from the heavens. Prophetically, the story ends on a hopeful message of saving grave, with the words "The Beginning" superimposed over the final fade-out, signaling that humanity has been given a second chance.

Because of its limited budget, *Day the World Ended* doesn't quite live up to its ambitious premise. It's a talky affair that fails to fully utilize its colorful cast of characters. The bickering of ex-lovers Tony and Ruby quickly takes a turn into soap opera, and the hook of the final reel—the mutant's attack—undermines the serious premise so carefully estab-

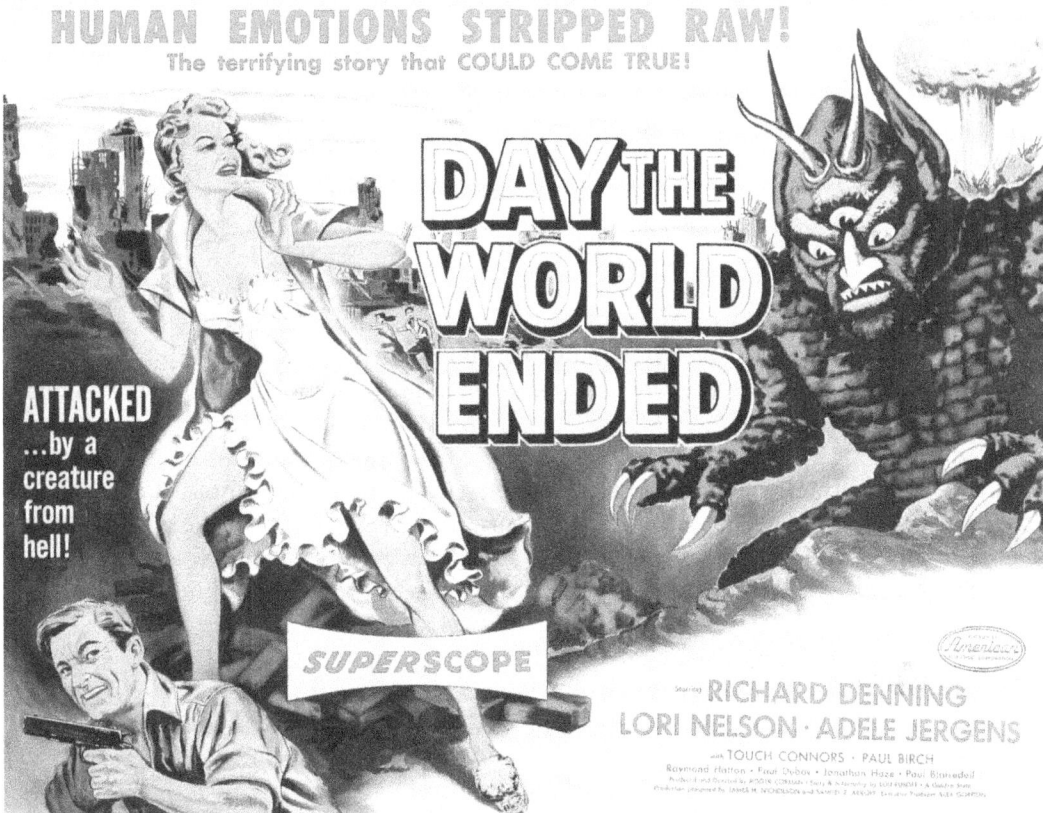

Day the World Ended (1955), director Roger Corman's first science fiction thriller, is an energetic combination of atomic-attack survival guide, monster movie, and somber reflection on the perils of total war. The lively poster art is by Al Kallis.

lished early in the story. But on the other side of the ledger, the film resonates with enough ideas to keep a viewer thinking for weeks. Renowned filmmaker Roger Corman, laboring on one of his early directorial efforts, displays his knack for making the most of meager resources. Although *Day the World Ended* sidesteps the details of Cold War politics (no specific enemies are named and no blatant agenda is endorsed) it earns points for exploiting the Big Fear that dominated thinking. And it does so in an admirably honest way that productions from the larger studios seldom attempted.

FILMOGRAPHY

Day the World Ended—American Releasing Corporation; Released December 18, 1955; Black and white; 79 min.

    Credits: Producers: Alex Gordon, Roger Corman; Director: Roger Corman; Screenplay: Lou Rusoff; Director of photography: Jock Feindel; Editor: Ronald Sinclair; Music: Ronald Stein; Art director: Harold Rief; Creature design: Paul and Jackie Blaisdell

    Cast: Richard Denning: Rick; Lori Nelson: Louise Maddison; Adele Jergens: Ruby; Touch (Mike) Connors: Tony Lamont; Paul Birch: Jim Maddison; Raymond Hatton: Pete; Paul Dubov: Radek; Contaminated man: Jonathan Haze; Creature: Paul Blaisdell; Opening narration: Chet Huntley

Take Us to Your Leaders—So We Can Kill Them

Columbia Pictures joined the "invasion from space" bandwagon in 1956 with *Earth vs. the Flying Saucers*. Although not as ambitious as the decade's best sci-fi efforts (and, as a consequence, not as highly regarded), the film does provide solid entertainment, thanks principally to the superbly crafted effects work of stop-frame animator Ray Harryhausen. And in a modest way, the movie visualizes the fearful anxieties that fed Cold War politics.

Flying saucer sightings accelerated quickly following private pilot Kenneth Arnold's encounter above Washington State in 1947. Interest in the UFO phenomenon ran high throughout the following decade, and *Earth vs. the Flying Saucers* wastes no time tapping into this mania. Dr. Russell Marvin (Hugh Marlowe) and his new bride, Carol (Joan Taylor), are closely involved with Project Skyhook, a Washington initiative to launch multiple satellites into earth orbit as a precursor to manned space exploration. While traveling to the project's desert-based locale, they experience a close encounter with an enormous flying saucer of, as we shortly discover, extraterrestrial origin. Unbeknownst to the pair, the aliens hoped to arrange a meeting concurrent with the launch of the next satellite. When launch day arrives and the saucers land at the Skyhook complex, all hell breaks loose and our military forces open fire. The aliens easily prevail, unleashing frightful ray weapons and utilizing electronic screens that protect the saucers. In an impressive sequence that skillfully blends stop-frame animation with copious footage of various aviation and industrial disasters, the spacemen flatten the Skyhook site, forcing the project to an early, unscheduled termination, and sending Marvin and Carol deep into a sub-basement.

Early scenes vibrate with fears of sabotage and subversion. Something has been bringing down the Skyhook satellites—but what? Lacking (for the moment) evidence of extraterrestrial invaders, officials discuss human mischief. From Alger Hiss to the Rosenbergs to the Silvermaster spy ring, Communist sympathizers inside the U.S. exposed atomic secrets and other secret information to unfriendly eyes. Although the ultimate damage caused by these security breaches is debatable, the panic they engendered, both in government circles and among the general public, was substantial. America's nascent space program was jealously guarded, so contemporaneous audiences got a sickly thrill when the film reveals that Project Skyhook has been interfered with by a powerful alien enemy. As with the other films covered in this essay, an outside power with a hidden agenda uses force to ensure that its interests prevail.

The plot develops pretty much as expected (the aliens decide to subjugate our planet, forcing humankind to develop a weapon that can best their superior technology) until the climactic battle in the skies above Washington, D.C. To observe alien spacecraft crash into such familiar landmarks as the Capitol Building and the Washington Monument is both exhilarating and alarming, a visual reminder of what would be at stake during a full-fledged invasion by a well-armed foreign power. (In a perverse act of cheekiness, one saucer gently settles on the White House lawn.) In real-life 1956, a belligerent Nikita Khrushchev uttered the phrase "we will bury you" to ambassadors of the Western world—a promise not of death but of something even more frightening: the eventual triumph of a remorseless Communist ideology over the world's democracies.

When a few people are taken aboard a saucer and flown thousands of miles in moments, an American general (Morris Ankrum) is held fast by an immobilizing ray

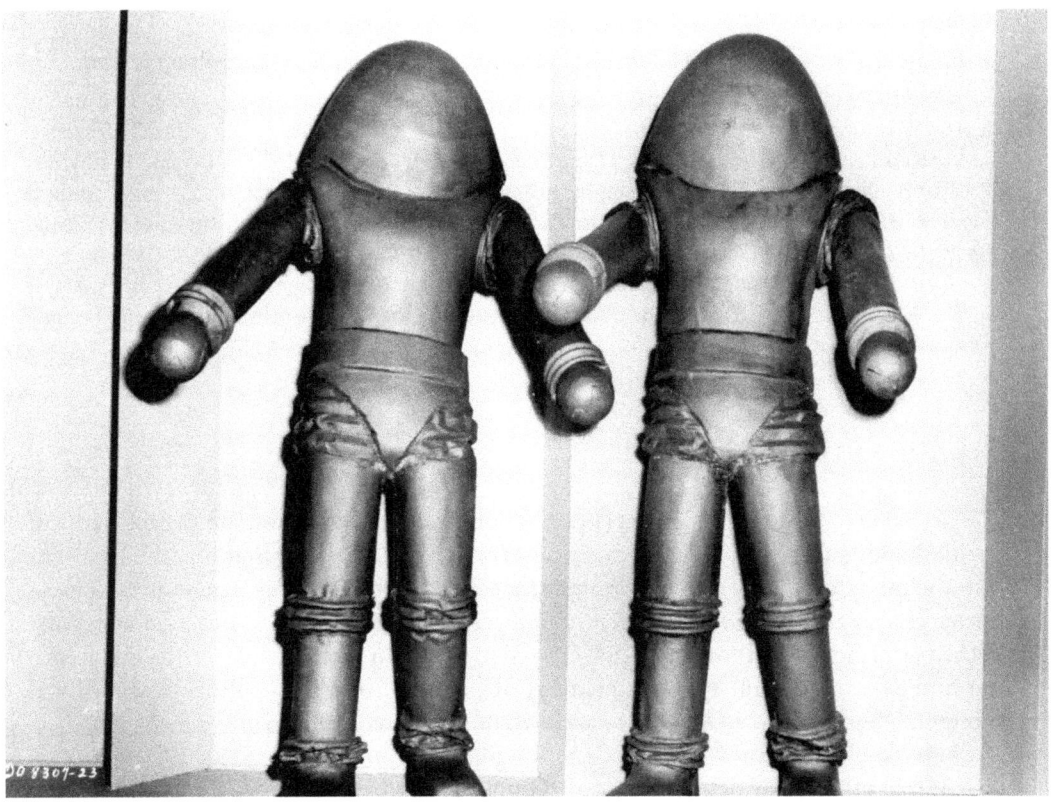

There was no negotiating at all with the brutal and acquisitive invaders of *Earth vs. the Flying Saucers* (1956). Although physically inadequate (like the Martians of *The War of the Worlds*), the aliens encase themselves in weaponized armor, and employ their enormous saucers and other heavy ordnance to kidnap, kill, and destroy. Their goal: complete subjugation of Earth.

that probes his head, revealing his brain and draining it of information. When the process is complete, the aliens dump the general's body from the craft, like garbage. This pictorial representation of an ugly Communist trick from the Korean War, "brainwashing," remains unsettling after more than sixty years. Although the aliens fall short in their goal of burying us, they do enough damage to treasured American institutions to sober us, and to suggest that Washington and everything represented there must be defended.

As a movie thriller, *Earth vs. the Flying Saucers* is derivative, with story elements and twists that echo plot points of earlier, better films. (Especially brazen is an overly talky sequence—lifted almost line for line *The War of the Worlds*—in which the capabilities of captured alien technology are demonstrated.) Regardless, the sight of America's capital city reduced to ruins remains one of the decade's science fiction movie highlights. And crouching beneath this noisy mid-century mayhem is the endless real-life saber rattling of various Cold War powers. *Earth vs. the Flying Saucers* suggests what can happen when the sabers are no longer rattled, but used in anger. Indeed, hardly more than four months after the film's American release, Soviet tank troops in Hungary brutally crushed a countrywide citizens' uprising, killing 2,500 Hungarians, and arresting and imprisoning more than 20,000. The brunt of the Soviet destruction was absorbed by Budapest, Hungary's capital city.

FILMOGRAPHY

Earth vs. the Flying Saucers—Columbia; Released July 4, 1956; Black and white; 83 min.

Credits: Producers: Sam Katzman, Charles H. Schneer; Director: Fred F. Sears; Screenplay: George Worthing Yates, Bernard Gordon (blacklisted Gordon credited as Raymond T. Marcus), loosely based on the non-fiction book *Flying Saucers from Outer Space* by Maj. Donald E. Keyhoe; Director of photography: Fred Jackman, Jr.; Editor: Danny Landres; Music: Mischa Bakaleinikoff (supervisor of stock music); Art director: Paul Palmentola; Special effects: Russ Kelley; Visual effects: Ray Harryhausen; Sound: Josh Westmoreland.

Cast: Hugh Marlowe: Dr. Russell A. Marvin; Joan Taylor: Carol Marvin; Donald Curtis: Major Huglin; Morris Ankrum: Brig. Gen. John Hanley; John Zaremba: Prof. Kanter; Tom (Thomas) Browne Henry: Vice Admiral Enright

"You're next!"—Yes, You!

Invasion of the Body Snatchers (1956) is unquestionably a milestone in SF cinema of the 1950s. One part invasion tale and one part exercise in pure paranoia, the film taps into the mood of unease and uncertainty that masked the cheerful facade of the Eisenhower era. To this reviewer, *Invasion* remains a solid piece of entertainment—a tribute to the performers and filmmakers that crafted it. Critics and commentators still reference the film as a minor, but pointed, element of postwar American culture and political thought. Offering style and fertile ideas in equal measure, *Invasion of the Body Snatchers* is a remarkable piece of work.

While other films depict the destruction of the world in physical terms, *Invasion* conveys that tragedy on a uniquely person level. Dr. Miles Bennell (Kevin McCarthy) returns from a medical conference to find that his hometown of Santa Mira has experienced a subtle change. A number of townsfolk believe that a close relative is somehow different. The relatives look, sound, and act the same but something—a special look, a tiny spark of humanity—is gone. Just as surprisingly, the crisis passes a few days later and everything appears to be back to normal. Miles and old beau Becky Driscoll (Dana Wynter) puzzle over the situation but shrug it off as a likely case of mass hysteria. Before long, however, Miles and Becky realize that the story is bigger, and the stakes are higher, than they ever realized.

The pace, and the sense of paranoia, escalates impressively when Miles receives an emergency call late one night. At the home of mutual acquaintance Jack Belicec (King Donovan), Miles is astounded when he is shown the inchoate form of a not quite human body, in eerie repose atop Jack's pool table. All the anatomical features are correct but the body has no lines or other flaws, no "character," and no fingerprints. The mood shifts to horror when wife Teddy (Carolyn Jones) realizes that the figure matches Jack's frame and body type. The moment shocks but what really sells it are the reactions of the cast—Jack's fearful disbelief, Teddy's hysteria, Becky's panic, and Miles's rationalizations as he tries to process what he sees. So good is director Don Siegel's staging and the cast's performances that one's suspension of disbelief is total.

Later, Miles has a hunch, and discovers Becky's duplicate growing in the cellar of her house. The next day, inside his shadowed greenhouse, he discovers a bumper crop of synthetic bodies, himself and the Belicecs included. Never for a minute do we question the innate absurdity of this scenario. The final sting is that the replacements occur when

One of the great movie thrillers of the Cold War era, Don Siegel's *Invasion of the Body Snatchers* (1956) is predicated on a hideous alien scheme to infiltrate the minds and bodies of humans, one person at a time, and one small group at a time, turning the victims into emotional neuters that live not for joy, but for brute survival. This rarely seen original-release poster captures much of the tale's frenzied paranoia.

the human victims sleep; in other words, we are destroyed when we are most vulnerable.

A growing sense of isolation heightens the film's tension. Little by little, Miles and Becky come to understand that no one in Santa Mira can be trusted. Everyone they know—friends, neighbors, and relatives alike—have become alien replicants intent on replacing the human race with lookalike doubles. Miles soon discovers that any hope of help from the local authorities is in vain. Roads are blocked, phone lines are unresponsive, and the town's police force has been overrun by the invading horde, making it impossible to get word to the outside world. Soon, Miles and Becky are in a footrace for their lives with an army of otherworldly pursuers close behind them.

The human tragedy intensifies when Miles and Becky are confronted by the alien duplicates of their most trusted associates, Jack and Dr. Kauffman (Larry Gates). "While you're asleep they absorb your minds, your memories," the doctor remarks. He promises that they will be "reborn into an untroubled world" where there will be "no need for love." The alien credo is almost an anathema for normal human instincts. "Love, desire, ambition, faith—without them life's so simple, believe me," the doctor says in coolly measured tones. Miles and Becky console each other as they reach the film's darkest, and saddest, moment. "I want to love and be loved," sobs Becky. "I want your children. I don't want a world without love or grief or beauty. I'd rather die…"

Finally driven almost to madness, Miles darts onto a busy nighttime highway, straddled by passing cars and trying in vain to get drivers' attention. "You're next!" he screams. "You're next!"

Other science fiction thrillers of the early Cold War era dazzle with their special effect or impress with their sociopolitical implications. But *Invasion of the Body Snatchers* scores simply by taking the implications of an alien invasion to its logical conclusion, and presenting the terror of this scenario through the eyes of the characters whose lives are directly affected by it. For audiences of the 1950s, bombarded with anti–Communist government propaganda and everyday anti–Red cultural cues, the potential loss of basic human drives resonated on a primal, instinctive level.

Don Siegel had hoped to call his movie *Sleep No More*. Allied Artists nixed that, of course, but because the title has been preserved by film historians, we can appreciate its multiple meanings: do not let down your guard; remain alert; if you are helpless, enemies may take you—and if that happens, untroubled sleep and life's other everyday pleasures will be denied you. You will have been absorbed by the Other.

Filmography

Invasion of the Body Snatchers—Allied Artists; Released February 5, 1956; Black and white; 80 min.

Credits: Producer: Walter Wanger; Director: Don Siegel; Screenplay: Daniel Mainwaring, b/o the novel *The Body Snatchers* by Jack Finney; Director of photography: Ellsworth Fredericks; Editor: Robert S. Eisen; Music: Carmen Dragon; Art director: Edward (Ted) Haworth; Special effects: Don Post (pods), Milt Rice.

Cast: Kevin McCarthy: Dr. Miles Bennell; Dana Wynter: Becky Driscoll; Larry Gates: Dr. Dan Kaufman; King Donovan: Jack Belicec; Carolyn Jones: Teddy Belicec; Jean Willes: Sally Withers; Virginia Christine: Wilma Lentz; Tom Fadden: Uncle Ira Lentz; Whit Bissell: Dr. Hill; Richard Deacon: Dr. Bassett

Fatal Vows

Cultural critics have long maintained that family is the true backbone of society. This premise is given a genre twist in Paramount's 1958 release, *I Married a Monster from Outer Space*. Ignore the risible title; this smart and moody picture by director Gene Fowler, Jr., is a well-executed thriller that stands on equal footing with the best science fiction thrillers of the decade. Although the damage that unfolds is limited mainly to interpersonal relationships, the implied threat to our world is considerably greater, particularly insofar as the invaders use subterfuge rather than a massive display of force.

From early on, the narrative casts marriage in an unflattering light. The night before he is to tie the knot, Bill Farrell (Tom Tryon) bids goodbye to his bachelorhood with friends at a local watering hole. They claim to be celebrating but the affair feels more like a dirge. "Everyone one of us is married, was married or is about to get married," laments one of the gang in hangdog fashion. Other episodes throughout the film reinforce the idea that marriage is something that women desperately long for and men avoid at all costs. This pejorative dismissal of the traditional man/woman pairing scheme sets an uneasy undercurrent for the events to follow.

Despite one of the silliest titles in movie history, *I Married a Monster from Outer Space* (1958) is a moody and intelligent SF thriller about stolen identity, predicated on a foreign culture's violation of marriage, and destruction of the family—primal themes that resonate no less strongly today than during that era of Communist subversion. In order for the scheme to succeed, young husbands and authority figures must be neutralized, as seen in this unsettling tableau inside the invaders' spacecraft.

Things become personal when Bill, on the way home from the party, has an otherworldly encounter and his body becomes the host to an alien presence. The wedding goes ahead as planned, with Bill claiming Marge (Gloria Talbott) as his bride. Soon though, there is trouble in paradise. A year passes and the union fails to produce a child. Even worse, Marge senses that some great change has taken over her husband. "Bill is not the man I fell in love with," she pens in a letter to her mother. "He's almost a stranger." It sounds like the story of a thousand other marriages gone wrong, as husband and wife experience a growing disconnect that continually pushes them apart. But the science fiction twist gives the story an added weight, and forces the narrative into personal territory.

In time, Marge learns the truth about the stranger whom she has taken for a husband. The aliens' motivations, she learns, aren't totally unreasonable. Like so many SF visitors from space, they fled a dying planet in search of a new home for their imperiled race. But their decision to colonize the earth will have serious consequences for Earth. The alien women, used for breeding purposes only, perished before their flight to the stars could begin. But through the miracle of alien technology, the biological differences between the species can be overcome. "Along with these bodies we inherited other things as well—human desires, emotions," Bill tells a concerned Marge. "Eventually, we will have children with you."

"What kind?" she asks softly.

Bill gives her a passionless gaze and answers, "Our kind."

Marge is understandably cool to the idea. Married or not, she is reluctant to jump into the cosmic gene pool.

Fear and tension are generated on a number of levels—sexual objectification, identity confusion, spousal abuse, paranoia, the death of emotion, and betrayal of trust. Sympathy is factored into the mix as well. "I've never known happiness or love or any emotion," alien-possessed Bill confesses moments before he is liquidated. "I'd just begun to learn."

Tom Tryon is impressive as the alien in human guise, displaying a surface level of normalcy that barely masks his emotionless inner core. Gloria Talbott delivers a fine performance as the young wife who experiences the world's worst case of a marriage gone wrong. In an uncertain world, trust and intimacy are basic and comforting human traits. Marge's oldest friend in town, the police chief (John Eldredge), has been taken over, and secretly contrives to use her fears against her. And although Bill has a raft of guy friends, Marge has no idea which ones can be trusted. Surrounded by heartless catspaws, she is alone.

In *Invasion of the Body Snatchers*, the physical disposition of the supplanted human bodies remains unknown, but here, inside the aliens' shadowed spaceship, the true bodies of Bill, the chief, and other local men hang suspended above discrete machines designed to—keep them alive? Drain their memories? Probe their anatomies? Whether used for all of those reasons or just some, the devices are subliminal visualizations of brainwashing, false imprisonment, and torture—each a widely reported element of Communist cruelty.

I Married a Monster from Outer Space suggests that when intimate trust is violated—the covenant between husband and wife, and between citizen and state—we have reached the beginning of the end. Conservative pundits cite the destruction of the traditional family as a sure way to speed the ruin of a society. Without proper families, these critics insist, we are not simply lost and vulnerable, but alien to ourselves.

FILMOGRAPHY

I Married a Monster from Outer Space—Paramount; Released September 29, 1958; Black and white; 78 min.

   Credits: Producer: Gene Fowler, Jr.; Director: Gene Fowler, Jr.; Screenplay: Louis Vittes; Director of photography: Haskell Boggs; Editor: George Tomasini; Music (stock; Leith Stevens, et al.); Art directors: Henry Bumstead, Hal Pereira; Special effects: John P. Fulton; Creature design: Charles Gemora;

   Cast: Tom Tryon: Bill Farrell; Gloria Talbott: Marge Ferrell; John Eldredge: Police Capt. H. B. Collins; Ken Lynch: Dr. Wayne; Maxie Rosenbloom: Max Grady; Valerie Allen: Francine; Creature(s): Charles Gemora

Ideology of the Undead

We conclude our overview of Cold War science fiction thrillers with a low-budget DVD favorite, *Invisible Invaders* (1959). Typical of the lower-end SF thrillers of the period, the film borrows liberally from earlier and noticeably better productions. But almost in spite of itself, *Invisible Invaders* reflects the era in which it was made and, along the way, makes salient points about life in the Cold War atmosphere.

Earth is once again threatened by alien beings who object to our nuclear testing and space programs. The novel and gratuitously gruesome twist is that the extraterrestrial fiends can make themselves invisible and inhabit the bodies of the recently deceased. Thus possessed, an army of corpses is sent forth to implement the invaders' scheme to destroy the human race. Military envoy Maj. Bruce Jay, played by genre stalwart John Agar, assists a trio of researchers who labor around the clock to find the aliens' weakness, eventually thwarting them with a hastily invented high-energy ultrasonic weapon. Echoes of *The Day the Earth Stood Still*, *The War of the Worlds*, *Earth vs. the Flying Saucers*, *Creature with the Atom Brain*, and others are readily apparent. But in a surprising way, *Invisible Invaders* has a certain pop legitimacy, anticipating the "undead" premise that drives *Night of the Living Dead* by almost a decade. Nothing is more unreasonable and remorseless than a reanimated dead person, depicted here as a parade of men, invariably dressed in suits (fresh from the funeral parlor or recent burial, one assumes), their gait stiff, their eyes dead, and their discolored faces layered in old blood and the discoloration of rot.

Director Edward L. Cahn filled out the picture's running time with copious newsreel and World War II footage of collapsing buildings, houses torn asunder, seething flood waters, and raging fires. The old footage, though grainy and mismatched, helped save the budget, but also draws our attention to the flat, stage-bound quality of most of the narrative. The slack pace of the film's non-disaster sequences doesn't do it any favors, either. The problems are compounded because top-billed Agar doesn't appear until the thirty-minute mark, and popular character player John Carradine is relegated to a mostly off-screen role as the voice of the aliens. (He's on screen for mere moments at the beginning, and then he accidentally blows himself to bits.)

Despite the threadbare budget, unengaging pace, and perfunctory direction, *Invisible Invaders* does manage one impressive feat. Dr. Adam Penner (Philip Tonge), the scientist who is instrumental in defeating the alien menace, has a social conscience, a rare quality in movies of this type. In the first reel, he lectures a military representative on the need

56 Part 1: Space Invaders

Perhaps some Americans found comfort in the popular conception of Communists as mindless automatons: such creatures cannot think for themselves, and can be defeated. Then again, Russia could field *a lot* of those automatons, and prevail with sheer numbers. *Invisible Invaders* (1959) seems to want it both ways. Leading this group of well-dressed dead men is actor Hal Torey.

to end nuclear tests, arguing that testing should be "limited to experiments for peace." Upset by the death of Carradine, Dr. Penner resigns from a high-profile nuclear commission, only to resume his work when the survival of the planet is at stake. But even when defeat of the aliens appears inevitable, Penner remains committed to his high-minded ideals. "If we get through this," he reasons, "the nations of the world will realize that it's possible to work together as they're doing now, instead of trying to destroy each other with nuclear bombs."

It's entirely possible, of course, that the script offers Penner's viewpoint merely as a sop to liberal sensibilities, or as simply a novel change from the gung-ho belligerence that's almost invariably encoded in the DNA of films from this period. Still, the character's commitment to peaceful coexistence is the voice of a thoughtful culture that is contemplating a way out of the combative standoff of Cold War politics. Not bad for a movie that was quickly relegated to the drive-in circuit.

In the low-budget arena that spawned *Invisible Invaders*, filmmakers were content to fall back on ideas that had been pioneered by earlier, bigger pictures. But in some cases, the freedom from studio restrictions proved liberating for everyone involved. *Invis-*

ible Invaders falls somewhere in the middle of this scale. Its recycled plot points and timeworn clichés are apparent to anyone who has even a loose familiarity with such stuff. We can be grateful, however, for the few nuggets of gold that shine through the pyrite. In its own economy-minded way, the film reflects not just the fears of the day, but Americans' hope for a better, more livable world. "The nations of the world could work and fight together," the narrator tells us at the conclusion, "side by side, in a common cause." Tokenistic and rote, yet nevertheless a message worth hearing.

FILMOGRAPHY

Invisible Invaders—Premium Pictures/United Artists; Released May 15, 1959; Black and white; 67 min.

Credits: Producers: Edward Small, Robert E. Kent; Director: Edward L. Cahn; Screenplay: Samuel Newma; Director of photography: Maury Gertsman; Editor: Grant Whytock; Music: Paul Dunlap; Art director: William Glasgow; Special effects: Roger George; Special makeup: Phillip Scheer; Sound effects editor: Henry Adams

Cast: John Agar: Maj. Bruce Jay; Jean Byron: Phyllis Penner; Philip Tonge: Dr. Adam Penner; Robert Hutton: Dr. John LaMont; John Carradine: Dr. Karol Noymann; Hal Torey: Farmer; Paul Langton: Lieutenant General Stone; Narrator: Carl Princi

Politics of Evolution

Time passed, taking with it the entire Soviet Union. Although the USSR's military might transformed that nation into a formidable world power, internal structural weaknesses rendered the Soviets less of a long-term menace then their adversaries once anticipated. And as the chilly atmosphere of the Cold War warmed into the spring of détente and political realignment, the paranoia and suspicions of that earlier time likewise passed into the back pages of history. American entertainment culture reflected this as well; stories of Communist infiltration and Soviet double agents, which had been a reliable staple of television and the movies, soon went the way of westerns and other genres that had fallen out of favor. From this distance, it all seems like a curious interlude of American history.

American society evolved in the ensuing decades as well. Although culture wars are sure to continue, doors of opportunity once restricted by race or gender are now open to more people than ever before. Technology continues to transform the way we work, travel, learn, and live. Openness has become the hallmark of successful modern organizations. And, most importantly, social revolutions that had once been unthinkable are routine facets of American life.

But those who lived through the Cold War know that not all the subsequent changes have been positive. In an ironic way, many of the social breakdowns that cultural critics feared have become accepted norms of our way of life. Marriage rates have steadily declined in recent decades and divorce rates, which began to spiral upward in the late 1960s, remain distressingly high. The percentage of children living in traditional, two-parent families is near an all-time low. U.S. poverty rates still show a distinct bias over racial lines. Economic inequality threatens to erase decades of progress for people at the lower end of the wage scale. Sexually transmitted diseases have reached epidemic proportions, drug use is a plague that continues to vex the modern world, and violent crime has become a chronic issue without an obvious solution. On the geopolitical front, proxy wars and other conflicts rage in hot spots around the globe. American relations with a handful of key world powers, most notably modern Russia, have deteriorated. The problems of contemporary society have no single cause, of course, so it is futile to draw direct correlation between specific events of the past and our current litany of political and social ills. Yet it is difficult not to feel that, when contrasting the (possibly illusory) certitude of the 1950s to the dysfunctional society of today, the baby was somehow thrown out with the atomic bathwater.

The world as we knew it was destroyed long, long ago, not by extraterrestrials and certainly not by communism, but by time itself. Outmoded ideas and cherished, long-standing beliefs were tossed away without a shot being fired, a bomb being dropped, or the landing of an alien spacecraft. And no one ever bothered to look back.

Works Cited

DVD/Video

The Day the Earth Stood Still. 20th Century-Fox. 2003. DVD.
Earth vs. the Flying Saucers. Sony. 2008. DVD.
I Married a Monster from Outer Space. Warner Archive Collection. 2013. DVD.
Invasion of the Body Snatchers. Olive Films. 2012. Blu-ray.
Midnite Movies: Invisible Invaders/Journey to the Seventh Planet. MGM. 2003. DVD.
Samuel Z. Arkoff Collection Cult Classics: Day the World Ended/The She-Creature. Lions Gate. 2006. DVD.
The War of the Worlds. Paramount DVD. 2005.
When Worlds Collide. Paramount. 2001. DVD.

Part 2

Red Mischief Here, There and Everywhere

"A nation can survive its fools, and even the ambitious. But it cannot survive treason from within."

—Marcus Tullius Cicero

"Frankie, is there the possibility that someone besides yourself would like to get ahold of that rocket?"

—Roy Rogers to Frankie Manning (Penny Edwards); *Spoilers of the Plains* (1951)

Happy Trails in Cold War Valley
Bells of Coronado *and* Spoilers of the Plains

TED OKUDA

> "Nowadays, Roy Rogers seems almost too good, but you buy it from him somehow. I find myself being moved by his common decency.... His code is his code. The whole world can change, and it doesn't change his code."
> —Quentin Tarantino[1]

In *Hollywood Canteen* (1944), Warner Bros.' star-studded tribute to the charitable establishment of the title (a club that provided food, dancing, and entertainment for wartime servicemen and women), a host of luminaries lend their presence in support of the cause: Bette Davis, John Garfield, and Barbara Stanwyck; Joan Crawford, Ida Lupino, and Joan Leslie; Sydney Greenstreet, Peter Lorre, and Jack Benny; Joe E. Brown, Eddie Cantor, and Jack Carson; Jane Wyman and the Andrews Sisters, among others.

Yet the star who meant the most to the target demographic—young soldiers hailing from small-town America—was not under contract to any major studio but rather on loan from a comparatively low-rent operation on the opposite end of the industry's prestige spectrum. Roy Rogers, the "King of the Cowboys," along with his horse Trigger, receives one of the warmest welcomes from the onscreen crowd, and there's no doubt the response is genuine. No other star in *Hollywood Canteen* exemplified the ideal of an honest-to-goodness American role model more than Rogers.

King of the Cowboys

From an early age, Rogers, born Leonard Franklin Slye in 1911 in Cincinnati, Ohio, sang and played the guitar to entertain family and friends. In 1931 he joined the country music group the Rocky Mountaineers. Following short-lived gigs with other groups, he was instrumental in forming the Pioneers Trio in 1933, which would soon evolve into the Sons of the Pioneers.

The success the Sons of the Pioneers achieved from radio exposure and recordings resulted in supporting roles in movies, with Rogers billed as Len Slye. When Rogers decided to go solo, Republic Pictures renamed him "Dick Weston" and cast him in a couple of inexpensive westerns, one of which, *The Old Barn Dance* (1938), starred the screen's reigning singing cowboy, Gene Autry.

At the time, Gene was Republic's main box-office draw, and the business-savvy Autry was fully aware of his status. Studio chieftain Herbert J. Yates balked at Autry's demand for a pay hike; Autry walked out and Yates retaliated by creating a new cowboy star. Len Slye/Dick Weston was rechristened Roy Rogers (the surname inspired by humorist Will Rogers) and given his own starring vehicle, *Under Western Skies* (1938). Yates's gamble paid off. The film was a big hit and established Rogers as a serious rival to Autry. Coincidentally (?), Autry and Yates resolved their differences and Republic wound up with *two* profitable singing cowboys in their stable.

Republic Pictures specialized in "B" movies (short feature films designed to play the bottom half of double bills, in support of prestigious "A" pictures) and serials (action-oriented short subjects in which a continuous narrative unfolded over the course of twelve to fifteen installments or "chapters"). Though branded a "Poverty Row" studio (industry slang for a low-budget independent operation), Republic turned out slick-looking productions on economical budgets, thanks to impressive contributions by ace cinematographers, special-effects artists (notably Howard and Theodore Lydecker), an expert stunt crew, and other in-house talents. Outdoor location filming—at such California settings as Simi Valley and Santa Clarita—gave the movies an expanse and grandeur that belied the limited resources. Republic tackled a variety of genres but excelled at westerns and serials. Major studios were hard-pressed to equal the sheer energy and excitement of a Republic action sequence.

When Gene Autry enlisted in the U.S. Army in 1942, Republic concentrated on turning Rogers into the screen's premier singing cowboy, going so far as to title one Rogers vehicle *King of the Cowboys* (1943). In the process, Rogers went from being a popular performer to a beloved icon, establishing a strong connection with moviegoers of all ages, just as Autry had done. (Unlike many B movies, Rogers's films—and Autry's—frequently secured top-of-the-bill bookings at first-run theaters in major cities.) By this point, Roy always played a character named "Roy Rogers," fusing real life with reel life.

Although Rogers may never have been anybody's go-to choice to play Richard III, he was a better actor than he was usually given credit for. Or to put it another way, no one could have been a better Roy Rogers than Roy Rogers. His on-screen decency, kindness, modesty, and good-natured disposition registered as authentic. Indeed, by all assessments of the off-screen Rogers, it was. His public persona was an extension of the private man. As an actor, he learned how to deliver dramatic dialogue with conviction and comedic lines with flair. He could also project ferocity when duking it out with assorted villains. An accomplished horseman and trim athlete who possessed a fine singing voice, he looked just as natural and at ease in his cowboy garb as Fred Astaire did in top hat, white tie, and tails. Rogers was the perfect western hero.

Any motion picture cowboy worth his salt had a trusty steed: Tom Mix had Tony the Wonder Horse, Ken Maynard had Tarzan the Wonder Horse, and Gene Autry had Champion the Wonder Horse. Not to be outdone, Roy Rogers had a golden palomino named Trigger (formerly Golden Cloud, seen in *The Adventures of Robin Hood*). In a field—or rather, corral—overrun with Wonder Horses, Trigger was billed as "The Smartest Horse in the Movies." It was a claim that rang true, given the high volume of commands, tricks, and stunts Trigger executed flawlessly.

Rogers' filmography (consisting of more than ninety westerns) falls roughly into three categories: "Historical" westerns (1938–41) that had only loose parallels to actual history (*Billy the Kid Returns, Frontier Pony Express, Young Buffalo Bill, Jesse James at*

Bay); light entertainments (1941–46) that alternated between song-laden musical revues—Roy's old pals, the Sons of the Pioneers, were occasional co-stars—and fast-paced action tales (*Hands Across the Border*, *The Yellow Rose of Texas*, *The Cowboy and the Senorita*, *Sunset in El Dorado*, *Don't Fence Me In*); and "serious" entries (1947–51) that combined the usual music and comedy elements with a harder-edged approach marked by increased violence and make-believe fatalities (*Down Dakota Way*, *The Golden Stallion*, *Trigger, Jr.*, *Trail of Robin Hood*). Beginning with *Apache Rose* (1947), some of the productions were photographed in Trucolor, a limited-hue color process that nonetheless enhanced the look of the films.

Typical Roy Rogers pictures downplayed romantic subplots in favor of action and songs, even with such comely leading ladies as Carol Hughes, Lynne Roberts, Peggy Moran, Ruth Terry, Jane Frazee, and Penny Edwards. (On-screen, impish Roy was not above resorting to pranks and teasing to knock a snobby filly's ego down a peg or two.) Rogers's best—and best-known—leading lady was Dale Evans, whom he married in 1947. They shared a natural rapport that managed to win over even the youngest fans resistant to "mush."

The Write Stuff

By the late 1940s, overworked screenwriters who churned out one script after another must have (quietly) rejoiced at the onset of Cold War paranoia, if only for the opportunity it afforded to slap a new coat of paint on the shopworn good guys/bad guys formula. Bank robbers, cattle rustlers, stagecoach outlaws, gold raiders, and out-of-date Nazi saboteurs could be substituted with the more topical threat of Communist infiltration, in the form of "agents of unfriendly powers." In *Under Nevada Skies* (1946), perhaps the first western to acknowledge the atomic bomb, Roy and Trigger thwart a plot by said agents seeking a rich deposit of pitchblende, used in the making of A-bombs. The foolhardy no-goodniks don't realize they're up against two of America's mightiest defense weapons—all six legs of them. Yet our enemies refused to call it quits.

And so, during 1950–51, Roy Rogers turned political.

To Be Ore Not to Be

> "Ride the devil's highway with Roy Rogers and Trigger ... on the trail of atomic ore hi-jackers! Here's something excitingly new in western thrills with Roy pitting his wits and courage against the killer cunning of the most dangerous of men—outlaws who turn traitors."
> —from the theatrical trailer for Bells of Coronado

Photographed in semi-glorious Trucolor, *Bells of Coronado* (1950) opens with George Perez (Jack Low), co-owner of the El Coronado Grande Mine, transporting a wagonload of high-grade uranium ore. An outlaw gang, led by Ross (Clifton Young), hijacks the shipment and chases Perez into the reservoir of the Coronado Dam. (This well-staged sequence was filmed at Littlerock Dam in Pearblossom, California.) Perez's subsequent death is ruled an accident and his partner, Craig Bennett (Grant Withers), assumes full possession of the mine.

Bennett files a claim with the Great Southwest Insurance Company; in turn GSIC assigns special investigator Roy Rogers to the case. Posing as an unemployed rancher and with Trigger in tow, Roy travels to Coronado, which just happens to be his hometown (for the sake of this plotline, anyway). After a fifteen-year absence (!), he reconnects with old friends Sparrow Biffle (comic sidekick Pat Brady) and Dr. Frank Harding (Leo Cleary), who helps Roy secure a position as a lineman for Bennett's Coronado Light & Power Company. Riding out to an electrical-tower site, Roy meets Pam Reynolds (Dale Evans), Bennett's secretary, whose car is stranded on the side of the road. The ever-gallant Roy offers assistance but Pam fears criminal intent (she's carrying company funds) and she curtly dismisses him, which only makes Roy more persistent. Pam feigns an ankle injury; after Roy dismounts to come to her aid, she distracts him then rides off on an uncharacteristically disloyal Trigger. (He may be the smartest horse in the movies, but evidently his allegiance could be easily swayed.) At the general store, run by Ross (whose criminal activities are unknown to all except mutual outlaws), Pam phones Bennett to warn him of the "desperate-looking stranger" who "threatened" her. Roy is eventually identified as a new employee and, gee willikers, is Pam's face red. (Or is it just the Trucolor?) Even by the standards of "meet cute" set-ups in previous Rogers-Evans films, this one is pretty contrived. Regardless, it isn't long before Pam stops giving Roy the stink eye and succumbs to his innate charms, joining him in a rendition of the title song.

Roy confides to Sparrow, who's in charge of the powerline crew (warblers Foy Willing and the Riders of the Purple Sage), that he's working undercover to find the missing uranium ore. The ore doesn't have much value to the U.S. government (the reason *why* is never explained), although Roy observes, "To some unfriendly power without a uranium supply, it'd be worth a fortune."

On the pretext of checking the electrical transformer and meter, Roy and Sparrow ride out to the mine and witness two men leaving with another wagonload of ore. Sparrow comments he's never seen them before, and notes that the mine seems strangely deserted. Upon further investigation, they find the real miners bound and gagged in a shack. Roy catches up with the wagon, subdues the thieves and delivers the ore to a warehouse in town. Shot in the shoulder during the pursuit, Sparrow is taken to Doc Harding's office. Under anesthesia, Sparrow spills the beans about Roy's secret mission. Bennett immediately fires Roy, who confirms Perez's death was no accident. Bennett is arrested after Roy files a murder charge against him.

With Bennett languishing in jail, the real mastermind behind the uranium-smuggling outfit is unveiled: it's none other than kindly old Doc Harding, who sure looks awfully sinister once he removes his eyeglasses. Conspiring with Ross and the other henchmen, Harding plots to steal the ore from the warehouse to fulfill a deal with "the other side."

Harding hosts a party at his place, inviting Roy, Pam, and the company crew to cheer up the wounded Sparrow. With everyone distracted by the festivities, the Harding gang disables a power line; the resulting blackout allows them to raid the warehouse.

Roy discovers that George Perez died of strychnine poisoning in Harding's office, and that Harding gave Sparrow sodium pentothal—"truth serum"—instead of a regular anesthetic, to uncover the real purpose behind Roy's return to Coronado. Fortunately for national security, Roy remains one step ahead of his foes. He and Bennett suspected Harding from the get-go but didn't have enough evidence on him. So they arranged to have Bennett framed for murder, thereby allowing Harding and his gang to continue their shady activities.

Roy tries to arrest Harding but henchman Jim Russell (Robert Bice) gets the drop on Roy, who is (seemingly) knocked cold in the ensuing brawl. Harding receives a phone call alerting him that Jim is an undercover federal agent. (Jim somehow managed to convey this information to Roy between punches during their slugfest.) In a struggle with Jim, Harding is shot and killed with his own gun.

Roy and Jim race to a dry lake bed appropriately named Dry Lake (they like to keep things simple in Coronado), where an airplane carrying a foreign smuggler, who must be racking up plenty of frequent flyer miles, is scheduled to land. Roy leaves a note for Sparrow to have the sheriff and a posse meet them at the rendezvous point but, to heighten the suspense, the note goes unnoticed for a few minutes, delaying the reinforcement. As Ross and the remaining members of the Harding gang are about to turn over the stolen ore to the aforementioned (and still unspecified) "unfriendly power," Roy and Jim decide to shoot it out to prevent the transaction from being completed. The posse arrives in the proverbial nick of time. As the outlaws are rounded up or mowed down, Roy chases after Ross, who climbs up an electrical tower but loses his grip and falls to his death.

Few film personalities of the 1950s possessed the likeability and innate decency of cowboy star Roy Rogers. For him to mix it up with Communists, then, suggested to audiences that the Red threat had real weight. *Bells of Coronado* (1950) hinges on efforts by minions of "an unfriendly power" to control a local uranium mine.

With the evildoers vanquished and peace restored to the valley, Roy and Trigger ride off into the distance, to the strains of the title tune.

Suspicion and Professionalism

Even if this sort of sagebrush saga isn't your cinematic cup of tea—or sarsaparilla—one has to admire the technical panache and production polish on display. The folks involved knew precisely what audiences had come to expect from a Roy Rogers western and they deliver the goods. It may be formulaic, assembly-line filmmaking, yet it's also a well-crafted, crowd-pleasing commercial "product."

More pertinent to our discussion here is that the villains look and sound like everyone else, and blend in effortlessly. If any single element of America's Red paranoia is especially unsettling, it is this: you can trust no one. Kindly Doc Harding, the pharmacist on the corner, the clerk at the post office, your neighbor, your brother-in-law—*anyone* might be a Red agent, hiding in plain sight, plotting your destruction.

Bells of Coronado was one of twenty-seven Roy Rogers movies directed by William Witney, who honed his skills helming a number of first-rate serials the likes of *Spy Smasher, Adventures of Captain Marvel, Dick Tracy vs. Crime Inc., Perils of Nyoka*, and *The Crimson Ghost*. In addition to his ease in handling actors—even the four-legged kind—Witney knew how to adapt the scripted material to the screen for maximum effect. Taking a cue from the choreographed shots in Busby Berkeley's musical numbers, Witney enlivened fight sequences by filming them in carefully staged segments rather than with the customary approach of shooting the action straight through from start-to-finish.

No less an authority than Quentin Tarantino considers Witney to be a forgotten master:

> He's a visual stylist, but he's a visual stylist in the way that a lot of those guys were back then.... His camera movements, when they happen, are so cool. They're either completely artful, in a cool, don't-call-attention-to-yourself kind of way, or they're visually about how to tell the story. These guys were storytellers. They knew how to move the camera to convey information so they didn't have to shoot another dialogue scene to explain something.[2]

The screenplay by Sloan Nibley (who wrote most of the Roy Rogers adventures from this period) alludes to an unfriendly power without directly mentioning Communists, Soviets, the Red Menace, or other fellow travelers. Nevertheless, it posits that such a power can't function without cooperation from traitors, and that there are no greater enemies of the USA than those eager to betray our country.

Beyond the patriotic posturing, the plot doesn't bear close scrutiny. For instance, how did the unfriendly power and the Harding gang hook up in the first place? Did Harding take out a classified ad in the local newspaper? Does Coronado have a worldwide reputation for being the Uranium Ore Capital of the United States? And didn't any of the foreign smugglers grumble, "If we're the ones shelling out big bucks for this stuff, how come *we* have to go pick it up ourselves? Don't we have a source closer to home? I *hate* dry lakes!" But then, serious ruminations are ludicrous when applied to a western in which the local powerline crew doubles as backup singers for a fellow they hadn't seen hide nor hair of for the past decade-and-a-half.

No matter. Roy and his pals protect Coronado—and the rest of America—against traitors and an unspecified foreign power. On to the next showdown…

Whose Pipeline Is It Anyway?

> Roy and Trigger [fight] our enemies, men who are after our country's newest secret weapon! Roy and his pals have never before fought such vicious killers! It's rocket fast excitement combined with rollicking western song in the first western rocket picture!
> —from the theatrical trailer for *Spoilers of the Plains*

Spoilers of the Plains (1951) gets off to a blazing start—literally—as Roy and the crew of the Mesa Valley Pipeline Company race to put out an oil fire from a leaking pipeline. (The sight of Roy and Trigger wearing white asbestos suits may be the most bizarre and unsettling visual in all of Roy's pictures.) Extinguishing the flames just in time to prevent an explosion, they are informed by Roy's comic-relief pal Splinters Fedders (Gordon Jones, "Mike the Cop" on *The Abbott and Costello Show*), who works for a government-sanctioned experimental station camped nearby, that the damage was caused by a wayward missile launched by the station. The missile, also referred to as a rocket, is equipped with a long-range weather forecasting device, "the most advanced mechanism in the world today ... worth a lot of money."

Watching from a distance is the owner of the Camwell Oil Company, Gregory Camwell (Grant Withers, this time playing a bona fide villain instead of the red-herring role he essayed in *Bells of Coronado*). The introductory close-up of his leathery, scowling face instantly establishes that this ornery bastard is not to be trusted. Camwell drops by the station and strikes a cost-cutting oil deal with government rep Dr. Jonathan D. Manning (William Forrest), and Manning's bespectacled, spinsterish daughter Frankie (Penny Edwards), who formally addresses her sullen father as "J.D." Camwell's real motive, however, is to get his hands on the missile device.

Frankie goes to the pipeline company to reimburse them for damages. Roy accidentally douses her with a chemical spray and, boy, does *that* ruffle her uptight feathers. Remorseful Roy offers to buy her a new outfit and instructs Splinters to "take her over to the beauty shop and tell 'em to give her the works." The makeover reveals that beneath the owlish exterior lies a darn purdy gal who's ecstatic about her metamorphosis. Far less euphoric is Dr. Manning, irate that some prairie Pygmalion has taken his daughter away from "important business."

When Frankie mentions the station's deal with Camwell, Roy is surprised that a formerly dry well is pumping oil again. Roy, with Trigger and a German shepherd named Bullet, pays a visit to Camwell's company, hoping to land a new client for the pipeline service. Upon arrival, Roy is attacked by a Doberman guard dog (subdued by Bullet), beaten up by Camwell's main henchman, Ben Rix (Don Haggerty), and tossed out for trespassing. All these strong-arm tactics are meant to prevent Roy from discovering the truth: the well *is* dry, and to fulfill the 500-gallon government order will require Camwell to steal oil from the pipeline.

The theft results in a drop in pipeline pressure. When Roy investigates, both he and Bullet are ambushed by Camwell's gang and left for dead. Trigger gallops to the campsite for help and manages to enlist Frankie's assistance. Roy recuperates at the station infirmary, where a musical interlude provides proof that his vocal cords haven't been injured. Ol' Doctor Grumpy is livid because, in his view, Frankie has abandoned her scientific training to waste valuable time with Rogers ("A worthless, irresponsible saddle tramp!")

68   Part 2: Red Mischief Here, There and Everywhere

In *Spoilers of the Plains* (1951), Roy and friend Frankie (Penny Edwards) survive a time bomb, only to be braced by unscrupulous oilman Camwell (Grant Withers). What's on Camwell's mind? Possession of missile technology undergoing tests at a nearby government facility—technology he intends to hand over to his "customers."

and his cowpoke cohorts ("And that Splinters! That submarginal idiot! Why, if he had twice as many brains as he has, he'd still be a half-wit!").

Camwell learns the details of the next rocket launch from loose-lipped subnormal idiot Splinters. After the rocket is fired, Frankie tracks its trajectory but Camwell intercepts it before Manning's retrieval team (headed by, oddly enough, subnormal idiot Splinters) can arrive at the location. Camwell explains to Ben Rix why he's so interested in the device: "With this invention of his, [Manning] can predict weather conditions months ahead.... It can also be used in case of military moves, knowing the weather beforehand. The people I represent would pay anything for that. Even sacrificing a few lives."

Then Camwell drops the other shoe (or cowboy boot) and announces he'll be replacing the instruments in the rocket with a nitroglycerin-packed booby trap: "Gettin' that rocket was only half the job. The other half's gettin' rid of that scientific data and the balance of those rockets at the camp." For Rix, this act of sabotage crosses the line: "I don't mind a little rough stuff once in a while. After all, a guy has to make a living. But like you said, Dr. Manning's worth a lot to this country.... I'd doing my country a favor if I had nerve enough to blow us all up. *Don't tempt me!*" A bullet in the back brings Rix's patriotic filibuster to an abrupt halt as he dies in a blaze of redemptive glory.

Dr. Manning concludes that the disappearance of his coveted rocket is the fault of his daughter's ineptitude, the result of her "moping over that Rogers when you should have had your mind on your work." Undeterred, Frankie and Roy ride out to the spot that Frankie had tracked and find the rocket, repositioned by Camwell and fitted with a time bomb. Roy, Frankie, and the retrieval team use a horse-drawn wagon to haul it back to the campsite—singing "Happy Trails in Sunshine Valley" along the way—where the ever-alert Bullet calls their attention to the ticking sound emanating from within the rocket. (The others would have probably heard the ticking too, if they hadn't been doing all that singing.) Roy hops on the wagon and drives the rocket over a ridge, with barely enough time to unleash the horses and escape the explosion.

Realizing Camwell is orchestrating the nefarious activities, Roy tells Splinters to round up an armed posse and meet him at the oil company. But as soon as Roy, Trigger, and Bullet depart, Splinters is knocked unconscious by one of Camwell's eavesdropping henchmen. Upon Roy's arrival, the villains get the drop on him, and Camwell signals the Doberman to attack Bullet. After a vicious dogfight, Bullet kills his opponent and makes it back to camp, where he assists in reviving Splinters.

Camwell and his gang load Roy onto a wagon with the stolen device and head for the rendezvous point. Splinters's wagon, filled with government lawmen, catches up with Camwell and a rip-roaring brawl ensues, with heroes and villains leaping from wagon to wagon. As his men fall by the wayside, Camwell jumps onto one of the team horses and heads back to his oil well. Roy also jumps on a horse, then onto Trigger, who has been racing alongside the wagons throughout the chase. Camwell climbs up the oil derrick and after a tussle with Roy, winds up falling to his death. (Why do western heavies try to elude Roy by scampering up tall structures? The answer lies in the fact that Roy never kills anyone. The villains often cause their own demise.)

With America safe and secure once again, Roy bids a cheery farewell to everyone at the campsite, where presumably the rocket experiments will continue without further interruption.

Make-Believe and Reality

Another one directed by William Witney and scripted by Sloan Nibley, *Spoilers of the Plains* doesn't precisely delineate Camwell's "customers." Camwell makes references to "the people I represent" and "my connections," encouraging us to assume that any party that would strike a deal with a crook like Camwell doesn't have our nation's best interests at heart. The strongest allusion to anti–Americanism is when Ben Rix's conscience gets the better of him and he begins to run off at the mouth.

Still, a real-life timeline of events is provocative, for when *Spoilers of the Plains* came to American theaters in February 1951, New York "atom spies" Julius and Ethel Rosenberg had been in federal custody for six and five months, respectively, startling Washington and shocking the general public. Illustrative of the "hiding in plain sight" concept discussed earlier, the Rosenbergs lived unassuming lives on New York's Lower East Side, working ordinary jobs (Julius owned a small, struggling machine shop) but conspiring with Ethel's brother, David Greenglass, to obtain American nuclear secrets and pass them on to Soviet agents in New York. Julius had been a civilian engineer with the Army Signal Corps from 1940 to 1945, and Greenglass had worked as a machinist at Los Alamos during development of the atomic bomb. Though naturally limited as to where he could wander at the facility, Greenglass nevertheless drew and smuggled simple technical drawings to Julius Rosenberg.

On January 31, 1951, just two days before the release of *Spoilers of the Plains*, a federal grand jury indicted the Rosenbergs, David Greenglass, and four others (including the USSR's vice-consul in New York, Anatoly Yakovlev) on charges of espionage. (The Rosenbergs and others had been arrested in the summer of 1950.) Audiences that saw this latest Roy Rogers adventure, or any other movie with anti–Communist over- or undertones, were stunned. Does *Spoilers of the Plains* inadvertently foresee when pulpy make-believe would become reality? Yes, when Frankie asks Roy "who around here" might be working for an unfriendly power. Roy replies, "You never can tell, it might be your next-door neighbor."

Because production of *Spoilers of the Plains* took place some months before the arrests of the Rosenbergs and the others, the film minimizes the "unfriendly foreign powers" angle, opting for fast-paced storytelling, upbeat songs, cornball comedy, and exciting action sequences. The climactic wagon chase (staged by legendary stuntman/stunt coordinator Yakima Canutt) is thrilling in its execution, and it's impossible not to gasp at the sight of a stuntman who, while attempting to leap from one wagon to the other, slips and falls under a wagon wheel.

Spoilers of the Plains marked the debut of Bullet the Wonder Dog, a solid addition to Roy's courageous animal companions. While Trigger was deemed "The Smartest Horse in the Movies," the praiseworthy Bullet was not granted a comparable canine accolade, perhaps due to heavy Hollywood competition from Rin-Tin-Tin, Lassie, Asta, and Pete the Pup. Along with Trigger, Bullet—who literally takes one in this film—would figure prominently on television's *The Roy Rogers Show* (1951–57).

It's easy to dismiss films like *Bells of Coronado* and *Spoilers of the Plains* as innocuous fodder for undiscriminating kids. Yet the recurring themes of good vs. evil and us vs. them acquire added resonance because Good is represented by Roy Rogers, the embodiment of the American ideals of decency, justice, and fair play. In an era when loyalty to our country could repeatedly be called into question, Rogers's patriotism was undeniable.

Because television was calling, Rogers made just four more star feature vehicles following *Spoilers of the Plains*, none of which have an espionage element. The real-life Rosenberg revelations of 1950–51 and after effectively pushed Rogers out of the foreign-intrigue business. His persona could no longer function in such an arena.

Regardless, to American audiences, Roy's enemies were *our* enemies. And each triumph scored a victory for every upright, God-fearing U.S. citizen. With Roy on our side, those unfriendly powers got themselves roped and branded, just as they deserved.

"*Goodbye, good luck and may the Good Lord take a likin' to you.*"—Roy Rogers's signature farewell to his audiences

Filmography

Bells of Coronado—Republic Pictures; Released January 8, 1950; Trucolor; 67 min. (TV-syndicated prints run 54 min. in black and white)

    Credits: Producers: Herbert J. Yates, Edward J. White; Director: William Witney; Screenplay: Sloan Nibley; Director of photography: John MacBurnie; Editor: Tony Martinelli; Music: Dale Butts; Art director: Frank Hotaling

Cast: Roy Rogers: Himself; Dale Evans: Pam Reynolds; Pat Brady: Sparrow Biffle; Grant Withers: Craig Bennett; Leo Cleary: Dr. Frank Harding; Trigger: Himself

Spoilers of the Plains—Republic Pictures; Released February 2, 1951; Black and white; 63 min. (TV-syndicated prints run 54 min.)

Credits: Producers: Herbert J. Yates, Edward J. White; Director: William Witney; Screenplay: Sloan Nibley; Director of photography: Jack Marta; Editor: Tony Martinelli; Music: Dale Butts; Art director: Frank Arrigo

Cast: Roy Rogers: Himself; Penny Edwards: Frankie Manning; Gordon Jones: Splinters Fedders; Grant Withers: Gregory Camwell; Don Haggerty: Ben Rix; Trigger: Himself; Bullet the Wonder Dog: Himself

NOTES

1. Rick Lyman, "Whoa, Trigger! Auteur Alert!," *The New York Times*. September 15, 2000.
2. *Ibid.*

WORKS CITED

Book

Miller, Don. *Hollywood Corral*. New York: Popular Library. 1976.

Web

b-westerns.com (*The Old Corral*, Boyd Magers).

DVD

Bells of Coronado. Good Times Video. 2003.
Spoilers of the Plains. Good Times Video. 2004.

The Flying Saucer
Top Secret Travelogue
DAVID J. HOGAN

When I was a kid growing up in Cleveland in the early 1960s, the city's CBS-TV outlet ran a locally produced afternoon show called *Adventure Road*. Host Jim Doney welcomed Cleveland-area residents who had traveled to exotic locales and returned with 8- or 16mm movie footage of their trips. The stuff had invariably been shot silent, so the show consisted of the traveler sitting in the studio with Doney, and narrating for the audience at home the scenes that unspooled on the monitor.

"Yes, Jim, that's the Great Wall of China," a typical guest might say. "As you can see, it's really big and long, and almost nothing of its majesty comes across in my homemade movie."

Adventure Road came to mind as I watched *The Flying Saucer*, actor Mikel Conrad's 1950 Alaskan travelogue masquerading as a Red-panic science fiction thriller.

"Yes, Jim," star/producer/director Conrad might intone, "here's *another* scenic lake, and there I am in the skiff, slowly motoring across the placid water."

"Looks like a great, leisurely day. What brought you to Alaska, Mike?"

"Well, Jim, I was up there doing a picture called *Arctic Manhunt*, and during down time I shot my own nature footage. And then, before I knew it, I had nine hundred feet of saucer footage that Washington classified as 'top secret'!"

"Say, that's impressive, Mike. So all of that is in official government records?"

"Absolutely. Plus, it's in the pressbook."

"I can see how you'd be excited by a flying saucer."

"Boy, was I! You know, 'flying saucers are the hottest topic of conversation in the country today.' That's from the pressbook, too."

"Tell us a little about the plot, Mike."

"Well, I play a cynical, dissolute playboy who's inexplicably recruited by the U.S. government to travel north to check out reports of a Communist flying saucer. See, the government's worried that the Soviets could use saucers to A-bomb major American cities."

"Sounds serious, Mike."

"Like a heart attack. So who better than a drunken polo player to safeguard the American people?"

"Gee, nobody that I can think of."

"Exactly. Now, Alaska's a pretty fabulous place, so although I sighted the saucer near Juneau, I just couldn't toss away the delightfully endless footage of me spending a lot of time elsewhere, on rowboats, seaplanes, and just wandering around—climbing hills and hiking in the woods."

"Yes, I can see you spent a lot of time outdoors. Pretty quiet there, isn't it?"

"Well, Jim, I suppose some people might not want to look at reel after reel of me in all that uninhabited space, but believe me, if you were there, you'd probably feel differently."

"Now, who's this, Mike?"

"Ah, that's Vee, and like all female agents of the U.S. government, she's young, blonde, and very pretty."

"She certainly looks lovely in that sweater."

"Two of the nicest peaks in Alaska, Jim."

"Golly, you really did spend a lot of time boating and hiking."

"Sure, and with Vee along, it was double the fun. You know, we wore out five or six pairs of hiking boots. And I just couldn't bear to leave one single mile of that scenery on the cutting room floor."

"Uh oh, who's this shifty-looking character, Mike?"

"Oh, that's Hans. He passed himself off as a guide but he's really a Red. Get a load of the size of that knife."

"Gee, that's a big one. Good thing that passing ferryboat blew its whistle and scared him before he could plunge the blade into Vee's back."

"A lucky break for sure, Jim, although why a hard-bitten Soviet agent would be deterred by a little boat whistle is beyond me."

"Say, looks like you and Hans had some trouble of your own."

"Yeah, as you can see he was really eager to shove my head into that seaplane's whirling propeller."

"Boy, it's pretty exciting, at least until Hans just kind of gives up and falls down."

"Yes, another lucky break for our side, Jim."

"Wait a minute, Mike, what was that sudden blur of movement?"

"Flying saucer, Jim! Did you see how it just swoops out from that wooded area and streaks across the screen?"

"I'm not sure, Mike. I blinked and I may have missed it."

"Well, don't worry, Jim. After another fifteen or twenty minutes of hiking and boating, you'll be able to enjoy another nanosecond of thrilling saucer footage."

"I'm sure audiences are going to be panting for that. Say, here's another dangerous-looking fellow."

"That's Turner, a so-called American who thought he'd steal the saucer and fly it to Russia. I tell you, I hate a traitor almost as much as I hate a bartender that cuts me off after a dozen highballs."

"Uh oh. Looks like the Communists have captured you and Vee."

"A tight spot for sure, Jim."

"Mike, this looks like the exciting climax of your trip, when the Communist agent machine-guns one of his own. Ooh, I bet *that* hurt!"

"The only good Commie's a dead Commie, Jim."

"I can't help but notice that the machine-gun bullets don't penetrate to hit you, even though you're pressed right against the victim's back."

74   Part 2: Red Mischief Here, There and Everywhere

Actor Mikel Conrad (bottom left), eager to exploit the "flying saucer" craze that took hold in 1947, refashioned himself into a producer and director with *The Flying Saucer* (1950), an anesthetizing travelogue blending Alaskan scenery, Red spies, and a briefly glimpsed flying disc.

"Reds manufacture a lousy grade of bullet, Jim. And they can't put together a flying saucer, either. That was an invention of one of *our* guys. When the Reds kidnapped Vee and me, they grabbed the doc, too."

"Ah, yes, the fellow in the wing tips and overcoat who's climbing the glacier. Golly, look at the snow that's been jarred loose by the gunshots."

"Oh, yeah, we searched for at least a day to find that swell stock footage."

"The avalanche appears to have buried the Communists."

"Yeah, just a bunch of Redsicles, frozen forever."

"Mike, thanks so much for coming by today. We certainly enjoyed your boring yet strangely repetitious footage of Alaska. What's next for you?"

"Well, Jim, first I'll get drunk and then hurt myself when I fall off my polo pony. Then I'm going to reconnoiter Vee and that sweater. After that I'll travel the country to ceaselessly flog the picture, making it sound way better than anyone can imagine, and establishing myself as an artsy but rugged two-fisted American adventurer."

"Jack London and Orson Welles in one package, eh, Mike?"

"Say, I like that, Jim."

"Do you plan to cut any of the travelogue footage at all—you know, just to pick up the pace a little?"

"Not on your life, comrade."

Mikel Conrad's claim of nine hundred feet of top secret saucer footage became the centerpiece of the film's 1949–50 publicity blitz. Worried (Conrad said) that the footage might fall into unfriendly hands after Washington examined and returned it, he secreted the reel in a bank vault.

The Realart Pictures pressbook prepared for the 1953 re-release of *The Flying Saucer* suggests that theater owners dress staff like "Men from Mars," sponsor a saucer-model contest (to be judged by "a few prominent scientists of your town"), and "[c]ontact the Army, the Navy and the Air Force and obtain permission to exhibit newly-designed defense weapons"—the last an absurd and most unlikely event in that Cold War era.

The Flying Saucer was the first feature directed by producer/star Mikel Conrad. He never directed or produced another, and had the lead in just two other pictures, the earlier *Arctic Manhunt* (1949) and *Untamed Women* (1952). He passed away in 1982, twenty-six years after his final screen appearance.

The melodramatics of *The Flying Saucer* aside, Washington had a keen awareness of Alaska's proximity to Soviet Russia, and maintained an Alaskan espionage and self-defense plan called Operation Washtub during 1951–59.

FILMOGRAPHY

The Flying Saucer—Colonial Productions/Film Classics. 1953 re-release: Realart; Released January 5, 1950; Black and white; 69 min.

Credits: Producer: Mikel Conrad; Director: Mikel Conrad; Screenplay: Howard Irving Young; Director of photography: Phillip Tannura; Music: Darrell Calker; Editor: Robert Crandall; Art director: Charles D. Hall

Cast: Mikel Conrad: Mike Trent; Pat Garrison: Vee Langley; Hants Von Teuffen: Hans; Roy Engel: Dr. Lawton; Erle (Earle) Lyon: Alex Muller; Lester Sharpe: Col. Marikoff; Denver Pyle: Turner

WORKS CITED

Print

The Flying Saucer re-release pressbook. Realart Pictures. 1953.

DVD

The Flying Saucer. Image Entertainment. 2001.

The Whip Hand
Accidental Template for Fear and Paranoia

Mark A. Miller

In 1951, for his follow-up to the now-classic RKO *noir* thriller *The Narrow Margin*, producer Stanley Rubin wrote an entertaining if wildly fantastic script about a secret Nazi operation inside a small, secluded Minnesota town—six years after the death of Hitler. The completed RKO movie, *The Man He Found*, is apparently lost, yet over half of its footage survives in an easily accessible film, *The Whip Hand*. Through a fateful combination of socio-political events, a decision made by the owner of RKO, and Rubin's stubborn adherence to his artistic integrity, *The Whip Hand*—an oddball hybrid that is 75 percent Rubin's *The Man He Found* and 25 percent work by others—unwittingly became a seminal Red Scare picture. As such, it inspired or at least influenced many of the decade's science fiction pictures. We knew, after all, that an extraterrestrial is just a Communist in disguise.

In 1951, the year of *The Whip Hand*'s release, the U.S. economy was thriving, and, after the lean war years of the previous decade, the American Dream assumed a fresh dimension. Postwar prosperity elevated huge numbers of couples into the middle class. The hungry Depression-era kids became adults who got hitched younger and made more babies than their parents produced—on average, three per family. So began America's Baby Boomers. Dads went to college on the G.I. Bill and used their educations to find good jobs or start new businesses. With more money to spend, they wanted houses for their families, and so the wartime housing shortage became history, with the help of Veterans Administration mortgage loans and an unprecedented home construction bonanza that added tremendous momentum to the economy. Suburban living as we know it today first mushroomed in the early 1950s, and "suburban sprawl" was born. With cash instead of ration coupons in hand, homeowners consumed, consumed, consumed—refrigerators, washing machines, dryers, kitchen appliances, furniture, clothes, and a relatively new gadget called television.

Prosperous young Americans purchased cars, too, millions of them. Detroit's Big Three automakers, which had been devoted solely to the machinery of war since early 1942, retooled for automobile production at war's end. At General Motors alone, six million cars rolled off the assembly line in 1950. Consumers bought cars furiously, as if they were, well, houses.[1] Men needed transportation from their new suburban homes to their city jobs, and wives needed cars to shop and socialize.

Trouble Abroad

The economic recession of 1948–49 resolved itself quickly, but America faced larger troubles. Our new decade's consumer economy that yielded optimism and the joy of luxury and plentitude was prized all the more in a Cold War climate in which America's free market was challenged by the managed economies of Communist Russia and its East European satellites. By 1949, Americans' fear of communism began to spread faster than communism itself. That fear was not unfounded. The Soviets had painted East Germany and Eastern Europe Red after World War II, reasoning (correctly) that the West would have no stomach for physical opposition after four years of wartime casualties. In September 1949, the Soviets leveled the military playing field with a successful test of their own atomic bomb, and China fell to Mao Zedong's Communist rebels. Already criticized for having "lost" mainland China to the Reds by failing to offer active support to Chiang Kai-shek's Chinese Nationalists, President Truman could not stand idle as North Korea invaded South Korea in June 1950. The Korean hot spot resulted in 200,000 newly drafted young American men entering the Army and 62,000 reservists returning to active duty.[2] Red China quickly entered the military conflict on the side of the North. It was us against them now.

America's fear induced a domestic panic fueled by ambitious, career-minded politicians. The message went like this: the Communists threatened to spread their virus worldwide and destroy America's freedom and prosperity—blessings that had been earned at a high price of lives and misery. Red baiting and witch hunts found traction because the politicians' claims seemed plausible. After all, in January 1950 a German scientist, Klaus Fuchs, who had helped the Americans and British build the atomic bomb, confessed to passing nuclear secrets to the Soviets—secrets that had toppled our atomic monopoly (and eventually sent Julius and Ethel Rosenberg to the electric chair). The House Un-American Activities Committee (HUAC), mandated to rout out suspected Communists in government and the arts, gained significant credibility after accusing Alger Hiss, head of the Carnegie Endowment for International Peace, and a former State Department official, of espionage. After two trials on charges of perjury, Hiss was convicted. Communist sympathizers and spies did operate in the U.S., but now, with public hysteria brimming, unscrupulous politicians could conveniently multiply the number of Reds and place them anywhere prudent for their reelections on an anti–Communist platform.

Panic

No one applied the pink spray paint more prolifically or carelessly than Senator Joseph McCarthy (R–Wisconsin). In a now infamous statement, made off-the-cuff at a Republican Women's Club meeting in Wheeling, West Virginia, on February 9, 1950, the senator waved a piece of paper above his head and claimed, "I have here in my hand a list of 205 that were known to the secretary of state as being members of the Communist Party, and who nevertheless are still working and shaping the policy of the State Department." The piece of paper was a prop, and reporters asked again and again to see it, to no avail. As the days rolled on, the number of Communists cited by McCarthy changed, as did his descriptions of their transgressions. But the damage was done. For three years, despite sloppy research and the groundless nature of his accusations, McCarthy led a national crusade against communism without offering evidence. President Truman called him "the greatest asset that the Kremlin has."³

Hollywood was not immune to the Red hunts. In 1947, HUAC conducted nine days of hearings into the film industry's alleged Communist propaganda. Resting on their Fifth Amendment right to refuse to answer some of the committee members' questions were ten men: Alvah Bessie (screenwriter), Herbert J. Biberman (screenwriter/producer, name given by Budd Schulberg and Edward Dmytryk), Lester Cole (screenwriter), Edward Dmytryk (director), Ring Lardner, Jr. (screenwriter), John Howard Lawson (screenwriter), Albert Maltz (screenwriter), Samuel Ornitz (screenwriter), Adrian Scott (screenwriter/producer, name given by Dmytryk), and Dalton Trumbo (screenwriter/director). Most of them spent a year in jail, and all of them were blacklisted, although Dmytryk later got his name off the list by becoming a "friendly witness" and naming names.

On April 10, 1950, the U.S. Supreme Court upheld the contempt of Congress convictions of the film capital's "Hollywood Ten."

In another development from 1950, three ex–FBI men and a television producer named Vincent Harnett published a pamphlet, *Red Channels*, a list of film, television, and radio artists who, Hartnett and his accomplices alleged, had at one time or another been members of subversive organizations. Copies of the pamphlet went to movie studios gratis, making the blacklist seem more "official" than ever.

Studio chiefs perused *Red Channels* and fired or refused work to any tainted individuals whom they had not already sacked. This list of about 150 artists eventually grew to over 320, and included Leonard Bernstein, Charlie Chaplin, John Garfield, Edward G. Robinson, Howard Da Silva, Dashiell Hammett, Burl Ives, Arthur Miller, Dorothy Parker, Joseph Losey, Zero Mostel, Orson Welles, Paul Robeson, Richard Wright, and Abraham Polonsky.

Also on the list was an RKO producer/screenwriter named Paul Jarrico, who was quickly dismissed by Howard Hughes. But more on these two later.

The Little Studio That Could

During this latter portion of Hollywood's "classic era," RKO stood apart from the other Big Five studios—MGM, Warner Bros., Paramount, and Twentieth Century-Fox—because it lacked something the others possessed: a house style. For example, MGM (the most prosperous studio and home to "More Stars than there are in Heaven") made its reputation with opulent production value, while Warner Bros. made gritty, tough films "torn from today's headlines!" In contrast, RKO's twenty-seven years of production existed, in the words of *The RKO Story* authors, Richard B. Jewell and Vernon Harbin, in a "perpetual state of transition: from one regime to another, from one set of production policies to the next, from one group of filmmakers to an altogether different group.... It failed to develop a singular guiding philosophy or continuity of management for any extended period. As a result, RKO's films tended to reflect the personality of the individual in charge of the studio at any given time—and since this time was always short, a dizzying number of diverse individuals became involved in RKO's creative affairs over the years, and the pictures never evolved an overall style unique to the studio."⁴

RKO offered, therefore, an alternative to the more predictable fare of the other majors, and granted opportunities to a diverse and ever-changing group of artists. The rich RKO catalogue encompasses Wheeler and Woolsey comedies and Astaire-Rogers musicals; *King Kong*; Orson Welles's *Citizen Kane*; and numerous film noir classics like *Out of the Past*. The studio made breezy detective series (Dick Tracy, the Saint, and the Falcon); sophisticated comedies like *Love Affair*; B-westerns; Val Lewton's subtle, psychological horror thrillers; and Hitchcock's *Notorious*. And then there are *Gunga Din* and other heart-pounding adventures; Oscar champion *The Best Years of Our Lives*; and great melodramas like *Five Came Back*. Yet these films really do not "look" like the product of a single studio in the manner that would be true of another major. This was not a liability, however, but a strength that usually meant interesting, entertaining films showcasing a bracing variety of editing, lighting, and directing styles. You knew what you would be seeing as soon as MGM's lion roared, but that beeping RKO radio tower didn't give away a thing.

Mr. Hughes

Then, in 1948, a change came to RKO that would turn the studio into a burlesque of itself. That change's name was Howard Hughes, a multimillionaire (later billionaire) who had already dabbled in movies after successful ventures in toolmaking, aviation, electronics, and other areas.

According to Elliott Reid, star of *The Whip Hand*, "Howard Hughes was like an old-time potentate, and what he wanted was what had to be. And, of course, he had the money to back it up."[5]

Not long after Hughes purchased a controlling interest in RKO, studio production chief Dore Schary quit because of Hughes's constant interference. Meanwhile, Hughes demanded that 75 percent of the studio's labor force be laid off, and production kept to a minimum. Most of RKO's 1948–49 releases were carryovers from Schary's tenure.[6] As described in *The RKO Story*, Hughes "became notoriously difficult to reach when vital decisions had to be made, while continuing to insist that he and he alone would pass judgment on all important projects.... A film studio run on the lines of RKO could not survive for long, no matter how rich the madman in charge happened to be."[7] In 1949, a consent decree between the U.S. government and the vertically integrated studios stripped the Big Five of their monopolistic control of production, distribution, and exhibition. The studios were forced to sell off their theater chains, and the eventual collapse of the studio system would begin its slow, inevitable course. When RKO sold off its exhibition arm in 1950, it lost the studio's only corporate component that turned a profit.[8] Because Hughes micro-managed studio activity, his production chiefs kept quitting on him. In the resulting turmoil, production and profits continued to decrease, partly due to television, which offered free entertainment right in the comfort of Americans' living rooms.

Hughes's despotic and unorthodox style encouraged the production of ludicrous turkeys like *The Conqueror* and *Jet Pilot*. (In 1982, Vincent Price told director Pete Walker that Hughes made *Son of Sinbad*, in which Price appeared, only to appease the many starlets he had promised parts to, casting them as the harem!) The often told story—true or not—that Hughes visited the studio only once, in the middle of the night while it was mostly deserted, and reacted with only two words, "Paint it," epitomizes his peculiar management style. By about 1951, RKO's best films tended to be independently produced pick-ups, such as *The Thing from Another World*, *Rashomon*, and *Face to Face*.

Hughes approached the Communist threat with the same fervency and hysteria as the worst of the witch hunters. His declaration of war was a better-dead-than-Red laugh riot called *The Woman on Pier 13* (aka *I Married a Communist*, 1950), a $650,000 loser at the box office.[9] In April 1951, shortly after completing his script for RKO's *The Las Vegas Story*, Paul Jarrico was summoned before HUAC. He refused to testify, proclaiming, "If I have to choose between crawling in the mud or going to jail like my courageous friends of the Hollywood Ten [mostly screenwriters], I shall certainly choose the latter."[10] Hughes not only fired Jarrico (under the pretense that the screenwriter had violated his contract's morals clause), but also had his name removed from *The Las Vegas Story*'s credits after commanding other studio screenwriters to remove all of Jarrico's contributions to it.[11]

What happened next reveals the power of eccentric billionaires. Hughes's treatment of Jarrico violated RKO's collective bargaining agreement with the Writers Guild of America. In a preemptive strike, Hughes filed a lawsuit against the Guild, after which the Guild and Jarrico filed separate lawsuits against RKO. Hughes forestalled a Guild strike at RKO by placing a great many of his employees on a (permanent) leave of absence, and creating a security department to examine remaining employees' backgrounds to eliminate any so-called subversives. (Another job of this department was to remove the names of blacklisted artists from the credits of any RKO film slated for re-release.) Remarkably, Hughes's lawyers defeated both the Guild and Jarrico in what many probably perceived (certainly Hughes did) as a public blow against Hollywood Reds.[12]

In 1951, a young, unknown writer-producer named Stanley Rubin, who had started at Universal as an associate producer, entered the gates of RKO with high hopes of moving up. He had written a script for *Macao* that the studio's top-line contract stars, Robert Mitchum and Jane Russell, accepted. Pleased with that, the studio bought the rights to a story called "Targets," which Rubin wished to produce as a movie.[13] Titled *The Narrow Margin*, the taut film noir (concisely directed by Richard Fleischer) garnered considerable positive buzz and attention at the studio even before its release. (A model of B-movie efficiency, tight scripting, and taut pacing, *The Narrow Margin* impressed Hughes so much that he delayed its release as he considered re-shooting it with an A-cast.)

While editing of *The Narrow Margin* proceeded, RKO rewarded Rubin with a green light to choose another property, and an opportunity to write and produce the picture. Rubin found a story and wrote a script based on it called *The Man He Found*. The project's projected budget was about the same as *The Narrow Margin*, under $250,000, but Rubin got to choose his cast and director.[14] Under the heavy hand of Howard Hughes, he was enjoying something rare at the studio: relative autonomy.

Rubin made an interesting choice of William Cameron Menzies, a respected production designer who also had directed, to do both jobs on *The Man He Found*. The studio's ace cinematographer, Nicholas Musuraca, one of Hollywood's most imaginative and evocative directors of photography, had lit RKO's *Out of the Past* and Val Lewton's suburb horror films. Musuraca would prove a perfect match for Menzies's talents.

Rubin's unusual selection for the heroic leading man was thirty-one-year-old Elliott Reid, a busy radio actor who, at age seventeen, had been a member of Orson Welles's Mercury Theatre. (Reid is best remembered today as Jane Russell's hapless suitor in *Gentlemen Prefer Blondes*, and as Fred MacMurray's insufferable romantic rival for Nancy

Olson in *The Absent Minded Professor*.) Because Reid was an unknown actor who did not look or act tough, he lacked the two-fisted, fearless appeal of someone like Robert Mitchum. But audiences, Rubin felt, would worry much more about Reid's character escaping with his life than they would about a tough-guy in the Mitchum mold. Heroes of that sort looked after themselves, and nearly always triumphed. But an ordinary, Everyman fellow like Reid's Matt Corbin invited no preconceived notions about the character's survival. Even when we like and care about them, non-star central characters like Reid's are expendable for dramatic purposes, especially in a spooky, suspenseful low budgeter like *The Man He Found*. And so the casting of Reid as the protagonist brings suspense. *Who is this guy, and what's going to happen to him?*

Reid's leading lady was Carla Balenda, a pretty but undistinguished ingénue who is believable as Janet Keller, the sister of a small town doctor (Edgar Barrier, another Mercury Theatre alumnus). The only familiar face in the cast was that of future *Perry Mason* star Raymond Burr, by this time already an established heavy in *Desperate*, *Raw Deal*, *Pitfall*, and other solid noir thrillers of the late 1940s.

The Original Idea

In Rubin's script, vacationer Matt Corbin (Reid) slips and hits his head while fishing for trout in a lake near Winnoga, a sleepy little Minnesota town. In pouring rain and thunder, he drives for help, but an armed guard threatens him when he happens upon the estate of Dr. Peterson (Lewis Martin) to ask for assistance. He continues his journey until he reaches Winnoga, where a young man, who seems suspicious of him, directs Matt to the town's physician, Dr. Edward Keller (Barrier). Keller and his sister Janet bandage Reid's head, but the doctor is nervous and asks Matt prying questions. Sent to the town's inn for the night, Matt meets the owner, Steve Loomis (Burr), who explains that because the trout all died of a virus a few years ago, the once-busy tourist location is now a ghost town. Loomis, too, seems unusually interested in Matt and explains Peterson away as the local eccentric.

When Loomis asks about Matt's occupation, he reveals that he is a writer-photographer for *American View* magazine. No one seems happy about that news. The next morning Matt meets a friendly general store manager named Luther (Frank Darien), who tells Matt that most of the people in town were bought out two years ago after the town's fortunes crumbled. Luther is one of the few left. This surprises Matt because Keller and Loomis have led him to believe that they have been around much longer. Matt begins to wonder why outsiders would buy all of a dying town's property. Meanwhile, a young, smart-alecky man named Nate (Peter Brocco) keeps a close eye on Luther and Matt. Nate, Loomis, and Keller seem to be in cahoots about *something*. That evening, Matt takes Janet to a movie, and sees Loomis enter the theater and summon Keller away with him.

Janet is friendly enough, but her manner is uncomfortable, worried. Later that evening, near the inn, Matt spies Loomis and Keller climb out of a boat with a third person (later revealed as Peterson), who says, "Remember, my orders are to be carried out exactly." Matt waits for them in the inn's tavern and catches them in a lie when he asks about their leaving the theater. After that, Matt is more curious than ever about all of this strange behavior, and so the next morning he announces that he has decided to stay

in Winnoga for a while to write a human-interest story on the town's misfortune and decline. He is watched more closely now, and is caught taking photos of Peterson's secret estate. After Matt confides in Luther for help, the old man is killed by an injection administered by Keller. The story is that Luther died of a heart attack.

To complicate things further, Matt's increasing romantic interest in Janet has been noticed by Keller and Loomis.

Matt convinces Janet that her brother is caught up in something sinister and that both their lives are in danger. Janet, in fact, knows her brother has been involved in something horribly wrong, but, like Matt, she is clueless as to what that could be. Because Matt's car has been sabotaged and Loomis controls all outgoing telephone calls, Matt and Janet decide to escape at night in a canoe. As they paddle past Peterson's estate, they see something shocking. Reid described this revelatory scene in a 2003 interview: "[I]t was Wagnerian, almost—suddenly this madman comes out onto the little balcony of a man-

The original premise of *The Whip Hand* (1951)—with a climax calculated to shock audiences holding vivid memories of World War II—was dumped at the insistence of RKO owner Howard Hughes, and reworked into an anti–Red polemic. Atmospheric and highly pictorial, *The Whip Hand* is a true curiosity.

sion on an island in this lake. And it's *Hitler*! Out comes Hitler, raving mad and screaming and half his face has been burned away by the fire in the bunker. *That* was the original ending."[15] In fact, that is the ending we will never see.

Working Creatively

William Cameron Menzies's set-ups create extreme paranoia and hysteria. In the film's first half, he constantly frames two-shots and three-shots of Reid and one or two others. After a pleasant exchange of dialogue, Reid will walk out of the frame and then the conspirator(s) left in shot will show a complete change of demeanor behind his back that expresses danger, anger, and contempt. No one expresses this better than Raymond Burr, who artificially laughs, smiles, and chuckles throughout his dialogue with Reid. Then, as soon as Reid turns or walks away, Burr's expression turns to menace. If *two* conspirators are left in the frame, they give each other knowing glances, as if to say, *We're going to have to do something about this guy*. Although not exactly subtle, these indicators of a conspiracy offer lip-smacking excitement and suspense. Adding to their chilling effect is that Nicholas Musuraca photographs almost every set-up in low-key, high-contrast lighting that establishes an aura of unease. Something diabolical is going on around here, and it's *der Führer*—evil incarnate.

Rubin's script is a blueprint for the you-can't-trust-your-neighbor conspiracy plot, and Menzies highlights the shock of the betrayed with close-ups of the most unlikely of betrayers. When Matt and Janet are on the run, they come upon a woodsy cabin occupied by a sweet old lady, Mabel. The actress was Olive Carey, who started making movies in 1912, so picture your kindly grandma here. Mabel courageously offers her help, and all three climb into Mabel's truck, grateful and relieved, and before long are delivered safely—to Loomis! Menzies's close-up of her mission-completed face is horrifying in its implication. No one can be trusted in such a universe—not mothers, fathers, siblings, or grandparents—no one.

For one sequence, Menzies and Musuraca bring the paranoia into the bright light of day, at a deserted hatchery with shrunken, sun-bleached, vertical planks for siding. Inside, Matt hopes to elude one of the approaching Nazis, the planks silhouetted against thin lines of luminous sunlight that crosshatch the floor. Menzies cuts to an interior close-up of two planks with the space between them centered in his frame. In the same shot, outside, through that space, is the Nazi in full shot as he walks toward the camera—toward Corbin (and us), in effect—until his face is in close-up, peering in. The tightly blocked shot makes Corbin's entrapment in the hatchery intense and claustrophobic. Menzies's purposeful set ups reveal his smart commitment to angles, lighting, and choreography that serve theme and mood.

Evidently, the economics of low-budget filmmaking and Menzies's time-consuming dedication to the movie's meaningful, highly textured appearance left him little or no time for his cast. "I thought he was absolutely the best production designer in the business," says producer Rubin. "And, I liked him very much personally. But by the time he finished shooting the picture, I had decided ... that he was a better production designer than he was a director.... [H]e was more interested in his set-ups, in the angles, the design, the look of the scenes, than he was in the performances."[16]

Reid calls Menzies a "very, very gifted man" and says the film "had some *good* things

In *The Whip Hand*, magazine writer Matt Corbin (Elliott Reid, left) stumbles into a peculiar Minnesota town that appears to hold many secrets. Matt's curiosity will lead to the murder of the friendly fellow (Frank Darien) who owns the local general store—but that's just the prelude to a Communist scheme to conquer North America via germ warfare.

in it, starting with a ... good script by Stanley Rubin, and the great black-and-white photography of Nick Musuraca. It's really beautifully photographed thanks to ... Menzies and Musuraca. But Menzies never directed me, *ever*. He was very involved with the set-ups, with the look of it. I think his focus was more on the visual aspect of a film."[17]

Despite Menzies's reluctance to guide his actors, they all give more than adequate to fine performances. Most of them were experienced players capable of nuance, which suggests that they studied more than just their dialogue. They were professionals. No one under- or overplays (with one exception, later). Much of each performance, in fact, is expressed through Menzies's shot selections and cutting, the true grammar and syntax of moviemaking.

As Reid would later note, "*The Whip Hand* began life as *The Man He Found,* a B movie that had real quality and a great denouement—until it was traduced, trampled upon and totally destroyed by Howard Hughes."[18]

Before it could be released, *The Man He Found* was screened for Hughes in a penultimate final cut.[19] He liked the film, but, like many on the right, he was personally at war with Communists, not Nazis. Hughes ordered Rubin to complete the script changes needed for reshoots. Some cast members, including Reid, would be paid their entire salaries a second time.[20]

Rubin turned Hughes down flat, quit the production, and asked that his name be dropped from the credits. "This was about 1951," Rubin recalls, "and there was a lot of anti–Communist hysteria going on around the country and particularly in Hollywood at that time. The anti–Communist hysterics in Hollywood, as led by John Wayne, Ward Bond, Hedda Hopper, etc., were extreme. *I didn't want to do that.*"[21]

Auf Wiedersehen *to Hitler*

Producer Lew Rachmil took over the production reigns and hired writers George Bricker and Frank L. Moss to write the script changes in a manner to retain most of the existing footage (75 to 80 percent, Rubin reckons[22]). Because the original film is a well-paced mystery that does not reveal the villains (Hitler and his henchmen) until the end of the film, the reshoot and fresh edit were not as involved as they might have been. Menzies and Musuraca stayed on to design, light, and direct the new scenes, which gave the newly titled film, *The Whip Hand*, an essential continuity of style.

A German actor named Otto Waldis was hired to play the replacement lead villain, Dr. Wilhelm Bucholtz, a Nazi-turned-Communist. Hitler (Bob Watson, who played Hitler in nine films including this one) was left on the cutting room floor. Besides adding Bucholtz, the reworked film picked up a horror element: a lab full of Dr. Bucholtz's grisly human experiments with germ warfare. Covered in bandages and displaying grotesque make-up effects, they stumble, groan, and, in the end, collectively beat Bucholtz to death before he can unleash a bomb designed to spread enough deadly germs to destroy the country. (The plan seems a little shortsighted in that the germs would presumably kill all of the Communist operatives in the U.S., too, and then spread to Red countries as well.) Waldis (well-liked by genre fans as Dr. Heinrich Von Loeb in *Attack of the 50 Foot Woman*) plays his death scene with unrestrained bombast, spouting familiar, Hollywood-scripted Red gibberish. But the situation is so preposterous that the approach seems appropriate. Reid says that Waldis "felt terrible guilt doing this [part], because this was when the anti–Communist furor was starting, and the McCarthy era. Hollywood was making anti–Communist pictures, *I Was a Communist for the F.B.I.* and all those [other] things, all this junk, in this dark period in our history."[23]

Mixed Reviews

With the added production expense, *The Whip Hand* budget swelled to $376,000. Unfortunately, Hughes's newest volley against the Reds lost $225,000 at the box-office.[24] (That's nearly enough money to make another movie like *The Narrow Margin*!) Some critics liked the film and didn't seem to notice that almost everyone in town was blond and Aryan. "*The Whip Hand* emerges a near masterpiece in suspense," beamed *Daily Variety*. "Fascinating in theme, expertly presented and beautifully enacted by a cast of comparative unknowns, [the] film is perhaps the best modestly produced melodrama of the season. Peak interest is sustained throughout." The review cannot really be faulted except for one (major) comment about the film's suspense. Writers Bricker and Moss added an opening scene set in the Kremlin, where a military man standing in front of a large map of the U.S. rants in Russian and then directs his pointer to a small town in

Minnesota. Other military types observe. Unfortunately, then, what's going on in Winnoga is no mystery from the start. Most of the picture's suspense is lost from the start.

In Britain, a *Monthly Film Bulletin* critic saw what *The Man He Found* had become: "The explicit characterization of the villain as a Nazi turned Communist; Bucholtz's violent expressions of hatred for all things American ....; the extreme, almost hysterical nature of the plot, together with its improbability, make this a curious example of propaganda carried to excess."

Pod People

When Rubin wrote and produced *The Man He Found*, he could not have known that he created the essential combination of elements that could tampered with to evoke what would become the archetypal conventions of many of the decade's Red scare science fiction films. Science fiction is the perfect genre to cloak controversial issues in metaphor, however thinly. (Fans of the 1960s iterations of *The Outer Limits* and *Star Trek* will attest to this.) Such thrillers as *Invasion of the Body Snatchers* (1956), *I Married a Monster from Outer Space* (1958), Menzies's own *Invaders from Mars* (1953), and others that belong to the aliens-inhabit-human-bodies subgenre substitute the ultimate "foreigners" for their Communists.

These aliens often do not possess human emotions or desires. Like the Communists, they wish to destroy our way of life. They start their covert operations in little, middle-class suburban areas, where decent American families with new houses and cars live good, white, Christian lives. The "foreigners" stealthily infiltrate by quietly replacing each citizen, one-by-one, with one of their own, and when an outsider enters town, these aliens that masquerade as perfectly normal humans secretly give each other knowing, portentous glances. In effect, each of these movies takes place in Winnoga, Minnesota. Many science fiction invaders of the 1950s are stand-ins for Communists who act like your good next door neighbor—or at least they try to. Their "cultural" differences (in other words, a lack of Americanism) eventually exposes them.

Many of the decade's alien-infiltration films owe at least something to *The Whip Hand*'s template; you see it in *Creature with the Atom Brain* (1955), *It Conquered the World* (1956), *The Gamma People* (1956), *The Quatermass Xperiment* aka *The Creeping Unknown* (1956), *Beast with a Million Eyes* (1956), *Not of this Earth* (1957), *Kronos* (1957), *The Brain Eaters* (1958), *The Brain from Planet Arous* (1958), *The Space Children* (1958), *Invisible Invaders* (1959), and many others.

At the end of the day, the most terrifying element of *The Whip Hand* is not the Communists that secretly live among us, or the mad scientist's threat of germ warfare. What truly terrifies is how easily and seamlessly Howard Hughes changed the face of the enemy to suit his personal agenda. A film about Hitler and Nazis after World War II is turned into an I-told-you-so confirmation for Red-baiters that exploited fear under the guise of Americanism. It sounds too fantastic. And yet, on September 11, 2001, nineteen of Osama bin Laden's Al-Qaeda terrorists hijacked four commercial airline jet liners. None of the hijackers were Iraqi, but by March 20, 2003, a U.S. president and his administration had convinced many of their fellow Americans—via fear, panic, and lies—that Iraqi dictator Saddam Hussein was the face of the enemy. As a result, the U.S. made an unprecedented first-strike invasion of a sovereign nation.

And with that, we utilized a trick favored by real-life Nazis and Communists.

Filmography

The Whip Hand—RKO; Released October 24, 1951 (some sources claim October 1); Black and white; 82 min.

Credits: Producers: Howard Hughes, Stanley Rubin (uncredited),[25] Lewis J. Rachmil.; Director: William Cameron Menzies; Screenplay: Stanley Rubin (uncredited), George Bricker, Frank L. Moss; Director of photography: Nicholas Musuraca; Editor: Robert Golden; Music: Paul Sawtell; Production designer: William Cameron Menzies; Art directors: Albert S. D'Agostino, Carroll Clark

Cast: Carla Balenda: Janet Keller; Elliott Reid: Matt Corbin; Edgar Barrier: Dr. Edward Keller; Raymond Burr: Steve Loomis; Otto Waldis: Dr. Wilhelm Bucholtz

Notes

1. David J. Hogan, ed. *The Fifties Chronicle*. Lincolnwood, IL: Legacy Publications, 2006.
2. *Ibid.*
3. *Ibid.*
4. Richard B. Jewell and Vernon Harbin. *The RKO Story*. New York: Arlington House, 1982.
5. Tom Weaver. *Earth vs. the Sci-Fi Filmmakers*. Jefferson, NC: McFarland, 2005.
6. Jewell and Harbin.
7. *Ibid.* After operating RKO to ruin, Hughes sold the studio to General Teleradio, Inc., in 1955, but by then the studio could not recover. New film production halted permanently in 1957 (Jewell and Harbin).
8. *Ibid.*
9. *Ibid.*
10. Doug Ireland. direland.typepad.com. "The Howard Hughes Scorsese Doesn't Tell You About." *Direland.* 27
11. *Ibid.* After he was blacklisted and fired by Hughes, Paul Jarrico produced and Herbert Biberman (one of the Hollywood Ten) directed an acclaimed, award-winning film about striking Mexican-American mine workers, *Salt of the Earth* (1954). Made independently of the Hollywood system with a cast of real mine workers, the low-budget film was condemned by HUAC while in production, and never had a prayer of proper release in the U.S. Hughes got in on the act with his letter to HUAC member Rep. Donald Jackson (R-California) to explain that "the studios could effectively kill the picture if they denied the production access to the facilities they needed to edit, dub, score, and otherwise prepare the movie for theaters" (Ireland). The film received brief runs in only New York and San Francisco before it disappeared. Reviewing it for *Sight and Sound* at the time, Pauline Kael described it "as clear a piece of Communist propaganda as we have had in many years."
12. Jewell and Harbin; Ireland.
13. Weaver.
14. *Ibid.*
15. *Ibid.*
16. *Ibid.*
17. *Ibid.*
18. *Ibid.*
19. *Ibid.*
20. *Ibid.* Producer Stanley Rubin left RKO after *The Whip Hand* to accept Darryl Zanuck's offer to produce three films at Fox. Rubin had a long, successful career as a film and television producer that includes *River of No Return* (1954, Otto Preminger) and *White Hunter Black Heart* (1990, Clint Eastwood).
21. *Ibid.*
22. *Ibid.*
23. *Ibid.*
24. Jewell and Harbin.
25. By requesting his name be removed from *The Whip Hand*'s credits, Rubin forfeited his residuals.

Works Cited

Books

Dunning, John. *On the Air: The Encyclopedia of Old-Time Radio*. New York: Oxford University Press, 1998.
Halberstam, David. *The Fifties*. New York: Villard Books, 1993.
Hogan, David J., ed. *The Fifties Chronicle*. Lincolnwood, IL: Legacy Publications, 2006.
Jewell, Richard B., and Vernon Harbin. *The RKO Story*. New York: Arlington House, 1982.
Warren, Bill. *Keep Watching the Skies*, Vol. I. Jefferson, NC: McFarland, 1982.
_____. *Keep Watching the Skies*, Vol. II. Jefferson, NC: McFarland, 1986.
Weaver, Tom. *Earth vs. the Sci-Fi Filmmakers*. Jefferson, NC: McFarland, 2005.

88   Part 2: Red Mischief Here, There and Everywhere

Web

Ireland, Doug. direland.typepad.com. "The Howard Hughes Scorsese Doesn't Tell You About." *Direland*. 27
moria.co.nz. Scheib, Richard. Moria Science Fiction, Horror and Fantasy Film Review.

Video

The Whip Hand. Private collection.

Artists and Models
The Day the Slobs Saved Democracy

Ermine DeGraffenried

> Two pals quietly starving in Lower Manhattan—a frustrated fine artist and a would-be author of children's books—are pulled into the wild world of comic book publishing, whirlwind romance, and the Communist menace.
> —author's synopsis

Following a lively main-title sequence, the first image in writer-director Frank Tashlin's *Artists and Models* (1955) is a woman's mouth: a half-open, frankly unappetizing orifice with small pearl-like teeth arrayed behind full lips glazed a glistening crimson. The mouth dominates the screen frame. So enormous is it, in fact, that it dwarfs Dean Martin, who plays the billboard artist who has just painted it, at a plum spot high above a busy Manhattan boulevard. This Brobdingnagian maw is designed to sell cigarettes (mechanicals behind the image work a smoke-producing bellows), but what it's really selling is, of course, sex—as well as the dignity of all movie-going women disinclined to reward Tashlin for being a brilliant vulgarian.

As for that main-title sequence that precedes the giant mouth, picture six pairs of shapely bare legs (sporting the glow of suntans, naturally) with no torsos above; a dozen pampered feet shod in strappy, open-toe high-heeled sandals and backless mules, with six left legs artfully bent at the knees, ankles turned, so that we can peer at the showy perfection of that twelve-pack of fabulous stems. Across this fleshly panorama, in casual white letters boldly accentuated with black drop-shadow, is the film's title: *Artists and Models*.

Following this, the credits are displayed on separate "cards" occupied by stunning models wearing even more stunning gowns—in a riot of colors. (All credit to cinematographer Daniel L. Fapp, who shot in widescreen VistaVision and Technicolor with marvelous care.) The first time I witnessed this sequence I wanted to bite it, as if it were cotton candy or a juicy apple. It's that dazzling.

* * *

But all right, just to be clear: the problem that women have with Frank Tashlin isn't that a great deal of his humor is jejune and just plain silly (that's a good thing), but that so much of his wit is based in objectification of the female body—or rather, in the objectification of *pieces* of bodies, particularly legs and feet, in which Mr. Tashlin displays a

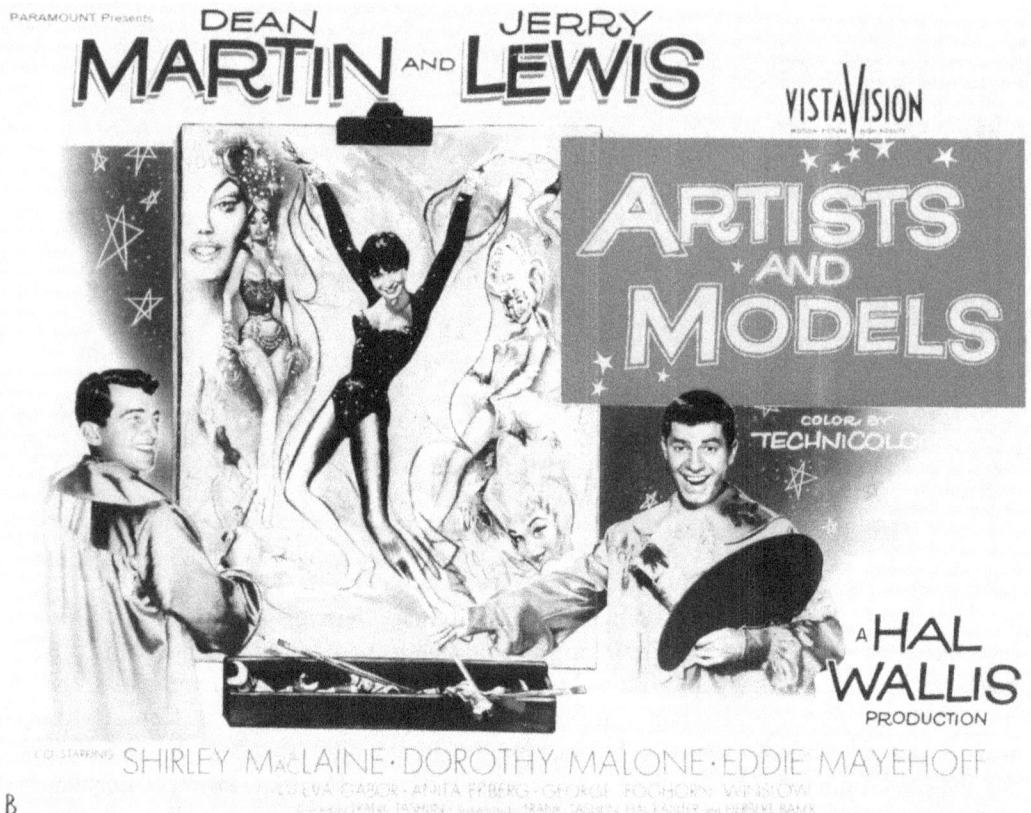

Splashy and deliciously absurd, Frank Tashlin's *Artists and Models* (1955) is the penultimate Martin and Lewis picture, and one of the team's best. The comedy celebrates America's love of joyous nonsense—not least, advertising, fetishized sex, comic books, and good-natured vulgarity—constructing a flamboyant contrast to the goofy (but grim) Communist ideology that dominates the film's final thirty minutes.

robust interest. During the course of this hugely funny and frequently disturbing comedy, *Bat Lady* comic book artist and sometime advertising illustrator Abby Parker (Dorothy Malone) takes a shower, in order to wrap herself afterward in a wee towel that displays her long legs and pretty feet. And Tashlin clearly intends for us to focus when she kicks off her mules to dry her lower legs, revealing splendid arches and petite toes. (Doesn't every woman put on mules immediately after bathing, so she can take three steps and then take them right off again?)

Our first look at Abby's friend and model, Bessie Sparrowbush (Shirley MacLaine) isn't of the entirety of Bessie, but is rather a lingering, carefully framed aft view that pulls our gaze to her ass, legs, and heels, as she poses in a skimpy Bat Lady costume while Abby draws. Only after we enjoy a good long look does the camera pan up to reveal Bessie's torso, head, and aggressively posed Bat Lady limbs and talons—*grrr!* Bessie is sexy, and like many sexy women who are refreshingly assertive, she's vaguely menacing—or so Hollywood has liked to tell us. In the manner of the fictional Bat Lady, Bessie is a sort of confection, valued more for her accouterments than for her true, inherent Bessiness.

Later at Murdock Publishing, home of *Bat Lady* and where Bessie works as a secretary, Bessie hikes her dress, raises one leg, and leans backward across a desk while taking a phone call, her breasts straining against her blouse, and the audience surely encouraged to let its gaze travel northward along Bessie's shapely calves to her thighs. Mind you, Bessie has no reason at all for all the contortions—she just arrays herself that way because she's pert and oversexed and a real handful for the fellow she falls for, an aspiring children's book writer and full-on comic book addict named Eugene Fullstack (Jerry Lewis). In one of the best movie jokes of the 1950s, Eugene feels no physical attraction whatever to Bessie—a great laugh because twenty-one-year-old Shirley MacLaine looks and behaves more deliciously than any male might reasonably hope. No, skinny Eugene is in love with Bat Lady, and has a sexual response to Bessie only while she wears the Bat Lady mask and costume. (Yes, this is fetishism.)

Like many of Tashlin's films, notably a brilliant pair of vehicles for Jayne Mansfield, *The Girl Can't Help It* (1956) and *Will Success Spoil Rock Hunter?* (1957), *Artists and Models* is about sex. It is preoccupied with sex. It is, in fact, obsessed with sex. As the lunatic narrative unreels, Abby goes all atremble whenever touched by Eugene's roommate and best friend, an unfulfilled fine artist named Rick Todd (Dean Martin); if Bessie wants sex too much, Abby hasn't allowed herself to want it enough.

While Abby struggles with her attraction to Rick, Bessie—barely dressed—literally drapes herself on furniture and staircases inches from Eugene, hoping to get that not-so-metaphoric rise out of him. (So flexible is she that she seems to have no bones!) Bessie later finds herself half-dressed (yet again) and tied to a chair backstage at the splashy Artists and Models Ball, stripped of her Bat Lady costume and held fast, one long leg pinioned on this side of the seat, the other long leg pinioned on the other. (Does every male have a secret wish to tie a woman to a chair, or to a bed, or to something else? Movies certainly seem to suggest as much.) Tashlin engineers things so that Bessie finally turns herself, and the chair, ninety degrees, bending at the waist and offering us another aft view, this one a startlingly intimate look at her spread legs and barely concealed lady parts.

To ensure we don't lose focus, Swedish bombshell Anita Ekberg ambles here and there throughout the film, squeezed into a ridiculous corset and bursting from her bodice. Gorgeous babes are *everywhere*, and if I were a male voyeur, I'd cherish this movie.

A sexy Red spy (Eva Gabor) with the unlikely nom de plume Mrs. Curtis has swiped Bessie's stimulating Bat Lady costume (this is why Bessie is restrained in that chair) and then leans in to seduce Eugene, her rounded breasts rising and falling as she blows cigarette smoke in his face and lays hands on him.

Why does this Communist want to seduce Eugene Fullstack? Because Eugene's audible nightmares have given Rick the plots for comic book adventures, and one detail that got into print, secret formula X34–5R1, happens to be the first part of a *real* secret formula created by the United States and much desired by the Reds. The spy stuff, then, comes down to which faction arouses Eugene first.

* * *

Artists and Models is the sixteenth of seventeen features Dean Martin and Jerry Lewis made as a team. The tuxedoed crooner and "the monkey" got together in 1946, slaying 'em in nightclubs as Jerry bounced around the stage, frantically interrupting and otherwise annihilating Dean's songs. The pair earned an NBC radio series in 1949, the

Artists and Models milks considerable humor from the inability of Eugene Fullstack (Jerry Lewis) to respond romantically—or even sexually—to lovestruck Bessie Sparrowbush (Shirley MacLaine). Bessie makes side money posing for the artist of the *Bat Lady* comic book. Eugene is obsessed with Bat Lady. Notice his understandable surprise when his heroine opens the door to the apartment upstairs. Hollywood's Production Code, by the way, wasn't amused that Eugene's last name was originally to be "Fullstick."

year of their first picture, *My Friend Irma*, a tepid comedy that gave the boys show-stealing supporting parts. A subsequent long-term contract with producer Hal Wallis and Paramount put Martin and Lewis on the treadmill of two pictures a year, a grind that transformed the duo into kings of Hollywood, accountable to no one and eager to indulge their appetites. Dean and Jerry's great success also made them increasingly sensitive to each other's quirks.

Before Tashlin, the better Martin and Lewis comedies were directed by George Marshall and Norman Taurog. A 1952 entry, Taurog's *The Stooge*, is a comedy-drama about a failed solo entertainer (played by Martin) who finds success only after teaming with a comic stooge (Lewis). Much of the story focuses on the entertainer's frank exploitation of his stooge, and on the stooge's unquestioning love for his partner. Although capped by a happy rapprochement, *The Stooge* is eerily predictive of the ego-created sinkhole that eventually swallowed Dean and Jerry, and that finally drove them apart in 1956. Martin resented the common industry wisdom about Jerry being the real star of the act; pundits insisted that without Jerry, Dean would have no film career at all. And Jerry fancied himself a Renaissance man eager to act, write, direct, produce, and even sing. He wanted to get out from beneath Dean's handsomeness and easy charm, in order to show that he had those qualities, too.

* * *

Frank Tashlin had been a director of animated shorts at "Termite Terrace," the fabulous Warner Bros. cartoon unit, during 1933, 1936–38, and 1942–44. *The Stupid Cupid* (1944), an Elmer Fudd–Daffy Duck farce, is undeniably a sex comedy (and a brazen one, at that); another with Daffy, *Nasty Quacks* (1945), is one of the Warner unit's best, with the obnoxious, hyper duck raising holy hell in a household—and driving the homeowner to madness and violence—after being adopted by a little girl. And with *A Tale of Two Mice* (1945), Tashlin "worked with" another great comedy duo, Abbott and Costello, reimagined here as mice (one too dumb to live, the other cruelly aggressive) that covet a piece of cheese guarded by a housecat.

All of Tashlin's cartoon work being, well, cartoons, the rules of logic, physics, and everyday morality do not apply—an attitude that the writer-director enthusiastically brought to his later feature work. He broke into features as a screenwriter in 1945, and co-directed his first movie, *The Lemon Drop Kid* (starring Bob Hope), in 1951. He functioned as a "movie doctor" on that one, going without screen credit and shooting new scenes to goose the laughs after previews of the picture went badly. Tashlin got his first solo directorial credit on *The First Time* (1952), and had his first big success later the same year with another Bob Hope comedy, *Son of Paleface*. As events played out, Tashlin became vitally important to Jerry Lewis's hugely successful solo career, co-writing and directing *Rock-a-Bye Baby* (1958), *Who's Minding the Store?* (1963), *The Disorderly Orderly* (1964), and three others. Lewis, a serious student of film, observed Tashlin closely throughout their association, absorbing much of the older man's comic and visual sensibilities. Lewis's finest achievement as a director-star, 1963's *The Nutty Professor*, rocks with brilliant structural, sonic, verbal, and visual gags that are straight out of the Tashlin style guide.

Artists and Models is the first Martin and Lewis comedy directed by Tashlin; his second and last with the boys, *Hollywood or Bust* (1956), is also the last of the Martin and Lewis series.

The usual critical complaints about *Artists and Models* are (1) the movie is just too damn long at 109 minutes and (2) the spy stuff—which doesn't pop up until 78 minutes of story have gone by—feels tacked on and arbitrary.

Although 109 minutes is a prolonged running time for a fluff comedy, we beg to differ about the movie's spy element: what may seem like an unrelated narrative appendage is actually closely related, thematically, to everything that has come before. In the world of *Artists and Models*, everything is for sale—including bodies—because selling is American and thus good (I believe that this is so), and because communism is grim and joyless and, really, no system for anybody that enjoys fun and color and high spirits. Further, a debased American culture as exemplified by horror comics, sexy models, and advertising is good, too, because our system lets us *choose* to be debased. As far as we can discern, the government isn't telling us how to conduct our daily lives, or what to spurn and embrace. If we elect to be shallow dopes, that's great because what is freedom, after all, but the opportunity to be ridiculous?

* * *

Existing parallel to the worlds of sex and espionage is the issue of racy and violent comic books, a hot topic across America when Tashlin shot *Artists and Models* in the early months of 1955. Fredric Wertham, a humorless, thin-lipped German psychiatrist working with felons at Bellevue and with troubled children at Harlem's Lafargue Clinic, developed a deep interest in comic books because nearly all of the children he encountered read them. Practically every kid in America read comic books, but Wertham met only the ones that had broken into stores or caused ruckuses at home and at school. Encouraged, he recklessly concluded that comics had precipitated the bad behavior of his charges. According to Wertham, some of the boys and girls entertained violent fantasies. Some of the tots struggled to suppress unseemly sexual urges. Others, Wertham said, had hurt animals and even other children. In a series of widely read magazine essays, Wertham blamed bad juvenile behavior on the pernicious influence of what he called "crime comics." (Horror, western, superhero, cops and robbers, adventure, war—they were all crime comics to Dr. Wertham.) His hardcover polemic against comics, *Seduction of the Innocent*, was published in 1954 and became a best-seller. Here, at last, was a book telling parents that it wasn't they who had failed their troubled children; no, their children had been ruined by comic books. Mom and Dad, you're off the hook!

Few people will argue that a baseball game played on a field marked with human entrails and with a human head used for the ball is exactly good for children—but EC Comics published the tale anyway. (Nobody got chopped to bits later on their local sandlots.) And "headlight" comics devoted to busty crime-busters and gun molls undeniably trafficked in immature, reductive images of women. A lot of comic book material of the day was rote, obvious, violent, and crude. Many publishers—like *Bat Lady*'s Mr. Murdock (a hilarious Eddie Mayehoff), who implores his artists to give him "more gore" and "rivers of blood"—were cynical crumbs. But then, millions of America's comic book readers were not kids at all but young men who had picked up the habit in the service. Comics were accessible and cheap, and so without being aware of it, Wertham argued as strongly against form as against content. Because comics were printed in primary colors on cheap paper, and sold for a dime, they were trash.

In more recent years, *Seduction of the Innocent* has been an object of mirth, not least for the doctor's contention that Batman and Robin's daily life is "a wish dream of two homosexuals living together," and because Wertham equates the "S" on Superman's chest with the atrocious runes of the Nazi SS. But in 1954, with many wayward children whose fathers had been absent during World War II now old enough to roam the streets, the book struck a nerve. Bad enough that international communism gazed greedily at the U.S.; now the country faced this four-color threat from within. Many parents accepted Wertham's offer of a free pass.

The consequence of the book's success is that the impossibly crowded comic book market thinned itself, with some publishers exiting voluntarily, and many driven out. A purportedly voluntary self-policing body headed by a judge, the Comics Code Authority, was actually censorship that arrived as extortion: join the Code or no wholesaler will distribute your comics, and any that do find their way to retailers will be refused by the vendors. (An investigatory comic book Senate subcommittee headed by Estes Kefauver, the Tennessee senator famous for his coonskin caps, also got into the act.)

It is against all of this real-life commotion that Tashlin staged a particularly funny sequence in *Artists and Models.* Abby, who has grown disenchanted with Bat Lady and Vincent the Vulture (a Murdock comic book hero literally dreamed up by Eugene), has Eugene in tow when she appears on a television panel show discussing the comic book menace. Here is Jerry Lewis in his glorious element, dull and unsure before the TV cameras, mouth agape and eyes half-closed, stumbling his way through an incoherent explanation of the deleterious effects of comics. In a rare lucid moment, Eugene proudly explains that comic books taught him, among other things, "how to prepare rat poison so it spreads like peanut butter." For comics' critics, Eugene is Exhibit A.

Naturally, the television program informs viewers that comic books must go.

To Frank Tashlin, who began his professional life as a print cartoonist and later created those wonderfully pugnacious animated cartoons, the comic book controversy seemed an insulting absurdity. Throughout his Hollywood career, he found himself at odds with the Production Code, by which anything with even a hint of "illicit" sex and other subversion was scrubbed from scripts and, if necessary, from finished movie prints. Tashlin had no patience for humorless bluenoses. Censorship made him mad, and he developed a habit of retaining bits of business that he had led the Code to understand would be cut. (*Artists and Models* has one of those moments: already in the snare of the beautiful spy, Eugene—wearing a hideous, snowball-shaped Freddie the Fieldmouse costume—follows her across a massive foyer at the Reds' hideout, his elongated mouse tail dragging on the floor. When the woman starts up the stairs and Eugene follows, the tail is suddenly, stiffly horizontal (and at the center of Tashlin's frame). Production Code: *Cut that gag.* Tashlin: *Will do.* The gag: still there.

Dialogue given to the Communists establishes that they are an unsmiling bunch guided by robotic groupthink. Slaves to a gray Soviet system (yet sufficiently hypocritical to set themselves up in a Scarsdale mansion), they wish to steal that secret formula, and then turn all of *us* into joyless gray things, too. Living with Red-style censorship and fed pre-masticated, state-approved diversions, Americans would lose the ol' joie de vivre. No more crime comics. No more bikinis. No more movies. No more fun.

A fate of that sort is in defiance of the movie's love of imagination. When Eugene has only a single baked bean for supper, he carefully cuts it with a knife and savors each teeny bite, as if it were the world's most tender filet. Then he wraps his hand and forearm with a linen napkin and struggles to pop an imaginary cork before pouring himself an imaginary class of champagne. (Roommate Rick can only look on in silent incredulity.)

When the bean is gone, Eugene wishes for a steak. Rick tells him to keep his wishes to himself. And then the couple in the flat above begins to argue (in parody *Honeymooners* voices) about dinner; Eugene sticks his head from the window and in another moment a thick steak drops into his hands.

Abby and Bessie give the imaginary Bat Lady a career and even physical reality. Eugene imagines Vincent the Vulture and the character becomes real. Freddie Fieldmouse lives only in Eugene's mind until Abby prepares a pastel sketch, and when Eugene puts on the Freddie costume, the character exists in three dimensions.

The film closely ties imagination to upward mobility, a fiercely desired postwar condition that has eluded Rick before he meets Abby. Upward mobility motivates the publisher Murdock (who plots to divorce his wife while retaining his lifestyle), and he's upward in his sexual relationships, too: at a fancy lunch intended to woo Rick to the comics business, Murdock introduces a silent blonde as his daughter. (So dedicated is the blonde to her eating that her hand reaches in from screen right to remove food from Rick's plate; having all the food you want is part of being upwardly mobile, too). The blonde shows up again much later, and this time Murdock introduces her as his cousin.

The Murdock Publishing office is decorated with expensive furniture and a splashy, wall-sized mural of Bat Lady; when the office is invaded by a little boy (George "Foghorn" Winslow) whose mind has been ruined by Murdock's comic books, you laugh at the kid's physical insults against Eugene while worrying that that beautiful office is going to be trashed.

The lipstick billboard that opens the movie suggests an upward path to pleasure and beauty. When Abby sketches a rough for a magazine print ad, she draws a young man and young woman locked in a kiss: buy this product, the ad suggests, and climb the stairway to sex and love.

Even the Communists aspire to a mansion.

Left unsaid (and yet made very clear) is that if the Reds take over, the American march to the good life of material and sexual goodies that Tashlin finds so funny will end because dreams and imagination itself will be crushed flat.

* * *

The slapstick climax vanquishes the Communists physically, but also hands the villains a sharp philosophical rebuke. Because the spies' undoing takes place inside the mansion—a durable representation of Anglo-Saxon "old money"—the Reds are out of their element. When a clot of burly spies begins to push up the staircase, Rick and Eugene shove suits of armor down on them, a typical Tashlin absurdity (the suits of armor seem to be struggling to walk) that cements the notion of Anglo-Saxon superiority.

The Reds don't belong inside the splendid house, and are doomed to failure there. In other words, the predatory system worshipped by the spies is no match for the American way. Rather like the USSR, ultimately bankrupted by a financially unsustainable Cold War, the spies of *Artists and Models* are undone by the fruits of capitalism.

Did Frank Tashlin plan all of this symbolism? (Did he even believe that the Anglo-Saxon tradition trumps all others?) Sixty years out, it's difficult to say, but the fact is that because Manhattan gives access to grand houses built from old money, and because grand houses often have suits of armor (at least in the movies), the film's final battle becomes a clear explication of East vs. West. Whether Tashlin "knew" what he was doing in this regard or not, America's heritage and the American spirit—superiority complex included—are on display when Rick and Eugene fight back. With the cheerful, innocent smugness that characterized American public thought in the 1950s, audiences of 1954 laughed during the climax of *Artists and Models* and thought, *We win!*

* * *

The movie's final, post-climax sequence is set at the Artists and Models Ball, Tashlin's take on ostensibly charitable, real-life events cooked up by agents and publicists, and mounted in New York and Los Angeles during the 1950s and '60s. If you had a movie to promote or a modeling career that needed a boost or maybe a record to push, this was the event for you. Show up dressed like a Zulu, show up painted like an Oscar statuette (Rock Hudson once did just that), show up nearly naked (pin-up queen Bonnie Logan made a splash at one particularly memorable ball), but just show up. Sometimes called Artists and Models, sometimes called Photographers Balls, the lively extravaganzas attracted every salaried and freelance photographer in town.

As imagined by Tashlin, the ball is a giddy swirl of bodies and color. No woman appears to be over the age of twenty-five, and every one of them is, you guessed it, good-looking and half-dressed. *Artists and Models* is a bit of a musical, highlighted by Rick singing "Innamorata" to Abby as he rubs her with suntan oil. Music at the ball is more expansive and less intimate; it's a celebration of youth and high spirits. Dean and Jerry take turns painting mustaches on each other, and then slather their brushes with bright colors and utilize the naked backs of various beauties as canvases for a cartoon heart, funny faces, and a game of tic-tac-toe. Even a cute pair of knees gets the paint treatment. (Sure, all of this amounts to another shockingly reductive shtick, but I smiled anyway.)

Despite the boggling array of colors in this sequence, three—red, white, and blue—are dominant. Here we arrive at more uncertainty about intentionality. Is it an accident that these colors frame our happy protagonists? Well, Tashlin used color masterfully in this movie, exploiting not just its "prettiness" but the sheer surprise of it. He shot the film's urban exteriors on scrupulously lighted sound stages, where colors become far more striking than in life. Passing automobiles sparkle like gems, and when three men standing beneath the giant billboard are plastered by cans of paint, viewers are as delighted by the eye-candy vividness as by the slapstick. So the emphasis on red, white, and blue didn't just happen. The all-American colors are there because our protagonists have found upward mobility and the rest of the American dream—not least, the pleasures of sex. Rick learns that sex is better when it's an expression of love. Abby trusts her instincts and allows herself to be physical. Eugene finally abandons Bat Lady and reacts positively to Bessie's lunging amorousness. And Bessie is, at last, loved for her Bessiness.

Those Reds never had a chance.

FILMOGRAPHY

Artists and Models—Paramount; Released November 7, 1955; Technicolor; 109 min.

Credits: Producers: Hal B. Wallis, Paul Nathan; Director: Frank Tashlin; Screenplay: Frank Tashlin, Hal Kanter, Herbert Baker, b/o the play *Rock-a-Bye Baby* by Michael Davidson and Michael Lessing; Director of photography: Daniel L. Fapp; Editor: Warren Low; Music: Walter Scharf; Art director: Hal Pereira, Tambi Larsen

Cast: Dean Martin: Rick Todd; Jerry Lewis: Eugene Fullstack; Shirley MacLaine: Bessie Sparrowbush; Dorothy Malone: Abby Parker; Eddie Mayehoff: Mr. Murdock; Eva Gabor: Mrs. Curtis/Sonia; Anita Ekberg: Anita; George "Foghorn" Winslow: Richard Stilton

Works Cited

Books

de Seife, Ethan. *Tashlinesque: The Hollywood Comedies of Frank Tashlin*. Middletown, CT: Wesleyan University Press, 2012.
Garcia, Roger, and Bernard Eisenschitz, eds. *Frank Tashlin*. London: British Film Institute, 1994.
Marx, Arthur. *Everybody Loves Somebody Sometime (Especially Himself): The Story of Dean Martin and Jerry Lewis*. New York: Hawthorn Books, 1974.
Neibaur, James L., and Ted Okuda. *The Jerry Lewis Films: An Analytical Filmography of the Innovative Comic*. Jefferson, NC: McFarland. 1994.

DVD

Dean Martin & Jerry Lewis Collection Volume Two (*Artists and Models* disc). Paramount Home Video. 2007.

The Girl in the Kremlin
Can a Monster Change Its Face?

Zsófia Bodnár-Hamilton

My first look at Zsa Zsa Gabor on television at home in Ithaca, New York, must have happened when I was very small, for my mother—like Zsa Zsa, a native Hungarian—glanced at the screen and then tossed her head before making a dismissive noise that sounded like *Prbbt!* She disapproved of Zsa Zsa, not because Gabor was beautiful and had been Miss Hungary 1936, but because Zsa Zsa (through no magical powers of foresight or other scheming on her part) had settled in America in 1941, thus avoiding Hungary's grim postwar experience of domination by Soviet communism. Depending on the date of my first glimpse of Zsa Zsa, the actress would have been on her seventh or eighth husband. There were nine in all, and my mother didn't approve of that, either.

Almost nothing of my life has anything to do with Zsa Zsa Gabor (although we will return to her in this essay). A great deal, however, has to do with events that took place in 1956—nearly fifteen years before I was born.

On November 4, 1956, Soviet tanks clattered into Budapest to crush the ferocious but short-lived October-November armed uprising that came to be known as the Hungarian Revolution. During the Soviet drive toward Budapest (which began on November 3), more than 200,000 troops poured into Hungary, along with 4,000 tanks and other vehicles encompassing nineteen divisions. Fighting grew especially fierce in Budapest, and in the end, some 2,500 Hungarian citizens died in the streets (taking with them about seven hundred Russian troops). Hundreds more died in subsequent weeks because of malnutrition. Although a series of Hungarian national strikes dissolved, isolated military skirmishes continued into December 1956.

Ignoring condemnatory declarations issued by the UN General Assembly and U.S. President Dwight Eisenhower, Moscow proceeded to install a new puppet government in Budapest, and undertake deportations of "reactionary counterrevolutionaries" to the USSR. With trickery, the Soviet occupiers coaxed former Prime Minister Imre Nagy, as well as his family and inner circle, from the sanctuary of the Yugoslav embassy. Soviet soldiers immediately fell upon Nagy and spirited him away. (The Russians eventually took this reformist leader of Hungary to another Soviet satellite, Romania, and secretly tried and executed him there in 1958.)

Soviet premier Nikita Khrushchev, peeved that he expended considerable military and political capital just to return Hungary to where it had been (more or less) before the uprising, cynically stoked global fears by suggesting that a simultaneously unfolding emergency, French, British, and Israeli meddling in the operation of the Suez Canal (the Suez Crisis of 1956), might have to be resolved with Soviet nuclear arms. After that, America's attention locked onto the Middle East. Hungary's failed revolution, although not forgotten, was put into the books as another stalemate in the ongoing Cold War.

* * *

As the drama unfolded in Hungary over that handful of days, my mother and father found themselves in a peculiar quandary: they were relatively conservative socially and politically (the perceived excesses of America and other Western nations did not—as you might already have guessed—appeal to them), and yet, given their status as young professors at Technical University of Budapest,[1] the epicenter of student unhappiness with Soviet rule, they could have been suspected, by association, of bad behavior.

On a more intimate note, they had two young children, for whom they feared greatly.

Through chance and the merest dribble of a shared bloodline, my parents were not purged. A midlevel functionary in the new, Soviet-installed government of János Kádár was a distant cousin to my father, and it was because of that relationship—or perhaps, simply, that neither Moscow nor the Kádár faction could summon much alarm over a pair of unassuming young academics—that the Bodnárs were left alone.

I am the youngest of five Bodnár children, and the third born in the United States. Mother and Father emigrated in 1961, when the Kádár government still held anti–Communist activists as political prisoners. My early awareness of Hungary 1956 came mainly from my parents, of course, but also from a latter-day paperback edition of James Michener's sober account, first published in 1957, *The Bridge at Andau*. (I still own that paperback, and have never tired of the black-and-white news photo of Budapest freedom fighters on the cover, situated against a field of dark orange.) That the Revolution was part of our American household, if not of my personal experience, made me sensitive to Soviet-style communism and other repressive political systems, and helped me become attuned to the longing of people to live freely and express themselves openly. Because of the massive influence of American popular culture, I am particularly interested in how Communist doctrine is depicted in movies and other consumer media.

And so this essay returns now to Zsa Zsa Gabor, and my thoughts about a starring vehicle she worked on during 1957, an American movie called *The Girl in the Kremlin*.

The film's plot is so simple as to border on the diagrammatical: in 1953, Soviet dictator Josef Stalin (Maurice Manson)—worried that the Politburo will shortly sentence him to death—works with a few intimates to liquidate his body double, passing the corpse off as himself[2] and then undergoing plastic surgery so that he can rule Russia and her satellites in secret. When hints of the scheme reach the West a few years later, the CIA calls in a freelance American investigator named Steve Anderson (former movie Tarzan Lex Barker). The agency dispatches Anderson to Berlin, and then to Greece, to locate Stalin and resolve an ancillary Red plot, the kidnap and extortion of a noted scientist.

As the narrative prepares the shift to Greece, Anderson encounters Stalin's older son, Jacob (William Schallert), a former Red Army soldier thought to have perished in a German concentration camp during the war.[3] Anderson is assigned to work with an affable, claw-handed CIA agent Mischa (Jeffrey Stone); the two of them run into a pair of nuns in jackboots; a whip-wielding torturer named Olga (Elena Da Vinci); and a well-traveled Red assassin (Michael Fox) with an umbrella that shoots like a rifle. A beautiful

The Girl in the Kremlin (Bodnár-Hamilton) 101

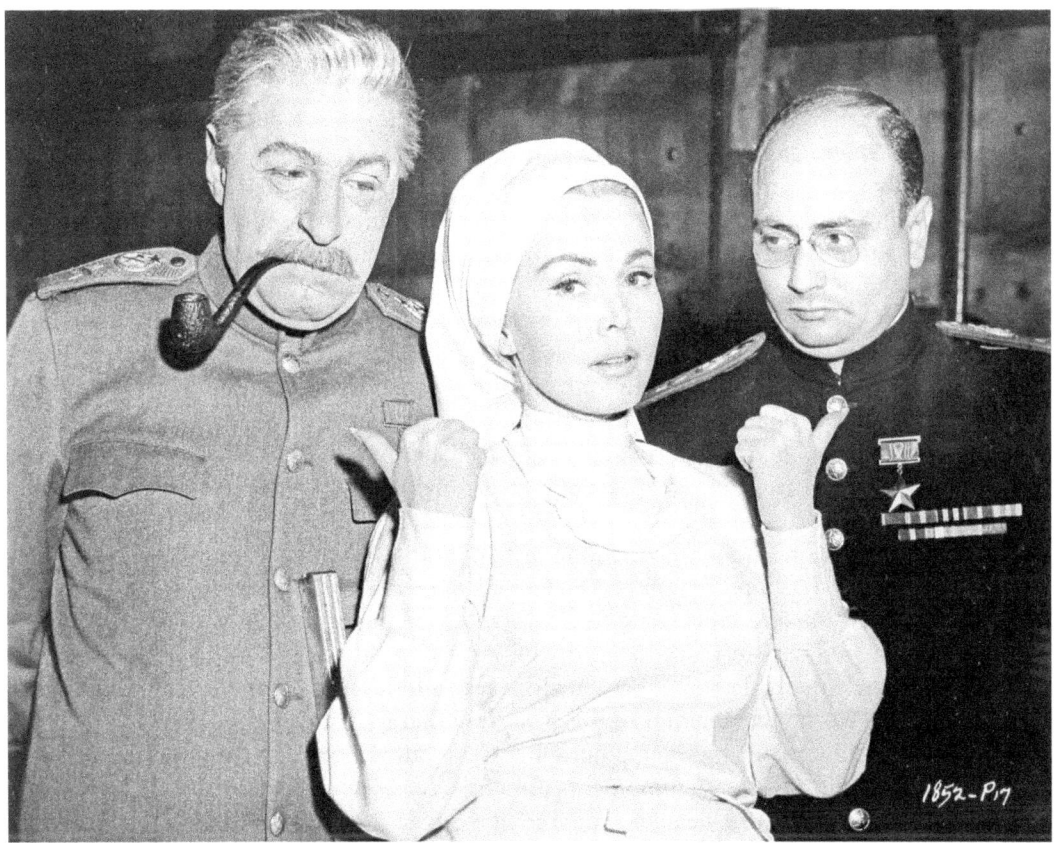

Even in the 1950s, few Americans believed that Soviet dictator Josef Stalin did not die in 1953. And yet we have *The Girl in the Kremlin* (1957), all wrapped up in the notion of a *living* Stalin hiding out in 1957, a premise that intrigued almost nobody. In this publicity photo (which is only barely different from what unfolds on screen), Stalin (Maurice Manson, left) regards Greta Grisenko (Zsa Zsa Gabor), the nurse who will assist in a complete re-do of Stalin's face. The dictator's ill-fated toady, Lavrenti Beria (Aram Katcher), looks on.

woman named Lili Grishenko (Zsa Zsa Gabor) finds Steve, too, and in one of those situations that happen only in comic books and bad movies, she identifies herself as the twin sister of Greta, a nurse who assisted in the murder of Stalin's double, and in the leader's later plastic surgery. (Nurse Zsa Zsa is an incidental but visible player in the story's opening minutes.)

The CIA suspects Stalin is still alive—and so they inexplicably broadcast their opinion over Radio Free Europe. This sends the disguised Stalin and his minions into a panic, encouraging a certain recklessness that puts their stolen fortune in dollars, pounds and rubles in danger. A climactic face-off inside a dank monastery uncovers the surgically altered Stalin, who kills his son and then dies horribly during a very bad bit of driving.

Steve Anderson regards the mess and says, "The Devil has gone back to Hell."

The Girl in the Kremlin is not a good movie. It exists only so that Universal-International had a brief second feature to play on double bills beneath more prestigious releases. The producer, a former attorney named Albert Zugsmith, pursued a peculiar path through Hollywood during the 1950s and early 1960s, supervising quality melodramas that include *Man in the Shadow, Slaughter on Tenth Avenue,* Jack Arnold's *The Incredible Shrinking Man,* Orson Welles's *Touch of Evil,* and a pair by Douglas Sirk, *Written on the Wind* and *The Tarnished Angels*. Alternatively, Zugsmith catered to the crowd that liked to leer rather than simply watch, with such oddities as *Captive Women, The Beat Generation, Sex Kittens Go to College, Girls Town, The Private Lives of Adam and Eve,* and the humorously perverse *High School Confidential!*

Within this canon, *The Girl in the Kremlin* sits somewhere in the middle, merely mediocre rather than satisfyingly good or amusingly bad. With the exception of the invariably dependable character player William Schallert, the cast is competent and no more. Lex Barker does not seem for a moment to engage with either the material or with Gabor. He strides through his scenes, looking handsome and seeming very empty. Zsa Zsa had already done good work in John Huston's *Moulin Rouge,* but she remained more successful as a personality than as an actress. At 5'4" she appears comically invisible next to 6'4" Mr. Barker, and must perpetually bend back her neck like rubber to speak to him. To American ears, her Hungarian accent is charming, but it is delivered with a voice that is thin and wispy.

The film's emptiest plot device—the revelation that Stalin's nurse and Lili are long-separated twins—is stupidly framed as a low-drama throwaway that emerges in conversation between Lili and Steve. And the inevitable meeting of the two women (achieved with simple split-screen and a back-of-the-head body double) lasts mere moments. Despite a quick physical altercation that climaxes with the exposure of Greta's bald head, the sequence has no tension and resolves nothing that is at stake in the plot.

Shadowplay created by cinematographer Carl Guthrie for the monastery climax has some texture. But other visual moments are undercut because neither the art directors nor set designers had the means to convincingly suggest Berlin or Greece.

Co-screenwriter Gene L. Coon (later an intelligent force behind the original *Star Trek* television program) carries partial responsibility for the movie's dramatic lacks, but the brunt must be borne by director Russell Birdwell, a newspaperman turned publicist[4] who promoted Hollywood stars and movies over a span of five decades, beginning around 1925. Birdwell directed four features between 1929 and 1957; *The Girl in the Kremlin* is his last. Lacking a superior cast, the film puts Birdwell's limitations on sharp display; most of the setups are static two- and three-shots in which people sit or stand, and look at each other and talk. Camera movement is limited, and one attempt to be clever—when the camera eye is situated inside a blazing fireplace, to observe two people chatting—is contrived and distracting. Too many other sequences meekly trail off rather than build to any sort of crescendo or even a small note of anticipation.

Universal-International publicity naturally emphasized the purportedly thrilling idea of a living Stalin. And yet an irony quite at odds with the film's intentions is that the death charade so thoroughly strips Stalin of his essential self that he evaporates as an existential menace and becomes just an oddball and a petty schemer, undone by an itinerant and rather lackadaisical American mercenary.[5] This fundamental misstep is a useful primer in how to ensure that the key character of your screenplay has no inner or outer life … but the movie has greater problems. What is most disappointing about *The Girl in the Kremlin* is that the modestly unorthodox premise of a living Stalin is barely developed … and has the added disadvantage of making no sense. Stalin's presence in the world of 1957 promises drama that no filmmaker could deliver. After all, what can this monster for the ages expect to make from his deception? He alters his facial features, assumes a fresh name, and goes into hiding far from Moscow. (Despite the film's title, the Kremlin is a mere bit player here.) He elects to become a non-entity. By giving up his public face and stripping away his cult of personality, Stalin effectively "kills" himself just as definitively as he kills his hapless double. And why might this self-created egoist who named himself "Steel" wish to do that?

The portion of screenplay set in 1953 suggests that Stalin is in danger of being murdered by his top-level underlings, but nothing in history (other than unsubstantiated claims and speculation) or in the film explains why that may be so. As scripted, Stalin longs to be an *invisible* puppet master who rules by proxy, like a supervillain in a 19th-century French pulp periodical, or an elusive master criminal in a Hollywood movie serial. That sort of facelessness, we are to believe, is more desirable to Stalin than open use of enormous, unquestioned power that checks every subordinate (and the entire globe) with fear. Such is the nonsense that is the core of *The Girl in the Kremlin*.

The film's concept of Stalin as a quixotic figure who revokes everything that defines him is clearly preposterous. But the plot premise is ultimately more disturbing than nonsensical. Because the story reduces Stalin from annihilating autocrat to a small figure living in nondescript, shadowed rooms, the film strips away Stalin's monstrousness. When

This lobby card for the Mexican release of *The Girl in the Kremlin* includes a peek into Stalin's torture chamber (center left), and somber-looking actress Natalia Daryll (right), who submitted to a real-life shaving of her head to illustrate Stalin's nonexistent head-shaving fetish. Co-stars Zsa Zsa Gabor and Lex Barker are seen in the center image, and at lower left and lower right.

he abandons the fiendish "Uncle Joe" persona and becomes just another middle-aged man in a baggy suit, we are no longer sobered by his malevolent heft. To the contrary, he becomes approachable; he now seems like us. Hannah Arendt's useful ruminations on the banality of evil aside, the fact is that not every person is capable of indescribable evil. Despite the legions of bureaucrats and pencil pushers that facilitated the everyday operations of the Third Reich and Stalin's Russia, despite the commonplace origins of Hitler and Himmler, Stalin and Molotov—despite, even, the concept of original sin— none of us are born with the seed of evil. Evil is a characteristic, not an infection. You do not *become* evil; you have to work at it.

And you work at it for just one reason: because you want to.

The diminished Stalin of *The Girl in the Kremlin* is woefully man-sized. Even his appetites are shoddy and tedious, as we see during a peculiar four-and-half-minute sequence in which Stalin keenly watches while a beautiful young woman (Natalia Daryll) is held in a chair, shorn of her waist-length hair, and then shaved as smooth as a pear.[6] Some may argue that this depiction of Stalin as deviant but otherwise nondescript is desirable, because despots need to be dressed down to expose their inherent smallness. But Stalin was small only in that he was flesh, and had a heart that one day stopped beating. In other regards, he was large. He was not one of us. He exploited a hateful ideology for his own ends, betraying legions of friends, associates, and even family members. He purposely starved millions of his countrymen, and purged thousands more. His capacity for wickedness, and his dedication to its care and development, was infinitely greater than yours and mine.

Stalin died alone on March 5, 1953, four days after suffering a severe stroke that rendered him insensible and incontinent. So deadly was his power and so in thrall to it were his lieutenants that they did not immediately attend to him, other than to move him from the floor to a sofa, and call doctors for a diagnosis. Stalin was left to die in the room where he had fallen, not because he was small, but because he was enormous and the other men were afraid.

At his death, Stalin entered the ages as a symbol: a face on banners in the post– Stalin USSR, and a model and inspiration for Malenkov, Bulganin, Khrushchev, and most of the others that followed.[7] In death, as in life, his essence is neither approachable nor fully understandable. But we can retain perspective and preserve historical truth when we recall the immense scale of Stalin's depravity, and condemn him as an outsized aberration of history.

FILMOGRAPHY

The Girl in the Kremlin—Universal-International; Released April 11, 1957; Black and white; 81 min.

Credits: Producer: Albert Zugsmith; Director: Russell Birdwell; Screenplay: Gene L. Coon, Robert Hill; Director of photography: Carl Guthrie; Editor: Sherman Todd; Music: Joseph Gershenson (supervisor of stock music); Art directors: Alexander Golitzen, Eric Orbom.

Cast: Lex Barker: Steve Anderson; Zsa Zsa Gabor: Lili Grisenko/Greta Grisenko (some sources incorrectly claim "Grishenko"); Jeffrey Stone: Mischa Rimilkin; Maurice Manson: Josef Stalin/Count Molda; Aram Katcher: Lavrenti Beria; William Schallert: Jacob Stalin; Michael Fox: Igor Smetka; Natalia Daryll: Dasha (girl with shaven head); Elena Da Vinci: Olga; Phillipa Fallon: Olga's assistant

Notes

1. Now named Budapest University of Technology and Economics.
2. Although the Soviet government did not release details of Stalin's final days and hours, they made very clear to the Soviet public and the world that he had died. Because Stalin had been in no danger of prosecution for his crimes, and never considered going on the run or into hiding, no romance about a living Stalin ever developed after 1953. *The Girl in the Kremlin*, then, attaches itself to an idea that was just a wisp, considered by almost no one. Conversely, ridiculous accounts of the 1945 escape and postwar life of Stalin's arch-enemy, Adolf Hitler, were predicated on the appealingly miserable scenario of a hunted, sociopathic brute running for his life. The tales took hold close at the end of World War II and had vigorous life for more than forty years, until so much time had passed that Hitler's continued existence was a physical impossibility. In the eight years that remained to Stalin following the war, he instructed the propagation of rumors of a living Hitler. Such rumors were useful because they offered Stalin one more reason to keep Red forces in East Berlin and Eastern Europe: a living Hitler could rouse old loyalists and establish a Fourth Reich.
3. Yakov Dzhugashvili, the eldest of Stalin's three sons, did not get on well with his father. A lieutenant in the Red Army during World War II, Yakov fell into German hands in the summer of 1941 (whether by capture or surrender is unclear). The Germans made hay from having Stalin's son, and printed his photograph on leaflets intended to encourage Red troops to surrender. When Germany offered a prisoner exchange—Yakov for Field Marshal Paulus—Stalin publicly (and contemptuously) declined; accounts differ as to whether he secretly ordered attempts to rescue his son. In the event, Yakov remained an uncooperative captive who died in 1943 at the Sachsenhausen concentration camp in Oranienburg, Germany, a probable suicide.
4. Birdwell concocted publicity for many clients, including Zsa Zsa Gabor. He made a significant contribution to Hollywood marketing by creating Selznick International's highly publicized "search" for an actress to play Scarlett O'Hara in *Gone with the Wind* (1939). A few years later, in the hire of Howard Hughes, Birdwell arranged low-cut photo shoots of actress Jane Russell to promote the then-controversial western, *The Outlaw* (filmed in 1941, wide release in 1946).
5. A pre-release publicity stunt sent actor Maurice Manson, in full Stalin costume and makeup, on a walking tour of downtown Los Angeles, where "Stalin" seemed especially small and insignificant. According to *Los Angeles Examiner* writer James Bacon, Manson/Stalin caused barely a flutter among passersby, though he did receive an acceptable greeting from a wino.
6. Stalin had no hair fetish, but bald women and the sexual abuse of forced shaving appeal to somebody; aficionados can select from among no fewer than a dozen YouTube posts of the movie's hair-cutting scene.
7. In a bid to destroy the cult of Stalinism, as well as to set the stage for his own ambitions, Party First Secretary Nikita Khrushchev denounced Stalin's many crimes during a loosely "secret" 1956 speech to delegates of the 20th Party Congress in Moscow. Revelations from that address shortly reached the Soviet satellite nations.

Works Cited

Books

Békés, Csaba, and Malcolm Byrne, János M. Rainer. *The 1956 Hungarian Revolution: A History in Documents*. Budapest: Central European University Press, 2000.
Borkowski, Mark. *The Fame Formula: How Hollywood's Fixer, Fakers and Star Makers Created the Celebrity Industry*. London: Sidgwick & Jackson, 2008.
Michener, James. *The Bridge at Andau*. New York: Bantam Pathfinder, 1969.
Montefiore, Simon Sebag. *Stalin: The Court of the Red Tsar*. New York: Knopf, 2003.
Rubenstein, Joshua. *The Last Days of Stalin*. New Haven, CT: Yale University Press, 2016.
Sebestyen, Victor. *Twelve Days: The Story of the 1956 Hungarian Revolution*. New York: Pantheon, 2006.

Newspapers

Bacon, James. "Joe Stalin Here! So Wh-a-t[.] Takes Stroll Downtown, Gets Wino Howdy[.]" *Los Angeles Examiner*. February 22, 1957.
Rau, Neil. "Stalin's Shady Life." *Los Angeles Examiner*. March 3, 1957. [This publicity-focused article identifies *The Girl in the Kremlin* by its preliminary title, *The Secret Diary of Joseph Stalin*, and claims, erroneously, that the dictator favored head-shaving as a punishment.]

Paper

Ürményházi, Attila J. "The Hungarian Revolution-Uprising, Budapest 1956." Hobart, Tasmania: 2006.

Video

The Girl in the Kremlin. Private copy.

Web

conelrad.blogspot.com

Atomic Thrillers and the Danger at Home

ARTHUR JOSEPH LUNDQUIST

In August of 1945, people awoke to the news of the atomic bombing of Hiroshima, and to the question of what it meant to live in a world in which science fiction was now a part of everyday life.

Almost immediately that question became fodder for movies. The wartime espionage thriller *The First Yank in Tokyo* (1945) changed its script in mid-production to accommodate an ending of angry atomic clouds. In the years that followed, atomic mayhem became the theme of some martial dramas with historical pretensions like *The Beginning or the End* (1947), *The Flying Missile* (1950), and *Above and Beyond* (1952). However, action movies and thrillers with an espionage bent would be the first mainstream films to evidence how the popular mind on this side of the Iron Curtain was actually beginning to digest the implications of life with the atomic bomb. Most are relatively forgotten today, having been superseded by a wave that became the true mythology of the Cold War, the science fiction films of the 1950s. Yet in the relatively restrained, more "real" thrillers covered here are images and themes that would grow, and inform that mythology. And watching them today, we can observe ourselves stepping warily into the Atomic Age.

Seven Days to Noon

In the suspense thriller *Seven Days to Noon* (1950), we witness the dawn of the Atomic Age through the weary eyes of post–World War II England. Although a British production, the film's plot reflects American fears not just of cross–Atlantic mischief but the possibility of atomic extortion on American soil. A British nuclear weapons scientist steals a portable atomic bomb and threatens to detonate it in the heart of London unless the prime minister orders immediate nuclear disarmament. British security forces mount an effort to find the scientist or, failing that, to evacuate London. As the British bureaucracy lumbers into action, ordinary people on the London streets begin to notice the increased troop presence, accepting it with the easy assurance of people who have seen these things before.

In the economically exhausted, slightly shabby Britain of 1950, the personal expe-

Atomic Thrillers and the Danger at Home (Lundquist) 107

Things are a bit dodgy for fugitive atomic scientist Prof. Willingdon (Barry Jones), who has threatened to blow up London unless Britain scraps its nuclear weapons—and now finds his face plastered across the city. *Seven Days to Noon* **(1950) draws keen drama from the notion of a trusted atomic steward who suddenly goes off the deep end.**

rience of war was not remote. Everyday conversation expressed in *Seven Days to Noon* includes casual references to food rationing (still in effect in 1950), or to being "called up," or to personal recollections of Dunkirk. Here the blare of an air raid siren announcing an "all clear" can be a familiar, even comforting sound.

Over these almost nostalgic recollections hang hints of the shadow of a darker future. In a penny arcade people play a pinball machine sporting a rear panel emblazoned with an impressively rendered mushroom cloud, over which the game's name, "Atomic Racer," is proudly emblazoned. A pub patron complains, "I'm telling you, there won't be no declaration of war this time. Someone presses a button and it's goodbye Sally." Another responds, "Oh, so what? There's nothing we can do about it, is there?" The fatalism in this banter is described by the anti-hero of *Seven Days to Noon* as coming from people "moving like sleepwalkers towards annihilation." For these pub patrons their unvoiced fear is that the finger on that button may not even be of their own government, and their lives may simply be pawns in some war of distant super-powers. It is the same fear George Orwell articulated in his 1949 novel *Nineteen Eighty-Four*, of a future so subsumed by global states that Britain itself is known only as "Airstrip One."

With the extortion deadline approaching, evacuation begins and London's streets empty of human beings. These vacant boulevards, colored by our awareness of the nuclear threat hanging over them, take on a haunting quality, planting images in the popular mind that later dominated the post-nuclear cities of *Five* (1951), *On the Beach* (1959), and *The World, the Flesh and the Devil* (1959). Paul Dehn, the co-author of *Seven Days to Noon*'s original story, returned to this theme in his screenplay for *Goldfinger* (1964); and arrived at a similar feel of ultimate despair in his screenplay for *Beneath the Planet of the Apes* (1970).

And yet the admittedly grim landscapes of *Seven Days to Noon* are not devoid of hope. Once evacuated, the streets are patrolled by columns of armed troops that carry on the search right to the brink of zero hour. For an audience still warm with the memory of wearing khaki, this sight of soldiers marching against the night adds Atomic Age unease to what British political cartoonist David Low sought to convey with his drawing of the darkest days after the fall of France: "Very well, alone."

FILMOGRAPHY

Seven Days to Noon—London Films/Boulting Bothers/British Lion; Released September 14, 1950 (UK); December 18, 1950 (USA); Black and white; 94 min.

Credits: Producers: John Boulting, Roy Boulting, Peter De Sarigny; Directors: John Boulting, Roy Boulting; Screenplay: Frank Harvey, Roy Boulting; Director of photography: Gilbert Taylor; Editors: John Boulting, Roy Boulting; Music: John Addison; Art director: John Elphick.

Cast: Barry Jones: Professor Willingdon; Olive Sloan: Goldie; Andre Morell: Superintendent Folland; Sheila Manahan: Ann Willingdon; Hugh Cross: Stephen Lane

The 49th Man

The 49th Man (1953), produced by Sam Katzman's B-picture unit for Columbia, imposes a *Seven Days*–like plot onto the more prosperous United States of 1953. Here, the actual face of war is more remote: everyone drives huge cars, their clothes are newer, the standard of living higher than for so many in *Seven Days to Noon*. Yet this material comfort does not seem to bring with it a sense of ease and security. In fact, in this America the threat and the fear of nuclear weapons seems closer to everyday reality.

In *The 49th Man* atomic bombs are routinely tested in the atmosphere, altering the tone of everyday life. American counterespionage forces, more proactive than those of *Seven Days to Noon*, seem to be everywhere, routinely keeping track of suspicious people and events. While investigating one event, they uncover a plot to smuggle parts for a nuclear weapon and assemble them in a major American city.

Early in the film, one of the protagonists assembles public officials in a room and announces, "Rather than just tell you, I've brought over some film to show you what'll happen if the atomic bomb hits this country." A movie projector starts up, screening images of pedestrian-filled urban streets city. A narrator intones, "It'll be any American city. Some normal day around noon, maybe. People looking for work, others working. Kids coming home from school. Rush hour. When, with no warning…" Footage of a mushroom cloud is superimposed onto a shot of a city street, followed by stock footage of collapsing buildings, running crowds, screaming people, and a few shots of nuclear test footage. And then scenes of devastation from various disasters and wars depict, "An entire city suddenly reduced to rubble." This sequence is about as close as any mainstream

Hollywood thriller of the early 1950s could come to addressing the ultimate nightmare of the Cold War.

In pursuing that nightmare there is, in contrast to the British reserve of *Seven Days to Noon*, something surprisingly fearful, even hysterical, about the developing menace, making *The 49th Man* kin to the immediate period's only other American thriller covering the doomsday scenario, 1952's *Invasion USA*. As U.S. agents follow the threads of espionage to France and back to the United States, and all the way to the nation's capital, the web grows and grows, until in full view of the Capitol dome they become the tentacles of an all-encompassing conspiracy right out of *Invasion of the Body Snatchers*. Then, as if shocked by its own excess, the film abruptly backtracks, abandoning its labyrinthine conspiracy for one reassuringly smaller and more reasonable.

Along the way, someone remarks, "Sounds like a science fiction plot, doesn't it?" Indeed, when the film's narrator (Gerald Mohr) declares, "From the Pacific to the Atlantic coast, straight up into the sky, deep into the heart of the country, watchful eyes watched and probed and checked and hunted," we are only inches away from the "Watch the skies!" battle cry that concludes *The Thing from Another World* (1951). In fact, the style and themes devised for this Cold War espionage thriller, full of shadows and location shooting, recur eerily in American science fiction films of the next ten years that explore, or perhaps we should say exploit, the more disturbing anxieties that *The 49th Man* shies away from. Without the more distancing lens of science fiction, the harrowing implications of the nuclear nightmare were really more than any Hollywood popcorn thriller could comfortably support, at least until audiences were ready for more explicit dramas like *On the Beach* and *Fail-Safe* (1964), at which point the classic 1950s SF movie would abruptly fade away.

In fact, the crew that created this minor programmer accounts for a huge percentage of Hollywood's output of 1950s science fiction. *The 49th Man* was scripted by Harry Essex, who is credited with *It Came from Outer Space* (1953) and *Creature from the Black Lagoon* (1954); based on an original story by Ivan Tors, screenwriter of the charmingly gadget-obsessed trilogy *The Magnetic Monster* (1953), *Riders to the Stars* (1954), and *Gog* (1954). (Tors also produced a quintessentially optimistic 1950s SF television series, *Science Fiction Theatre*.)

Producer Sam Katzman had tickled very young baby boomers with the Columbia movie serials *Superman* (1948) and *Batman and Robin* (1949). With the coming of the 1950s, Katzman encouraged the shadow of the atom to creep into Saturday-morning serials the likes of *Atom Man vs. Superman* (1950), *The Mysterious Island* (1951), and *Captain Video, Master of the Stratosphere* (1951). Katzman and *49th Man* co-producer Charles H. Schneer later created the rude visitors featured in *It Came from Beneath the Sea* (1955) and *20 Million Miles to Earth* (1957). With director Fred F. Sears, Katzman collaborated on *The Werewolf* (1956), *The Night the World Exploded* (1957) and *The Giant Claw* (1957)—increasingly outlandish thrillers expressing fears about the consequences of misused or misunderstood science. And Katzman, Schneer, and Sears teamed to create *Earth vs. the Flying Saucers* (1956), one of the most emblematic and scarifying of all Cold War daydreams.

Of all of these Katzman-Columbia diversions, *Earth vs. the Flying Saucers* (see chapter 3) makes blatant the super-science terror that is noted but sidestepped by *The 49th Man*. The latter picture's relative realism simply did not allow, in 1953, full expression of nuclear terrorism.

FILMOGRAPHY

The 49th Man—Columbia; Released May 20, 1953; Black and white; 73 min.

Credits: Producers: Sam Katzman, Charles H. Schneer; Director: Fred F. Sears; Screenplay: Harry Essex; Director of photography: Lester White; Editor: William A. Lyon; Music: Mischa Bakaleinikoff (stock); Art director: Paul Palmentola

Cast: John Ireland: John Williams; Richard Denning: Paul Reagan; Suzanne Dalbert: Margo Wayne; Robert Foulk: Commander Jackson; Touch (Mike) Connors: Lieutenant Magrew

The Atomic City

From its title, you may think that *The Atomic City* (1952) is balls-out science fiction melodrama, happily rolling in sensationalism. Like *Night of the Iguana* or *Island in the Sky*, its title seems designed to grab the hungry eyes of young SF addicts. However, I can attest to the overwhelming sense of disappointment *The Atomic City* gave me as a boy whenever it popped up on television in the 1960s. In spite of being directed by journeyman Jerry Hopper (who did a huge number of episodes of *Voyage to the Bottom of the Sea*) and scripted by Sydney Boehm (a noir specialist credited the previous year with *When Worlds Collide*), the film struck my child's mind as a perfectly ordinary drama. Growing up in the Atomic Age, I did not appreciate just how science fictional so many aspects of the everyday life depicted in the film were for audiences of the 1950s. And that is what makes *The Atomic City* worth watching today.

The Atomic City begins as the story of a boy whose dad works at the tightly guarded Los Alamos, New Mexico, nuclear weapons research facility. Tommy (Lee Aaker) lives in a house luxuriously stocked with modern American conveniences that would have been an impossible dream to many of the poor–Brit the characters of *Seven Days to Noon*. He spends his afternoons playing near fenced-off areas where signs announce "DANGER CONTAMINATED AREA DO NOT ENTER." When playing at home, neither he nor his mother (Lydia Clarke) seem to notice when a shock wave roars through their modern, well-kept house. After all, it's just another test. Occasionally, though, ominous aspects of the Cold War surface, as when Tommy innocently announces, "Mom, if I grow up, do you know what I'm going to do?"

Tommy's dad (Gene Barry) is tightlipped and secretive, as Depression/World War II generation fathers tended to be. But the burdens on Tommy's dad are special, as they would be for all fathers who must be examined by Geiger counter as they arrive at work. Casual conversation between Tommy's parents is always a little constrained. When one of his co-workers is burned by radiation, Tommy's dad cannot confide his feelings to his wife because the details are classified. Every now and then Tommy's mother will sigh and ask, "Don't you ever get tired of the barbed wire, Frank?"

Neither of them is aware that some of their closest friends and co-workers are in fact government agents whose real job is to keep a watchful eye on their every move. And a good thing too, as we learn when Tommy is kidnapped by foreign agents intending to blackmail his father into turning over the secrets of the hydrogen bomb.

Here the film switches its focus, as American forces begin to hunt down the conspirators using a host of ultramodern technological aids: wiretaps, television cameras, and that most futuristic of postwar technological toys, a helicopter (so new in 1952, the bad guys mispronounce it HEEL-i-cop-ter).

The sheer scope of America's ongoing espionage war is suggested as we watch FBI agents review film footage of a surveilled suspect. Hidden in the shadows of the screening room, we cannot see their faces, but a voice pipes up, "That vendor. We were party members together in Illinois." Then a second voice, this one female, concurs: "That's right! I knew him in Detroit." In simple, almost perfunctory style, these voices in the darkness create in our minds a world where agents of our own government move silently among us, watching others—enemies—that move among us, too.

One tool in the arsenal of espionage, however, does not work with Atomic Age efficiency. As are so many heroes in espionage films of the Cold War, notably John Wayne's HUAC operative in *Big Jim McLain* (1952), society's protectors are handicapped by America's occasionally bothersome Bill of Rights. In particular, they are not allowed to subject suspected foreign agents to torture—an interrogation technique that *The Atomic City* suggests is the most effective way to gain information. Tommy's father, a surrogate for us, voices his impatience: "Rules? Who cares about your rules? I care about Tommy!" Ultimately, it is up to this red-blooded American dad to take the law into his own hands and beat the truth out of a suspect.

Unlike *Seven Days to Noon* or *The 49th Man*, *The Atomic City* never directly mentions the atomic nightmare that its agents of order work so hard to avert. Yet it leaves its audience with the unambiguous implication that against the possible consequences of atomic secrets, considerations of privacy or due process or even the life of Tommy himself are of relatively little importance. As his father is told, "Even you can't be permitted to get in the way of what has to be done." If Tommy must die, it will be for the greater good.

Still, nothing too shocking is going to happen in *The Atomic City*. An exciting climax in and out of the elevated crags of a barren mesa is satisfying but not apocalyptic. A B-plus release from Paramount, *The Atomic City* was designed, in part, to mollify America's moms, who in those days usually decided which movies the family would see. Nation—and family—are preserved.

FILMOGRAPHY

The Atomic City—Paramount; Released May 1, 1952; Black and white; 85 min.

Credits: Producer: Joseph Sistrom; Director: Jerry Hopper; Screenplay: Sydney Boehm; Director of photography: Charles B. Lang Jr.; Editor: Archie Marshek; Music: Leith Stevens; Art directors: Hal Pereira, Al Roelofs

Cast: Gene Barry: Dr. Frank Addison; Lydia Clarke: Martha Addison; Michael Moore: Russ Farley; Nancy Gates: Ellen Haskell; Lee Aaker: Tommy Addison; Milburn Stone: Inspector Harold Mann

Split Second

A fear of brutes taking over the world was nothing exclusive to films of the 1950s. It played a prominent part, for instance, in the 1936 drama *The Petrified Forest*. Surprisingly, the theme plays very little part in *Split Second* (1953), a nuclear thriller usually accurately described as "*The Petrified Forest* in a nuclear test site." As in the earlier film (and stage play), the protagonists of *Split Second* are held captive in a desert location by fugitive gangsters. However, the setting of *Split Second* is a western ghost town that at dawn will be ground zero of an atmospheric atomic test. The kicker is that neither the gangsters nor their captives realize their situation until time has nearly run out.

112 Part 2: Red Mischief Here, There and Everywhere

The irresistible hook of Dick Powell's *Split Second* (1953) is that fugitive gangster Sam Hurley (Stephen McNally, right) takes hostages and drags them to a Nevada ghost town—unaware that the whole area is about to be vaporized by an A-bomb test. For the moment, Sam hangs out confidently with chums Bart (Paul Kelly, left) and Dummy (Frank de Kova).

Split Second is bookended by two images touching the elemental fears of the Atomic Age. As its opening credits roll, a bright light like a setting sun shimmers on a barren desert of cracked and dried mud, over which desperate figures run. At film's end, one of its handful of survivors says, "Let's take a look at the world of tomorrow," emerging from their hiding place to gaze upon a landscape of smoking, radioactive rubble.

In between, as in *Seven Days to Noon*, we spend much of the film waiting in empty buildings as its captives pass the night away until zero hour. But *Split Second*'s ghost town setting, not merely abandoned but crumbling into ruins, brings overtones even more disturbing than the vacant but still intact London of *Seven Days to Noon*. Against this stark backdrop, the captives of *Split Second* reflect on their lives. Larry (Keith Andes), a newspaper reporter, and Dottie (Jan Sterling), a cynical nightclub dancer, a share an intimate moment:

> LARRY: Sooner or later one of us has got to learn to fight.
> DOTTIE: Take up judo in the next world.
> LARRY: Our last chance may have gone with that gun.
> DOTTIE: Well, it wasn't much a life, anyway.

LARRY: You mean that?
DOTTIE (looking at Larry): As a matter of fact, I thought things were just beginning to look up.
LARRY: I thought so too.

In this, *Split Second* is one of the first motion pictures to bring to life a mood I remember growing up with during the Cold War, a feeling of living at the end of time, contemplating the past with the awareness that there may be no tomorrow. The feeling is treated almost wistfully here, but in other movies it could erupt into a flailing violence; later science fiction films, such as *La Jetee* (1962) and *These Are the Damned* (1963), explore the theme far more explicitly.

FILMOGRAPHY

Split Second—RKO; Released May 2, 1953; Black and white; 85 min.

Credits: Producer: Edmund Grainger; Director: Dick Powell; Screenplay: William Bowers, Irving Wallace; Director of photography: Nicholas Musuraca; Editor: Robert Ford; Music: Roy Webb; Art directors: Albert S. D'Agostino, Jack Okey

Cast: Stephen McNally: Sam Hurley; Alexis Smith: Kay Garven; Jan Sterling: Dottie Vale; Keith Andes: Larry Fleming; Arthur Hunnicut: Asa Tremaine; Paul Kelly: Bart Moore; Robert Paige: Arthur Ashton; Richard Egan: Dr. Neal Garven; Frank de Kova: Dummy

Shack Out on 101

Writer-director Edward Dein's *Shack Out on 101* (1955) opens on a sunny beach where an attractive young woman sunbathes in a two-piece bathing suit, her sleep undisturbed by the touch of the *From Here to Eternity* surf. In a surprisingly carnal close-up, she lies in profile that gives equal prominence to her upturned face and breasts; from far in the distance, a man approaches. He kneels down to steal a kiss and immediately they are in a savage tussle. For a few moments it's hard to tell if we are witnessing a rape or if she is simply playing rough. At last he tosses her off him into the surf. Unable to despoil the woman, he settles for plucking her petticoat from the sand and soiling with his grimy hands.

That is the jaw-dropping opening to what is a consistently jaw-dropping piece of exploitation from B-movie studio Allied Artists, the slightly more respectable offshoot of Monogram.

The shack of the title is a greasy spoon located somewhere on Highway 101, a picturesque route running along the beaches just north of Los Angeles. The clumsy Romeo seen in the opening sequence is the establishment's cook, Leo (Lee Marvin)—or as he is referred to throughout the film, "Slob." His employer describes Slob as a fellow with "an eight-cylinder body with a two-cylinder mind," and of whom it can be said, "Even when you're clean, you look dirty." The young woman from the beach is waitress Kotty (Terry Moore), who is regarded by the shack's salivating male customers and vendors as "the Tomato" and "the Chicken."

The diner is run by George (Keenan Wynn), whose fellow D-Day veteran Eddie (Whit Bissell) struggles to overcome a war-born aversion to "blood and violence." Every figure that passes in and out of the diner seems to harbor a dark secret, and struggle with uncontrollable impulses to act—or not act at all. They scrape by in an existence where "life's ninety percent walking through slop to get to the roses," in an atmosphere of lust,

Grab a roast beef sandwich and a piece of pie at the *Shack Out on 101* (1955). Nuclear physicist Sam Bastion (Frank Lovejoy) is a frequent customer, chatting up feisty waitress Kotty (Terry Moore) and passing time with other interesting friends, too. Yes, this seaside dump is an unlikely place for espionage—which helps generate the oddball charm of this fevered little movie.

barely suppressed violence, and unexpected (and unexpectedly funny) homosexual subtexts revolving around Slob. (When Slob and a deliveryman roll up a towel, take each end in their jaws, and engage in a bare-knuckles fistfight, the pair look like Neanderthals in a courtship ritual. Later, Slob and George strip to the waist and labor to outdo each other during a sloppy weightlifting interlude with much talk of "pecs" and calves.)

If this grimy underside of 1950s America seems an unlikely arena in which to enact the conflicts of the Cold War, be advised that the narrative becomes somewhat more plausible because of another character, Sam Bastion (Frank Lovejoy), a prominent nuclear scientist who regularly stops by the shack to woo Kotty and, perhaps, Slob (the men share a giddy enthusiasm for seashells). As it turns out, Sam and a huge number of the shack's denizens are agents of the federal government, sent to Highway 101 to root out agents of an unnamed foreign power. Amidst the chili, hamburgers, and flying pheromones, then, is a real war of civilizations.

Sam explains at the film's climax, "Can't you see what's happened? The apes have taken over. While we were busy watching television and filling our freezers they've come out of the jungle and moved in. And what's worse is they've begun to dress like us and pretend to think like us. We're just where we were in the beginning. The animals have begun to hunt man."

Slob counters, "They are all apes. Every last one of them. But you're so desperate for security that you'll take any promise that vaguely resembles it. Oh, I don't blame you for looking down at the apes. But you overlook one important fact: their leaders are not apes."

And so we have *Shack Out on 101*'s weird and wonderful thesis, a struggle for civilization led by the Stanley Kowalskis of the world. It sums up a fear I remember being expressed by people of my grandparents' pre–1929 generation, of an Atomic Age aggravated by the coarsening of popular culture, by the slow decay of American cities, and by the erosion of public morality in a sexualized culture partly driven by homosexuality and by, well, movies like *Shack Out on 101*.

FILMOGRAPHY

Shack Out on 101—Allied Artists; Released December 4, 1955; Black and white; 80 min.

Credits: Producers: William F. Broidy, Mort Millman; Director: Edward Dein; Screenplay: Edward Dein, Mildred Dein; Director of photography: Floyd Crosby; Editor: George White; Music: Paul Dunlap; Art director: Lou Croxton

Cast: Terry Moore: Kotty; Frank Lovejoy: Professor Sam Bastion; Keenan Wynn: George; Lee Marvin: Slob; Whit Bissell: Eddie

Kiss Me Deadly

Now if you *really* want to watch the saga of society's apes flailing about in the Atomic Age, you are directed Robert Aldrich's 1955 adaptation of the Mickey Spillane novel *Kiss Me, Deadly* (comma in the book title; no comma in the movie title).

The good-looking protagonist of *Kiss Me Deadly* is Mike Hammer (Ralph Meeker), a private detective described as "one of those self-indulgent males who thinks about nothing but his clothes, his car." His main sources of income are divorce investigations in which Hammer and his attractive lover-secretary Velda (Maxine Cooper) alternately seduce and blackmail both subject and client. By chance, Hammer's relentlessly petty existence briefly intersects with that of mental-hospital escapee Christina (Cloris Leachman); in just minutes, Hammer and Christina are waylaid by gangsters, Hammer is nearly killed, and Christina is tortured to death. The gangsters work with particular urgency because they seek a unique prize that's also coveted by the feds.

Hammer senses that Christina's life contained "something big," and he pursues that something as if it might give meaning to his own. As his investigation unfolds, the mystery begins to consume Hammer's life, one acquaintance at a time. Or as Velda explains it, "First you find a little thread, the little thread leads you to a string, the string leads you to a rope, and from the rope you hang by the neck."

Along the way, we glimpse the rich 1950s America around Hammer, a world of blues singers and petty gangsters, prize fights and badly sung opera, second-rate abstract art and all-night gas stations. Hammer bulls his way through all of this with surly indifference, smashing a valuable record of Caruso's *Pagliacci* with the same unconcern he shows while bribing or threatening people who may provide him with a useful clue to his objective.

The gangsters treat Hammer with equal contempt, saying (in an example of the film's strange pulp poetry), "What's it worth to you to return your considerable talents back to the gutter you crawled from?" As he closes in on the mystery, the faux-erudite

116 Part 2: Red Mischief Here, There and Everywhere

Private dick Mike Hammer is unprincipled, well groomed, and prosperous, but he's also clueless about the hideous nature of the intrigue he's stumbled into. Robert Aldrich and A. I. Bezzerides's thrillingly innovative *Kiss Me Deadly* (1955) proposes that we are victimized by incomprehensible forces spun by a world out of control. Here, Hammer (Ralph Meeker, center) and gal Friday, Velda (Maxine Cooper), are briefed by Pat Murphy (Wesley Addy), a smart cop who knows that the cocksure Hammer is in way over his head.

leader of the thugs, Dr. Soberin (Albert Dekker), taunts him: "What is it we are seeking? Diamonds? Rubies? Gold? Perhaps narcotics? How civilized this Earth used to be. But as the world becomes more primitive, its treasures become more fabulous."

To both sides in this game, human beings are expendable pawns. As Velda puts it, "They? A wonderful word. And who are *they*? They are the nameless ones who kill people for the great whatsit."

In this world where nothing seems to matter, Hammer follows a trail of bodies that soon includes some of his closest friends. Finally, he arrives at last at the center of the mystery: a leather-buckled metal box which, when barely opened, emits a blinding light that burns Hammer's wrist. From this point, our anti-hero becomes progressively more and more tired. It is possible that he is dying.

When his sometimes ally Pat (Wesley Addy), a lieutenant of the LAPD, notices Hammer's burned flesh, he begins one of Cold War cinema's creepiest monologues:

> PAT (slowly): Now listen, Mike. Listen carefully. I'm going to pronounce a few words. They're harmless words. Just a bunch of letters scrambled together. But their meaning is very important. Try to understand what they mean. Manhattan Project. Los Alamos. Trinity.

At the sound of these words, Mike Hammer's desires, his goals, his vendettas, and all the lives he has fed into his search suddenly dwindle into insignificance, and he cooperates with the authorities for the first and only time. He sees his place in the Atomic Age, living a trivial existence while forces beyond his comprehension continue a silent struggle that could at any moment tear the world apart.

And at the conclusion of *Kiss Me Deadly*, as with the conclusions of all the films discussed in this essay, we are left to return to our own lives, carrying with us jigsaw puzzle pieces of the unspeakable.

Filmography

Kiss Me Deadly—Parklane Pictures/United Artists; Released May 18, 1955; Black and white; 104 min. (original USA release); 106 min. (unedited cut)

Credits: Producers: Robert Aldrich, Victor Saville; Director: Robert Aldrich; Screenplay: A. I. Bezzerides, b/o the novel *Kiss Me, Deadly* by Mickey Spillane; Director of photography: Ernest Laszlo; Editor: Michael Luciano; Music: Frank De Vol; Art director: William Glasgow

Cast: Ralph Meeker: Mike Hammer; Albert Dekker: Dr. Soberin; Paul Stewart: Carl Evello; Maxine Cooper: Velda Wickman; Gaby Rodgers: Lily Carver; Juano Hernandez: Eddie Yeager; Wesley Addy: Lt. Pat Murphy; Marion (Marian) Carr: Friday; Nick Dennis: Nick; Cloris Leachman: Christina Bailey; Jack Elam: Charlie Max; Jack Lambert: Sugar Smallhouse; Percy Helton: Doc Kennedy; Strother Martin: Harvey Wallace

Works Cited

DVD

The Atomic City. Olive Films. 2011.
The 49th Man. Sony. 2012.
Kiss Me Deadly. Criterion. 2011.
Seven Days to Noon. StudioCanal. 2010.
Shack Out on 101. Olive Films. 2013.
Split Second. Warner Archive. 2010.

Memo to the State Department
Seven Overlooked Cold War Films

CHASE WINSTEAD

As Americans grappled with international turmoil during the first decade of the Cold War, Communist ideology seemed to fester everywhere: in the jungles of troubled Southeast Asia and deep beneath Asian seas; in labor unions at home and abroad; and in the power centers of Moscow and the hapless satellite states of Eastern Europe. Red dogma had enslaved much of the world, and Communist mischief carried out by catspaws threatened the social order up and down North America, from Canada to Southern California's sunny Pacific shore. As we will see, Communist crosshairs targeted the American family, America's children, and the American economy. And as sure as the Red Army had brutalized the females of Berlin, the virtue of American women and girls was at risk, too.

Worst of all, perhaps, is that Americans' cars, kitchen gadgets, television sets, and new ranch-style houses and Cape Cods could be taken away. Yes, everything that epitomized the American way of life, all the material pleasures that relieved us of thought and discomfort, might vanish.

Nobody could pretend to be exempt from Red predation, neither politicians nor untrustworthy intellectuals; neither the weak nor the virtuous.

Not every maker of anti–Communist films produced in Cold War America was paranoid, but all of them knew how to prick the paranoia of audiences. Below, we look at seven often-neglected film productions that—with varying degrees of commitment—rip bare the crimes of international communism.

Make Mine Freedom

Between 1923 and 1946, the long-term direction of General Motors fell to a dynamic CEO, Alfred P. Sloan. Recalled for his insistence on planned obsolescence and aspirational marketing, Sloan seduced two generations of auto buyers with naked appeals to glamour and status. Body styling that changed annually encouraged impulse purchases, and GM's product line—from entry-level Chevrolet to the heady Cadillac—could theoretically be negotiated by any American go-getter, with stops along the way at Pontiac, Oldsmobile, and Buick. Discrete models of each make frequently sat on identical platforms; differentiation was achieved via styling touches to bodies and interiors, luxury touches, and engine choices, but under the skins, the cars were very similar. In that regard, GM's business plan was brilliant—never mind that the company's marketing was a bit of a con.

Ford Motor Company, Chrysler Corporation, Studebaker, and other volume automakers of the interwar years patterned their manufacturing and sales strategies after GM's example. American carmakers of the period were alike in another way, too: they regarded labor unions with horror, and dealt harshly with union organizers. General Motors made free use of police as strikebreakers. In Detroit in 1937, Henry Ford's union-busting goon squad nearly killed union organizer Walter Reuther during the infamous "Battle of the Overpass." Pro-union workers that could not be intimidated found themselves unemployed and blackballed at other automakers. Corporate dons tarred union agitators, and even union sympathizers, with the "Communist" brush.

The irony here is that even while American car manufacturers strove to entice car buyers, positioning automobile ownership as a necessary element of the American way of life and one's self-worth, they actively undercut American tenets of worker freedom, assembly, and happiness.

GM's Alfred Sloan established an eponymous foundation in 1934. Although retired by 1946, he understood that the real glory days for automakers and the rest of American industry lay ahead, in the postwar era. As 1950 approached, immediate-postwar unemployment lessened. Detroit's car companies had accepted the inevitable and recognized workers' right to organize in 1937–38 (GM and Chrysler) and 1941 (Ford). Automakers finally grasped that American workers in all industries, made sanguine by increased wages and improved working conditions, would spend freely on new cars, houses, white goods, and other big-ticket items that had been generally unavailable during wartime America's focus on defense manufacturing. With the war won, millions of babies on the way, and the economy reset for explosive growth, America became a synecdoche for *production, selling*, and *buying* just as surely as it stood for *individual choice*.

Communism was anathema to this mentality. With its elevation of workers to (in the eyes of American conservatives) dangerous heights, communism's manufacturing and retailing delivered little beyond impractical ideology: few goods, shoddy quality, and—on top of everything else—general unavailability to a poorly paid workforce captive to a centrally managed economy. Electing to focus on economics and business, the Sloan Foundation (as well as numerous other industry-oriented foundations) worked with high-level politicians and corporate leaders to help ensure the perpetuation of the American way of manufacturing, marketing, and consumption. But everyday citizens had to be reached, as well.

Thanks partly to the animation unit at Warner Bros. (home to the sophisticated antics of Bugs Bunny, Daffy Duck, and friends), the appeal of animated shorts to teenagers and adults was clear; foundation-think came to be reflected, then, in a rush of ostensibly educational animated cartoons focused on military training, health, dating, worker safety, and other "social" topics.

Around 1947, the Sloan Foundation awarded a grant to Harding College (founded 1924; now Harding University), a conservative Christian school in Searcy, Arkansas, named for Protestant missionary and pacifist James Harding. The Sloan grant—amounting to at least $300,000 and possibly as much as $600,000—financed a series of animated cartoon shorts promoting the American way of business. Before becoming Harding's president in 1936, George Stewart Benson (who held the post until 1965) had been a

Protestant missionary in China. But he was chased from that troubled country in 1936, when Mao Zedong established himself as leader of Communist activity there. Benson developed an aggressive dislike of communism, as well as anything that, to him, smacked of it, such as socialism or liberal economic and social values. By the late 1930s, just a couple of years into his tenure as president, Benson turned the emphasis of Harding's curriculum and broader activities to the promotion of America's corporate brand of capitalism and industrial productivity.

With Sloan Foundation money in hand, Harding representatives that approached Burbank-based Walt Disney Productions were referred to John Sutherland Productions, an animation studio established in 1945 by onetime Disney writer-animator John Sutherland. Early on, JSP divided its time between "Daffy Ditties" cartoon shorts distributed by United Artists, and low-budget, live-action feature mysteries (1948's *Lady at Midnight* is one) released by Eagle-Lion. The greater part of the studio's activity, though, eventually became instructional cartoons.

Sloan money allowed Harding College to finance four shorts made at Sutherland. The first, a nine-minute cartoon called *Make Mine Freedom* (1948), is the most overtly anti–Communist. Sparkling with Technicolor, the cartoon was directed by William Hanna and Joe Barbera, who revolutionized cartoon animation a decade later—and not for the better—with a limited-motion technique personified by the likes of television's Huckleberry Hound. But in 1948, Hanna and Barbera stood tall with Tom and Jerry, MGM's hugely popular theatrical cartoon series starring hapless cat Tom and ingenious mouse Jerry. *The Truce Hurts*, a cartoon released just two months after *Make Mine Freedom*, pivots on the unlikely truce of Tom, Jerry, and Tom's canine antagonist, Butch. As you might anticipate, the group's cooperation is short-lived, and finally replaced by comic violence.

The Truce Hurts has no raison d'être other than laughs fashioned from mayhem. Technically artful and philosophically artless, it succeeds because it has no goal beyond the startled guffaw. *Make Mine Freedom* has some slickness of execution but none of the visceral assets of *The Truce Hurts*. Worse, *Make Mine Freedom* has a serious point of view, and worse still, it's determined to make that point of view *our* point of view. Nicely animated (though not as fully as the MGM unit's other theatrical cartoons), it skates by on craft, while assuming that American audiences are a bunch of dummies to be gulled with visual and textual clichés that pass as wit.

The cartoon trots out zany characters aplenty, summoned to illustrate America's plain folk in quick vignettes: teenagers jitterbugging at the malt shop; a lavishly bearded old gent who snoozes on his front porch; a "Dad" golfer who bungles a drive and angrily wraps his club around a tree; a gruff "worker" type; a Southern senator; "cracker barrel" philosophers seated around the wood stove at a general store; and cigar-sucking "tycoons in Wall Street." These figures are manipulated to illustrate Americans' right to due process and a speedy trial (exemplified here by an all-male jury directing wolf whistles at a sexy female defendant); and freedom to assemble, worship, and vote. Public schooling is celebrated in a brief, tokenistic glimpse of a grade-school classroom filled with kids of "all races, creeds, and religions."

With the boilerplate patriotism out of the way, *Make Mine Freedom* gets into the real meat: the adversarial positions of labor and capital. Neither side seems inclined to budge. Enter Dr. Utopia, a swarthy, Brylcreemed snake in a zoot suit and skimmer who wishes to sell bottles of "ISM" (pronounced IZ-m), a substance that "will cure any ailment of the body politic." Well, Utopia's doctorate suggests pointy-headed intellectualism, and his outrageous attire recalls Hispanics or Negroes. We're meant to understand that he isn't a real American at all.

Utopia, though, is a slick talker. His prospective customers are the worker, the capitalist, a farmer, and a politician. Utopia promises that anyone can have a swallow of his salubrious stuff, *after* signing a simple form: "I hereby turn over to ISM, Inc. everything I have, including my freedom and the freedom of my children, and my children's children, in return for which, said ISM promises to take care of me forever."

In a bid to reach audience members who haven't been paying attention, the top of Utopia's printed form is topped by a caricature of a grinning bull (bullshit)—complete with a ring in his nose (slavery).

The four citizens are joined by a fifth gentlemen (there are no women in this cluster of decision-makers). This is John Q. Public, a calm, deliberate type who digests Utopia's declaration and dismisses it as "imported doubletalk." Utopia's ISM is not home grown. No, it's foreign, and anathema to America's heritage.

Via flashback, John Q. Public reminds the others of "Joe Doakes," who invented a horseless carriage fifty years ago. Joe found investors among his friends and family, and transformed his employee, Willie Lumpkin, into a well-paid skilled laborer. John Q. asserts that the same dynamic continues today, on a grander scale, as American citizens enjoy more "food, clothing, travel, and entertainment" than any other people on Earth. "With only seven percent of the world's population," the narrator reminds us, "we drive seventy percent of the world's automobiles." This is what trumps all of that imported doubletalk: things, and our possession of them.

Because John Q. Public isn't convinced that his companions really grasp the value of America's material bounty, he encourages the others to swig from the bottle of ISM, go ahead! The effect is almost psychedelic: the suddenly chained worker agitates for higher wages and a proper union—only to be gripped around the body by an enormous blue hand and held fast. The farmer learns that his farm is now a collective, its activities planned by the state. His yields will be appropriated. The capitalist is ordered to surrender his business, which becomes State Factory #29. Finally, the politician is tossed into State Concentration Camp #5, and then smashed on the head with a phonograph that repeats, "Everything is fine, everything is fine, everything is fine, everything is fine...."

John Q. sums up, warning against veiled calls for "class warfare, race hatred, or religious intolerance," which are the work of people who wish to "rob us of our freedom, and destroy our very lives. And we know what to do about it!" At that, the group flings the bottles of ISM at Dr. Utopia, who cowers and then dashes out of town.

Significantly, the menacing blue hand does offer the worker a union, with membership announced by a rubber stamp that brands the worker as State Union member 1313. So there are unions and then there are unions. There are unions that roll over for management, and there are unions—full of ISM—that antagonize management and purportedly abuse the workers.

Over a montage of John Q. and the others marching at sunrise with the stars and stripes before the Lincoln Memorial (with fife and drum accompaniment), the narrator concludes with this: "Working together to produce an ever-greater abundance of material and spiritual values for all—*that* is the secret of American prosperity."

This is pro–American business painted in broad strokes, propelled by stereotypes that respond only to John Q. Public—who is, of course, every sensible American. Only by subscribing to John Q.'s model of production and consumption can the worker and the others become "real" Americans.

The other three Sloan-financed John Sutherland cartoons produced with Harding College explore increased worker productivity to beat inflation (*Why Play Leap Frog?*, 1949); worker cooperation with management (*Meet King Joe*, 1950); and the perils of centrally planned economies (*Albert in Blunderland*, 1950). Following his association with Harding College, Sutherland created cartoon shorts for another twenty years, in association with the American Stock Exchange, General Electric, the Automobile Manufacturers Association, the New York Stock Exchange, Frigidaire, United States Steel, the American Petroleum Institute, DuPont, the U.S. Department of Commerce, and other government organizations and large businesses.

The Sloan Foundation liked the propagandistic efficacy of cartoons. In the mid-fifties, the organization established a relationship with Warner Bros. that resulted in three pro-business cartoons starring Sylvester Pussy Cat.

Animation aficionados do not adore them.

FILMOGRAPHY

Make Mine Freedom—John Sutherland Productions; American Studies Institute at Harding College; MGM (distributor); Released February 25, 1948; Technicolor; 9 min. 27 sec.

Credits: Producer: Fred Quimby; Directors: William Hanna, Joseph Barbera; Music: Scott Bradley, Paul J. Smith.

Voice Cast: Billy Bletcher: Worker; Frank Nelson: Dr. Utopia; John Hiestand: Narrator and John Q. Public; Daws Butler: Various

Fuelin' Around

The pure joy of *Fuelin' Around* (1949), the 116th Three Stooges two-reeler produced by Columbia Pictures, is that Larry, the perennial "Stooge in the middle," has a rare turn in the spotlight. Mistaken for a real-life scientist and kidnapped, Larry can award or deny a belligerent Eastern European nation a new "super rocket fuel." (In the shorthand of the Cold War, Eastern Europe connotes communism, and "rocket fuel" evokes "rocket delivery system," which inevitably leads to "atomic bomb.") Held in the "State of Anemia"—described by comedy historian David J. Hogan as "an Eastern Bloc hellhole with a capital that looks like an 18th-century stone fortress by way of comic operetta"—Larry struggles to pass himself off as Professor Sneed, and Moe and Shemp as his assistants.

Edward Bernds directs with jaunty flair, mixing up his shots and deftly highlighting the short's verbal and physical gags. The built-in pretension of brutally ideological dictatorships becomes ripe for laughs; likewise, the central issue of mistaken identity. (Larry is mistaken for Sneed because of his "magnificent head of hair," characteristic of Sneed and, of course, Albert Einstein.) While the trio fumbles in the lab, Shemp funnels a combustible liquid concoction into Moe's sleeve instead of a bottle. Moe upends the mixture and inadvertently burns a hole through a tabletop. With the faux fuel safely corked and handed over to a delighted Captain Rork (Philip Van Zandt), the boys assume it's time to get back home. "Oh, think nothing of it," Larry says cheerfully, "drop us a line and let us know how you come out."

Ah, not so fast. The narrative takes a dark turn when a general (Vernon Dent)

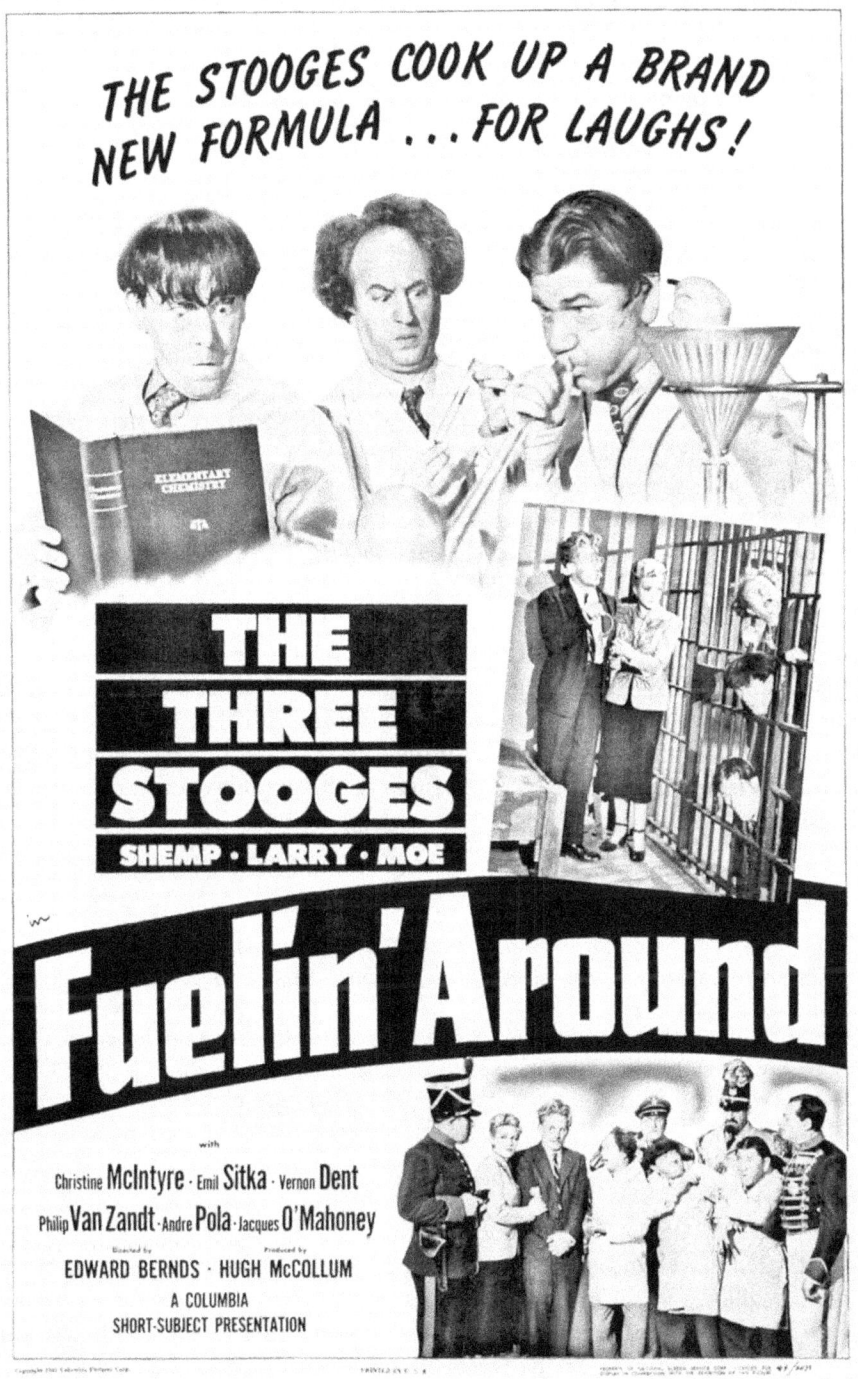

Rocket science and mistaken identity cause Moe, Larry, and Shemp to be spirited to a Communist hellhole somewhere in Eastern Europe, where Larry is ordered to produce fuel for a Red rocket program. *Fuelin' Around* (1949) is one of the best postwar Three Stooges shorts, boasting good production values and clever physical and verbal gags. But when the real scientist is discovered and brought to join the Stooges, the boys face the possibility of execution.

appears, herding the real Prof. Sneed (Emil Sitka) and Sneed's daughter, Hazel (Christine McIntyre), into the lab. The Stooges have been found out, and are ordered to convince Sneed to produce the genuine fuel. The professor and his daughter are removed to a dungeon to reflect on their fate. Left alone in the lab, the boys pace and worry.

> SHEMP: Say Moe, do you think the professor'll give in?
> MOE: Not for us he won't. It's all over but the shootin'.

This is the short's least funny dialogue exchange, and the most central, as well. Earlier sequences of the Stooges ineptly laying carpet at Sneed's house are forgotten; now the boys must contemplate death, because Sneed is a good American who will allow five to die in order to save millions. Subsequent comic business, including Hazel's sweet-talking of a handsome young guard (Jacques O'Mahoney) and the boys' noisy escape from the lab via a hole they burn through the floor, climaxes with a getaway in a jeep gassed up with Larry's explosive mixture. Disasters political and personal are averted, but be assured that when the shadow of death fell over the Stooges and the others, contemporaneous audiences may have felt a little uneasy.

Columbia released *Fuelin' Around* to theaters on July 7, 1949. Barely seven weeks later, atop a tower at the Semipalatinsk test site on August 29, the Soviet Union exploded its first atomic bomb. The United States had long suspected that traitors inside the U.S. atomic program had been feeding technical secrets to the Soviets. In that regard, the test came as no surprise. Nevertheless, analysts at the CIA's Office of Research and Estimates had insisted that the Soviets could not manage a successful test before the middle of 1953. Washington was stunned, and President Truman did not reveal the blast to the American public for a full month. Score a big one for the Russians. Purloined data and, perhaps, a captured Professor Sneed or two, allowed them to shock the world, and make the Cold War considerably hotter.

FILMOGRAPHY

Fuelin' Around—Columbia; Released July 7, 1949; Black and white; 16 min. 50 sec.

    Credits: Producer: Hugh McCollum; Director: Edward Bernds; Screenplay: Elwood Ullman; Director of photography: Vincent Farrar; Editor: Henry Batista; Music: stock; uncredited; Art director: Robert Peterson

    Cast: Moe Howard: Moe; Larry Fine: Larry; Shemp Howard: Shemp; Emil Sitka: Professor Sneed; Christine McIntyre: Hazel Sneed; Philip Van Zandt: Captain Rork; Jacques O'Mahoney (Jock Mahoney): Guard; Vernon Dent: General; Hans Schumm: Colonel

Tokyo File 212

The United States and other Allied nations learned the painful lesson of the 1919 Treaty of Versailles, a force-fed declaration that placed onerous reparations on a defeated Germany: humiliate your defeated enemy, and that enemy will eventually fall to pieces and re-form as something more dangerous than before. So, then, U.S. policy toward a defeated Japan in 1945 was (literally) constructive rather than punitive. The American presence was stern yet benevolent, with Japan remade in the mold of American democracy. A democratic Japan would be a serene Japan. Further, such a nation would protect American interests in the Far East, chiefly as a bulwark against Asian communism.

Although neither Japan's political integrity nor physical safety were seriously threatened by the Korean War of 1950–53, Communist activity on that peninsula alarmed Americans and some Japanese, who feared a Far East domino effect (never mind that Asian nations are widely separated geographically, and are fundamentally very different from each other).

Filmmaker George Breakston appreciated the business possibilities offered by the postwar island nation. A onetime Hollywood child actor of the 1930s and '40s, Breakston entered film production in the late 1940s, and devoted the next ten years to making movies in Japan. (He also filmed in Kenya and elsewhere in Africa.) In 1950, partnered with American attorney Melvin Belli and B-movie specialist Dorrell McGowan, Breakston successfully negotiated with the U.S. Department of Defense, U.S. Army Far East Command, the Tokyo Metropolitan Police, and the Civil Education section of the Occupation Government to make the first American film shot in postwar Japan: a 1951 anti–Communist thriller called *Tokyo File 212*. (During the same period, Breakston produced *Ori-*

Expat American producer George Breakston made numerous English-language films in Japan during the 1950s, none quite as timely as *Tokyo File 212* (1951), a modestly budgeted melodrama about Communist labor agitation in early postwar Tokyo. Despite some tired elements, including a hotshot young American agent and the obligatory woman of intrigue (Florence Marly, right), the picture's novel structure (it opens with the story's climax, and then backtracks), as well as interestingly shabby Japanese locations, provide some spark. The real-life labor element is handled with reasonable accuracy.

ental Evil [1951], concerning smuggling in Japan; and *Geisha Girl* [1952], a peculiar comedy involving Japanese Communists, a pair of bumbling U.S. servicemen, and pill-sized explosives capable of destroying all of Tokyo. At decade's end, Breakston produced his best-known picture, *The Manster* [1959], a creepy, determinedly peculiar horror thriller about an American in Japan who grows a second head.)

In general outline, the modestly budgeted *Tokyo File 212* is at once familiar and (ostensibly) up-to-the-minute. U.S. government agent Jim Carter (Robert Peyton) is in Tokyo on assignment, masquerading as a journalist and keeping tabs on a local workers' group that espouses communism as well as labor rights. He particularly wishes to locate Taro Matsuto (Katsuhiko Haida), the leftist son of an old friend, Mr. Matsuto (Tatsuo Saitô). Leads to Taro run hot and cold. As Carter presses his investigation, he's ambushed in his hotel room by Japanese men who, Carter later learns, had been in the company of Russians.

Lounging unannounced one day in Carter's hotel room is an East European woman named Steffi Novak (Florence Marly); she describes herself as a sort of guide capable of leading Carter to whatever and whomever he wishes. (American film fans are best familiar with the cat-eyed Marly as Bogart's love interest in *Tokyo Joe* [1949], and as the alluring and malevolent extraterrestrial in Curtis Harrington's *Queen of Blood* [1966].) We've seen quasi-exotics like Steffi in numerous other films—the glib, faintly ratty seductresses who trade on their round-heeled natures for money, food, and a place to stay. Guided by Steffi and his government handlers, Carter narrowly avoids being poisoned during an expensive dinner with a cryptic businessman named Oyama (Tetsu Nakamura), and discovers that Taro trained as a kamikaze in the waning days of the war. Shamed and infuriated because he never had the opportunity to sacrifice himself, Taro became ripe for conversion to communism.

Events begin to close in on Taro when Namiko (Reiko Otani), the stage actress he cares for, is kidnapped by his own Communist colleagues. The message: If you want to see Namiko alive again, hold your tongue. Further complications arise when Steffi admits to Carter that she's been helping Oyama and other Communists. Why? To earn the release of her captive sister from North Korea. Shocked when Carter shows her proof that her sister has already been executed, Steffi agrees to turn against Oyama, and facilitate the breakup of a violent labor strike led by Taro. Nationwide labor violence is narrowly avoided when the older Matsuto renounces his son's ideas, and insists upon order and democracy.

Tokyo File 212 has a couple of novel elements (besides Steffi's habit of referring to herself in the third person); the historically most interesting is the location shoot, which was the first by an American production company postwar. Although neither as humidly evocative as the Tokyo locations of Akira Kurosawa's *Stray Dog* (1949) or Sam Fuller's later CinemaScope and Technicolor noir, *House of Bamboo* (1955), *Tokyo File 212* successfully shows a crowded, very busy city split by broad avenues and crisscrossed with side streets and alleyways.

Not surprisingly, nothing about the city appears prosperous. Even the businessman Oyama functions in cramped, worn environments. Although not quite the "Commie rat's nest" claimed by one democratically minded Japanese character, the city of *Tokyo File 212* is very much a hotbed of dissolution and intrigue. Shabby and raucous a mere five years after war's end, it bustles with workers, schemers, petty hoodlums, gamblers, tattooed yakuza, and drunks. Nevertheless, the film's introductory monologue (spoken in voice-over by Peyton) describes Japan as "the last outpost of democracy in the Far East." Still struggling to recover physically, but up for grabs because of geography, the Japan of *Tokyo File 212* is important—because America says so.

The film's other novelty is its story construction, for the narrative *begins* with the tale's literally explosive climax, when a Communist bomb goes off on a pedestrian island in a busy street where Carter, Steffi, and Mr. Matsuto wait for Taro. Nearly all but the film's final few minutes, then, are flashback. When we finally come full circle, the group again gathers near the bomb. As a clock's hands approach the doomsday hour of noon, Taro violently, tragically redeems himself, and precipitates the destruction of Oyama. Distracted by the commotion, Carter, Steffi, and Mr. Matsuto run to Taro. Mere moments later, the bomb (in an alarming, real-time mechanical effect) explodes very closely behind them.

Dorrell and Stuart McGowan's screenplay (from a story by Breakston) suggests that postwar Japan is rife with Communist subversion, which encourages drama but doesn't paint an accurate picture. When General Douglas MacArthur landed at Atsugi airfield on August 30, 1945, he stepped onto the soil of a defeated Japan. For nearly the next six years, he would live and work in that country, as Supreme Commander of Allied forces there. Although politically right of center, MacArthur devoted himself to crafting a new Japanese constitution that renounced war, gave women the vote, opened free economic markets and empowered urban and rural labor, established a free press, and quashed oppressive police practices. Above all, political power—heretofore concentrated in the hands of an aggressive Japanese military and the Emperor—would be decentralized.

Postwar Japan had a Communist Party, and MacArthur tolerated it, reasoning that American support for the rights of women and workers trumped any promises local Communists might make. MacArthur's stance was proved correct. The general also agitated with President Truman for a reduction of U.S. troop presence in Japan; the fewer American soldiers, the less opportunity for the Japanese Communist Party to recruit new members from among resentful Japanese. MacArthur's program of rapid land reform undercut the Communists' entreaties to "exploited farmers." Japanese women, enjoying a more emancipated status than ever before, had no interest in communism. Young Japanese, put to work in a growing, if modest, manufacturing sector, were likewise unmoved. And MacArthur's early support of strong Japanese labor unions largely eliminated yet another common Communist talking point. Still, in 1946 Japan's Communist Party had a membership of 60,000.

Despite those numbers, and furious at being stymied in their other goals, Party leaders threatened a general strike for February 1, 1947. Rather than follow the obvious—and politically disastrous—course and quell the labor unrest with U.S. troops. MacArthur waited until hours before the strike deadline to simply remind Japan that he was Supreme Commander, and that he would "not permit the use of so deadly a social weapon in the present impoverished and emaciated condition of Japan and have accordingly directed [the labor leaders] to desist from furtherance of such action."

Occupation historian Seymour Morris, Jr., has written that "so great was MacArthur's prestige, and so forceful was his message, that the workers capitulated. The union leaders … were helpless. Efforts to rally their followers fell short."

And that—*Tokyo File 212* notwithstanding—marked the end of the only serious Communist threat in postwar era Japan.

The musical score of *Tokyo File 212* is the work of a prolific B-film composer named

Albert Glasser. On Thursday, April 19, 1956, Glasser sat down before House Un-American Activities Committee investigators inside the Los Angeles Federal Building. A member of the Communist Party in 1943 (when pro–Soviet U.S. propaganda was at its peak), Glasser shortly became disenchanted and walked away. Now, he sat as a friendly witness, publicly ruing his past and happy to provide the names of film-community colleagues who had been Party members with him. As he gave up former associates, Glasser helpfully spelled peoples' surnames for his HUAC interrogators.

During a thirty-year career, Glasser scored about one hundred low-budget pictures ranging from *The Gas House Kids in Hollywood* to *The Amazing Colossal Man*, bringing a recognizably dissonant, frequently clangorous orchestral approach to his work. His themes for *Tokyo File 212* are more euphonious than many of his others, and he seemed proud of the work, and of the film, too. Glasser explained to HUAC:

> Most of these pictures, *Tokyo File 212*, *Invasion U.S.A.*, and *Huk*, which I just completed two months ago, are very strong, very dynamic anti–Communist pictures.... *Tokyo* was made completely in the Orient, in Tokyo, and showed how some of the Communist Party methods operate, what they have done in various ways, and shows their machinations, how they can accomplish certain purposes and how it was stopped by the Japanese government.

Glasser's testimony, like his brass-heavy film scores, is over-emphatic. *Tokyo File 212*, although guilty of exaggeration for dramatic effect, nevertheless succeeds in suggesting an actual fear, if not reality itself.

FILMOGRAPHY

Tokyo File 212—RKO (USA); Tokyo Eiga Haikyuu (Japan); Released January 26, 1951 (Japan); May 31, 1951 (USA); Black and white; 84 min.

Credits: Producers: Melvin M. Belli, George P. Breakston, Dorrell McGowan; Directors: Dorrell McGowan, Stuart E. McGowan; Screenplay: Dorrell McGowan, Stuart E. McGowan; Director of photography: Herman Schopp, Ichirô Hoshijima (uncredited); Editor: Martin G. Cohn; Music: Albert Glasser; Art director: Seigo Shindô

Cast: Florence Marly: Steffi Novak; Robert Peyton: Lee Frederick; Katsuhiko Haida: Taro Matsuto; Reiko Otani: Namiko; Tatsuo Satô: Mr. Matsuto; Satoshi Nakamura: Mr. Oyama

Hell and High Water

Sam Fuller's *Hell and High Water* (1954) is Cold War conflict imagined with adolescent brio—a large-scale "mission" adventure that is predictive of better-known films the likes of *The Guns of Navarone* and *Operation Crossbow*. The climactic *Hell and High Water* set piece, on and near a mysterious, supposedly uninhabited island in the North Pacific, anticipates the high stakes and lavish visual excitement of the James Bond films. Of all the pictures directed by Fuller, this one is at once the most obviously commercial and the most whimsical.

The disappearance of a noted American émigré atomic scientist is actually deception, and part of a plan originating in Washington: the scientist is to be taken, by decommissioned submarine, to a supposedly uninhabited island in the North Pacific, where he will advise the sub's captain on how to destroy a secret Communist atomic lab. Following a violent adventure on a heavily fortified Communist island that *is not* the one in question, the sub locates the lab island, putting an end to a Communist scheme to ratchet up the Cold War.

In keeping with Hollywood war-film tradition, the sub commander (Richard Widmark) is a man with a past: a problem with authority that led to his postwar dismissal from the Navy. But now, as a civilian contractor, he's needed. And for more only-in-the-movies logic, the valuable scientist (Victor Francen) arrives on board with his attractive daughter (Bella Darvi), who innocently inflames the crew and gets under Widmark's skin, too.

Of the most stylistically aggressive directors of Hollywood's late classic period, Sam Fuller also remains one of the most idiosyncratic. His life experience included stints as a teenage crime reporter, World War II combat dogface, novelist, and Hollywood story man, screenwriter, producer, and director. When he relocated to Europe after 1980, he continued to direct, and became a screen actor. During the Fox relationship that produced *Hell and High Water*, Fuller wrote and directed *Pickup on South Street* (1953), a potent thriller combining Cold War politics and film noir. Although Fuller liked and admired Fox chief Darryl Zanuck, he never felt completely comfortable with big-studio work. He invariably described himself as a storyteller, and if he could tell his stories on small budgets, as an independent filmmaker, that's what he would do, exemplified by such stuff as *I Shot Jesse James* (1949), *The Steel Helmet* (1951), and *Park Row* (1952; one of the best-ever movies about rough-and-tumble tabloid journalism).

After 1957, his big-studio days mainly behind him, Fuller settled into the quasi-underground with vigorous melodramas dismissed by many at the time as mere exploitation: *The Crimson Kimono* (1959; interracial romance), *Verboten!* (1959; diehard Nazis in postwar Germany), *Shock Corridor* (1963; medicine's failure to effectively treat mental patients), *The Naked Kiss* (1964; prostitution and pedophilia), and *White Dog* (1982; a furious attack on American racism that so frightened the participating studio, Paramount, that it was barely released, and allowed to go unseen for decades).

As a thirtyish G.I. during World War II, Fuller witnessed and experienced episodes of brute, elemental tragedy and sacrifice. It's no surprise, then, that some of his most effective movies focus on soldiers in combat. *Fixed Bayonets!* (1951) and the aforementioned *The Steel Helmet*, two of the best pictures about the Korean War, are also among the most honest of all Hollywood delineations of combat, particularly how soldiers wrestle with their own fear in order to meet their obligations to their buddies. *China Gate* (1957), produced by Fuller's Globe Enterprises, is an early Hollywood rumination on the violent and complicated civil war in French Indochina—a place better known to Americans as Vietnam. And Fuller's late-career triumph, *The Big Red One* (1980), is an autobiographical account of the U.S. Army's fabled 1st Infantry Division, and its hellish, spirit-sapping progress through Germany in the closing days of World War II.

Although *Hell and High Water* looks closely at issues of command and sacrifice, it also is the most overtly fanciful of Fuller's war dramas. We've already noted the presence of actress Bella Darvi; on top of that are crewmen so persistently "colorful" that you begin to wonder just who's attending to the sub. Cameron Mitchell, horny, lavishly tattooed, and straining to be a figure of humor, seems especially artificial.

The most preposterous element, that the Chinese and/or North Koreans plan to drop an A-bomb on America from a purloined American B-29, is treated with great gravity—as if a scheme so wild could 1) be executed in the first place, and 2) would not bring disastrous consequences upon the perpetrators.

The film's first set piece, a nighttime attack against a barren outpost island held by Communists (perhaps Chinese, perhaps North Korean), is a slickly choreographed bedlam of automatic rifle and machine gun fire, tracer bullets, and artfully placed explosions. The brief battle is exciting, but Sam Fuller surely knew that few instances of combat are as tidily executed.

The climax, as the full complement of crewmen standing on the deck of the surfaced sub trains its small-arms fire on a swiftly moving target, is a gem of choreography, sound effects, and cutting. As the object moves right to left across the screen, the crewmen are filmed from behind, deck guns belching, and rifles and machine guns tracking the target with their muzzles. In reverse shots, in which we see the crewmen's faces, the small arms (weapons Fuller knew best) track across the screen in the opposite direction, without losing the visual context of the physical situation. This is kinetic, even thrilling visual storytelling, and a suitable climax to one of the Cold War's most "fun" anti–Communist adventures.

FILMOGRAPHY

Hell and High Water—20th Century-Fox; Released February 1, 1954 (New York City); February 6, 1954 (wide); Technicolor; 103 min.

Credits: Producer: Raymond A. Klune; Director: Samuel Fuller; Screenplay: David Hempstead (story); Jesse L. Lasky Jr., Samuel Fuller; Director of photography: Joe MacDonald; Editor: James B. Clark; Music: Alfred Newman; Art directors: Leland Fuller, Lyle Wheeler; Special photographic effects: Ray Kellogg

Cast: Richard Widmark: Capt. Adam Jones; Bella Darvi: Denise Montel; Victor Francen: Prof. Montel; Cameron Mitchell: "Ski" Brodski; Gene Evans: Chief Holter; David Wayne: "Tugboat" Walker; Richard Loo: Hakada Fujimori

A Bullet for Joey

The whole point of *A Bullet for Joey* (1955)—other than that Communists are awful people—is that even an egregiously antisocial American hoodlum can square up against the Red menace and die on the side of the angels.

Joe Victor (George Raft) is an American mobster of middling status, recently released from prison and now self-exiled to Canada. Like most such hoodlums who enjoy dames, good clothes, and handsome cars, Joe is perpetually on the lookout for a score. He has busied himself for years with gambling, the numbers racket, smuggling, and "an occasional rubout." Because he accepts such risk easily, he's unfazed when a stranger named Garcia (Steven Geray) offers $100,000 if Joe will appropriate and deliver an important piece of goods. *A Bullet for Joey* is essentially a heist thriller, in which the coveted item is not currency or jewels but a man. Garcia's handlers want to procure (for reasons that do not interest Joe) a nuclear physicist named Carl Macklin (George Dolenz), a courtly fellow of handsome middle age, ensconced in a lab near Montreal and engaged in U.S.-Canadian weapons research.

Garcia explains to Joe that simply conking Dr. Macklin on the head will not do. No, the scientist must accompany Joe willingly. He must want to go to where Joe leads.

Joe gets on the phone. He knows people in New York, L.A., and Havana, and within days he's gathered a surveillance expert, a couple of strong-arm boys, a bedroom creeper, and—most vitally—a woman with a history of getting men to follow her anywhere. Joe puts his plan in motion, with the creeper, handsome and murderous Jack Allen (Bill Bryant), sent forth to coax information from Macklin's mousy, love-starved secretary,

Political ideology and one man's struggle for redemption drive *A Bullet for Joey* (1955), a Communist-themed melodrama that catches tough and charismatic George Raft during the downside of his star period. Joe Victor (Raft, left) is a selfish, midlevel hood who thoughtlessly involves himself in atomic espionage. It is left to RCMP Inspector Raoul Leduc (Edward G. Robinson, seated, right) to uncover Joe's better nature—that is, if Joe has one. Joe's playmates are actors John Cliff (left) and Joseph Vitale.

Yvette (Toni Gerry). A stimulating blonde named Joyce Geary (Audrey Totter) has been called up from Cuba to develop a "chance" romance with Macklin himself. Joe directs his operatives closely but coolly, keen on getting his final payment and concerned not at all that his employer, an icy, Aryan type named Hartman (Peter van Eyck), wants Macklin for military-political reasons.

As Joe's careful pursuit of Macklin develops, RCMP inspector Raoul Leduc (Edward G. Robinson) pursues a simultaneous parallel course, becoming intrigued when various events—the killings of an RCMP trooper and a nameless man near Macklin's apartment, the apparent murder of Macklin's secretary, and that new romance in Macklin's life—dovetail too neatly to be coincidence.

In familiar Hollywood police-procedural style, an RCMP Identi-Kit and some clever forensics (that discovers monkey hair) not only identifies the anonymous murder victim as an organ grinder, but also as the man that killed the trooper.

When Leduc and other RCMP investigators gather in a desolate, stubbled lot to view the forlorn body of Yvette, the corpse is obscured beneath a police sheet, very like the body of Elizabeth Short, the real-life "Black Dahlia" murder victim of 1946 who also was abandoned in a vacant lot. The visual link between that infamous L.A. case and the murder of Macklin's secretary establishes the brutality of not just Joe's professional lothario, but the raw criminal nature of the Communists. In their pursuit of Macklin, anything goes.

Procedural details continue with a police transmitter affixed to a moving truck, which allows the RCMP to keep tabs on Joe and Macklin—until the signal weakens and gives out.

Finally, during a climactic meeting aboard a steamer that's cast off from Montreal harbor, Joe discovers that he is as much an unwilling passenger as the captured Macklin and Leduc. Although Joe hasn't given a damn about political philosophy, Inspector Leduc tries his best to reach the mobster.

> LEDUC: Men like Hartman are masters of deception. They tell lies, they corrupt people's minds.
> JOE: That's no skin offa my nose.
> LEDUC: No, it's more than the skin of your nose that's in danger, Joe. It's you, *all* of you, all of us, all of humanity.
> JOE (indecision on his face): Aw, shut up for a while, will ya? I'm tryin' to think.

Leduc presses his advantage:

> LEDUC: Joe, you've pulled all kinds of deals during your lifetime.... But all these are petty crimes to the one you committed when you handed Macklin over to this mob. [pause] Why don't you do something decent for a change?
> JOE (uncertainly): Like what?

Joe's abrupt concern for the USA and geopolitical stability, plus his determination to get himself off the damn boat, encourage him to plug a few of Hartman's minions—even as Hartman, who knows the game is up, prepares to destroy Macklin. Joe saves the scientist by gunning Hartman, only to be mortally wounded by one last bullet from the dying Communist's gun. A bullet for Joey, yes.

During the melee, Leduc managed to locate a Very pistol and send up a distress flare. Now, cradling Joe, he listens soberly as the mobster asks that his ashes be scattered *on the American side of the border.* Ah, an evolution from thug to self-sacrificing patriot in just eighty-five minutes.

Little of this would be even remotely believable if not for the sheer authority and acting skill of Edward G. Robinson, and that great wooden—and hugely charismatic—presence known as George Raft. The two had been under contract at Warner Bros. throughout the 1930s and '40s, forging paths of solo stardom and appearing together in *Manpower*, a 1941 Warner melodrama about rival power-line workers in love with the same woman.

Joey director Lewis Allen spent most of his thirty-five-year career in television, though he's recalled for one of Hollywood's best ghost stories, *The Uninvited* (1944), and a pair of efficient crime thrillers starring Alan Ladd: *Chicago Deadline* (1949) and *Appointment with Danger* (1951). Nevertheless, Allen's feature career began to unravel with *Valentino* (1951), a biopic that flopped at the box office and remains one of Hollywood's legendary, high-profile misfires. His handling of *Joey* is competent, but marked by a disinclination to move the camera; it's left to Robinson, Raft, and the others to propel the narrative. The picture was probably not a challenge for anybody in the cast, though perennial small-part player Bill Bryant makes a potent impression as the cruel seducer of Macklin's secretary. And Toni Gerry, as that victim, brings a vulnerable longing to the role. When Leduc tells Joe that Communists are "masters of deception," he casts the secretary as a synecdoche representing the totality of free men and women endangered by pulp Hollywood's vision of communism.

Co-scripters A. I. Bezzerides and Daniel Mainwaring (credited under his frequent pseudonym, Geoffrey Homes) had considerable flair for shock melodrama; Bezzerides's novel, *The Long Haul,* had been adapted by others in 1940 for one of George Raft's best pictures, *They Drive by Night.* Bezzerides himself scripted the adaptation of another of his trucker novels, *Thieves' Market,* for release as *Thieves' Highway.* In 1955, the same year as *A Bullet for Joey,* he and director Robert Aldrich challenged conventional Hollywood filmmaking with *Kiss Me Deadly,* a ferocious—and ferociously funny—adaptation (and improvement of) Mickey Spillane's pulp novel.

Mainwaring impresses with his scripts for a trio of noir thrillers, *The Big Steal, Out of the Past* (from his novel, *Build My Gallows High*), and *Roadblock;* as well as *The Lawless* (small-town newspaper editor vs. murderous, anti-immigrant racists) and *The Phenix City Story* (politicians vs. gambling and prostitution interests that viciously dominate an Alabama town; based on a true story). And then there is Mainwaring's superb, sharply observed adapted script for the original *Invasion of the Body Snatchers.* In that film, too, as in *A Bullet for Joey,* innocent or oblivious people are endangered by frightful interlopers. The stakes are high, and the Italian distributors of *Joey* properly pushed back against the gangster element to emphasize the tale's political overtones, titling the picture *Spionaggio atomico—Atomic Espionage.*

Filmography

A Bullet for Joey—Bischoff-Diamond Corporation; United Artists; Released April 15, 1955; Black and white; 85 min.

Credits: Producers: Samuel Bischoff, David Diamond; Director: Lewis Allen; Screenplay: Geoffrey Homes aka Daniel Mainwaring, A. I. Bezzerides; Director of photography: Harry Neumann; Editor: Leon Barsha; Music: Harry Sukman; Art director: Jack Okey

Cast: Edward G. Robinson: Inspector Raoul Leduc; George Raft: Joe Victor; Audrey Totter: Joyce Geary; George Dolenz: Dr. Carl Macklin; Peter Van Eyck: Eric Hartman; Toni Gerry: Yvonne Temblay; William Bryant: Jack Allen; Morrie: John Cliff

Shack Out on 101

The grungy, ten-day wonder known as *Shack Out on 101* (1955) insists that America and the rest of the free world are in peril because Slob, a reedy, dippy cook at a Southern California greasy spoon, is a mastermind of atomic espionage. A place that has few customers other than a couple of wiseacre deliverymen from Acme Poultry (guys who are really government agents), the diner nevertheless is a locus of compelling human activity. Owner George (Keenan Wynn) believes fiercely in the American dream of small business—even though his place looks to be grossing about forty-two dollars a week. His waitress, Kotty (Terry Moore), is a petite and curvy all-American type: young, perky, and with an agreeable patina of I'm-in-this-on-my-own wariness. She's a toughie, but a good American girl too, studying for the civil service exam, and looking forward to a job with the government.

George is frequently visited by Eddie (Whit Bissell), a former soldier who distinguished himself during D–Day (in the company of George), only to fall into postwar jitters that have made him timid, and terrified of violence. Popular culture and the news (including the USSR's great unhappiness with the West's 1954 remilitarization of West Germany; and the spring 1955 Warsaw Pact, the Soviet counter to NATO) had already conditioned audiences to be wary of a pacifistic mindset. In the brutalities of the Cold War and Korea (where the sacrifices of G.I.s fighting in impossible weather and on harsh terrain remained a fresh and painful public memory), there is no good place for an American man who cannot kill.

The most novel of the diner regulars is Sam (Frank Lovejoy), a stolid but friendly guy in a wool suit. Sam is a nuclear physicist, and when he needs a break from his top secret work at a lab up the highway, he falls by for coffee and conversation—and a cuddle with Kotty, whom he's been romancing since before we came in. (In a very amusing scene that anticipates the elliptical dialogue of novelist Richard Condon's *The Manchurian Candidate*, Kotty and Sam make love talk by exchanging humid questions and answers about the Bill of Rights and other topics Kotty will find on her exam.)

If Kotty only knew that Sam sells atomic secrets to Slob!

Whether any of this strikes the audience as unlikely is irrelevant; certainly, writer-director Edward Dein (otherwise best known for an amusing horror thriller called *The Leech Woman*) is too busy plowing forward to care. Although shot almost entirely on a plain "diner" set (with occasional—and effective—use of true beachside exteriors), *Shack* torques along with the subtle grace of a rock-crusher transmission. The opening sequence is one of those genuine exteriors, a sweet left-to-right pan from breaking surf to a pair of pretty feet, along nicely formed legs, and finally to the remainder of Kotty (supine in the sun, encased in a suggestion of a bikini, and snugged so close to the camera that you can see every pore). Floyd Crosby, who shot *High Noon* three years earlier, establishes Kotty's horizontal splendor via gorgeous deep focus that reveals Slob waaay down the beach. Does he notice Kotty?

Yes, Slob notices Kotty. As the girl's body gently sways in surf that curls beneath her legs and along her back, Slob ambles the considerable distance separating him from the camera eye, discarding a sea shell along the way and finally kneeling over the girl to plant his mouth on hers. A similar scene played out romantically two years earlier in *From Here to Eternity*, but on this isolated beach the woman resists with such vigor that Slob is forced to retreat. And so Dein establishes the sexual tension that undergirds the better part of *Shack Out on 101*. Although you wonder why an earthy chick like Kotty is turned on by straight-arrow, single-breasted Sam, the opening sequence establishes that Kotty pursues playtime on her own terms. Meanwhile, the surf crashes and moans, and near the film's climax, the diner is rattled by a howling storm.

Others in this disheveled blend of Steinbeck and Odets include Professor Dillon (an amusingly miscast Frank de Kova, who almost invariably played thugs). Like Sam, Dillon is a Red dupe, and although he finally comes to his senses about Communists ("They preach liberty and practice slavery!" he tells Sam), Dillon barely has time enough later to gasp when Slob slides a knife between his ribs. Then there's the perpetually damp fishmonger, Perch (hawk-nosed Len Lesser); like Slob, he's a deep-cover Red agent.

But wait. Is Dr. Sam—the man, after all, whom Kotty loves—*really* a Red agent? Well, of course not. By the time the pair enjoy a post-climactic clinch, the right people have been disposed of, and the espionage ring broken up.

Shack Out on 101 catches fourth-billed Lee Marvin early in his film career, when *The Big Heat*, *The Wild One*, *Bad Day at Black Rock*, and other pictures began to establish him as a go-to villain. Although delineated during most of *Shack* as a crude buffoon,

A few moments into the bracing opening sequence of *Shack Out on 101* (1955), thick-headed short-order cook Slob (Lee Marvin) takes liberties with his sunbathing co-worker, Kotty (Terry Moore). Because she's self-reliant and American-tough, Kotty tells him where to get off, unaware that Slob is a highly trained Communist agent.

Slob is considerably more dangerous than the sadistic gangster, boozy biker, and small-town bully he portrayed in those earlier pictures. Slob's small genius is that by encouraging others to laugh at him, he becomes invisible, hiding in plain sight while plotting murder and other, more existential crimes.

Marvin and Keenan Wynn developed an offhand, easy rapport on-screen, and it's easy to believe that George and Slob have been in each other's orbit for quite a while. The picture's oddest and best-liked interlude is the ad-libbed weightlifting sequence, in which George and Slob strip to the waist when the diner closes and wrestle with barbells and dumbbells—each fishing for compliments from the other, and displaying a riotously funny narcissism. According to a 2014 interview given to historian Eddie Muller by Terry Moore, writer-director Edward Dein had little interest in guiding his cast, and allowed Wynn and Marvin to invent their dialogue and bits of business. Both men foolishly lift their barbells from the floor by bending at the waist, with legs straight, inviting serious back trouble. There is much verbal back and forth about muscles and bodily contours ("How many times do I haveta tell you not to call 'em muscles," George says irritably. "Call 'em pecs!"), and some evaluative prodding of flesh. When George crows about his abs (flat but undefined), Slob sucks in his breath and wheezes, "Are they as hard as mine?"

George sticks out a finger and gives Slob's abdomen a desultory poke. "That's a matter of opinion," he mutters.

George reflects on becoming the envy of Muscle Beach. Slob, apparently eager to establish his bodybuilding bona fides, answers back, "I don't go for those guys on Muscle Beach, their waists is so thin there's no room for any food!" After struggling cartoonishly to execute a few behind-the-neck barbell presses, Slob admits, "You know what I really want? A big, thick neck!"—illustrating his wish by grimacing, and lacing all ten fingers below his jaw.

Although Terry Moore has recalled that Wynn and Marvin ad-libbed, the sequence was nevertheless planned; sets of barbells didn't end up on the set by the whims of the actors. But in the amusing, foolish narcissism of the exchange, George and Slob capture some mid-century American qualities that, according to Dein (and many social critics, as well), put the nation at risk. George is wrapped up in chasing the American dream, and is oblivious to the perfidy unfolding around him. Slob—playing, we must remember, a role for the benefit of George and the others—is vain, delusional, and unwilling to work hard, despite having a fund of big ideas.

The film's low budget ($100,000 is a fair guess) restricts the physical action of *Shack Out on 101*, and results in a highly theatrical, almost anti-cinematic feel, with key action choreographed on various areas of the diner interior. The characters' purposeful entrances and exits treat the edges of the frame as a proscenium (in other words, nothing exists beyond the margins of the frame, and the players provide much of the action in lieu of an active camera). The cutting emphasizes full-figure two- and three-shots (as a stage audience would observe the players). Tart, sharply batted dialogue emphasizes characterization and theme over setting. In all of this, *Shack* has an intriguing artificiality. Certainly, its hothouse of emotions is reflected by the dramatically contrived physical setup of the diner, with Kotty living in a room off the diner floor, and horny Slob ensconced in a shack on the beach behind. Sam's laboratory is never seen, but dialogue suggests that the facility is just up the highway. The fishmonger and the Acme Poultry fellows show up with sufficient regularity to suggest that their routes are very small. Even combat-troubled Eddie, respectable and blandly middle-class in his suit and tie, lives nearby. The continual crowding of the characters and restriction of physical action has a subliminal effect: despite the international implications of the tale's Red-spy narrative, we are invited to regard the small diner as the nexus of everything that really matters in the world.

As the climax unfolds, George—the struggling small-businessman so enamored of his ramshackle diner—takes a big breath and expresses the film's central preoccupation:

> Don't you see what's happened? The apes have taken over. While we're watching television and filling our freezers, they've come out of the jungle and moved in. And what's worse is they've begun to dress like us and pretend to think like us. Just the way we were in the beginning: the animals have begun to hunt man.

The secretly eloquent Slob has a retort: "They *are* all apes. Every last one of them. But you're so desperate for security that you'll take any promise that vaguely resembles it. Oh, I don't blame you for looking down at the apes. But you overlook one important factor: their leaders are *not* apes."

Sam replies, "Don't look now, but a foreign government has just invaded our country and this is the beachhead." Kotty then addresses Slob: "What have we ever done to you, why do you want to change *our* lives? You've got your own place, build it up, tear it down, if you want to eat each other, eat each other, just leave us alone!" But it's too late for that.

Early in the story, George displays his new harpoon gun. When Eddie gives the thing a wary glance, you understand that this weapon, like those delightful "ladies' guns" revealed in Act One of so many drawing-room mystery plays, will figure prominently in the film's Act Three. And so it does, as Slob rushes out of frame, the harpoon fired by Eddie trailing out of frame after him. Slob dies out there in the wings, where we can't see him—but by this time Slob is hardly the issue. The point is that Eddie, America's Eddie, meets his moment of crisis, and triumphs. Rather like a man who has had no orgasm for a long time, and finally achieves one, Eddie is exultant, not because of sex, but because of sex's most pointed sublimation. Eddie is joyful because he can once again do his duty and kill.

The film's purposely stagey quality encourages us to excuse the screenplay's didacticism and inherent artificiality, and embrace the characters that are brought so close to us. Free of physical reality, *Shack Out on 101* lives, successfully, on the strength of its message: the interlopers are close to you, every day. You look at them, and do not truly see them, but you have no choice but to see them now.

FILMOGRAPHY

Shack Out on 101—Allied Artists; Released December 4, 1955; Black and white; 79 min.

Credits: Producers: William F. Broidy, Mort Millman; Director: Edward Dien; Screenplay: Edward Dien, Mildred Dien; Director of photography: Floyd Crosby; Editor: George White; Music: Paul Dunlap; Art director: Lou [Lucius] O. Croxton

Cast: Terry Moore: Kotty; Frank Lovejoy: Sam Bastion; Keenan Wynn: George; Lee Marvin: Slob; Whit Bissell: Eddie; Jess Barker: Artie (Acme Poultry); Donald Murphy: Pepe (Acme Poultry); Frank de Kova: Claude Dillon; Len Lesser: Perch (fishmonger)

Five Gates to Hell

The trailer for writer-director James Clavell's *Five Gates to Hell* (1959), with voice-over by the great announcer Art Gilmore, opens with big block letters—ATTENTION PLEASE!—that flash against a black screen. The words fade and the screen returns to black as Gilmore intones, "Today the screen has broken down many old taboos. But even so, we have never yet presented a picture quite so shocking as 20th Century-Fox's *Five Gates to Hell*!" With this, a title card comes up, and the visual portion of the trailer begins. Against a backdrop of quickly edited snippets of grinning Asian soldiers and struggling, terrified Anglo and Asian women, Gilmore continues:

> Five nurses and a disguised nun captured by the bloodthirsty, women-hungry guerrillas of Indochina, facing mass violation from men so sadistically cruel, they make suicide seem the easy way out. But this is not like movies you've seen before. These girls *actually go through* the five gates to Hell, before your startled eyes.... So degraded in body and soul that they have only one way out—to cast off every restraint of sex and fight back with the weapons—the bloodlust—of men.

As the women fight back in the trailer clips, more block letters unfurl across the screen: THE NAKED FURY OF WOMEN BATTLING MEN IN A SPECTACLE OF UNPARALLELED SAVAGERY!

In quick cuts, one nurse, and then another, let loose on their tormentors with M3 "grease gun" machine pistols. A Vietminh tears open the blouse of that disguised nun. A nurse tosses a hand grenade—*kaboom!* The "virile young warlord" who has instigated all the mayhem threatens to take the women alive—and you know what *that* means.

Not every film from the Cold War period that featured Communists manipulated those bogeymen as the raison d'être. To the contrary, *Five Gates to Hell* (with story set in the recent past, 1950) exploits not ideology but a racist sexual fear: the violation of white women at the hands of yellow beasts—a notion of sexual relations straight out of the men's "sweat" magazines of the day. Still, because audiences understood communism to be "bad," every whim and action of the warlord and his men is duplicitous. The guerrilla fighters' childish desires mark them as unrestrained creatures of the id, with a propensity for violence that, in essence, endows a gang of two-year-olds with the willingness and ability to murder.

Typical of casting conventions during this period of Hollywood filmmaking, the Vietminh warlord is played by Caucasian actor Neville Brand, who enjoyed a good career playing Native Americans, Arabs, surly Eastern Europeans, and garden-variety thugs. His lean physique and frankly brutish features—an overhanging shelf of brow, splayed nose, and thickened lips—encouraged casting as quasi-exotics. Although not a star at the time of *Five Gates to Hell*, Brand had achieved the level of star character actor. He had been a familiar face since 1950; audiences knew him and had a general idea of what to expect when he appeared on screen. Brand's casting allowed audiences a thoughtless expectation of brutality. Relieved of the responsibility to look for nuance, audiences allowed the rote depiction of evil to wash over them. Because the actor had played ogres so many times before, filmgoers accepted the Vietminh warlord's excesses as both false (*That's Neville Brand up there*) and "real" (*Look how that guy abuses those women*). In the end, the impossibility of anyone believing that Neville Brand had any DNA relationship with Asia becomes irrelevant. In the false and stylized reality of the movies, Brand became Vietnamese, and Communists became animals.

All of the foregoing aside, *Five Gates to Hell* is remarkably plot-free. Somewhere in an area of Indochina that has been abandoned by French troops, a Vietminh squad abducts doctors and nurses of a mobile hospital. The doctors are unable to save the life of a cancerous old Vietminh leader. Arguments and blame ensue, and the doctors perish, leaving the women with the guerrillas.

Chen Pamok (Brand) sets his sights on an American, the classically named Athena (Dolores Michaels). She resists his sexual advances ... and then she doesn't. A neurotic nun called Sister Maria (Shirley Knight) is raped. A British nurse named Joy (Patricia Owens) screeches at a plain–Jane French nurse (Nancy Kulp) that the only way for a woman to survive is to "use her sex!"

A German nurse, Greta (Gerry Gaylor), is accepted by the others as one of the group, but a Japanese, Chioko (Nobu McCarthy), is viewed with some suspicion, particularly by the vengeful, ever-screeching Joy, whose husband died in the Pacific. Again, then, the issue isn't politics but race.

With three hundred guerrillas conveniently away in battle, only Chen and a handful of troops remain with the captives. Athena gets fed up and shoots Chen in the head. Chioko seduces her would-be lover and then stabs him in the neck with a hairpin. The nurses pick up machine guns and kill slouchy guerrillas that had laughed at them. The women escape. Joy adjusts her nylons.

The women make night camp and talk about men, in a sort of can't-live-with-'em, can't-live-without-'em way. Joy admits that during the war her husband abandoned her to the mercies of a Japanese bordello.

With rebel leader Chen (inexplicably) recovered and closing in, the plain Jane blows herself up with a hand grenade, taking a few guerrillas with her. Joy screeches at the nun, and finally sells the idea of killing.

Chioko says, "Athena, your slip is showing."

A nurse studies herself in her compact. Linda Wong, playing an adorable "half-caste," puts on a cute little hat before the final battle.

Sister Maria sacrifices herself. Greta does some damage with hand grenades before being gunned by what remains of Chen's group.

Chen and Athena face off. He has the drop on her, but can't bring himself to shoot. But Athena can.

What does she do now? She's pregnant with Chen's child.

Of course, the baby won't be a Communist baby. It will be a half-Vietnamese baby.

Here, then, are the Cold War life choices forced upon us in *Five Gates to Hell*: subjugation by enemy ideology; shame by enemy DNA. In 1959, one fate seemed considerably more damning than the other.

James Clavell, Australian by birth and a much-abused POW in the Pacific during World War II, had an unsurprising interest in all things Asian. Preoccupied with political-economic applications of individual rights and fair competition, Clavell hated political, military, and mercantile tyranny. Although most famous for his "Asian Saga" novels that began with *King Rat* in 1962, Clavell is remembered also for his screenplay for *The Fly* (1958; adapting George Langelaan's short story), co-writer credit on *The Great Escape* (1963) and *The Satan Bug* (1965), and his greatest film success, as writer-director of the 1966 hit, *To Sir, with Love*. In the last, a teacher encourages British hoodlums to redeem themselves. But as we see in *Five Gates to Hell*, shots fired in vengeance are the best medicine for Communist oppression.

Filmography

Five Gates to Hell—20th Century-Fox; Released September 23, 1959; Black and white

Credits: Producer: James Clavell; Director: James Clavell; Screenplay: James Clavell; Director of photography: Sam Leavitt; Editor: Harry W. Gerstad; Music: Paul Dunlap; Art directors: John B. Mansbridge, Lyle R. Wheeler

Cast: Dolores Michaels: Athena; Patricia Owens: Joy; Neville Brand: Chen Pamok; Ken Scott: Dr. John Richter; Nobu McCarthy: Chioko; Benson Fong: Gung Sa; Shirley Knight: Sister Maria; Irish McCalla: Sister Magdalena

Works Cited

Print

Aaker, Everett. *The Films of George Raft*. Jefferson, NC: McFarland. 2013.
Cameron, Ian. *Samuel Fuller*. New York: Praeger, 1970.
Epstein, Dwayne. *Lee Marvin: Point Blank*. Tucson: Schaffner Press, 2013.
Fuller, Sam, with Christa Lang Fuller and Jerome Henry Rudes. *A Third Face: My Tale of Writing, Fighting, and Filmmaking*. New York: Knopf, 2002.
Hogan, David J. *Film Noir FAQ*. Montclair, NJ: Applause, 2013.
_____. *Three Stooges FAQ*. Montclair, NJ: Applause, 2011.
Investigation of Communist Activities in the Los Angeles, California, Area—Part 9. Committee on Un-American Activities, House of Representatives, 84th Congress, Second Session. April 19, 1956. United States Government Printing Office. Washington, D.C.: 1956.
Lentz, Robert J. *Lee Marvin: His Films and Career*. Jefferson, NC: McFarland, 2000.

Morris Jr., Seymour. *Supreme Commander: MacArthur's Triumph in Japan.* New York: Harper, 2014.
Yablonsky, Lewis. *George Raft.* New York: McGraw-Hill, 1974.

DVD

A Bullet for Joey. Included in *Film Noir: The Dark Side of Cinema.* Kino Lorber. 2016.
Five Gates to Hell. 20th Century-Fox Cinema Archives. 2016.
Fuelin' Around. The Three Stooges Collection Vol. 6, 1949–1951. Sony Home Entertainment. 2009.
Hell and High Water. 20th Century-Fox. 2009.
Shack Out on 101. Olive Films, 2013.

PART 3

Dupes, Victims and Crusaders

"Men, like musical instruments, seem made to be played upon."
—Christian Nestell Bovee

"We have something in common. We both seek out lepers."
—leper colony physician to HUAC investigator Jim McLain
(John Wayne); discarded scene, *Big Jim McLain* (1952)

Big Brains and Betrayal
Walk a Crooked Mile

BRUCE DETTMAN

> There was a crooked man, and he walked a crooked mile,
> He found a crooked sixpence against a crooked stile;
> He bought a crooked cat which caught a crooked mouse,
> And they all lived together in a little crooked house.

It wasn't America alone that had drawn a huge line in the sand against the so-called International Communist Conspiracy. The way it appeared following World War II, opposing teams from across the entire globe were rallying together in a universal draft of commitment, the whole of Western civilization signing up for what could conceivably be the last big showdown, a possible nuclear endgame of good versus evil, right versus wrong, the godly versus the godless. This time around there would be no fence-sitting; the sidelines were not an option, not even for Hollywood, which had earlier taken its sweet time in suggesting the truth about the Third Reich. But now Hitler and the Nazis were old news. Tinseltown had its eyes on a new villain, and the film industry was eager to capitalize on this terrifying and immediate threat.

Walk A Crooked Mile, put together in 1948 by independent producer Edward Small, directed by Gordon Douglas and released by Columbia Pictures, stars the always solid, always likable (and underrated) Dennis O'Keefe (*T-Men*, *Raw Deal*) as Dan O'Hara, an FBI agent on the track of persons behind a highly dangerous security leak: the theft of high-level information from a Los Angeles-area atomic plant.

The breach is ultimately tied to a group of Communists operating with impunity in America. Lending a sense of international cooperation to the investigation is O'Hara's new and temporary partner, a savvy and jocular Scotland Yard operative named Philip "Scotty" Grayson, winningly played by Louis Hayward (an actor whose worldly and bemused persona greatly aided him during a long career that included *The Man in the Iron Mask* and *The Saint*). O'Keefe and Hayward are a convivial team, playing representatives of the same partnership that had helped licked the Nazis, and now taking on the Reds. Grayson jokingly refers to the collaboration as "reverse Lend-Lease."[1]

The hands-across-the-water plot setup that puts an FBI agent in the driver's seat could not have, on the face of it, disappointed the House Un-American Activities Committee (HUAC), which set Hollywood's teeth on edge with a highly publicized 1947

Walk a Crooked Mile (1948) supposes that Scotland Yard sends an investigator (Louis Hayward, top left) to Los Angeles, where he teams with an aggressive FBI agent (Dennis O'Keefe, bottom left) to stop thefts of secrets from an atomic facility. FBI chief J. Edgar Hoover had no disagreement with that, but did object strongly to some of the story's other elements.

investigation of communism in the film industry. In this, producer Edward Small acted cleverly, positioning the film when public awareness of HUAC was high, and approaching the subject with appropriate mock seriousness.

During this immediate postwar period, one of the signposts alerting movie viewers that what they were about to see was not only serious but based (at least in part) on true events was actor Reed Hadley, providing opening voice-over comments and occasional narrative tidbits as the tales unfolded. And then, a final wrap-up. Familiar as an on-screen presence in things as varied as *The Bank Dick*, *I Shot Jesse James*, and *Zorro's Fighting Legion*,[2] Hadley discovered this second career as a stentorian narrator on such pictures as *Guadalcanal Diary*, *The House on 92nd Street*, *Boomerang*, and *He Walked by Night*. His authoritative voice brings reality and gravitas to *Walk a Crooked Mile*, promising that the tale will show American and British law enforcement at their finest.

The picture is frequently classed as a film noir; surely, the chiaroscuro lighting of cinematographer George Robinson and stark compositions by director Gordon Douglas encourage this, and then there are Howard Bristol's textured, shadow-marinated sets. Nevertheless, the film is more closely related to police procedurals the likes of *The Naked City*, *The Undercover Man*, and (especially) the aforementioned *The House on 92nd Street*, an earlier anti–Communist melodrama that aspired to a documentary flavor and procedural realism. Like that movie, *Walk a Crooked Mile* highlights the arduous maneuvers that bring criminals to heel. This time, the murder of an FBI informer leads investigators to the atomic facility. O'Hara and Grayson painstakingly investigate, closely scrutinizing the small body of male scientists and a female assistant—the only ones with direct access to the compromised material.

As in most Cold War thrillers that cast dedicated Communists as the villains, *Walk a Crooked Mile* skimps on the Reds' characterization and motivations—a noticeable lack that leaves us searching for the political philosophy that drives their behavior. They exist as simple, superficial creatures, ruthless and slavishly devoted to their tasks, with little if any regard for their victims. The concept of "shared humanity" seems to have escaped them. One conspirator proudly boasts, "The individual counts for nothing." Take away the accents and telltale political nomenclature (everyone addresses everyone else as "comrade") and this could be any run-of-the mill group of gangsters from a standard American crime film. Violent and animalistic, they're the kind of misfit screen psychotics usually busy with armored-car robberies and bank heists. Although exposition given to Hayward and O'Keefe establishes the Communists' dream of global domination, the Reds rarely, if ever, discuss politics or the reasons behind their actions. The script sets them up as straw men, devoid of humanity, and intent on terror and destruction. It isn't difficult for filmmakers to knock down bad guys who are, in the end, mere sketches.

One scene in particular provides a telling demonstration of Communist techniques and character. O'Hara and Grayson have been caught and made prisoner in a seedy boarding house where the aging landlady, an obvious European immigrant (superbly played by the uncredited Tamara Shayne), sacrifices her life to save the agents. As the landlady dies, she offers a final message that is a renunciation of her killers: "Don't worry about me. I see plenty of fellows like these before I escaped to this country. This is not the first time I have been asked questions the same way.... My whole family was questioned to death. I am happy I can do such a small thing for my country, a country that has done so much for me." The inference is obvious. The Communists (never once actually called this in the film) are no different than the Nazis. They are constructed from the same single-minded allegiance to a totalitarian way of life, bereft of any regard for human principles. They will pursue any strategy, however abhorrent, to achieve their communal goals. No act is too monstrous, no lie too large, no inflicted pain too excessive. We are expected to agree that these monsters must be destroyed.

On the other hand, neither O'Hara nor Grayson is a well-developed character. The two don't waste time trying to explain their quarry. These investigators, though intelligent and dedicated, are essentially incurious, running their investigation by the book and showing little interest in what makes their adversaries tick. But in the familiar movie tradition of freedom-loving he-men, our heroes have jaunty senses of humor, and aim occasional quips at their foes. Grayson evaluates the artistic skill of one of the Reds (a skill used for espionage), and remarks, "Could make a pretty fair painter." O'Hara comes right back with, "If there wasn't so much *red* in his work."

One sees that O'Hara and Grayson don't reflect on their jobs, or on the battling political philosophies. They want to do nothing other than to shut down the Communists, lock 'em up, and throw away the key. Or, as O'Hara says to the main culprit after the crumb is finally unmasked, "Keep your seat until we can put you in a hotter one."

The closest the film comes to a political square-off is the final confrontation of the Boston-bred Red leader and O'Hara, Grayson, and the agents' superiors. While undergoing the third degree, the villain tries to wiggle out of his culpability, and demands the "protection of the democratic due process of law."

> GRAYSON: And the country you try to betray will see that you get it.
> O'HARA (quickly): We once had another American like you. His name was Benedict Arnold.

When O'Hara forces open the traitor's clenched fist, we see an equation, written in pen on the palm.

FBI director J. Edgar Hoover learned of the traitor angle when *Walk a Crooked Mile* was still in production. He did not disapprove of movies that suggested homegrown communism. By this time, the U.S. Army's Venona project had broken the KGB code that allowed exchange of messages between Moscow and Red agents in the States. The FBI and other investigators were already zeroing in on atom spies the likes of Julius Rosenberg and Klaus Fuchs. No, the plot point disliked by Hoover is the idea of a Red *inside an atomic facility*. A fictional character of that sort might suggest that the FBI had been remiss, and allowed the infiltration to happen. Another plot element, the murder of the fictional FBI informer, also rubbed Hoover the wrong way. His attempt to shut down the production was successfully resisted by producer Edward Small; thwarted, Hoover sent a letter to *The New York Times*, announcing that he was appalled by the notion of a Com-

Scotland Yard's Scotty Grayson (Louis Hayward) assists injured FBI agent Dan O'Hara (Dennis O'Keefe), minutes after Red spies have forced O'Hara's car off a cliff. This kind of red-meat action gave thriller audiences what they expected, but *Walk a Crooked Mile* also traffics in a thinly veiled anti-intellectualism—a self-defeating bias that took hold in America very shortly after World War II.

munist mole inside an American atomic facility. He added that the FBI did not assist or otherwise cooperate with Mr. Small.[3]

Walk a Crooked Mile gets a boost from the strong male leads and solid supporting players, most of whom, like Hayward and O'Keefe, are stuck in underdeveloped roles. Chief among the secondary cast are Onslow Stevens as Igor, the ringleader of the bunch; the hulking and goateed Raymond Burr—a decade before *Perry Mason*—as the enforcer, Krebs; Philip Van Zandt as Radchek, an early sacrifice for the cause; and Frank Ferguson as Carl, who fronts an all-night cleaner that holds classified material smuggled from the plant.

The brainy scientific community is led by continental Carl Esmond as the Viennese Dr. Ritter Von Stolb (whose name is a sideways reference to Operation Paperclip, the halfway secret U.S. program that brought German and German-Nazi scientists to the States after the war). Art Baker is the plant's chief, Dr. Townsend; Lowell Gilmore is Dr. Forrest; and Charles Evans plays Dr. Allen. Actress Louise Albritton is very effective in one of her best screen roles, as the faintly scheming Dr. Neva—although her motivation, love, seems unconvincing and inadequate.

Director Gordon Douglas rose from being a child actor to a gag writer, and then a director of Our Gang shorts, and finally to features. He was a highly capable journeyman active at RKO, Columbia, and Warner Bros. (His best-remembered assignment is the Warner science fiction classic, *Them!*) The narrative flow of *Walk a Crooked Mile* is measured and steady, with sharp, effective editing by James Newcom. Douglas apparently felt comfortable shooting on Southern California locations, and in San Francisco; the picture's pseudo-documentary feel is palpable.[4] The director's gift for realism and restraint is a big plus, though George Bruce's script forced him into a Hollywood cliché: an action-packed conclusion described by *Variety* as "highly contrived."

New York Times senior film reviewer Bosley Crowther finally got around to *Walk a Crooked Mile* about five weeks after the picture's release. Although his remarks are generally dismissive, he was struck (like Hoover) by the unnerving notion of Communist perfidy *inside* an American atomic facility. These "dark and disturbing reflections upon our own atomic men," he wrote, are "alarming." The timing of the film also bothered Crowther, given what he described as the "current agitation over the attempted 'purge' of scientists"—a veiled reference to America's resident atomic genius Robert Oppenheimer, whose public opposition to development of a hydrogen bomb alarmed many of his colleagues and enraged J. Edgar Hoover.

Film historian J. Hoberman has proposed that *Walk a Crooked Mile* may have been inspired by the experiences of American physicist Edward U. Condon, one of Oppenheimer's colleagues at the Manhattan Project. Postwar, Condon agitated for civilian control of atomic power, a point of view that encouraged HUAC to smear him with an insinuation of weakness on national security. Condon was able to crawl from beneath the shadow of slander by 1951, but he understood that everyday Americans were being led to a dangerous belief, one that is submerged but present in *Walk a Crooked Mile*: anti-intellectualism isn't nice, but maybe it's not a bad idea.

That is a revolting suggestion. Although *Walk a Crooked Mile* avoids the loudly hysterical tone that mars many anti–Communist films of the Cold War era, the picture nevertheless adheres to the propaganda template of the time, with its stunted interest in the broader and more complex issues surrounding global conflict, and in its skeletal depictions of patriots and enemies alike.

Filmography

Walk a Crooked Mile—Edward Small Productions/Columbia; Released September 2, 1948; Black and white; 91 min.

   Credits: Producers: Edward Small, Grant Whytock; Director: Gordon Douglas; Screenplay: George Bruce; Director of photography: George Robinson; Editor: James E. Newcom; Music: Paul Sawtell; Art director: Rudolph Sternad

   Cast: Louis Hayward: Philip "Scotty" Grayson; Dennis O'Keefe: Daniel F. O'Hara; Louise Allbritton: Dr. Toni Neva; Carl Esmond: Dr. Ritter von Stolb; Onslow Stevens: Igor Braun; Raymond Burr: Krebs; Charles Evans: Romer Allen; Art Baker: Dr. Frederick Townsend; Philip Van Zandt: Radchek

Notes

   1. In an amusing and calculatedly provocative 2010 piece done for her blog, mystery novelist and film noir enthusiast Christa Faust describes the Grayson and O'Hara relationship as a "seething cauldron of red hot man love." Faust seized on the pair's use of twin beds, a sweaty undershirt sequence with Grayson, and O'Hara's post-climax insistence that Grayson stay with him rather than return to Britain.
   2. Not long after his voice-over duties for *Walk a Crooked Mile*, Hadley did straight acting as star of the popular TV crime shows *Mr. District Attorney* and *Racket Squad*.
   3. Hoover's substantial power forced Small to abandon the film's shooting title, *FBI vs. Scotland Yard*.
   4. Although Louise Allbritton had been in pictures since 1942, *Walk a Crooked Mile* was her first experience with location shooting.

Works Cited

Books

Hoberman, J. *An Army of Phantoms: American Movies and the Making of the Cold War*. New York: The New Press, 2013.
Lingeman, Richard. *The Noir Forties: The American People from Victory to Cold War*. New York: Nation Books, 2012.
McNeil, Alex. *Total Television*. New York: Viking Penguin, 1984.

Newspapers

Crowther, Bosley. Review of *Walk a Crooked Mile*. *The New York Times*. October 13, 1948.
"Movie Memoranda." *The Bronxville Review-Press*. August 19, 1948.
"Walk a Crooked Mile." *Variety*. December 31, 1947.

Web

christafaust.com (posted April 12, 2010)

DVD

Columbia Pictures Film Noir Classics IV (*Walk a Crooked Mile*). Sony/TCM (Turner Classic Movies). 2014.

Cvetic Takes One for the Team
I Was a Communist for the F.B.I.

BRUCE DETTMAN

J. Edgar Hoover, the FBI's highly controversial director who reigned supreme for over thirty-five years, needed a substantially long time to get what he wanted out of Hollywood concerning portrayals of his beloved agents. Hoover ran a tight—some have suggested highly paranoid—ship, and foremost within this tightness was image, one meticulously crafted and then sold to the American public the way Madison Avenue sold new Chryslers, nylon stockings, and filter-tipped cigarettes. The slightest deviation on the part of his subordinates from the clean-cut, mature, and professional agent Hoover carefully designed and cultivated was cause for demotion or even dismissal. Naturally enough, he wished to promote this same image with positive portrayals of Bureau agents on cinema screens.

But early depictions of FBI agents in film showed colorless background figures, tight-lipped and gray-flannel drab, who occasionally showed up to aid the local police or, particularly at Warner Bros., throwing their weight around as streetwise, rule-bending James Cagney types. Neither of those conceptions corresponded to the image Hoover wished to promote. Mr. Hoover got a break with World War II: America's battle against the Axis provided a great centerpiece for the Bureau's crusade not just against domestic crime but at foreign enemies sworn to disrupt and even destroy the American way of life. Semi-documentary efforts, such as *The Street with No Name* and *House on 92nd Street*, both starring Lloyd Nolan as a no-nonsense, totally professional FBI agent, were much closer to what the Director had in mind—but still not *exactly* right.

Nonetheless, Hoover got lucky because one of his main duties was to legitimize increased Congressional funding for the Bureau—a task that might have been difficult given that World War II had been won and the threat of Nazi sabotage eliminated. But the postwar escalating danger—real and imagined—of Communist influence came along to provide Hoover with a new and possibly even more exploitable enemy. His FBI, he insisted, would safeguard the country; left unspoken was Hoover's plan to use the threat to solidify his position as the nation's top crime watchdog. Given the climate of the times and the paranoia that would grow out of concerns of an aggressive Communist attempt to subvert the American system, Hoover could not have asked for a better development. During the early days of his career in the Justice Department, J. Edgar cut his teeth on compiling lists of known or suspected radicals, and now, decades later, his Bureau would fight the Red Menace—while largely steering clear of the issue of homegrown organized crime, a more difficult and less manageable target.

* * *

As Hoover prepared to press the Bureau's public relations advantage, loudly outspoken anti–Red politicians labored to ferret out supposed Communists in Hollywood. The investigations of the House Un-American Activities Committee (HUAC) dated to 1947; partly to play along with the national mood, and partly to get HUAC off its back, the picture industry began to not only distance itself from claims of Red influence, and to turn its back on suspected Hollywood Reds, but to produce films that lambasted—usually with the subtlety of a hydrogen bomb—the so-called "international Communist conspiracy." During the early and mid–1950s large studios and independent companies rushed out politicized melodramas the likes of *Woman on Pier 13*, *My Son John*, *The Whip Hand*, *Big Jim McLain*, *Man on a Tightrope* and *Trial*.

While the majority of these efforts were fictions offering exaggerated depictions of Communist activity, a few offered supposedly factual accounts of Communist perfidy. One of the most notable of these was the sensationally titled *I Was a Communist for the F.B.I.*, a 1951 Warner Bros. production that tells the fact-based story of Matt Cvetic, a steelworker and clandestine agent for the Bureau assigned to expose American Communist Party activity in Pittsburgh.

As scripted, Cvetic's Communist affiliation upsets his family, whereas his work as an undercover agent is known only to the Bureau and a local priest. Cvetic's Party membership brings hatred and vilification from just about everyone in his orbit, including his apartment-building neighbor, who stops him from showing his boy how to use a bat and ball: "Stay away from my kid. Baseball is an American game!" Cvetic's brothers are hostile to him, particularly Joe (Paul Picerni), who denounces Cvetic as a "slimy Red." Naturally enough, all of this is painfully confusing for Cvetic's young son (Ron Hagerthy).

Cvetic struggles to handle his Bureau assignment and the stress it is causing him. The Bureau learns that the local Communist cell has been ordered to gain a foothold in Pittsburgh's labor community by creating disharmony and social unrest among the steel workers. "Move Pittsburgh an inch," one operative says, "and we can move this country a mile." The local Communists put particular effort into divide-and-conquer scenario among Pittsburgh's minority population. After riling up a mainly black audience at a union hall meeting, a cynical Red remarks, "Those niggers ate it up."

Matt Cvetic finally reaches his breaking point. He has been involved in this undercover work for nine long years. His whole family despises him, and his boy is rebelling, getting into trouble at school and wishing to disown his father. "Don't ever come near me again!" he spits. Cvetic's mother passes away and at the funeral his brother tries to goad him into a physical confrontation: "Put up your hands, you dirty Red!"

The priest (Roy Roberts) urges Matt to reveal his true motives but Cvetic refuses. Instead, he goes to his superiors at the FBI, explaining that he can't go on much longer. "You gotta wipe this red smear off of me!" he cries, as a pair of agents listen stoically and let him vent. Cvetic apologizes later for his momentary weakness and returns to the job. To this end he must continue his ruse, working as a manager at a steel plant, a place the narrative displays as a breeding ground for local Party members. An additional wrinkle is introduced in the form of Cvetic's chancy relationship with a teacher named Eve Merrick (Dorothy Hart), who has joined the Party out of an earlier naïve belief in the cause.

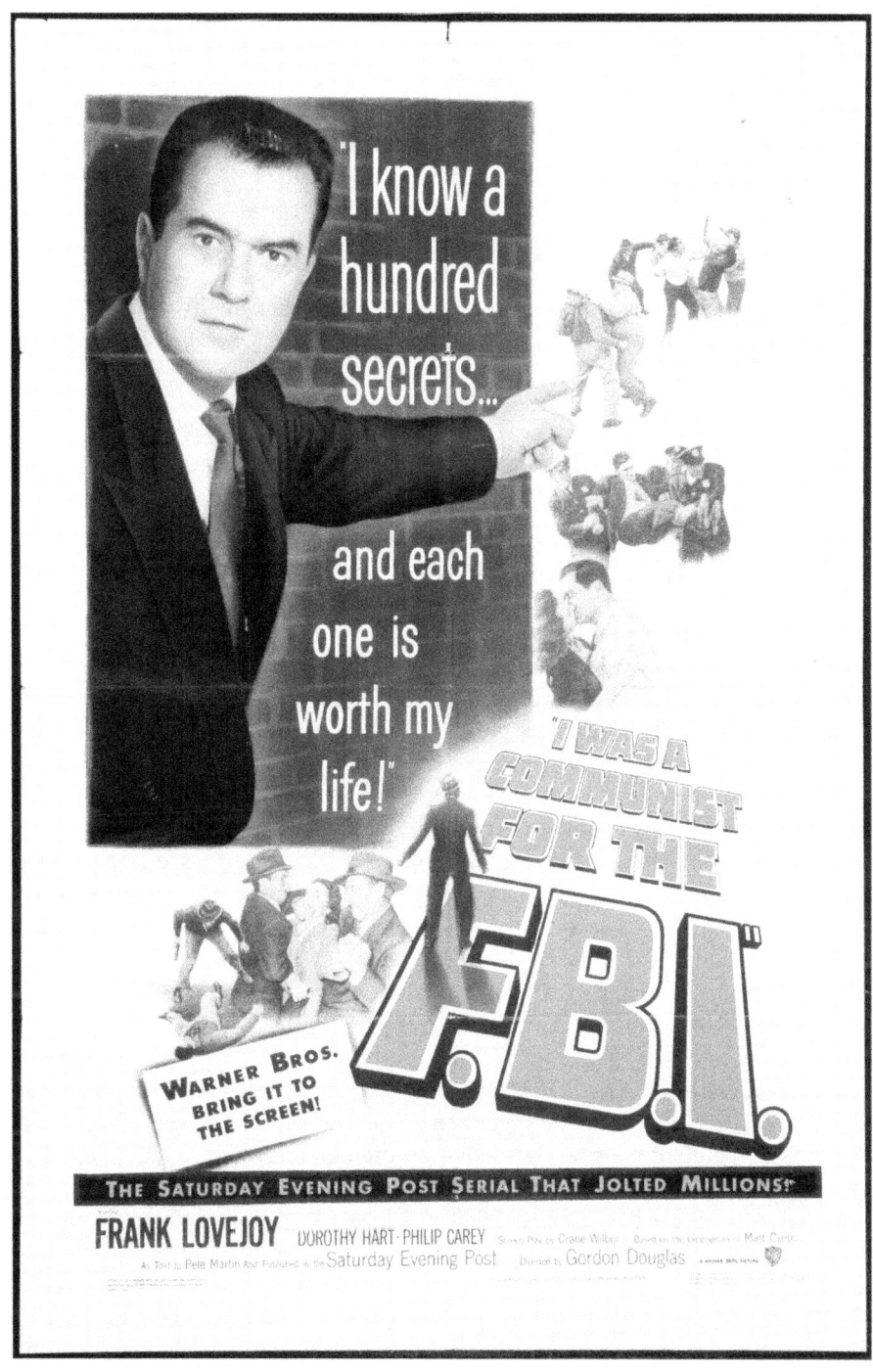

Undercover American "Communist" Matt Cvetic faded into obscurity by the mid–1950s, but when Warner Bros. released *I Was a Communist for the F.B.I.* in 1951, this real-life "mole" was a national celebrity. The movie polishes away Cvetic's rough edges, casting likeable actor Frank Lovejoy in the title role, and delineating Cvetic as a committed family man tormented by his inability to tell his disillusioned loved ones the truth of what he's doing.

She is assigned to check up on Cvetic, and seduce him, if necessary. "I came here because I thought you were lonely," she coos after following him to his apartment. "I'm lonely too."

Following protracted intrigue and contrived fistfights and improbable gun battles with several Party members, Cvetic is finally given the green light by the FBI to face those he has long wished to put away. He testifies, reunites with his son ("When you hated me I loved you for it," he tells the boy), and reveals to his family and friends his nine-year ordeal posing as a member of the Communist Party. "Now I can crawl out of my rat hole and live like a man."

Even naïve Eve Merrick sees the light. "Communism," she finally realizes, "is a mockery of freedom." The film ends with the strains of "Glory! Glory! Hallelujah!" and a close-up of a bust of Abraham Lincoln.

* * *

Because of the film's title there is no guesswork about the protagonist's role in this tale. We know from the get-go that Matt Cvetic is not a Communist sympathizer, that he is instead a clever plant working for the Bureau, and is under unbearable pressure. Early in the story, when Cvetic attends a birthday party for his aging mother, his brothers make no attempt to hide their disdain. Crane Wilbur's screenplay wastes no time before defiling and degrading Cvetic, making clear that nothing in the known universe is wickeder or more perverse than being a Communist save one thing: being an American who betrays his country and willingly becomes a Red. In this movie's universe, communism isn't an ideology, it's a disease.

Political issues aside, the plot plays out very much like a film noir. Cvetic, who often narrates the action in voice-over, is a man caught in the middle, squeezed from all sides with no one to turn to, yet unable to extricate himself. He can neither openly betray the Communists nor defy the FBI. Worse, he cannot betray himself. He must struggle to hold on to his own ethical code and principles, despite the endless recriminations from everyone in his world. That sort of rock-and-a-hard-place personal pressure defines many noir thrillers.

The noir factor is heightened by the depiction of the cadre of Communists, who seem like characters from a hardboiled detective story rather than sophisticated political players. Other than Eisler (Konstantin Shayne), the token big brain of the bunch, Matt Cvetic's playmates are thugs and pinheads. Their casual banter is glib and flip, marinated with American slang and macho braggadocio. "We're always in the red," they joke when discussing their deficient finances. None of their dialogue would be out of place at a racetrack, a gambling casino, or a hot pickup bar. When Blandon (James Millican), Cvetic's main contact, introduces Eve to other Party members, he addresses the men with, "How do you like this for a dish of cream?"

It's hard to imagine any of these hooligans having the brains or finesse to take over America; even their immediate target, Pittsburgh, seems beyond their grasp. None of them demonstrates philosophical or political savvy, only a gangster-like craving for power and the good life. Like teenage delinquents, they rejoice at their own nastiness, as when they amuse themselves by bringing "red" roses to the funeral of Cvetic's mother. In another scene, when Cvetic comments on the catered goodies the gathered Party members are devouring, he is reminded sardonically that "this is the way we're all going to live once we take the country over." Cvetic asks if America's workers are to enjoy the spoils after capitalism has been vanquished. Unfortunately, no: "The workers will still be the workers." Moreover, the Commies aren't brothers in arms but shallow bottom feeders not really interested in any amalgamation of efforts or solidarity within their own despicable ranks. Cvetic learns quickly that there isn't an ounce of humanity in any of these vermin, only hypocrisy and a dangerous and insatiable lust for power that he must help check and destroy.

* * *

The real Matt Cvetic was not quite the ethically pristine Cold War warrior seen in the film. He was a controversial figure, one whose career, motivation, and history remain blurred and uncertain. While he continues to have his supporters and champions, his image became tarnished even in his own lifetime. What is known is that in 1943, at the request of federal agents, Cvetic joined a Pittsburgh branch of the Communist Party, serving on numerous occasions as a plant, supposedly earning the descriptor "Pennsylvania's most significant mole." Because of what has been described as his "erratic behavior" he was later relieved of his duties by the FBI, but subsequently turned up to give testimony before HUAC. Journalists noticed him there and made him the subject of a series of articles that appeared in *The Saturday Evening Post*, co-written by celebrity profiler Pete Martin. Although the portrait and activities of Cvetic were exaggerated and even glamorized, Warner Bros, seeing a perfect vehicle to exploit the politics and tone of the time, went ahead with a film version. Cvetic, later discredited by the courts and labeled an "unreliable witness," ended up as a spokesperson for America's radical right. Just fifty-three years old, he died of natural causes in 1962.

* * *

Popular character star Frank Lovejoy won the role of Cvetic. Lovejoy had come to the screen via stage and radio work, carving out a very visible career playing solid, familiarly American characters—fellows not of great intellect or talent, but bedrock in their convictions and ethics. (There were a few exceptions, films like *Try and Get Me!*, in which he played a kidnapper and killer assisting criminal Lloyd Bridges, but even in this instance Lovejoy lent an Everyman quality to the vulnerable, down-on-his-luck workingman who is cajoled into helping commit the crime.)

Lovejoy excelled in *Home of the Brave* (1949), *In a Lonely Place* (1950), *Retreat Hell!* and Ida Lupino's *The Hitch-Hiker* (both 1953; in the last, Lovejoy is an everyday kind of guy who is terrorized by a psychotic killer). He would also play in two additional Communist-related films, *Shack Out on 101* (1955) *and Three Brave Men* (1957), the latter about a patriot (Ernest Borgnine) wrongly persecuted for bogus Communist affiliation.

Nearly all of Lovejoy's movie work dates to the 1950s. With his low-key, unassuming manner and unremarkable good looks, the actor came to embody a guy next door figure who could be depended upon to be there in a pinch. As Cvetic, Lovejoy is what one would expect an anti–Red crusader to be in a picture of this era: strong and stoic, invincible in his beliefs, and resolute in his goals despite the few shaky moments when he nearly breaks. The real Cvetic must have been extremely pleased with this flattering portrayal.

Costarring as Eve is Dorothy Hart, a former model and onetime Columbia contract player with a sophisticated, patrician beauty. She did feature-film work from 1947 to 1952, once playing Jane to Lex Barker's Tarzan and finding good if unremarkable roles in *The*

As filmed, Cvetic's life is a constant roil of tension caused by his faked support of the "hell brew of hate" created by Pittsburgh's Communist contingent. After the Communists commit murder and turn naively receptive teachers and "Negroes" into Red dupes, Cvetic (Frank Lovejoy, seated) has a critical meeting with his ruthless "comrades" (from left): Blandon (James Millican), Harmon (Eddie Norris), and Mansanovitch (David McMahon).

Naked City, Larceny, and *The Countess of Monte Cristo*. After three years of television work, Hart abandoned Hollywood (which she had come to loathe) and moved to New York, where she worked for the United Nations on behalf of children. She brings to her role of the dissatisfied Party member elegance and quiet intelligence.

Character player James Millican, cast here as the irredeemable racist who happily exploits black aspirations, had craggy good looks (highlighted by narrow eyes beneath a heavy brow), a sturdy physique, and sharp, resonant voice, all of which put him into many westerns and actioners. He had good roles in *Command Decision, High Noon, Fourteen Hours, Winchester'73* and *Warpath* (as General Custer). As the Communist Blandon he is unctuous, cynical, and menacing—as much a common hoodlum as a political operative. The FBI agents that manage Cvetic, Crowley (Richard Webb) and Mason (Phil Carey), bring the sort of humorless, resolute vigilance audiences of the day would expect. Although *I Was a Communist for the F.B.I.* had no official link to the Bureau, J. Edgar would probably have approved of these focused agents, not least because they give Cvetic moral guidance when he falters.

Others in the cast are better than competent, but didn't find much to work with in the script. They function mainly as types: sympathetic or angry; passionate or robotic. The actors are given no emotional or intellectual framework that might allow them to flesh out and humanize their characters. This is not the fault of director Gordon Douglas, a seasoned professional who brought proficiency to a wide variety of projects, including the much-lauded science fiction thriller *Them!*, the notable Cagney gangster thriller *Kiss Tomorrow Goodbye*, and later, the spy parody *In Like Flint* and a solid Sinatra vehicle, *The Detective*. No, the picture's shortcomings must be laid at Crane Wilbur's lively but single-note script, which, in its eagerness to paint Communist infiltration with a broad brush, allows its secondary characters little life.

Warner executives took no risks, crafting a product to reflect the days' headlines while adhering to the tried-and-true ingredients of more conventional crime thrillers. Cinematographer Edwin Depar seemed as well keyed-in to Lovejoy's strengths as Douglas; deep, low-key lighting emphasizes Cvetic's dreary isolation and seedy existence. The imagery makes clear that Cvetic functions in a nocturnal cloak-and-dagger world of small, drab rooms, shadow-marinated streets, and dark corners, all of which define the restricted nature of Cvetic's little universe. Even the opening credits, when Cvetic walks alone through an ominous archway, bold block letters on the screen behind him, suggest the character's claustrophobic and existential isolation.

* * *

Looking backwards through the convenient telescope of time, *I Was a Communist for the F.B.I.* appears two generations later as a garish, nearly hysterical exercise in political propaganda. Its slick and polished big-studio look, capable and often effective direction, and earnest performances by Lovejoy, Hart and others give it a peculiar legitimacy of purpose that it certainly doesn't deserve. Almost cartoonish in its simplicity, the film does have *this* lasting value: it reminds modern-day audiences of film's power to distort and persuade. Dangerously one-sided points of view do nothing to explicate complex issues, particularly when a film's narrative is freighted with phony dramatics and heroics.

Oddly enough, *I Was a Communist for the F.B.I.* (promoted with lurid poster art dominated by "I had to sell out my own girl—so would you" and "I learned every dirty rule in their book and had to use them") earned an Academy Award nomination for producer Bryan Foy in, of all things, the best documentary category! (The award went to *Kon-Tiki*.)

Syndicator Frederick Ziv purchased the title and expanded on the premise for a seventy-eight-episode *I Was a Communist for the F.B.I.* radio series that ran during 1952–54. With a big assist from screen star Dana Andrews, cast as Cvetic, the radio iteration created plenty of tension in a somewhat more subdued and less sensational approach to the central situation.

FILMOGRAPHY

I Was a Communist for the F.B.I.—Warner Bros.; Released May 5, 1951; Black and white; 83 min.

 Credits: Producer: Bryan Foy; Director: Gordon Douglas; Screenplay: Crane Wilbur, b/o the article "I Posed as a Communist for the F.B.I." by Matt Cvetic and Pete Martin; Director of photography: Edwin DuPar; Editor: Folmar Blangsted; Music: William Lava, Max Steiner (stock); Art director: Leo K. Kuter

Cast: Frank Lovejoy: Matt Cvetic; Dolores Hart: Eve Merrick; Philip Carey: Mason; James Millican: Jim Blandon; Richard Webb: Ken Crowley; Konstantin Shayne: Gerhardt Eisler

WORKS CITED
Periodicals
Cvetic, Matt, and Pete Martin. "I Posed as a Communist for the FBI." *The Saturday Evening Post.* July 15, 22, and 29, 1950.

DVD
I Was a Communist for the F.B.I. Warner Archive Collection. 2009.

American Virtue and *Big Jim McLain*

GAYE WINSTON LARDNER

A battle rages on this American movie screen, and it's an elemental one. Prostrate beneath the clouded night sky, a tropical beach is swept by hurricane-force winds, and the heavens are split by titanic bolts of lightning. Palm trees bow and the sea roils. This is the main-title sequence of *Big Jim McLain*, a 1952 John Wayne vehicle produced by Wayne and Robert Fellows for their Wayne-Fellows Productions.[1] As the storm continues, a clever optical effect sweeps successive credits from the screen, as if they were shreds of paper. Lightning flashes again and again, and—wait, can you hear it?—the title theme is interrupted by snatches of melody from "Yankee Doodle Dandy," "Columbia, the Gem of the Ocean," "Dixie," and other 18th- and 19th-century patriotic favorites. Voice-over narration invokes Benét's Daniel Webster, a fictionalized version of the 19th-century secretary of state. Benét's statesman threatens to leave his grave if "the state of the union" is not to his liking. *Big Jim McLain* concerns itself not just with American Communist activity of present-day 1952, but with the ideals of an imagined America that no longer exists.

Soft Island Breezes and HUAC

Following the main titles, representative members of the House Un-American Activities Committee (HUAC) are introduced. Voice-over narrator Harry Morgan declares, "We owe these, our elected representatives, a great debt." Enter a pair of HUAC's rugged investigators, Jim McLain (John Wayne) and Mal Baxter (James Arness). These two will spend the next hour and a half investigating Communist subversion in the Hawaiian Islands. Action, patriotism, laughs, good-looking dames, and even death await. Hawaii, this film wants us to know, is in deep trouble.

American fears of Communist skullduggery in the Territory of Hawaii surfaced very shortly after World War II, and were given voice in a 1947 speech by the opportunistic island governor, Ingram Stainback. The governor warned of a Red scheme to infiltrate and take over Hawaiian labor, and promised to fire any Territorial employees suspected of being Communists or actively sympathetic to Communist ends. The House Un-American Activities Committee, already engaged in its first investigation of Communist infiltration of Hollywood and the movie industry, turned its attention to Hawaii.

Some of the locals were already on the case: during a 1949 dock strike by Hawaiian members of the International Longshore and Warehouse Union (ILWU), some three hundred counter-protesters—mostly Caucasian women armed with brooms—showed up to "sweep" communism out of island labor.

The islands' so-called Big Five sugar cane companies, already in control of Hawaii's banks, exploited the local government's aggressively anti–Red stance, as well as citizens' growing fear, to get a leg up on island labor, the ILWU in particular. In gossip, in speculation, and in print, local labor leaders, as well as teachers and other intrinsically untrustworthy types, were labeled Communists. In 1950, some seventy persons, including Honolulu's ILWU leader, Jack Kanawo, were subpoenaed by HUAC investigators. Kanawo and thirty-eight others refused to testify, earning the sobriquet the Reluctant 39. But growing pressure from HUAC, plus Hawaiian newspapers' expressed certitude about the guilt of Kanawo and the others, encouraged Kanawo to change his mind. In June 1951 testimony given in Washington, Kanawo gave HUAC an earful, naming as many members of the Communist Party in Hawaii as he could recall, but identifying himself and ILWU regional director Jack Hall as the "only" Communists in the union.

Well, few politicians or citizens were prepared to believe *that*.

Ichiro Izuka, a reformed Communist and onetime ILWU vice president, published *The Truth about Communism in Hawaii*, a pamphlet that identified Jack Hall as a busy disseminator of Communist ideas and literature. Not much of a leap was required for the frightened, the uninformed, and the opportunistic to label all of the ILWU—as well as other Hawaiian labor organizations—as tainted by communism, or hopelessly subsumed by it.

During coordinated raids carried out across Hawaii in August 1951, federal agents arrested seven people—a group including a pair of newspapermen, a mechanic, labor officials, and the head of the Communist Party USA in the islands—and charged them with violations of the Smith Act: plotting to overthrow and destroy the government of the United States. The so-called Hawaii Seven had been under surveillance since 1945, and had conducted their activities in plain sight. In one of numerous things that *Big Jim McLain* gets right, the seven were not the most critically important Communists in Hawaii, but patsies, set up by their own comrades to take the fall so that more clandestine operatives could continue to work across the Hawaiian Islands.

HUAC and the Hawaii Seven were very much in the news when *Big Jim McLain* went into production during the spring of 1950. The timeliness of the subject was proved justified when the Seven came to trial in November 1952, barely eight weeks after the film's release. A dozen witnesses—seven "reformed," former Communists among them—helped the government build its case. The trial continued until the summer of 1953. The jury returned guilty verdicts; Judge Jon Wiig sentenced each of the six male defendants to five years in prison, plus a $5,000 fine. The only female defendant received a three-year prison term and a $2,000 fine. *Time* magazine, then a bellwether of conservative thought, celebrated the trial's end with this headline: "Communists: Aloha."

Vigorous legal appeals kept the seven from prison for more than five years. And then, in January 1958, the Ninth Circuit Court of Appeals reversed the convictions levied in 1953.

Of course, *Big Jim McLain* had long left America's theaters by the time all the legal maneuvers had played out, but the picture's initial timeliness helped propel it to a $2.6 million first-run gross (equivalent to more than $23 million in 2017 dollars), and a net

Because John Wayne takes the title role in *Big Jim McLain* (1952), the movie has been discussed more regularly than might otherwise be the case; it's also been erroneously tarred as a complete disaster. Although the picture positions itself firmly on the political right, its portrayal of Communist subversion in Hawaii is more accurate than many modern viewers realize. For Italian release, a specially dubbed soundtrack established that McLain is chasing after pot growers instead of Communists—hence the title on this poster.

profit (according to Wayne biographer Scott Eyman) of $261,641. Politics, Duke Wayne's box-office appeal, picturesque location filming, and two-fisted action struck a chord with moviegoers.

General nervousness about Hawaiian communism, which propelled some people into the theaters, had largely dissipated by August 1959, when Hawaii became the 50th state.

He Knows How to Smile

John Wayne and James Arness (at 6'7", three inches taller than Wayne) essentially play a single character: the stalwart American male motivated by love of country. Arness's Mal Baxter is the hot-blooded, impulsive aspect of this admirable male. Younger than McLain, Baxter bristles with impatience, projecting lively body language and an eagerness to mix it up with Reds. Although not incautious, Baxter becomes more absorbed in his mission than is wise, and plays fast and loose with his own safety.

Wayne's Jim McLain is considerably more temperate than Baxter, and to the credit of the Duke and director Edward Ludwig, McLain is a mildly startling departure from what had come to be accepted as the Wayne persona. The actor had played a recent succession of clench-jawed military men during and shortly after World War II (*Flying Tigers*, *The Fighting Seabees*, *Back to Bataan*, *Sands of Iwo Jima*, *Flying Leathernecks*, and others); an obsessive tyrant in the cattle-drive cum family drama *Red River*; an aging, floundering cavalry officer in *She Wore a Yellow Ribbon*; and a hurtfully stern father and husband in *Rio Grande*. And yet Wayne had also been recently seen as a kindhearted cattle rustler in *3 Godfathers*, and as an unexpectedly pacifistic gunman in *Angel and the Badman*. In this regard, the joie de vivre of the Jim McLain character isn't a complete about-face.

Wayne's tonal shift, then, is most remarkable not because of the actor's recent professional history, but because *Big Jim McLain* concerns itself with Communist infiltration and subversion, a subject almost invariably treated by Hollywood with grim—and frequently tiresome—rectitude. The small beauty of *Big Jim McLain* is that, although the Communist menace is made to seem very real (and, as we shall see, is even exaggerated), Wayne, Ludwig, and a trio of scriptwriters found the confidence needed to allow McLain a sweet, honestly developed romance, much of which plays out against picturesque Hawaiian locations that fascinated audiences in 1952. Further, McLain reveals an easy camaraderie with Mal Baxter (rather like a big brother who tries to look out for a younger one), and develops a friendly relationship with a local navy officer. Big Jim also takes obvious pleasure in his recurring, lightly sexualized banter with a secondary female character. (More about this below).

Most appealing of all is that, although McLain takes his assignment seriously, he doesn't take himself too seriously at all. When a burly punk threatens violence, McLain quietly demurs, saying that a fight isn't what he needs right now. But when the punk gets tough a second time, grabbing McLain's lapels and threatening to knock his ears off—insulting a lady in the bargain—McLain uncorks a left hook that sends the delinquent into a lengthy, backwards stagger step that pitches him right over a porch railing. The annoyance out of the way, McLain smooths his jacket and returns to what he was doing before the interruption.[2]

The Spectrum of Womanhood

And then there are Big Jim's interactions with the ladies. Two women figure prominently in the film, and they, too, are exemplars of American "types." McLain's lover is a sweetly pretty, faintly melancholy war widow named Nancy (Nancy Olson). Honest with herself and Jim about her feelings for him, and serene in her relative loneliness, Nancy has an emotionally cool appeal that is at once sexy and unthreatening. Although she looks smashing in short-shorts and in a scoop-neck day dress, she's mainly a philosophical creature, her thoughts turning to such proper "woman" things as the sadly ephemeral nature of relationships, and the merits of love and loyalty.[3]

A quite different woman is Madge (Veda Ann Borg), the sexy, agreeably hard-bitten Honolulu boardinghouse owner who eventually shares some useful clues with McLain.

Assigned by HUAC to root out Communists in Hawaii, investigator Jim McLain (John Wayne) finds an ally in Madge (Veda Ann Borg), a boardinghouse owner who has had some incidental contact with Reds. Confident, sexy, and tough, Madge is every bit an appealing American "type" as the Duke himself.

162   Part 3: Dupes, Victims and Crusaders

When Madge meets the investigator for the first time, she gives him a brazen up-and-down look and flirtatiously asks him his height. When he replies six-four ("That's a lotta man," she says), Madge dubs him "76," referring not just to McLain's size but—in a nod to our patriotic sensibilities—the Spirt of '76. (Remember those snatches of patriotic tunes beneath the main title?)

Madge is a tall, fortyish blonde, and clearly a woman who knows how to do what it is that men appreciate women doing. "Take it easy," she blithely tells McLain when he tries to rush her through dinner. "Relax. You always get the job done better if you take it real slow and easy." And later: "Oh, 76, what I think about you has to be said in the dark"—one of the most suggestive and best-delivered movie lines of the decade.

In a nice touch, Madge is drawn as neither a villainess nor an object of ridicule. To the contrary, she epitomizes that imagined American characteristic of being wholly comfortable in one's own skin—rather like McLain, come to think of it. She's not educated, which is a plus not simply because she's a woman but because her limitations suggest purity of motive. She's obviously proud of her come-hither features and sterling legs and figure, which she displays, during an amusing nightclub sequence, in a form-fitting evening dress that fits her form well indeed. She's randy and funny, and just saucy enough to keep McLain a little off-balance. Although Madge would not be comfortable in any of fantasy America's cherished small towns, she negotiates the urban current without effort, assisting McLain and, more importantly, providing a natural corrective to urban America's intellectuals and sophisticates, who think too much and are too often on the wrong side of the philosophical divide. Madge is the movie's celebration of America's coarse and kinder virtues, an authentic woman with real backbone. And like Nancy, Madge is a valued part of the American tapestry.[4]

Disease

The young punk described above is eventually revealed as part of the Honolulu Communist cell that Jim and Mal have arrived to root out and destroy. As played by blond, pug-nosed Hal Baylor, the young guy is a lout—but if you knew him, he'd probably be okay to have a beer with. And in that, the punk references all the "everyday" people with whom we work and socialize … and who are Communists.

The cell is headed by a tall, urbane gentleman named Sturak (Alan Napier). Impeccably dressed and holding court in an expensive *moderne* house lined with books, Sturak is the cold-blooded intellectual sort much disliked across large swaths of America sixty-plus years ago. The group also includes a shifty medical doctor named Gelster (Gayne Whitman), who becomes understandably peevish after being led to understand that Sturak is going to throw him under the bus in order to protect the rest of the cell. Well, good riddance to another pretentious fop, yes?[5]

The film's apparent anti-intellectualism extends beyond the cell: during a visit to a man who claims outsider knowledge of the conspiracy, Jim and Nancy are greeted (in another book-lined residence) by a pompously well-spoken, vaguely effeminate lunatic (Hans Conried) who has nothing to say other than that he is the inventor not just of "my own jet plane" but of air itself.[6]

These swipes at the educated class are obvious and calculated. But on the other hand, *Nancy's* residence is full of books, too, and even Jim and Mal's hotel room has a well-filled bookcase. Perhaps *Big Jim McLain* doesn't dislike erudition at all. Maybe the movie simply has a problem with erudition turned to bad purpose.

A few in the cell are Hawaiians, and some of those are of Japanese descent. A mere seven years after the end of World War II, "Japanese" remained a trigger for many American Caucasians, so the movie hardly has to work at all to establish a link between past perfidy and a dangerous new variety. Like the visible books, it's a lazy narrative device, yes, but also the best evidence of the movie's essential disinterest in Hawaiians as people.

Other than Communists, native Hawaiians that advance the plot are police and other minor functionaries on board with McLain's investigation, and completely without resentment about his presence or this latest of Washington's intrusions into Hawaiian affairs. All island activity that really matters, whether treasonous or righteous, is conducted by Caucasians, most of whom are not even on the islands; the natives are mere catspaws. Although far from a major current of the film, the situation nevertheless resonates subliminally, encouraging us to believe that the native islanders have no real ability (or business) to conduct their own affairs, and that protection and competence come only from white men.

The strangest—and most thoroughly "Hawaiian"—interlude of *Big Jim McLain* takes our hero to Molokai's leper colony, established in 1866 to hold native sufferers of viral leprosy, and their medical overseers. McLain has a few questions for a gentle Japanese-American nurse with peripheral knowledge of the Reds, and soberly listens to the woman's explanation of leprosy's highly communicable nature: mere association with lepers can infect you (a fallacy, by the way). The presumed "bug" that brings the ailment is a clear comment on the blight that is communism. Once allowed to establish itself in the islands (or anywhere), communism will infect the foolish, the ignorant, and the innately traitorous.

Big Jim McLain takes knocks for its loudly proclaimed endorsement of HUAC—and in retrospect it's impossible to deny that the film's fawning treatment of the committee's bullies is squirm-inducing. But if the Communist Party USA ultimately failed to overthrow the American system, it nevertheless caused real damage, providing the Soviets with information they were not entitled to have, and compromising America's security. One can argue, as well, that the Party's very existence brought out the worst in many Americans, lowered the level of American political investigation and discourse, and led to the persecution of many innocents.

Although an intelligent man skilled at reading people, Duke Wayne had no patience with ambiguity. As far as he was concerned, moral relativists and other weaklings deserved nothing but scorn. Wayne had not formally served during World War II (though he did make a good-faith but unsuccessful application to the OSS), and felt the embarrassment of that. Motivated by an honest love of country, he fought for America as he was best able—with his celebrity, and with ideas expressed in his movies.

The Duke's purity of motive aside, *Big Jim McLain* is awash in exaggeration. Daniel Inouye (a native Hawaiian of Japanese-American origins), Medal of Honor recipient for heroism in World War II Italy, and Hawaii's long-serving Democratic senator, witnessed the postwar upset caused by the islands' labor strife and other Communist agitation. In his 1967 autobiography, Inouye wrote, "No one with any sense of political reality denied that there were probably some Communists in the ILWU." In that, then, *Big Jim McLain* is accurate. But Inouye also observed the absurd leaps of logic made by some of Hawaii's more fervent anti–Red crusaders: "There were those who felt that the Democratic Party, by logical extension, was also controlled by Communists." By declining to get into that part of the controversy (that is, by not mentioning the Democratic Party at all), *Big Jim McLain* showed Democrats a certain respect, while concomitantly failing to explore the foolish meanness that spurred a segment of the Red haters. And with that omission, the film distorted history.

Some cinema historians and buffs excoriate *Big Jim McLain* for being boring, inane, wholly inaccurate, fascistic, and emblematic of John Wayne's far-right politics. Much of this criticism is of the latter-day variety, inadequately linked to history. Much is simple pique directed at Wayne because he was John Wayne. It should not have to be said that Wayne—like everyone else that ever lived—was more dimensional and complex than he may now appear. Even as his political beliefs grew increasingly strident and uncharitable as years passed, Wayne comported himself in good faith. The fictionalized but fact-based Operation Pineapple that propels the action of *Big Jim McLain* doesn't just root out Communists—it exposes what Wayne and many others perceived as communism's hypocrisy: Party members' quick willingness to turn on their own; their purported faith in economic equality co-existing with their fondness for quality booze and fancy digs; their abuse of the weak and uninformed.[7]

Did typical Communist Party USA members live luxuriously? No, but in presenting the leaders of Hawaii's Communists as selfish and pampered, the movie does suggest the cynical high living enjoyed by Party *nomenklatura* and selected *apparatchiks* in the USSR.

A Real Threat

The politics of *Big Jim McLain* now strike some viewers as stupidly far-right—and yet early-postwar Communist activity in Hawaii and on the mainland was very real, and not unthreatening. Further, the Communist Party USA took its orders from the Comintern (the Communist International) in Moscow—a fact that is forgotten by many of the movie's detractors, if the detractors even knew this in the first place. On the other hand, when *Big Jim McLain* began production in 1951, CPUSA influence was badly on the wane, its leaders prosecuted, its membership rolls in steep decline, and held in contempt by former members. (Washington's destruction of the Rosenberg atomic spy ring during 1950–53 helped discourage many onetime American Communists, who were shamed and sobered by the thought of an atomic USSR.) So the movie beats on an opponent who has already been pretty soundly thrashed.

Key to the narrative is that although Jim has rounded up a whole passel of Reds, every one of them takes the Fifth when hauled before HUAC. We learn a bit later that all have been set free. Not surprisingly, that doesn't sit well with Jim, who confides to Dan Liu (then the real-life Honolulu chief of police): "There are a lot of wonderful things written into our Constitution that were meant for honest, decent citizens. I resent the fact that it can be used and abused by the very people that want to destroy it."

McLain's selective interpretation of rights bestowed by the Constitution is shallow, of course, and the fact that the film's Reds walk away scot free is a most unlikely turn. The narrative, then, is rigged so that the film's philosophical points may be more easily pounded home. Like contrived elements discussed earlier, this is the work of professional screenwriters electing to be lazy.

Virtues and Stumbles

For all its faults, *Big Jim McLain* is a reasonably lively and entertaining melodrama; six decades on, it's still a lot of fun. Interest is maintained partly by the story's episodic structure: a series of pointed vignettes revolving around meetings, conversations, arguments, and the occasional punch-out. The pace slackens when Jim and Nancy pursue their relationship—but then, romantic interludes have slowed many action movies and other melodramas, making this film unremarkable in that regard.

Director Edward Ludwig was a versatile journeyman who began his career in 1920, helming comic shorts the likes of *Gridiron Gertie* and *Monkeys Prefer Blondes*. After eleven years of that, he graduated to features, moving easily between thrillers, adventures, westerns, even "women's pictures." No one ever accused Ludwig of being an "actor's director," but he had previously guided John Wayne in *The Fighting Seabees* (with an uncredited assist by Robert Florey) and *Wake of the Red Witch*. The latter is especially good, and the Duke felt comfortable bringing Ludwig onto *Big Jim McLain*. Although a film with a lot of talk, *McLain* perks along well thanks to lively and engaged performances by all,[8] and those then-unfamiliar Hawaiian locations, handsomely shot by Archie Stout in challenging natural light. The sense of local color is strong.

Despite the capable supporting cast, *Big Jim McLain* has (as its title suggests) just one figure of real focus. The movie was designed as a John Wayne picture for people who like John Wayne. And the Duke doesn't disappoint. As ruggedly handsome as we recall, amusingly self-effacing, and just entering the prime years of his career, Wayne is an irresistible presence. He demonstrates how star power can elevate material that's merely okay.

Philosophically, the picture is less noxious and far less naïve than the Duke's later conservative polemic, *The Green Berets*. Nor is it as daffy (or quite as charming) as *Jet Pilot*, an earlier Wayne vehicle produced by Howard Hughes during 1949–53, but not released until 1957. The scrumptious Janet Leigh is in that one, as a defecting Russian Yak pilot who finds herself in a romance with a Yankee jet jockey. *Big Jim McLain* is infinitely more watchable than either of these films, and because much of the present-day arguments against it are grounded in hindsight, it gets a partial pass on its politics.

Manipulative sentimentality is usually difficult to defend, though, and it's here that the movie falls flat with modern audiences. We have already noted the blips and bloops of patriotic song favorites heard beneath the main-title score. That device now seems awfully sappy, and the sin is compounded later, when patriotic music swells as McLain and Baxter visit the USS *Arizona*, and then when the camera lingers on a berthed aircraft carrier that disgorges grinning marines happy to be back home. Music for the latter sequence—"The Marines' Hymn (Halls of Montezuma)" and "Anchors Aweigh"—is provided by a navy band that happens to be on the dock when McLain and Nancy show up. Director Edward Ludwig shoots a close-up on the procession of leathernecks, each man (and for no explicable reason) announcing his name to the camera as he marches past: "Shulman! Gross! Donahue! Vasquez! Cohn! Brant!" (African American) "Green! Fellows! St. John!" (Japanese-American).

The inclusion of the black marine is a thin and painless acknowledgment of Harry Truman's 1948 integration of the U.S. armed forces, an executive order that was loudly decried by many politicians as well as by many in the military establishment and rank and file. And the Asian marine's "St. John" surname is a true marvel of tokenistic condescension. If the opening titles of *Big Jim McLain* suggest a yearning for a vanished

166 Part 3: Dupes, Victims and Crusaders

America, the subsequent narrative expresses a great uneasiness about America as it teetered in 1952, concluding with a clumsy—but well-intentioned—hope for a better, more secure tomorrow.

Filmography

Big Jim McLain—Wayne-Fellows Productions/Warner Bros.; Released August 30, 1952; Black and white; 90 min.

Credits: Producers: Robert Fellows, John Wayne; Director: Edward Ludwig; Screenplay: James Edward Grant, Richard English, Eric Taylor, b/o the article "We Almost Lost Hawaii to the Reds" by Richard English; Director of photography: Archie Stout; Editor: Jack Murray; Music: Paul Dunlap, Arthur Lange, Emil Newman; Art director: Alfred Ybarra

Cast: John Wayne: Jim McLain; Nancy Olson: Nancy Vallon; James Arness: Mal Baxter; Alan Napier: Sturak; Veda Ann Borg: Madge; Hans Conried: Robert Henried; Hal Baylor: Poke; Gayne Whitman: Dr. Gelster; Dan Liu: Himself, Honolulu chief of police; Gordon Jones: Olaf; Narrator: Harry Morgan

Notes

1. In 1954, Wayne-Fellows became Batjac Productions, with Robert Fellows remaining as Wayne's partner.
2. In this, Wayne's Jim McLain is reminiscent of the marvelous B-western star Wild Bill Elliott, who invariably (and with sincerity) declared himself "a peaceable man" in picture after picture, and who knocked heads or pulled the trigger only when goaded beyond endurance, or to protect others.
3. Nancy Olson came to *Big Jim McLain* following four co-star turns opposite William Holden during 1950–51: *Sunset Blvd.*, *Union Station*, *Force of Arms*, and *Submarine Command*. Although only the first two are important, Olson quickly established herself as an exemplar of understated sex appeal and, more importantly, honorable American womanhood.
4. Star character actress Veda Ann Borg steals her scenes with Wayne, an estimable feat made possible by her gifts, and because the Duke was a generous star who allowed himself to be upstaged when it heightened the moment. Borg made her living playing rough-edged dames who are sly, sensual, and almost invariably appealing. An August 1939 crash in a car with serial actor Dick Purcell catapulted Borg through the windshield, shearing off her nose and leaving deep cuts, particularly around her left eye. During the course of ten plastic surgeries, Borg gave up part of a rib and pieces of an earlobe to facilitate a new nose. When she returned to public life, she looked subtly different than before but no less pretty. Adults that saw *Big Jim McLain* in 1952 would have been familiar with Borg's travail, and thus predisposed to feel fondness for the Madge character.
5. When a character describes Dr. Gelster as "a renter of a personality," Gelster is meant to be seen as a cipher looking for an identity in cultism; here, the cult is communism.
6. The sequence with Conried is allowed to play out over six-and-a-half minutes—an excruciating interlude that labors to make its point, and tortures us in the process.
7. One briefly glimpsed female member of the cell is noticeably mannish, a coded characteristic suggestive of—to audiences of the day—perversion as well as disloyalty.
8. Comic character actor Gordon Jones is far *too* engaged, mugging violently as Madge's on-again, off-again boyfriend, gesticulating and huffing, as if he dropped in from a Depression-era campus comedy.

Works Cited

Books

Eyman, Scott. *John Wayne: The Life and Legend*. New York: Simon & Schuster, 2014.
Holmes, T. Michael. *The Specter of Communism in Hawaii*. Honolulu: University of Hawaii Press, 1994.
Inouye, Sen. Daniel K., and Lawrence Elliott. *Journey to Washington*. Englewood Cliffs, NJ: Prentice-Hall, 1967.
Smith, Jeff. *Film Criticism, the Cold War, and the Blacklist: Reading the Hollywood Reds*. Berkeley: University of California Press, 2014.

Newspapers and Periodicals

Borreca, Richard. "Fear of Communist infiltrators engulfed postwar Hawaii." *Honolulu Star-Bulletin*. October 18, 1999.

English, Richard. "We Almost Lost Hawaii to the Reds." *The Saturday Evening Post*. February 2, 1952.
"Wears new face." *Alexandria* (IN) *Times-Tribune*. March 15, 1941.

Web

archives.starbulletin.com (postwar Communist activity in Hawaii)

DVD

Big Jim McLain. Warner Home Video. 2007.

Trial
Love in a Time of Communism
ANTHONY AMBROGIO

"*Trial* is one of the most obscure movies ever made today." So claimed Don M. Mankiewicz, author of both the novel *Trial* and its screen adaptation, to Stephen W. Bowie during the course of a 2007 oral history, posted online at Bowie's classictv.com blog. (All Mankiewicz quotes come from this invaluable source.)

Indeed, *Trial* would not be the first film that springs to mind if one were compiling a list of titles for retrospectives devoted to its director and stars: Mark Robson, Glenn Ford, Dorothy McGuire, or Arthur Kennedy. Well, maybe Arthur Kennedy, at least to hear Mankiewicz tell it: "*Trial* is not a picture like *I Want to Live* [1958, also scripted by Mankiewicz], [which] you might have seen years after it was made. You didn't see *Trial*— it opened at Radio City, and it had its run, and that's it. Unless it gets on Turner Classic Movies. They play it once a year on Arthur Kennedy's birthday. They do that for dead actors." (Maybe so. The video copy used for this essay came from a TCM broadcast— though not on Kennedy's birthday.)

Trial was not one of the top twenty money-making movies of 1955, unlike Glenn Ford's big hit for that year, *Blackboard Jungle*, which ended up in the number-twelve spot, earning $5.2 million. But *Trial* did bring Kennedy his third Best Supporting Actor Oscar nomination (he lost to Jack Lemmon in *Mister Roberts*, the second-highest-grossing picture of 1955)—and he received a Best Supporting Actor Golden Globe for his *Trial* work, so maybe TCM *ought* to broadcast it annually on his birthday.

Though *Trial* had a respectable run at the time, Mankiewicz is right about its obscurity today, which is a shame, as it is one of the more interesting and nuanced anti–Communist pictures to come out of the 1950s. Like *Blackboard Jungle*, it was more of a "social-problem drama," dealing with race and justice, and how politics intermingles with and can taint the judicial system.

Given its author, it's not surprising that *Trial*—both the award-winning novel (1955 Harper Prize) and the MGM film—is not some simpleminded anti–Communist tract.

Mankiewicz is the son of celebrated scenarist Herman Mankiewicz and nephew of producer and writer-director Joseph Mankiewicz, neither of whom was known for creating one-dimensional characters. Mankiewicz himself was active in politics as a liberal Democrat, from at least 1948 on. ("I really wanted to be a congressman. That's what I decided when I was about fifteen.") His brother Frank became an important Democratic

Postwar Hollywood was seminal to the production of high-minded "social problem" dramas, and in a single year, 1955, Glenn Ford starred in two of them: *The Blackboard Jungle* (failed urban schools and juvenile delinquency) and *Trial*, which invokes murder, race hatred, and Red propaganda. Here, naïve defense attorney David Blake (Ford) has a jailhouse meeting with his frightened teenage client, Angel Chavez (Rafael Campos).

political operative: press secretary to New York Senator Robert Kennedy and manager of George McGovern's ill-fated 1972 presidential campaign (which is probably why Frank's name found its way onto Richard Nixon's enemies list).

Despite his political leanings and his familial associations (or maybe because of them), Don Mankiewicz was never a "knee-jerk" liberal. From an early age, he developed certain clear-headed ideas about groups on both sides of the political spectrum and how they worked, as illustrated by this "formative" story he told Stephen Bowie:

> I was young; I was sixteen and in high school, and I thought, "I should do something to prevent the Nazis from taking over the world," which it looked like they were going to in 1938. I joined the Hollywood Anti-Nazi League, which my father said was all right to do. "They're not Communists," he said, "'cause Oscar Hammerstein and Philip Dunne are in that, and they're certainly not Communists." Okay. I joined.

At the League's behest, he infiltrated a scary local Fascist organization, William Dudley Pelley's Silver Legion, aka Silver Shirts. As time went on, Mankiewicz feared his undercover status was going to be revealed ("even though my father assured me that I was perfectly safe because probably half of them were plants [by other leftist or government organizations]"). He stuck it out until late August 1939, when—convinced that the group was on to him—he told his control, "I don't want to do this anymore. It's too dangerous." No need, his handler explained: the Hitler-Stalin pact had just been signed (August 23, 1939), and "[we]'re not going to do this anymore, the Hollywood Anti-Nazi League.... we're going to have to change our name. We're going to be the Hollywood League Against Foreign Fascism."

170   Part 3: Dupes, Victims and Crusaders

Don Mankiewicz said, "That's very interesting. Where do I resign?"

He had to stand in line.

About this episode, Mankiewicz concludes:

> In the end the Communists took it over. They booted Oscar Hammerstein out, and they chased Philip Dunne away.... the battle was not between the right wing and the left wing. It was between the reformers—today they would be called liberals—and the radicals. They are natural enemies. Reformers want to improve the system, and radicals want to destroy it. It's always been that way.

With such a vivid example in Don Mankiewicz's own life of how people cut their conscience to fit this year's fashions, it's no wonder that he depicts the leftist and Communist organizations in *Trial* as less than honorable and more than a little self-serving. Not unexpectedly, the forces of reaction fare no better in his writing. (Although Mankiewicz doesn't think much of the Hollywood Ten's talent or scruples, he characterizes the organizers of the blacklist as "intolerant sons of bitches seriously mistreating and persecuting other intolerant sons of bitches. It should not be; the evil entirely was on the side of the blacklisters, no matter what these people did.")

Accommodations for Film

The novel concerns a court case in which honest law professor David Blake defends a Mexican-American teen accused of killing a white girl. Blake faces challenges from the right (bigots who wish to see "justice" done) and the left, who wish to manipulate the trial for their own gains. (In this regard, *Trial* shares certain affinities with Steinbeck's *In*

Defense attorney Barney Castle (Arthur Kennedy, far left) brings Blake into his practice, anticipating ways he can exploit the murder case—and manipulate Blake—to serve a money-driven Communist agenda. Seen with the attorneys are the defendant's mother (Katy Jurado) and the racist local sheriff (Robert Middleton).

Dubious Battle, where a good cause becomes a *cause célèbre* for the radical faction trying to control and exploit it.)

Much of the movie remains faithful to the book in plot and approach, successfully duplicating many of the novel's complexities. But—since it *is* a Hollywood film of the 1950s—Mankiewicz's screen adaptation plays up the anti–Communist angle to a greater degree, taking care to distance its hero from any Red taint. The film portrays David as an outspoken anti–Communist, with his law partner, Communist front-man Barney Castle, delineated as a more overtly despicable and brutal character than his calculating, Machiavellian literary counterpart (though this may have more to do with Arthur Kennedy's sneering on-screen interpretation than any real difference with the book). And the film adaptation supplies a boffo, crowd-pleasing courtroom showdown to replace the book's more desultory conclusion. (In this regard, Mankiewicz's novel shares certain affinities with the changes made to Walter Van Tilburg Clark's *The Ox-Bow Incident*, the 1943 film version of which bestows heroic stature on the novel's otherwise ordinary protagonist, and tries to soften some of its harsher edges.) Mankiewicz's rethinking of the ending shows his cinematic savvy; although the screen conclusion might be considered a "Hollywood" happy ending, it is infinitely more dramatic and perhaps, ultimately, more satisfying.

The movie's upbeat finale turns on a fine point of law, which is fitting because legal matters play a large part in Mankiewicz's work. He was a law student before World War II military service interrupted his university education, and when he began writing for television and the movies in the 1950s, he found his forte in courtroom drama. *Trial*, as its title indicates, is one such example.

Contemporaneous with *Trial*, Don Mankiewicz worked on a show called "On Trial," which he originally wrote for a 1955 broadcast of the NBC anthology *Star Stage*, and which became the 1956–57 CBS-TV series *On Trial* (aka *The Joseph Cotten Show*). Eager for the series to explore what Mankiewicz called "important points of law," he grew dispirited when NBC executives insisted that the program's finer points of law would begin and end with murder.

The Book's Tale

In novel form, *Trial* is a murder story. The basis of its courtroom case is an important point of law, a bit of legal esoterica: "felony murder," death as a result of an event growing out of a crime. Angel Chavez, a Hispanic teenager trespassing on a private, whites-only beach, encounters a girl there—Mary Wiltse, the underage, rheumatic sister of his school friend. (This relationship is omitted in the film.) She's looking for some excitement in a life circumscribed by illness, and he's excited by her attention. They kiss and begin petting; he awkwardly starts to go further than she's ready for; she panics and runs away—and her weak heart gives out. If the boy's intent was rape, then her death is felony murder.

Barney Castle lays out the defense's strategy: don't put Angel on the stand; make the state prove the boy was committing rape, if it can. Then he leaves the courtroom work to David and takes Angel's mother, Consuela, on a cross-country trip to raise court costs (and then some), once even summoning David to New York for a weekend rally hosted by leftist organizations, an act that brings David unwanted scrutiny from the state committee on subversion and disloyalty.

The book explores the machinations of the jury-selection process and other perfunctory but important aspects of trial. David falls in love with Barney's secretary, Abbe, and begins an affair with her. The case proceeds apace, in the defense's favor, until Barney returns and suddenly insists that Angel testify. The district attorney's brutal cross-examination sways the jury and destroys its sympathy for Angel. He's found guilty and ultimately executed. Consuela throws a fit in court when the verdict is read but makes sure to turn "her body so that the corner of the Judge's bench did not hide her from the [camera] lenses." Later, she attends a fund-raising memorial to her son "because Angel would have wanted me to."

Barney, the rally chairman, is present in court when Angel is convicted but physically disappears from the novel after that, though David has an epiphany about him later, realizing that Barney had planned from the outset to use Angel as a martyr to the cause. Abbe leaves David because he wouldn't step aside once Barney engineered Angel's suicidal testimony.

Still, the narrative provides a hint that David and Abbe might yet get back together: about to deliberately ram his car into a steel guardrail rather than appear before state senator Carl Baron Battle's Assembly Committee on Subversion and Disloyalty, David brakes at the last minute and goes to see Charles White, the newspaper publisher he fortuitously met on his plane trip to New York. White urges him to write an exposé of the trial and Barney's machinations, offering to print it in his newspaper and assuring David that it will cause the committee to back off and thus solve all of his problems; he even suggests that David hire himself a secretary to help out....

The Narrative on Film

The first half of the movie follows Mankiewicz's novel, though in compressed form. Mark Robson's direction and Mankiewicz's script streamline the source material and throw us into the action right away. The pre-credit sequence is an excellent example of economic storytelling, setting the tale in motion with a title laid over the action: "9:30 p.m. San Juno Village Beach, June 7, 1947." The camera dollies in on the crowded beach, lingering at the legs of a supine man and woman, and then tracks upward along their bodies as the man provides us with the only exposition we need about this gathering: "And I say, if no bass swims up that river, it'll still be a fine bass night because the opening of the bass season don't matter a-tall; it's all just an excuse to get out under the moon with a gal—" The woman giggles, and he puts a cigarette in her mouth and finishes his thought—"with a blanket and a bottle of somethin'." The man strikes a match on a sign, illuminating its words, "Private Beach; *Village Residents Only.*"

The camera moves on to pick up another beachgoer (who will testify later at the trial), who crawls to the shore to test his line—not for fish but for the mixer he's been keeping cool in the water. He uncaps the soda, adds liquor, and takes a drink. Suddenly, there's a call for help; the drinker reacts, as do others on the beach. Cut to a fellow (another witness seen later at trial), parked with his girl in a car, who turns on a spotlight to locate the source of distress. Beachgoers dash up wooden steps and halt, horrified, at the landing. A uniformed man elbows through and shines his flashlight on the platform, on the body of a young woman. The camera pans across her corpse, from the feet to the face, and then quickly pans up to the young man standing over her, whose face the guard pins with his beam. The film's title appears and enlarges itself: TRIAL.

Unlike the book, the film chooses *not* to depict what transpired between Angel Chavez (Rafael Campos) and the dead girl, Mary Wiltse. This decision simplifies the same scene in the novel, when Angel's fumbling efforts at heavy petting and to feel Mary's breast—which result in the dress being ripped—do not present him in the best light, and temper reader sympathy for him (Of course, that may have been Mankiewicz's original intention; nothing is simple in his novel). And anyway, the clinch would have been tricky to stage in the 1950s, and would have been an even greater impediment to audience sympathy.

The following scene in the dean's office—which transpires at that familiar time, "9:30 p.m., State University, June 7, 1947"—tells us all we need to know about David Blake (Glenn Ford) and his predicament. His "Legal experience: None"; he'll lose his university job as a law-school teacher unless he gets some "practical" courtroom experience over the summer. And then we're into a montage of David going from attorney's office to attorney's office, looking for someone to give him the opportunity he needs. His appearance in the office of Barney Castle (Arthur Kennedy), the lawyer who will take him on, begins with a close-up of the *San Juno Chronicle*, with headlines about the murder. David is already scanning these before he's invited in to see Barney.

The sequence in which Barney, his secretary Abbe (Dorothy McGuire), and David pay a jail-cell visit to Angel and his mother Consuela (Katy Jurado) is taken straight from the book, but it's a measure of Mankiewicz's powers of adaptation and Robson's skill with *mise-en-scène* to see how they make it come alive on film. The sequence lets us learn what transpired between Mary Wiltse and Angel from Angel's point of view—and allows Barney to badger him (the way the district attorney would do, Barney says). As a result, audience sympathy remains with the confused, innocent kid, and Barney's mean streak is revealed in the bargain. It also establishes the early stage of the hold Barney comes to have over Consuela.

As in the book, after Barney and company take Angel's case, they appeal to Mrs. Wiltse (Ann Lee), Mary's liberal mother, to conduct a quiet funeral service for the dead girl, to prevent stirring up passion in town. The local hatemongers show up anyway, including Cap Grant (Paul Guilfoyle), a Ku Klux Klan man from 'way back, and led by Ralph Castillo (John Hoyt), described in the book as "aristocratic-type bigot." (Mankiewicz must have intended some irony with the Spanish surname; could Castillo be descended from old Spanish hidalgos who resented Mexican peasants and immigrants?)

This group incites the townspeople to form a lynch mob, which is deterred not by a good man facing them down and appealing to their better nature, but by the speechifyin' of shady sheriff and good ol' boy Fats Sanders (Robert Middleton), who warns them of the economic consequences that befall towns known for lynching. Sanders neutralizes and charms the mob with his promise that Angel will be executed legally: "If the law don't hang that lousy Mex, I swear I'll quit my job and never run for public office again! ... I been twenty years on the public payroll [in the book: "twenty-seven years on the public tit!"]. Why, I'd starve to death on the outside!"

Barney leaves on the fund-raising tour with Consuela, and David is left to fall in love with Abbe and conduct the courtroom defense.

As in the book, the case is heard by an African American, Judge Motley (Juano Hernandez). A black judge presiding over the trial must have been stunning for 1950s audiences, many of whom probably didn't think such a creature existed. In the book, David has misgivings about Motley hearing the case, misgivings that Angel voices when he repeats another prisoner's assessment ("the judge will be a Negro ... because they can trust him to do his best to hang me—on account of his not being white either," a line repeated in the movie).

In another example of the film's portrayal of David as the righteous, fiery hero, David actually confronts the judge about this sinister motive: "I don't like you presiding. I think you were selected so that, after the conviction, they'd be able to say 'Of course, the Mexican had a fair trial; sure—he even had a Negro judge!'" And the judge, angered by the accusation, counters, "I'm sure that you consider yourself completely without race prejudice. But you'd bar me from the bench for this trial because of the color of my skin! You might think that over sometime"—leaving David chagrined and speechless. This exchange is significant because the judge plays a more important role in the film's conclusion than his rather ineffectual counterpart does in the book.

The movie devotes time to the legal maneuvering involved in jury selection and (as in the book) on the revelation that detectives working for the D.A. exceeded their authority and illegally questioned potential jurors, a maneuver David discovers and brings to the judge's attention in time to prevent a mistrial.

Rally to the Cause

Forty minutes into the movie, the "Communist element" is introduced with a vengeance when David attends the "Free Angel Chavez" rally. Up to this point, our naïve hero has had no idea where his legal fees are coming from. In the book, he's a little more savvy: before the trial commences, David expresses qualms about Consuela selling her life story to *Struggle*, a Communist organ, to earn cash for the defense fund, but he gets over it quickly enough when Abbe reminds him what her stockbroker grandfather always said: "Money Has No Morals." In the film, David doesn't catch on about the payments' source until he sees Barney wheeling and dealing with the leftists. "I don't want that kind of money," he tells Barney. "Of course you don't," Barney says mockingly. "You want nice honorable American money, not dirty Communist money"—but they can't raise enough to defend Angel that way.

David reluctantly concedes Barney's point and even agrees to speak at the rally, but he refuses to read the remarks (Communist propaganda, presumably) that Barney has prepared for him: "Not this speech," David says. "Not you or anybody else is gonna tell me what to say"—thus asserting our hero's individualistic Americanism. Barney seems happy to oblige.

That night, David barely has time for initial remarks. As soon as he launches into a righteous diatribe ("I've seen and I've heard a lot of things here tonight, and I don't—"), Barney cuts David's mic and urges the band to play. Forced to hold his peace, David sits and takes a good look around as the movie lays the propaganda on thick with quick cuts of signs and banners reading "JOIN," "PARTY," and "STRUGGLE." Barney comes to the mic to bilk the audience out of more cash and give them a rousing, amoral speech keynoted with, "Don't trust *anybody*!"

The David of the novel speaks at the rally and deviates from Barney's remarks, not out of protest but because he thinks a speech appealing for money no longer applies. He's not cut off; he just doesn't get much of a response from the crowd. And he doesn't leave the rally in disgust, as in the film. While he may be uncomfortable about the venue (and

Barney's tactics), he knows why he's there. The cab driver of the novel characterizes the rally thus: "Some nigger raped a white gal, and a bunch of yids are trying to get him off."

David's impulse is to thank the cabbie for what he had said. David has been so long in the company of Cheever and of Hopper (two of the rally organizers), and had become so aware of their failings of character, that it is with pleasure that he experiences this reminder that there are imperfections on the other side as well. The novel's David understands that he made common cause with the Cheevers and Hoppers for this reason: because not to do so would be to make common cause with people like the cabbie.

No cab driver appears in the film, and there's no racial or ethnic slur (unless you count Barney's description of a droning African American speaker as "a credit to his race," a line in book and movie). There is just the pre-rally finagling that indicates what a venal money-grubber Barney is, and how he'll stop at next to nothing to fill the coffers for the trial (fill them to overflowing, as it turns out).

In the film, the New York trip precipitates a crisis between David and Abbe, a crisis that they overcome through their mutual rejection of Communist doctrine. He feels she's lied to him and let him be set up. ("It was a trap. I stepped right into it. You could have warned me, Abbe." She counters, "You wanted that money for Angel." But David will have none of it, and Mankiewicz awards him an indignant speech worthy of a red-blooded American: "I ended up on the stage [with] Communists in front of me, Communist banners behind me. I tried to tell them what I thought of them, and I ended up just talking into a dead microphone with a brass band blaring."

The couple's relationship reaches a crisis. If Barney is a Communist, David muses as he looks at Abbe, "you must be one, too." Of course, that would be the end for them, because a mid-century movie hero must not love a Communist. Abbe insists she wasn't "a card-carrier," just "the perfect fellow traveler." She tells David about her flirtation with the Party, and how she's over it. "They told you everything," she explains. "Who to vote for, who to raise money for, who to carry banners for…"

"Who to stick the knife into?" David cuts in. Abbe answers:

> A lot of things have changed since then, David. I know love isn't the cure for communism. The cure is different in every case. The cure in my case was growing up. Long before I met you. I was glad they hadn't let me join the Party, that they hadn't given me a card. They said I was a hopeless bourgeois; they were right. I could never really accept the Party line. The way it kept changing. Monday's truth'd be Tuesday's lie. I could never really manage that.

"Like Barney can," David interjects, already softening, and realizing the distinction separating Abbe from Barney.

Mankiewicz cobbles together movie–Abbe's monologue from various sections in the book but embellishes the words to make clear that Abbe was *never* a Communist. In the book, she tells David she *was* a Party member but was gradually falling away from her "religion," partly through the Love of a Good Man. "I don't think meeting you was responsible for the final break," she says. "It only speeded it along."

Mankiewicz takes care that movie–Abbe expresses her individualism: "Then I started thinking for myself and asking questions, and then—you came along. I knew what they were doing to you. I knew I had to warn you, but somehow I couldn't. Warning you, telling, meant tearing down the last bit of anything I'd ever believed in. I was wrong." This admission is underscored by significant close-ups of each looking at the other. She tries to leave, to flee. "And then I let you go to the rally, and I let them serve the subpoena.

Now it's too late. I've let them destroy you. I can't bear to see you destroyed. I've got to...." David stops her; she's won him over again, and they embrace.

Nothing so dramatic occurs in the novel. Instead, when David returns from New York, *she* becomes irritated with him because he refuses to see the danger in the subpoena he's received from Battle. In the book, David's crisis with Abbe comes later, and leads to a split when he continues to pursue the case even after Barney has sabotaged it by forcing him to put Angel on the stand—a sacrifice to the cause that Barney planned from the beginning. But the film suggests that Barney changes tactics after receiving orders from above. As David mounts a futile argument against Barney's adamant intention that Angel testify (Barney has secured Consuela's permission), a drunken Abbe explains to David that "the Party line has changed" (and they both know Barney can change with it). The Party is "paying good money for a martyr—now they've gotta produce one." It's a toss-up as to which is more despicable—book–Barney, who calculates the kid's death, or film–Barney, who acquiesces when ordered.

In its depiction of the nefarious nature of Communists, *Trial* is not much different from other politicized films of the '50s. But in its treatment of un–American-activities committees, it is practically unique. (The only other contemporaneous movie that comes close is 1957's *Three Brave Men*, in which Ray Milland defends Ernest Borgnine, a man who lost his job because of alleged Communist leanings.)

The movie version of *Trial* doesn't make as much of the underhanded tactics of the state Committee on Subversion and Disloyalty as the novel does (the book includes an appearance by snarling Chairman Battle, brow-beating a "friendly witness" who's testifying to save his skin), but it does give us a taste of that right-wing mirror image of Barney Castle. The movie "covers itself" by having David say, "I know about investigating committees—how important they are, how much good work they do, but not the way Battle runs this committee. This isn't an investigating committee; it's a committee set up to crown Carl Baron Battle the little king of the anti–Communists." The *committees* aren't evil; only certain people who abuse their power are evil (which is not necessarily the same conclusion a viewer would draw from the picture's portrayal of Communists).

Equally naïve in this matter as he was about the Communists, David believes that if he simply tells the committee the truth, he'll be all right. Abbe eventually disabuses him of that notion in a well-written scene where she plays Battle and shows David how his truth will be twisted by Battle's lies. ("He won't let you tell the truth....") Her remarks are similar to the passage in the book, where Benson, a reporter, shows David what a Battle cross-examination is like. In this respect, Hollywood's *Trial* is a pretty devastating indictment of anti–Communist witch hunts not seen on screen until much later, as in *The Front* (1976), *Guilty by Suspicion* (1991), and *The Majestic* (2001).

The aftermath of the trial, which deviates substantially from the book, obviates the need for David to testify because his speech before the judge, asking for amelioration of the sentence, proves him to be the kind of formidable opponent whom Battle has no desire to challenge. Mankiewicz uses another fine point of law in his altered ending for the movie: he has David cite precedent to the judge, allowing him to mitigate the sentence, to sentence Angel to twelve months in a work camp instead of to his death. This big finish in the courtroom is tantamount to a witness's *mea culpa* before HUAC or McCarthy; because David explains in open court that "I was duped" by the Red schemers, the movie does have it both ways—though perhaps Mankiewicz intended David's courtroom outpouring as equivalent to the exposé David is *going* to write at the novel's end.

Movie-Consuela regrets her former behavior and moves away from the dark side. Barney shows his true colors, is severely reprimanded by the judge, and suffers the indignity of being arrested for contempt. With that act (by which our villain gets a kind of comeuppance), and the lenient treatment of Angel, the judge reveals himself as an independent-minded, free-thinking jurist.

Trial is a reasonably brave film, but it must not be overpraised on that score. After all, David's principled stand is an echo of journalist Edward R. Murrow's earlier confrontation with Sen. Joseph McCarthy, on March 9, 1954. Further, the Army-McCarthy hearings, televised from April 22 to June 17, 1954, had further dimmed the Red-baiter's star. And the Senate had finally censured McCarthy on December 2, 1954. All of that brought a more decent frame of mind to touchy political issues. Still, a certain amount of courage was required to bring this particular tale to the screen in 1955. That alone is sufficient for *Trial* to be acknowledged.

FILMOGRAPHY

Trial—MGM; Released October 7, 1955; Black and white; 105 min. (original cut); 109 min. (TV print)

Credits: Producers: Charles Schnee, James E. Newcom; Director: Mark Robson; Screenplay: Don Mankiewicz, b/o the novel *Trial* by Mankiewicz; Director of photography: Robert Surtees; Editor: Albert Akst; Music: Daniele Amfitheatrof; Art directors: Cedric Gibbons, Randall Duell

Cast: Glenn Ford: David Blake; Dorothy McGuire: Abbe; Arthur Kennedy: Barney Castle; John Hodiak: District Attorney Armstrong; Katy Jurado: Mrs. Chavez; Rafael Campos: Angel Chavez; Juano Hernandez: Judge Theodore Motley; Robert Middleton: Fats Sanders; John Hoyt: Ralph Castillo

WORKS CITED

Book

Mankiewicz, Don M. *Trial.* New York: Harper & Brothers, 1955.

Web

classictvhistory.com/OralHistories/donmankiewicz.html.

DVD

Trial. Warner Archive Collection. 2014.

The author is grateful to critic Brad Taylor,
who made it possible for him to re-view Trial *after some forty years.*

The Tears of a Clown
Chaplin's A King in New York

MARK CLARK

In a famous scene from Charles Chaplin's 1936 masterpiece *Modern Times*, the Little Tramp picks up a red flag that has fallen from the back of a passing lorry. As he waves the flag, trying to attract the truck driver's attention, a mob of working-class protestors rounds the corner, and the Tramp finds himself unwittingly at the head of a parade of agitators. He is promptly arrested. This sequence proved to be an eerie example of art foreshadowing life. Sixteen years later, in the waning years of the U.S. Congress's crusade to root out Communist "infiltrators" in all walks of American life, Chaplin was forced out of his adopted homeland due to his supposed socialist beliefs and other alleged misdemeanors. It was a stunning fall from grace for the legendary actor-director, who, during his silent movie heyday, had been not merely the most famous but also the most beloved man in the world.

After stewing over this ignominious turn of events for better than a year, a bitter and indignant Chaplin decided to strike back at his detractors, venting his pain and outrage through his final starring vehicle, *A King in New York* (1957). While the movie ranks among his weakest features, it is nevertheless a project of great passion and audacity, the only contemporary film to openly decry the anti–Red hysteria sweeping America at the time. It's also a picture that reveals more about its creator than many of Chaplin's earlier masterworks.

The People v. Charlie Chaplin

Chaplin, the movies' first international superstar, almost singlehandedly popularized film-going during the industry's infancy, and with the increasing sophistication of his works throughout the 1920s, helped legitimize the new medium as an idea-driven art form. *Modern Times*, Chaplin's final silent picture and the last to feature his Little Tramp character, met with tremendous critical and popular acclaim. Yet, he was omitted from the Hollywood Walk of Fame when that honorarium was introduced twenty-two years later, in 1958. Much had changed in the meantime.

Chaplin's first talking feature, *The Great Dictator* (1940), met with a mixed response, and audiences were even less supportive of his *Monsieur Verdoux* (1947) and *Limelight*

(1952). All the while, conservatives increasingly came to suspect the filmmaker of harboring Communist sympathies. Chaplin was an easy target because, despite having lived in the U.S. since 1913, he had never sought American citizenship. He also ran in intellectual, artistic circles, which many right-wingers viewed with distrust. These included FBI director J. Edgar Hoover, whose bureau maintained a file on Chaplin that eventually grew to nearly two thousand pages. According to Jeffrey Vance, author of *Chaplin: Genius of the Cinema*, Chaplin was introduced to socialist ideas in the early 1930s through friends, including Pulitzer Prize-winning novelist Upton Sinclair, but he never subscribed to any political party or system. Rather, Chaplin held that "humanity should be one, and that geographical and political distinctions should yield to what Vance describes as "a democratic whole." Chaplin sometimes referred to himself in simpler terms, as "a citizen of the world."

Chaplin held at least one passionate political conviction, however; he abhorred totalitarianism and looked upon the Nazi takeover of Germany with great foreboding. In *The Great Dictator*, his first talkie and most overtly political film, Chaplin lampooned Adolf Hitler through the proxy of Adenoid Hynkel, dictator of Tomania. Although now considered a classic, the movie—released in a year when most Americans still favored isolationism—wasn't as popular as his silent features. In the minds of many conservatives, the film cast further doubt on his politics. On the other hand, Chaplin's 1942 re-release of *The Gold Rush*, one of his silent favorites reissued with a self-penned musical score and voiceover narration by Chaplin replacing the original intertitles, met with great success. Audiences still loved the Little Tramp, and seemed to resent Chaplin for trying to play any other character.

But Chaplin's real problems began in 1942, when, at the behest of the Roosevelt administration, he replaced Joseph E. Davis, former U.S. ambassador to the Soviet Union, as the featured speaker at a San Francisco fundraiser for Russian war relief. Over the next year, Chaplin made appearances, either in person or by telephone, at several more pro–Russian fundraisers, including a large event at Madison Square Garden in New York. In the Cold War era, his pro–Russian activities were viewed with extreme prejudice, even though the Soviets were America's allies at the time. Chaplin's image took another hit when aspiring actress Joan Barry slapped him with a paternity suit in 1943. Barry eventually won the controversial case, which was tried again after the first jury deadlocked. A blood test revealed Chaplin was not the father, but Barry's attorney argued this evidence was inadmissible in the second trail. In 1944, the FBI brought Mann Act charges against Chaplin in connection with the Barry case, but Chaplin was acquitted.

Public opinion of Chaplin continued to sour with the 1947 release of his *Monsieur Verdoux*, a controversial black comedy about a Bluebeard-like wife-killer. That same year, Chaplin became one of the first nineteen Hollywood insiders subpoenaed to appear before the House Un-American Activities Committee (HUAC) as it investigated Communist influence within the film industry. Chaplin was scheduled to appear before the committee on three occasions, only to have his appearance postponed each time. When it became apparent that he would not meet the committee face to face, Chaplin issued a public statement declaring that he was not a Communist, but rather a "peace-monger." Nevertheless, conservatives continued to look askance at the rapidly falling star. The American Legion picketed both *Monsieur Verdoux* and Chaplin's sentimental backstage dramedy *Limelight* (1952), even though the latter film included no "objectionable" material.

Matters reached a head in October 1952, as Chaplin prepared to leave the U.S. to promote *Limelight* overseas. In order to earn his re-entry permit, Chaplin, and his family and staff, had to endure interrogation—including questions about his political views, his racial heritage, and his sex life—by immigration officials. Shortly after departing for England aboard the *Queen Elizabeth*, Chaplin received word via radio that his permit had been revoked. He later learned that the permit was yanked at the personal request of Attorney General James P. McGranery, who referred to Chaplin as "an unsavory character." Many, including gossip columnist Hedda Hopper, praised McGranery's decision. "Good riddance to bad rubbish," wrote Hopper, who claimed that Chaplin's views and actions "go against our customs, abhor everything we stand for, [and] throw our hospitality back in our faces." Due to the controversy, major theater chains, including Fox, Loews, and RKO, pulled *Limelight* after short runs. As a result, the picture wasn't widely seen in the U.S. until it was reissued in 1972.

Chaplin feared that, barred from re-entry, he would be unable to recover his personal fortune, most of which remained in the United States. In November, however, Oona O'Neill Chaplin was able to close out her husband's bank accounts and liquidate his other assets, including his legendary Hollywood studio (although he was forced to pay $425,000 in back taxes). In his autobiography, Chaplin wrote that by this time he was "fed up with America's insults and moral pomposity." He wouldn't return to the United States until 1972, when he received an honorary Academy Award.

The Ex-King

Chaplin made a bittersweet return to his native London for the British premiere of *Limelight*, and soon launched a promotional tour of other European countries before finally settling down on an estate in Switzerland, the fifteen-room Manoir de Ban at Corsier sur Vevey, where he would reside for the rest of his life. "I have never been political," Chaplin stated when confronted with reporters while disembarking from the *Queen Elizabeth*. "I have no political convictions. I'm an individualist, and I believe in liberty." Nevertheless, his behavior on the Continent continued to raise eyebrows. During his stay in London he crossed paths with Soviet premier Nikita Khrushchev, and the two embraced warmly. He was photographed with Chinese premier Chou En-lai at a party in Geneva in 1954 and accepted a prize from the World Peace Council, a Soviet organization, later that same year. "My prodigious sin was, and still is, being a nonconformist," Chaplin wrote in his autobiography. "Although I am not a Communist I refused to fall in line by hating them."

In Switzerland, Chaplin began to think seriously about his next screen project. In late 1954 he announced that his next movie would be *The Ex-King*, a musical about a deposed monarch seeking asylum in the United States. He denied that the film would be political, but inevitably his pent-up injuries and frustrations—including his loathing of America's anti–Communist witch hunt—seeped into the screenplay, which was completed the following year. Chaplin wrote a clutch of songs for the picture but eventually discarded the idea of producing a full-blown musical. The trappings expected of a musical by the mid–1950s, including widescreen color photography and elaborately choreographed dance numbers, were both outside Chaplin's métier and cost prohibitive. Chaplin faced many daunting obstacles in making the film, which would be entirely self-financed. By including material antagonistic to HUAC, Chaplin knew the movie could not be released in the U.S., the world's largest cinema market. Also, he would not have access to his familiar studio or trusted technicians; instead, he planned to rent space at Shepperton Studios in England and hire a British crew. Previously, it was not uncommon for Chaplin to halt production for hours, or even days or weeks, while he worked to improve a sequence. Since now, for the first time in decades, he would have to pay for every minute of studio time, Chaplin would be forced to abandon his previous idiosyncratic, perfectionist methods.

Casting presented further challenges. Given the dearth of expatriate American performers in England at the time, Chaplin had to identify British performers who could convincingly affect an American accent. He also struggled to fill two key roles. For the king's young American love interest, Chaplin originally wanted British musical-comedy star Kay Kendall, but finally settled for the lesser-known Dawn Addams, who had unsuccessfully auditioned for the female lead in *Limelight*. The actress went on to appear on British television and in fare such as *The Two Faces of Dr. Jekyll* (1960), *The Vampire Lovers* (1970), and *The Vault of Horror* (1973). To play a young boy whose parents are bullied by a Commie-hunting government committee, Chaplin—after much lobbying from Oona—chose his own ten-year-old son Michael. Shooting of the film now known as *A King in New York* began May 7, 1956, and wrapped on July 28, the shortest production of any Chaplin feature.

"One of the minor annoyances of modern life is a revolution," reads the film's opening card. Chaplin plays King Shadov, recently deposed ruler of Estrovia, who arrives in Manhattan with his ambassador and man–Friday Jaume (Oliver Johnston), and prime minister Voudel (Jerry Desmonde). Before fleeing the country, Shadov looted the Estrovian treasury, but Voudel absconds with the funds and checks into a swanky hotel suite while the king is processed through immigration. Much of the remainder of the film is devoted to the nearly destitute monarch and his ambassador trying to keep up appearances while struggling to raise money. Shadov attempts to sell his plans for peaceful applications for nuclear energy to the Atomic Commission, but the Commission is slow to respond. Shadov gains national celebrity after pretty Ann Kay (Addams) dupes him into appearing on her *Candid Camera*–like television program, *Ann Kay's Real-Life Surprise Party*, during which the king

In 1947, Charles Chaplin became one of the first Hollywood figures called by HUAC to testify about Reds in Hollywood. Unfairly vilified, he departed Hollywood for England in 1952, and would not return for twenty years. Chaplin's *A King in New York* (1957), the seriocomic tale of a deposed ruler and a troubled child, expresses Chaplin's disdain for political bullying.

performs Hamlet's "to be or not to be" soliloquy in bombastic fashion and generally makes an ass of himself. After his TV appearance, however, offers pour in for product endorsements, some of which he grudgingly accepts, including one for a vile-tasting brand of whiskey. Despite the duplicity, Shadov remains smitten with Ann, who encourages him to endure plastic surgery as part of another advertising scheme that goes awry.

The king also takes in the local nightlife and appears at diplomatic functions. He visits a night club with a cacophonous rock band so loud that he's forced to mime his request for caviar and turtle soup, and attends a cinema where he and Jaume strain their necks trying to view a western shoot-out on the wide Cinerama screen. More significantly, he tours a progressive boys' school, where he makes the acquaintance of a clever but pompous young boy named Rupert Macabee (Michael Chaplin), who espouses Marxist philosophy while other students pelt Shadov with spitballs and trick him into sitting on a frosted layer cake. Weeks later, Shadov discovers Rupert shivering in the cold rain outside the king's hotel. Rupert's parents, it seems, were jailed for contempt after being brought before a HUAC-like government committee and refusing to name names. Rupert was dismissed from school and has nowhere to go. Shadov takes him in, offers him a warm bath and a meal, and leaves with Jaume to purchase the boy some new clothes. While they're out, however, the Atomic Commission representatives finally arrive at Shadov's suite and meet Rupert. The boy tells them he's Shadov's nephew and launches into another Communist diatribe. Soon Shadov is subpoenaed to appear before the committee. On the way, he becomes entangled with a firehose and winds up accidentally blasting his accusers with water. Later, after (improbably) being cleared of wrongdoing, Shadov discovers that Rupert is back at school and his parents are free—because Rupert provided authorities with the identities of some of his parents' friends and associates. Although the schoolmaster praises Rupert as "a hero and a real patriot," the boy has lost his self-respect and seems despondent. Shadov, who is now preparing to leave for Europe, promises Rupert he will return once the "hysteria" has ended.

Clown v. Pamphleteer

A King in New York had its premiere in London on September 12, 1957. Anticipation for the film was keen, stoked by Chaplin's airtight security around the picture while it was in production. Journalists were barred from Shepperton's Studio C, and rumors swirled that the movie would be anti–American. This belief was reinforced when Chaplin announced that the film would not be released in the U.S. and American journalists would not be invited to its premiere. Critical reception was mixed. The *Daily Herald* and *Sunday Times*, among others, printed glowing notices. Esteemed author J.B. Priestley opined that Chaplin "has turned film clowning into social satire and criticism, without losing his astonishing ability to make us laugh." But some were less enthused. *Daily Mail* reviewer Cecil Wilson described *A King in New York* as "Chaplin the matchless clown fighting a losing battle with Chaplin the pompous pamphleteer." *Daily Express* critic Donald Gomery seemed at best lukewarm toward the picture and wondered if Chaplin might have "exaggerated the evil influence of the Committee on Un-American Activities." Meanwhile, American writers, most of whom hadn't even seen the film, wrote scathing articles about it. (The picture earned mostly sympathetic reviews from Stateside critics following its belated 1973 U.S. release. "I love the film," declared Andrew Sarris of the *Village Voice*.)

A King in New York views the larger American culture as fundamentally political, even when the politics are not overt. As the destitute king tries to make his way in New York, he meets Ann Kay (Dawn Addams), a television personality and marketing sharpie who convinces the king to do an endorsement advert for whiskey. To Chaplin's way of thinking, consumerism and cults of personality amounted to a squandering of Americans' freedom to choose.

In a particularly perceptive review, the London *Evening Standard* called *A King in New York* Chaplin's "most bitter" and "most openly personal" film. These are the picture's most striking qualities. All of Chaplin's previous features—even the dark *Monsieur Verdoux*—are lined with sweetness, often crossing into blatant sentimentality. In its icy cynicism, *A King in New York* stands apart. The only tenderness in the story arises from Shadov's pity for poor Rupert and the king's wistful affection for his estranged queen (which isn't strong enough to prevent him from pursuing a dalliance with Ann). None of the characters, apart from the steadfastly loyal and level-headed Jaume, are particularly likeable. That includes King Shadov, who serves as a thinly disguised stand-in for Chaplin himself.

Apart from the obvious parallels with Chaplin's HUAC problems and his real-life anxiety over the potential loss of his life savings, Shadov's disdain for widescreen movies mirrors Chaplin's resistance to advances in film technology. He was the last major Western filmmaker to make the transition to sound, and wouldn't release a widescreen color picture until *A Countess from Hong Kong* (1967), his final movie. Shadov's loathing of rock and roll reflects Chaplin's distaste for contemporary popular music. His *A King in New York* songs, apart from the faux rock number, could have been composed for a musical from the early talkie era. In California, Chaplin's son Michael attended a progressive school like Rupert's; presumably Shadov's antipathy for television, advertising, and plastic surgery also reflect Chaplin's feelings. Indeed, *A King in New York* may reveal more than its director ever intended. Shadov, although married, is attracted to a younger woman; following the breakup of his first three marriages, Chaplin wed younger women. Viewers may well wonder if the vain, snobbish, greedy, and deeply insecure monarch bears further comparison with the private Chaplin.

The film suffers from other deficiencies. Cinematographer Georges Perinal was a major talent who had worked with Rene Clair, Jean Cocteau, Carol Reed, and Michael Powell and Emeric Pressburger, among others, but the tight shooting schedule gave him little opportunity to demonstrate his gifts. As a result, *A King in New York* looks flat and bland. The picture's London exteriors and obvious stock footage make an unconvincing substitute for Manhattan. Chaplin and Addams have no chemistry, and Shadov's scenes with Kay—particularly one at a photo shoot, where the king attempts to grope the young woman—backfire, making Shadov seem like a predatory old reprobate. The project also would have benefited from some judicious editing. At 110 minutes it runs at least a half-hour too long. The dialogue is banal, and most of its comedic set pieces—Shadov's television appearances, the visit to the progressive school, his appearance before the Committee—prove disappointing, never achieving the heights of ingenious lunacy reached by the director's earlier films.

This being a Chaplin picture, however, it is not entirely devoid of laughs. The funniest scene is Shadov's mimed request for caviar from a befuddled waiter. First, he pretends to be a fish, then indicates having his belly slit open and eggs scooped out. "I think I'll have something else," reports a suddenly queasy Jaume. In another excellent sequence, botched plastic surgery turns Shadov into something that resembles Lon Chaney's Phantom of the Opera, but his face returns to normal when he "ruins" his facelift by laughing at the supper club antics of a pair of Laurel and Hardy-like comedians. Nevertheless, Chaplin seems off his game throughout, and receives little support from the rest of the cast. Michael Chaplin's work as Rupert is inconsistent, ranging from poor to passable. The finest supporting performance, by far, comes from Johnston, whose Jaume plays off Chaplin beautifully. Sidney James, soon to gain fame via the *Carry On* film series, also leaves a favorable impression as a fast-talking advertising agent.

If nothing else, *A King in New York* demonstrates that Chaplin was not as politically sophisticated as his enemies claimed. As an attack on McCarthyism, the film is mostly a missed opportunity—daring in its choice of targets but often missing the mark, and frequently reverting to old-fashioned slapstick. The climactic sequence in which Shadov confronts the Committee and accidentally blasts them with a fire hose could have originated in one of Chaplin's early Mack Sennett shorts. Many critics have complained that Chaplin diluted his satirical message by taking jabs at a number of targets in addition to HUAC, including widescreen movies, rock music, television, advertising, and plastic surgery. At this distance, however, these sequences (while not always effective) seem far more relevant and vital than the anti–HUAC material. In this 1957 feature, Chaplin judged American culture to be faddish, superficial, youth-obsessed, and materialistic. That indictment would stand even today.

Tears of Rage

The House Un-American Activities Committee was formed in 1938, following the outbreak of World War II, to investigate subversive activity by Nazi sympathizers and Communists in the U.S. Renamed the House Committee on Internal Security in 1969, the body wasn't disbanded until 1975. But its influence was greatest in the late 1940s through the middle 1950s, when it thrived in the paranoid, ultra-nationalist atmosphere created by Wisconsin junior senator Joseph McCarthy, chairman of the U.S. Senate's Permanent Subcommittee on Investigations, a separate but like-minded legislative entity. HUAC's greatest triumph was the conviction of accused Soviet spy Alger Hiss on perjury charges in 1948.

None of HUAC's film industry targets were convicted of a crime other than contempt of Congress, a charge many industry workers faced for refusing to cooperate with the investigation. Studio chiefs, under pressure from Congress, prevented those who ran afoul of the committee from working openly in Hollywood. The careers of (by some accounts) nearly three hundred writers, producers, directors, and actors were derailed due to blacklisting. Many European filmmakers working in Hollywood, such as Jules Dassin, returned to the Continent. Some Americans, such as Orson Welles and Paul Robeson, followed Chaplin and also moved to Europe. Others labored under pseudonyms or through "fronts" (working under the name of a trusted colleague). The careers of most never fully recovered. These included Chaplin, whose effective deportation proved catastrophic. As *A King in New York* revealed, it was virtually impossible for Chaplin to work outside of his personal studio in California. At age sixty-five, Chaplin was unable or unwilling to adapt his eccentric methods to conform to modern industry standards and expectations. He managed to direct just one more film, *A Countess from Hong Kong*, which was even less engaging than *A King in New York*.

For all its faults, *A King New York* remains a curiously compelling work. It still pulses like a raw nerve. There is nothing else quite like it in the filmography of another major director, except perhaps Ingmar Bergman's *The Rite*, a cinematic temper tantrum conceived in the wake of Bergman's ouster as director of the Royal Dramatic Theatre in Stockholm. *A King in New York* was also one of the few politically themed projects created by HUAC victims to see the light of day. In 1954, five members of the Hollywood Ten (the first ten film professionals to be held in contempt by HUAC) banded together to independently produce *Salt of the Earth*, a pro-union movie about striking mine workers, but the picture received almost no distribution. Other filmmakers challenged blacklisting and McCarthyism in subtler ways. Crusading producer Stanley Kramer's *Storm Center* (1956) struck back at censorship with the story of a small town librarian (Bette Davis) who refuses to remove a banned book on communism from her library's shelves. Other movies, such as Fred Zinnemann's *High Noon* (1952) and Don Siegel's *Invasion of the Body Snatchers* (1956), were read by some as coded indictments of McCarthy and HUAC. But no one was as straightforward and uncompromising as Chaplin. For that reason, or maybe because its protagonist is so nakedly autobiographical, *A King in New York* remains the only film of the era to convey a real sense of the pain of being blacklisted. Part of the reason the movie isn't as funny as it might have been is that it personalizes that experience for the audience, and plays at times like a howl of anguish and outrage. Chaplin made many better movies than this one, but none more heartfelt or more courageous.

Filmography

A King in New York—Attica Film Company/Archway (UK release); Classic Entertainment (USA release, 1972); Released September 12, 1957 (UK); March 8, 1972 (USA); Black and white; 110 min. (UK); 105 min. (USA)

    Credits: Producer: Charles Chaplin; Director: Charles Chaplin; Screenplay: Charles Chaplin; Director of photography: Georges Périnal; Editor: John Seabourne; Music: Charles Chaplin; Art director: Allan Harris

    Cast: Charles Chaplin: King Shahdov; Maxine Audley: Queen Irene; Dawn Addams: Ann Kay; Oliver Johnston: Ambassador Jaume; Jerry Desmonde: Prime Minister Voudel; Michael Chaplin: Rupert Macabee; Sidney James: Johnson

Works Cited

Books

Chaplin, Charles. *My Autobiography*. New York: Simon & Schuster, 1964.
Mitchell, Glenn. *The Chaplin Encyclopedia*. London: Batsford, 1997.
McDonald, Gerald, Michael Conway, and Mark Ricci, eds. *The Complete Films of Charlie Chaplin*. Secaucus, NJ: Citadel, 1988.
Robinson, David. *Chaplin: His Life and Art*. New York: McGraw-Hill, 1985.
Vance, Jeffrey. *Chaplin: Genius of the Cinema*. New York: Abrams, 2003.

Web

bergmanorama.webs.com/films/rite_parkinson.htm
charliechaplin.com/en/films/10-A-king-in-new-york/articles/9-Filming-A-King-in-New-York
imdb.com/title/tt0050598/

DVD

A King in New York/A Woman of Paris. Image Entertainment. 1993.

Riddle of the Pinks
Did The Fearmakers *Have* The Whip Hand?

REYNOLD HUMPHRIES

The title of this essay evokes two films which, in different ways, were part of the "anti–Red cycle" of the 1950s: *The Fearmakers* (directed by Jacques Tourneur, 1958) and *The Whip Hand* (William Cameron Menzies, 1951). Our purpose here is to show that, despite their clear anti–Communist message, both films can be (and have been) interpreted as representing points of view that sit uneasily with the straightforward "Reds under the bed"" discourse of most of the anti–Communist films produced by Hollywood from 1948 on. In the case of *The Fearmakers* certain questions arise, particularly: why produce this anti–Red melodrama in 1958, when the vast majority of these pictures were made in the period 1948–52? Why make a film in which the Korean War plays a crucial role five years after the end of hostilities? If one were to answer that the Communist menace still continued (for instance, the crushing of the Hungarian uprising in 1956 following revelations concerning Stalin's crimes), then it is legitimate to ask why *The Whip Hand*, although made during the height of the anti–Red cycle, evokes Nazi war crimes and returns to 1946, another date preceding the movie by five years. Is this justified simply because one of the characters is a Nazi war criminal high on America's wanted list? That answer would be satisfactory but for narrative elements of *The Whip Hand* that are uneasy bedfellows with the supposed Communist menace. These and other questions will be answered in what follows. Given that neither film is particularly well-known, a summary of their respective plots is necessary in order to facilitate the discussion.

The Fearmakers is focused on Alan Eaton (Dana Andrews), a former army officer who has just been released from the hospital, where he was treated for beatings and brainwashing administered by the Chinese during the Korean War. After returning to Washington to take up where he left off, as co-owner of a public relations firm, he discovers not only that his partner has sold the business to one Jim McGinnis (Dick Foran) without consulting him, but that the partner has been killed in a hit-and-run accident. Eaton reluctantly accepts a well-paid job working for McGinnis and soon begins to suspect that what had been an enterprise devoted to organizing and selling the results of opinion polls to politicians or businessmen to help them keep in touch with the sentiments of their constituents and customers has become a service that twists facts for clients, in order to impose a particular politician on the public. Eaton's suspicions are shared by an old friend, Senator Walder (Roy Gordon), both of whom come to the same

188 Part 3: Dupes, Victims and Crusaders

In Jacques Tourneur's *The Fearmakers* (1958), troubled Korean War vet Alan Eaton (Dana Andrews, center) returns to his D.C. public relations firm, only to learn that his partner is dead, and that the company has been sold to Jim McGinnis (Dick Foran, left). Despite the snooping of McGinnis's peculiar assistant, Barney (Mel Torme, right), Eaton discovers that the firm secretly manipulates polling data to advance the Communist agenda against America. Like Chaplin's *A King in New York*, *The Fearmakers* casts a disapproving gaze on American business and marketing—but this time, the stakes are the security of the United States.

conclusion: the PR firm is nothing but a front designed to help elect politicians engaged in treason—specifically, opposition to American nuclear policy, the better to advance the aims of the Soviet Union and Red China. The narrative climaxes with a car chase ending at the Lincoln Memorial, where Eaton confronts McGinnis and hands him over to the police.

The Whip Hand opens with journalist Matt Corbin doing a spot of fishing on one of Minnesota's lakes. A sudden deluge causes him to lose his balance and have a nasty fall. While attempting to reach the small nearby town of Winnoga, he hoped to find help inside a fenced-in property, only to be driven off at the point of a gun. This openly aggressive behavior finds a more insidious equivalent in Winnoga, the equivalent of a frontier ghost town, a once-thriving postwar community built on trout breeding, now nearly emptied of residents because the trout have been wiped out by disease. Corbin, whose injury has been treated by Dr. Keller (Edgar Barrier) and Keller's sister Janet (Carla Balenda), finds it odd that people should still be living there, especially as the few that do spend their time spying on him and the one small businessman left, the elderly Luther

Adams (Frank Darien). Despite his affable appearance, one denizen of the town, Steve Loomis (Raymond Burr), whose sister Molly (Lurene Tuttle) handles all incoming and outgoing phone calls, is clearly involved in something nefarious, as is Mr. Petersen (Lewis Martin), owner of the private property where Corbin received so unfriendly a welcome. Corbin manages to sneak onto Petersen's property and get sufficiently close to his home to notice the presence of physically handicapped men and a man he recognizes as Dr. Bucholtz (Otto Waldis), a Nazi war criminal wanted by the federal government. It transpires that Bucholtz fled behind the Iron Curtain in 1946 and that the little town of Winnoga has been taken over by American Communists who finance the doctor's experiments. Thanks to the doctor's discoveries, a prolongation of his activities under the aegis of the Third Reich, the Communist community intends to contaminate America's water supplies and bring the country to its knees. Warned by Corbin, the FBI storms Petersen's property and kills everyone there.

* * *

Apart from their dire warnings about the dangers of Communists inside America, *The Fearmakers* and *The Whip Hand* appear to be dissimilar. The former is a thriller with the Korean War as a backdrop, the other a film noir with science fiction elements. Although on the radar of some film cultists, neither movie is ordinarily discussed in relation to the other. Additionally, only *The Whip Hand* has been interpreted at its face value. Attention is systematically drawn to the fact that it was originally conceived as an anti–Nazi film, with *Hitler* hiding in Petersen's domain; scenes showing both the *Führer* and two German officers were deleted to make way for the anti–Communist message. This was due to RKO owner Howard Hughes, a leading witch-hunter who insisted on a revised script and expensive reshoots, to boost the picture's timeliness.

In *The Fearmakers*, however, anti–Communist discourse is subordinate to the film's interest in public relations, politics, and big business. We shall analyze *The Fearmakers* from this standpoint, but it is necessary at this juncture to highlight an aspect shared by both movies, one that seems to have gone largely unnoticed: the vexing question of spying on one's fellow citizens—how, for whom, and for what purposes. In *The Fearmakers*, "prying" would perhaps be a better term, though the activity still amounts to observation without the knowledge or consent of the individuals or the larger society in which this activity takes place. In *The Whip Hand* and *The Fearmakers* alike, American citizens are victims—less of Communist infiltration than of values presented as socially necessary. *The Whip Hand* is driven by distorted values presented as tools that combat communism; *The Fearmakers* proposes that institutional amorality gives allows citizens free choice in an open society. Let us start with this, the later film.

The opening sequences are articulated in such a way as to lay the groundwork for the film's political agenda; subsequent elements simply reinforce what is meant to be clear from the outset. Thus the credits unfold over shots of Alan Eaton being beaten by Chinese prison guards. Then we see his discharge from a hospital where he has been treated for shock, particularly the effects of brainwashing. The doctor warns him to anticipate recurring headaches and even blackouts, and urges him to seek medical help in D.C. in case of problems. The montage suggests Eaton's vulnerability, and the subsequent sequence on board the plane transporting Eaton to the nation's capital introduces the subtext of subversion and treason perpetrated by American Communists. Eaton is seated beside a passenger who suddenly engages him in conversation, one of those ruses screenwriters are well versed in and without which the film would grind to a halt. Even before he presents himself as Dr. Jessop, a specialist in nuclear physics, he is connoted for the spectator as an intellectual: he wears heavy, horn-rimmed spectacles![1] This harks back to a scene in an early anti–Red drama, *The Woman on Pier 13* (1950), in which a naive worker submits to a lot of talk—from a man strikingly similar to Dr. Jessop—about working conditions and labor strikes. Given the incestuous nature of Hollywood filmmaking (that is, what has worked in one film is likely to be imitated later), Jessop might be interpreted as an amalgam of two members of the Hollywood Ten, Dalton Trumbo (frequently photographed wearing spectacles) and John Howard Lawson (a dedicated Marxist theorist).[2] It is obvious, though, that Jessop's profession evokes real-life scientists Robert Oppenheimer and Linus Pauling. Both—particularly the aggressive Pauling—were considered security risks because of their political liberalism, and their increasing anxiety over the Bomb.

In the course of the relatively long conversation between Jessop and Eaton—whose expression soon displays distaste for what he hears, a sure sign that the audience must be on their guard—the scientist deplores the ever-closer link between science and the military, stating, "Science has brought us to the brink of world extermination." This was the opinion of yet another scientist whose radical views led to his being the object of surveillance by the FBI for years: Albert Einstein. It also surely echoes the opinions of another subversive who hid in plain sight, President Eisenhower, who excoriated what he called the "military-industrial complex."

Jessop is part of a campaign to abolish nuclear warfare and to put a stop to military encroachment on territory held by science. He concludes his monologue with a quote from Shakespeare, another sure sign of intellectual decadence. During the heyday of film noir a decade earlier, Jessop would have been connoted not as a Communist but as gay in order to mark him out as a villain. (See Waldo Lydecker in *Laura* [1944] and the wealthy art collector in *The Dark Corner* [1946], both played by Clifton Webb.)

Jessop's narrative function in *The Fearmakers* is multifold: besides establishing himself as an intellectual Communist, he gives Eaton a lodging address in Washington. Eaton takes advantage of this information when he finds himself without a hotel. The resulting sequence is as surreal as it is ludicrous, a perfect example of a script stacking the cards so that not even the most obtuse spectator can miss the point. It also shows a cavalier disregard for verisimilitude in the name of opportunistic ideology-mongering, not to mention total contempt for the spectator's intelligence. The address is a private house with rooms for rent, owned by Vivian and Harold Loder (Veda Ann Borg, Kelly Thordsen). Borg is lively as an aging floozy who expresses her loathing for her drunken husband by encouraging Eaton to beat him up after the husband has assaulted her. Mr. Loder is a thug who recalls similar characters in *The Woman on Pier 13*, *The Red Menace* (1949), *I Was a Communist for the FBI* (1951), and *Walk East on Beacon* (1952),[3] important earlier anti–Red melodramas. Loder is so seedy and vicious that even the least discriminating nightclub would shirk at hiring him as a bouncer. Eaton follows Mrs. Loder's suggestion, and as a former professional soldier, he makes mincemeat of the husband. Although the sequence validates Eaton as "tough," viewers are surely entitled to wonder how Jessop can possibly consort with people presented as the dregs of society. But then, *The Fearmakers* is not very subtle on such issues.

It is only in retrospect that audiences can read all the signs, although I would argue that Mr. Loder is just too bad to be true; no intelligent person (like Dr. Jessop), eager to

The displaced PR man (Dana Andrews, left) is fortunate to have an influential ally: a U.S. senator (Roy Gordon) who encourages Eaton to remain with the compromised firm, and discover its methods and intentions. *The Fearmakers* suggests that the Communist takeover may be achieved with ideas rather than bombs.

convince another of the rightness of a cause, would jeopardize a subversive set-up of the kind Jessop pilots by introducing a man with a distinguished war record (Eaton) to people like the Loders. We are in the realm here of pure ideology, where the only thing that matters is to make a crude point. By referring to Jessop and McGinnis as heading "fronts," and stating that the latter is possibly "a paid foreign agent," the film is not exactly making it difficult for the audience to catch on to the significance of their activities. However, the filmmakers obviously decided that, given the time at which the picture was made, something was needed to enable the spectator to identify with both plot and characters—to understand what's going on *and* draw the right conclusions about the Communist menace. The story's central irony is that the use and abuse of public relations, opinion polls, and advertising seriously compromises the entire political project, such as it is.

Eaton is invited to lunch with an old friend, Senator Walder. It is crucial that this meeting should take place prior to Eaton's going to stay with the Loders, since Walder has made remarks essential for pushing the audience in the right direction, and allowing them to interpret correctly, with the benefit of hindsight, the role of Jessop and the couple he recommends. The senator is chairman of a committee investigating how public opinion is being manipulated. He refers to "a highly financed, full-time organization" in

Washington whose purpose is "to pressure Congress" with "a professionally packaged campaign" larded with "high-sounding titles" and "fake front groups." As the senator sees it, there are "groups in this country out to sell peace at any price." He continues, using the word "fronts" a second time and adding that the organization has a "facade of respectability" designed to fool "the well-intentioned." Denouncing their "hidden loyalties," Senator Walder raises the specter of "a new Munich," that is, pacifistic capitulation to aggression. The word "fronts" points unambiguously to the Communist Party, an accusation leveled at the Party most vehemently in the early 1950s, when the House Un-American Activities Committee (HUAC) returned (after early snooping in 1947) to investigate Hollywood in February 1951. A horrified Eaton talks of "propaganda" and "treason." The latter term is particularly loaded, since it was common since the end of the 1940s to accuse the Communist Party of trying to overthrow the elected American government by violence (the definition of "treason").[4] We shall return to "propaganda" later.

It is during the discussion between Eaton and Barney (Mel Torme), the seemingly timid workhorse at the PR firm, that the film simultaneously reveals its hand concerning Communist attempts to manipulate both public and politicians, and introduces elements that totally displace the issue. With Barney, the film is hoist with its own petard. Although he works for McGinnis, he admires Eaton's work on advertising. Indeed, it is in his discussion with Barney that Eaton contradicts himself, and the film's ideological framework starts to crumble. For Eaton, public opinion polls are purely objective, serving politicians and public because the former need to know the latter's real feelings. This is idealistic at best and cynical at worst. Does the film really want its audience to accept that politicians want to know the public's feelings simply in order to carry out the policies the public is meant to want? The very phrasing of a question can obtain the answer one wants: "Are you against nuclear war?" is hardly likely to get a majority of people answering in the negative, however anti–Communist they may be. Similarly, "Do you believe in the sanctity of human life?" will also draw positive replies, including from those firmly in favor of capital punishment. And so on. (One is reminded of the story of the man who claimed any question could be answered by "yes" or "no." Challenged by a member of the audience to prove his theory, he unwisely accepted and was asked the following question: "Have you stopped beating your wife?")

Eaton has been accustomed to a world that has restricted selling to such stuff as soap and automobiles. He's put out when Barney informs him that politicians are now products. "It's still our job," Barney informs Eaton, "to sell the people a package."

Time has done nothing to diminish Barney's point of view. As in 1958, people and objects are interchangeable: "a package" can be a perfume, a home, or the local mayor—such is the intensity of reification and commodity fetishism in consumer societies. When Eaton denounces the tactic of asking people to express an opinion on an assumption that is not a fact, he puts his finger on something fundamental, but it has nothing to do with communism. When X hears that Y has been accused of pedophilia without an ounce of proof, X replies: "There's no smoke without fire." In which case, we are surely entitled to ask, "Then who lit the fire in the first place?" This is exactly what Eaton does when he asks Barney, "What's behind the billboard?" and "What's inside the package?" In other words: who's pulling the strings? For Eaton, Walder, and the filmmakers, the answer is simple. The puppeteers are Communists and fellow travelers.

Unfortunately for them, information of another kind was already available by the time the film was made. In 1957 Vance Packard published *The Hidden Persuaders*. Back-cover copy from the book's 1957 first edition describes what Packard called the Age of Manipulation, peopled by "the new breed of depth men, the motivational researchers," and how "they glide through your subconscious, charting your hidden urges, fears, frustrations, and wish fulfilments. [H]ow they are using this information to engineer your consent to buy, believe in, and even vote for what they want you to may well give you a slightly chilly feeling along the spine."

The Hidden Persuaders explicated the "eerie world of public-relations-men-turned-psychoanalysts." In the chapter called "Politics and the Image Builders," Packard refers to Stanley Kelley, Jr., a member of the Brookings Institution marketing think tank. Kelley wrote a book about the 1952 presidential campaign and concluded that General Eisenhower was handled by "professional propagandists" that used "strategy, treatment of issues, use of media, budgeting, and pacing" to sell Ike just as surely as ad men sold soap and candy bars. So where does *The Fearmakers* stand when it puts the word "propaganda" into Eaton's mouth to denounce the manifestly Communist pressure group the senator sees at work lobbying Congress? It is not a matter of saying the senator is wrong but of pointing out the simple fact that, years before the film claimed Communists resorted to such underhand tactics, American politicians and their handlers were doing exactly the same thing.

Packard quotes Leonard Hall, GOP chairman in 1956 (another victory for Ike) as stating that the Republican Party "has a great product to sell.... You sell your candidates and your programs the way a business sells its products." The film's Senator Walder denounces such tactics as un–American!

It is in this context that *The Fearmakers* highlights further contradictions. As already stated, the film presents Eaton as a victim of brainwashing, yet no evidence of this is produced; we see him being beaten by Chinese Communists, and the drunken Harold Loder beats him up in like fashion. Is this "proof" that Eaton is a Red? Do his headaches and temporary blackouts confirm brainwashing? Cinema's key affirmative answer to that question involves the Laurence Harvey character in *The Manchurian Candidate* (1962), who responds, zombie-like, to verbal stimuli planted in his unconscious. Can this be Eaton's plight as well?

These questions suggest subliminal advertising, long banned as immoral, and illegal in the United States. *The Fearmakers* reveals nothing that we can reasonably interpret as Communist brainwashing—yet it does show one character under the influence of subliminal advertising perpetrated by American business: Eaton himself! During the conversation on the plane, Jessop takes pains to insist on the beneficial aspects of science, a stance that probably is his attempt to cover up his subversive and treasonable denunciation of the dangerous links between science and the military. He refers to a "profession of mass persuasion" and mentions the gains made by science in establishing links between tobacco and certain "malignant diseases." In other words: smoking causes cancer. History has proved Jessop right, but we must stress here that Eaton is a chain-smoker. He cannot undertake any activity, such as combing the secret files in McGinniss's office, without lighting up. He's addicted. Given this, the film makes "brainwashing" manifest in the form of subliminal advertising: Eaton is unconsciously coded always to have a cigarette between his fingers. Unless we believe Communists had taken over Madison Avenue, the film cuts the ground out from under its own feet.[5]

Audiences, both then and now, might also find it difficult to imagine America as being in danger, even if people like McGinnis were to create millions of acolytes, if they all resembled hardworking Barney. A prototypical well-meaning nerd, he is utilized to show how easily people can be influenced, but he is so massively coded, confused, and impotent that even if there were *millions* like him, capitalism and democracy would have nothing to fear. Today, no doubt, he would be a movie zombie, lurching across country, munching everyone who got in his way. (*The Brain Eaters*, a no-budget science-horror thriller released the same year as *The Fearmakers*, can be interpreted as anti–Communist, while simultaneously opening up a different ideological vista.)

The Fearmakers is anxious to pillory left-wing intellectuals who toe the Party line, and woolly-minded liberals who go along because of the horrors of nuclear war. We have already argued that conservatives and anti–Communists could also see the wisdom of avoiding nuclear war. In 1951, year two of the Korean War, 76 percent of Americans favored a meeting between President Truman and Stalin, and yet after the war was over a majority felt the conflict had not threatened internal security. But what related information does the film give us about McGinnis? The senator believes that only a small step separates manipulating the public via opinion polls, to the election of a politician likely to become a "paid foreign agent" and sell out the USA. Eaton accuses McGinnis of "peddling fear," but was it not ideologues in the West who characterized nuclear weapons as a deterrent that would protect the West from Soviet aggression? Is this not a perfect case of "peddling fear"?[6]

Does the film prove that McGinnis is a Communist or fellow-traveler? On two occasions, McGinnis shows contempt for "the Chinese Commies," but what if McGinnis is a squalid opportunist, out to make a quick buck at everyone's expense? This is not just a rhetorical question.

* * *

We've seen that *The Whip Hand* morphed from an anti–Hitler screed into an anti–Communist tale. As rewritten, the Red angle is resolved when the FBI comes to the rescue in the nick of time. Still, *The Whip Hand* bears the mark of its origins, and suggestions of the rejiggered nature of the story. Hindsight suggests that the picture is a pivotal example of the period's political paranoia of the period, and that that paranoia arose from historical, as opposed to ideological, reasons. Whereas director Jacques Tourneur never gives the impression of having felt implicated in the *mise en scène* of *The Fearmakers*, William Cameron Menzies brought a considerably more stylized, film noir influence to *The Whip Hand*. The articulation of gloom, suspicion, and paranoia—as well as a hint of very different sorts of films to come—positions *The Whip Hand* as an intriguing document.

The story opens with a voice solemnly intoning, "At this very moment, behind the heavily-guarded walls of the Kremlin…." Cut to a Red Army officer pointing out various towns on a map of America to an attentive audience, finishing with the little town of Winnoga, Minnesota. So we know the Soviets are up to something dastardly and have chosen a tiny, out-of-the-way place for their scheme. And yet one can discern a flaw in the scheme. Behind the formulaic conceit of "the heavily-guarded walls of the Kremlin" hide other formulae in which "Kremlin" is replaced by "the Pentagon," "the White House," or "Fort Knox."[7] Indeed, one character refers to Mr. Petersen's secluded property as being "guarded tighter than the hydrogen bomb." This is an extraordinary remark that draws an explicit parallel between the secrecy endemic to the rulers of the Soviet Union and the "national security" mindset of secret-keepers in Washington. So the Kremlin and the

Despite having conked his head while fishing early in *The Whip Hand* (1951), journalist Matt Corbin's visit to Winnoga, Minnesota, promises to be nothing special—until he discovers that most of the locals, including the "friendly" innkeeper (Lurene Tuttle), are part of a monstrous Communist scheme to kill tens of millions of Americans.

White House behave in the same way, their every deed and word dictated by mutual fear and hostility. However, far more is involved in *The Whip Hand* than mere politics, and that is the crippling nuclear anxiety of America's John and Jane Doe.[8] One user of the Internet Movie Database points out that the surname of the doctor and his sister, Keller, evokes that of Hungarian-American Edward Teller, father of the H-bomb.[9] Dr. Teller is widely as the model for the title character of Kubrick's *Dr. Strangelove*, although given Keller's physical appearance and his guttural German accent, Dr. Henry Kissinger seems a more likely model. For the purposes of this essay, however, it is more cogent and pertinent to remember that Dr. Strangelove was a former Nazi now in the pay of the American government, whereas Dr. Bucholtz is a Nazi who has thrown in his lot with the Kremlin.

Otto Waldis, the actor who plays Bucholtz, also played the leader of the underground group working to reinstate Nazism in *Berlin Express* (Jacques Tourneur, 1948). That film takes place immediately after the end of hostilities in Europe and raises, among other issues, the denazification of Germany. There was, alas, much hypocrisy involved in the Allied attitude to this problem. On the one hand, the Nuremberg trials were a model for deciding who was responsible for the carrying out of acts of genocide and for determining the concepts of "war crimes" and "crimes against humanity." They completely eschewed the notion of revenge on a defeated nation (which had enabled Hitler to come to power following the victorious Allies' Versailles Treaty of 1919, conceived to punish and humiliate the German nation after the Great War). Summary executions, too, were prohibited. On the other hand, it was the small fry who were most commonly caught up in the denazification process, the German equivalents of John Doe who joined the Nazi Party out of fear or opportunism. We know that leading Nazis were either helped to escape (to South America) or were kept in power in the name of the new game: anti-communism. Thus Bucholtz's post–World War II escape behind the Iron Curtain should be put down to the doctor's desire for personal aggrandizement. The Soviets prepared themselves to use anyone and exploit any knowledge, in the conviction that they were right and capitalism doomed to destruction.

The unpalatable mixture of moral confusion and downright cant that characterized so much Allied thinking in the postwar period is as responsible for the question of confused identities in *The Whip Hand* as the film's switch from Nazis to Communists in mid-production. One of the town thugs is a young man with short blond hair that connotes him as a Nazi—in which case we can look behind the filmic text to the pro–Nazi German American Bund of the 1930s. Coded information even more obvious than the blond hair is the cap worn by one menacing character who appears suddenly, as if out of nowhere, whenever it is necessary to keep an eye on another character, such as the hero Matt Corbin and the storekeeper Luther Adams, who has miraculously survived the takeover by Communists. The simple cap suggests a proletarian—and therefore of a Communist! But it is made of leather, which is more likely to connote the Gestapo for original audiences for whom World War II was all too real, and too recent a memory to tamper with.

Besides trafficking in the rampant paranoia inherent in both film noir and the postwar climate of imminent Apocalypse,[10] *The Whip Hand* suggests germ war waged on America by Communists, an idea straight out of the science-horror genre. We have already mentioned *The Brain Eaters*, but earlier and more cogent examples exist: *The Thing from Another World* (1951), *It Came from Outer Space* (1953), *Invaders from Mars* (1953), and *Invasion of the Body Snatchers* (1956).[11] Only the first and last of these merit close attention here.[12] Produced by the conservative but often "politically incorrect" Howard Hawks, *The Thing* has its own Dr. Jessop in the shape of the scientist (= intellectual) who is ready to risk everyone's lives by elevating contact with the dangerous alien above all other concerns. Is this not an attack on the notion of peaceful coexistence that *The Fearmakers* is anxious to denounce?

Equally interesting is the curious coincidence that brings *The Thing* together with what is arguably the most unethical and repulsive film to come out of Hollywood during the period, *I Was a Communist for the F.B.I.*[13] The coincidence lies in the meeting of fiction and fact in the same place: the frozen North. The action of *The Thing* takes place at the North Pole and the main character of *I Was a Communist*, Matt Cvetic, was a real-life FBI informant who exposed Communist activity in Pittsburgh, Pennsylvania.[14] Cvetic's peculiar brand of patriotism, paranoia, and psychosis led him to claim that the Communists planned to invade the United States via Alaska. Another FBI plant in the local Communist Party cell, Joseph Mazzei, stated under oath that Party officers had taught him "how to blow bridges, poison water in reservoirs, and to eliminate people." Chief Justice

Earl Warren remarked that this testimony "has poisoned ... the reservoir and the reservoir cannot be cleansed without draining it of all impurity." Mazzei had been a particularly unsavory government informer since 1941, exposing Communists but developing self-aggrandizing fantasies anticipated by *The Whip Hand*, and reflected later in a vastly more subtle and intelligent science-horror film, Don Siegel's *Invasion of the Body Snatchers*.

Much has been written of the movie's ambiguity, interpreted as anti–Communist or anti–McCarthyist or both.[15] One detail common to both this film and *The Whip Hand* is crucial: just as Matt Corbin cannot get a message out of Winnoga by phone because the sister of Communist boss Loomis handles all phone messages, so the protagonist of *Body Snatchers* finds that the local telephone system is controlled by pods that frustrate his attempts to warn Washington. Siegel and screenwriter Mainwaring (a leftist who was briefly blacklisted prior to *Body Snatchers*) prepared and shot a decidedly disturbing and downbeat ending, with the hero lurching along a California freeway, attempting to warn people of the danger. Frenzied, he at last stares into the camera and cries "You're next!" But Allied Artists objected to the gloomy denouement, and insisted on an upbeat framing device by which the film opens with the hero trying desperately to convince a psychiatrist that he's not mad, and ends with news of a truck spilling its load of pods on a highway, a lucky accident that galvanizes the FBI into action.

One year after *The Whip Hand*, Hollywood came out with *Walk East on Beacon*, yet another entry in the anti–Red cycle. The film opens with a paean of praise to the FBI, whose help in making the film is acknowledged, and a call by the Bureau to all Americans: survey what's going on around you and, should you see anything suspicious, inform us. In other words, the FBI used Hollywood to encourage American citizens to spy on each other, on the assumption that even one's neighbor could turn out to be a Red. Conversely, *The Whip Hand* inadvertently reveals small-town America for what it was: not a hive of scheming Reds but a place where people behave precisely as the FBI encouraged people to behave. The fact that Winnoga lost its industry after the war must surely have resonated with many audiences that saw the picture. Communists moving to Winnoga and buying up homes cheaply corresponds exactly to what happened in Detroit in the 2000s: houses seized by banks and put up for sale for as little as $500! The real dread now evoked by the film's use of the word "takeover" is the chilliness of the corporate mentality, downsizing and outsourcing in the name of profit. Howard Hughes's switch from anti–Nazi to anti–Communist left a lot of semantic fallout that clouds the film's conscious message in ways that reveal the profound anxiety at work in America at the time.

This, of course, in no way changes the film's anti–Communist thrust. We would be wise not to impose too quickly a contemporary reading on entertainments that refuse to bend ideologically to our will. At this writing, a recent comment from the French cultural weekly *Télérama*, about the Paris reissue of Siegel's *Body Snatchers*, suggests that (in a famous photograph) the madly running hero and heroine are "fleeing McCarthyism." Although arguably true only with the benefit of hindsight, the remark does acknowledge postwar Americans' feelings of what continues to be a real threat, alienation and loss of identity. That said, the concept of Nazis or Communists taking over a small town as depicted in *The Whip Hand* is ludicrous. *It must mean something else*. Hence this essay's earlier interest in Joe McGinnis, the public relations front of *The Fearmakers*. He too can be viewed as basically just another representative of corporate capitalism, ready to sell anything to anyone, including his own country to the Soviet Union, if that swells his bank balance. Such an interpretation fits in more easily with the film's take on public relations, the subtext of which is the real problem facing America in the 1950s: the literal selling of the country for corporate profit, rather than selling it down the river, as if Soviet gunboats were about to appear on the Potomac.

If it is now far more difficult to place the Siegel film in the anti–Red cycle, there is a reductive tendency to do so with a contemporaneous film which is, generically, very close to *The Whip Hand*: Robert Aldrich's *Kiss Me Deadly* (1955). Because the latter turns on fissionable material (that is, the atomic bomb), *Kiss Me Deadly* is regarded seriously today. But when one considers the highly idiosyncratic, politically incorrect, corrosive, and socially committed cinema produced by Aldrich during the mid–'50s—*Apache* and *Vera Cruz* (both 1954), *The Big Knife* (1955), and *Attack!* (1956)—such a reading is perverse. Nary a Communist is in sight in *Kiss Me Deadly*, and the narrative is not one in which the hero turns "anti-communist and rout[s] atomic spies."[16] Granted that Dr. Soberin (another intellectual!) tells Gaby, his female companion in crime, that she cannot follow him where he is going, a remark that might be interpreted as a journey behind the Iron Curtain, or to South America, home to ex–Nazis (as Hitchcock showed us in *Notorious*, 1946). Soberin is not a creature ideology; his concerns are wealth and power.[17] Further, the brutish hoodlums (Jack Elam and Jack Lambert) of *Kiss Me Deadly* are not necessarily Reds in disguise. There is such a thing as genre, and introducing the Bomb into it need not bring spies and fellow travelers in its wake.

* * *

Because the *Télérama* writer wanted to deplore the American paranoia of the 1950s, he said that the principal characters of *Invasion of the Body Snatchers* are "fleeing McCarthyism." Since 9/11, a similar mindset is back with us. In the context of our analysis here, Athan Theoharis's 2002 book, *Chasing Spies: How the FBI Failed in Counterintelligence but Promoted the Politics of McCarthyism in the Cold War Years*, sums up both the real situation (there were pro-Soviet spies at work in the United States) and the ideological hay made of it by J. Edgar Hoover (to justify his persecution of anyone even mildly radical and non-conformist); and Senator McCarthy (who symbolized the Republican determination to destroy the social progress made under Roosevelt). The book's jacket shows a faceless figure, motionless and clad in hat and coat, standing in a street under a bridge. FBI agent? Communist courier? No way of telling.[18] The author has this to say about the period:

> Ideology led American Communists and Communist sympathizers to deliver classified documents to Soviet agents during the 1930s and World War II. These individuals made a conscious decision to convey such information to individuals whom they knew to be agents of a foreign power, even if they were temporary military allies. While not in every case treasonous, their actions violated the public trust and their responsibilities as federal employees to comply with the law and adhere to official policies.

Although that violation of trust, as well as activities of Senator McCarthy and HUAC have commanded intense interest, far less attention has been devoted to the FBI's politics of counterintelligence. Recently released—though heavily redacted—FBI records offer insights into both this counterintelligence failure and FBI officials' broader political purposes. They also raise disturbing questions about how secrecy, maintained ostensibly for counterintelligence reasons, undermined limited, constitutional government based on the rule of law and order.

In which case, neither the "fearmakers" nor those supposedly holding "the whip hand" were those excoriated by the two films under discussion here.

FILMOGRAPHIES

The Fearmakers—Pacemaker/United Artists; Released October 1958 (premiere); January 23, 1959 (wide); Black and white; 85 min.

Credits: Producer: Martin H. Lancer; Director: Jacques Tourneur; Screenplay: Elliot West, Chris Appley, b/o the novel *The Fear Makers* by Darwin L. Teilhet; Director of photography: Sam Leavitt; Editor: Paul Laune, J. R. Whittredge; Music: Irving Gertz; Art director: Serge Krizman

Cast: Dana Andrews: Alan Eaton; Dick Foran: Jim McGinnis; Marilee Earle: Lorraine Dennis; Veda Ann Borg: Vivian Loder; Kelly Thordsen: Hal Loder

The Whip Hand—RKO; Released October 1, 1951; Black and white; 82 min.

Credits: Producers: Howard Hughes, Lewis J. Rachmil; Director: William Cameron Menzies; Screenplay: George Bricker, Frank L. Moss; Director of photography: Nicholas Musuraca; Editor: Robert Golden; Music: Paul Sawtell; Art directors: William Cameron Menzies, Albert S. D'Agostino, Carroll Clark

Cast: Carla Balenda: Janet Keller; Elliott Reid: Matt Corbin; Edgar Barrier: Dr. Edward Keller; Raymond Burr: Steve Loomis; Otto Waldis: Dr. Wilhelm Bucholtz

NOTES

1. As does the character of Barney, who works for McGinnis but tells Eaton he admires his early work on advertising, opinion polls and how to measure public taste. However, the film forces our attention to Barney's glasses, which he spends his time taking off so that he can either clean them or mop his brow. He is very short-sighted, the film's none-too-subtle metaphor for naive liberals and left-wingers, always suckers for nefarious Red plots.
2. He was also a dedicated fighter against racism and the treatment meted out to African Americans, to the extent of getting himself arrested and imprisoned on two occasions in the South.
3. See Humphries 2006.
4. Nobody has ever provided a convincing scenario of how America's Communists were going to achieve this. With the help of the armed forces? Getting millions of discontented workers, presumably armed to the teeth, to march on Washington? Provoking a breakdown in law and order through speculating against the dollar and shares, using the sums amassed by Hollywood's Reds?
5. Apparently Andrews was a heavy smoker, but this sort of "real-life" anecdote is a nonstarter for explaining Eaton's compulsive smoking: Andrews couldn't do without cigarettes during the shooting of the film. There is something fascinating in the compulsive way Andrews-Eaton regularly lights up.
6. We have witnessed the same situation recurring nearer in time, the 1997 the creation of the neocon "think tank" Project for the New American Century, aimed at making populations accept the use of nuclear weapons; and the invasion of Iraq based on the lie created around so-called "Weapons of Mass Destruction."
7. In this day and age when money is paramount, it is perhaps considered more "normal" to guard Fort Knox than either the Pentagon or the White House. I refer readers to that fascinating cinematic document on contemporary ideologies, *Independence Day* (Roland Emmerich, 1996), and the way the film invites us to wallow in the destruction of New York, Washington, and Los Angeles.
8. This anxiety was exacerbated in 1957, when the Soviet Union showed its technological superiority by sending its Sputnik satellite into Earth orbit. There is an interesting contradiction here: on the one hand, the climate of fear existed because the Soviet Union had the Bomb; on the other hand, American ideology constantly repeated that the Soviet Union was backward in every way in relation to the U.S.
9. Author "the biologist," Gloucester, England, May 27, 2005. See "User Comments", www.imdb.com.
10. Today Christian fundamentalists on the far Right appear to have monopolized this discourse, stirring dangerous ethical and political fallout.
11. I shall not waste time on films such as *Red Planet Mars*, an inane piece of pseudo-religious nonsense.
12. For discussions of these and other films, see Humphries 2002 (Chapter 4, "Nuclear and other Horrors") and Humphries 2010 (Chapter 6, "The Anti-Communist Crusade on the Screen" where I discuss both the films of the anti-Red cycle and the various science-horror films listed above).
13. See note 3 and "Works Cited."
14. The home of the zombies in Romero's *Night of the Living Dead* (1968). To my knowledge, there has never been an anti-Communist zombie movie, one that *unambiguously* draws a parallel between zombies and "fellow travellers." There is, however, a joke comparing Democrats to zombies in the 1940 Bob Hope comedy *The Ghost Breakers*. (The clip can be viewed on YouTube.)
15. See Buhle and Wagner (2003: 73), Humphries (2002: 60–2), Kovel (1997: 184–7), Rogin (1988: 264–7).

200   Part 3: Dupes, Victims and Crusaders

    16. Michael Rogin similarly ropes the two movies together as anti–Communist (Rogin 1988: 269).
    17. The same could be said of the James Mason character in Hitchcock's *North by Northwest* (1959). In this later film, however, the character is clearly selling secrets to the Soviets, yet there is no indication that he is a dedicated Party member or even sympathetic to the Soviet Union. His sole motives are wealth and status.
    18. Sam Fuller's hard-edged *Pickup on South Street* (1953) nicely exploits the iconography of film noir by making it difficult for the audience to distinguish at the outset between the FBI and gangsters.

WORKS CITED

Books

Buhle, Paul, and Dave Wagner. *Hide in Plain Sight: The Hollywood Blacklistees in Film and Television, 1950–2002*. New York: Palgrave MacMillan, 2003.
Humphries, Reynold. *The American Horror Film: An Introduction*. Edinburgh: Edinburgh University Press, 2002.
_____. "Documenting Communist Subversion. The Case of *I Was a Communist for the F.B.I* (1951)." In *Docufictions. Essays on the Intersection of Documentary and Fictional Filmmaking*. Gary D. Rhodes and John Parris Springer, eds. Jefferson, NC: McFarland, 2006, pp. 102–123.
_____. *Hollywood's Blacklists: A Political and Cultural History*. Edinburgh: Edinburgh University Press, 2008.
Kovel, Joel. *Red Hunting in the Promised Land. Anticommunism and the Making of America*. London: Cassell, 1997.
Leab, Daniel J. *I Was a Communist for the FBI: The Unhappy Life and Times of Matt Cvetic*. University Park: The Pennsylvania State University Press, 2000.
Rogin, Michael. *Ronald Reagan, the Movie and Other Episodes in Political Demonology*. Berkeley: University of California Press, 1988.
Sayre, Nora. *Running Time: Films of the Cold War*. New York: Dial Press, 1982.
Shaw, Tony. *Hollywood's Cold War*. Edinburgh: Edinburgh University Press, 2007.
Theoharis, Athan. *Seeds of Repression: Harry S. Truman and the Origins of McCarthyism*. New York: Quadrangle Books, 1977.
_____. *Chasing Spies: How the FBI Failed in Counterintelligence but Promoted the Politics of McCarthyism in the Cold War Years*. Chicago: Ivan R. Dee, 2002.

DVD

The Fearmakers. MGM. 2011.
The Whip Hand. Warner Archive Collection. 2016.

Part 4

Total War

"Ours is a world of nuclear giants and ethical infants. We know more about war than we know about peace, more about killing than we know about living. The only way to win an atomic war is to make certain it never starts."
—Gen. Omar Bradley

"SEE NEW YORK DISAPPEAR! SEE SEATTLE BLASTED! SEE SAN FRANCISCO IN FLAMES! SEE PARATROOPS TAKE OVER THE CAPITAL!"
—trailer copy, *Invasion USA* (1952)

The End of Civilization and Its Discontents
Five *and* The World, the Flesh and the Devil, Two Films of Massive Post-Nuclear Depopulation

LYNDON W. JOSLIN

Americans of a certain age remember various aspects of growing up in one phase or another of the Cold War. One of my earliest memories is of seeing our bathtub filled with water during the 1962 Cuban missile crisis, so we'd have something to drink if the Bomb fell. A friend tells me he was sent to the principal's office for suggesting that the kids in his classroom were seated in alphabetical order so that their charred remains could be identified after the nuclear holocaust. A classmate in the early '60s said he believed the Earth would just "crumple up" during atomic war. I was puzzled by these views, since I was under the impression such a war had already taken place. Possibly I was dimly aware of the bombings of Hiroshima and Nagasaki; possibly, too, I was confused by the many declassified stock-film images of nuclear tests (including the spectacularly photogenic Baker test at Bikini Atoll in 1946) that had been incorporated into countless science fiction films of the '50s, which were starting to show up on TV by this time.

In any case, the Cold War was an inescapable backdrop to everyday life, its presence felt and seen in everything from television news reports about Vietnam to movies featuring James Bond and other fictional spies. A reactionary slogan of the times, "Better Dead than Red," indicated severe distaste for the prospect of life under a Communist regime, and hinted that it would be worth making the Cold War a hot one in order to prevent such an outcome. But given the burgeoning nuclear arsenals of the superpowers of the day, and the gradual proliferation of arms abroad, it became apparent early on that a nuclear World War III could mean the end of civilization, and indeed the end of all human life on earth. A balance of terror took hold, a nuclear standoff known as Mutual Assured Destruction. Much has been made of the acronym—MAD—of this scenario's matter-of-fact name; the irony is that, among nations populated by sane men who didn't wish to see things turn out that way, nuclear deterrence ultimately succeeded in preventing a global atomic war. (Whether or not the certainty of mutual destruction will deter a latter-day enemy who doesn't balk at strapping bombs onto his own body, or onto his own children, remains to be seen.)

Hollywood, Doomsday Fiction and the End of All Things

In the meantime, as they always do, the movies commented on this nervous state of affairs. Maybe it was American optimism—driven in part by the sort of underestimation of the Bomb's fury that led my parents to think a bathtub full of drinking water would tide us over until things got back to normal—or maybe it was hope springing eternal in the human spirit, which led to the creation of a subgenre of films that asked what would happen *after* World War III. (Maybe, on the other hand, it was the simple realization that if everybody in the world died, there would be no story to tell.) The world ends; what happens next? Billions die; what do the survivors do?

Movies in this category ran the spectrum from the exploitative (Roger Corman's mutant-haunted *Day the World Ended* in 1955) to the studied (1959's *On the Beach* from director Stanley Kramer, adapting Nevil Shute's novel). This essay looks at two films that fall somewhere between these two extremes of quality, and which, as samples of the day-after–Doomsday subgenre, bear similarities to and differences from each other, some of which are telling. The two movies in question are Arch Oboler's *Five* and Ranald MacDougall's *The World, the Flesh and the Devil*. Both are black-and-white studies of a handful of survivors, mostly Americans, after a nuclear apocalypse has depopulated the world. *Five* was released in 1951, *The World, the Flesh and the Devil* (hereinafter *World*) in 1959, so they bracket the decade in which Americans and others were coming to grips with the implications of the Cold War and its worst possible outcomes. Significantly, both films present postwar situations in which the Red Menace is irrelevant and completely forgotten, as survivors find they must deal with more immediate concerns. Both films address, in very different fashions, the question of race in a post-apocalyptic context. And both are seldom revived today, though each is available on commercial DVD.

Five, released by Columbia, is a low-budget indie with a cast of unknowns, written, produced, and directed by radio dramatist Arch Oboler and filmed mostly in and around his Frank Lloyd Wright home; *World* is a widescreen, comparatively big-budget prestige piece starring Harry Belafonte and released by MGM. (Its relatively obscure status today may be partly the result of its misfortune in being released the same year as the superior *On the Beach*.)

Five's prosaic title refers to the known surviving population of the world; if the pretentious title of *The World, the Flesh and the Devil* is meant to refer to its cast of three survivors, it's difficult to see how: the three titular entities are, in classic Christian teaching, an anti–Trinitarian grouping of the enemies of the human soul. Is the competent and confident Ralph "worldly"? Is the pretty blonde Sarah "fleshly"? Is the gun-toting Ben "devilish"? Are these characterizations cartoonish?

Various sources, including the Internet Movie Data Base (which has been known to include apocryphal information) and Kim Newman's book *Apocalypse Movies*, claim the screenplay for *World* was based in part on M.P. Shiel's 1901 novel *The Purple Cloud*. This claim is unsupported by the film itself, which credits director MacDougall with the screenplay and Ferdinand Reyher with the screen story, making no reference to Shiel. But that's not to say there aren't incidental similarities between novel and film; as we shall see, the same is true of *Five*.

The protagonist of Shiel's novel, Adam Jeffson, is an Englishman who successfully reaches the North Pole, a part of the globe still untrodden in 1901. He descends from the top of the world to discover—gradually—that the entire population of the planet (along with most animal life) has been killed by a volcanic cloud of peach-scented purple dust, active ingredient potassium ferrocyanide. He spends years traversing the globe in search of a single survivor. Both *Five* and *World* feature a widely traveling survivor. In *Five*, he's Eric (James Anderson), a man of uncertain European origin, safely atop Mt. Everest—a summit not conquered until 1953—when fallout from the war swept the globe. (The terrifyingly beautiful Baker test kicks off the action in a behind-the-titles nuclear montage.) Eric travels across Asia and sails the oceans until washing ashore under the noses of the other survivors. In *World*, the globe-trotting survivor is Ben Thacker (Mel Ferrer), who arrives in a boat and declares, "Wherever I've been, I was the total population. And I've been here and there the last six months." It turns out he's from right nearby the Manhattan location where the other two survivors, Ralph Burton (Belafonte) and Sarah Crandall (Inger Stevens) live. How he survived the cloud of "radioactive sodium isotope" released into the upper atmosphere by an unknown belligerent isn't revealed. Despite their similarities to Shiel's narrator, neither of these men is the protagonist of his film; indeed, the arrival of each man presents a complicating factor, potentially a deadly one, for the others.

Another remotely "Shielesque" aspect of both films is the hero's discovery of a lone female survivor. Adam Jeffson finds the literally nameless young woman after *years* of wandering the world; how she has survived is such an utter contrivance that Jeffson himself believes it must be providential. In both films under consideration here, the discovery is actually reversed, as the woman discovers the man: *Five*'s Roseanne (Susan Douglas)—who is pregnant, inconveniently enough—makes her way to the country home once owned by her aunt, and finds Michael (William Phipps) squatting there. In *World*, Sarah follows Ralph around deserted Manhattan for weeks, glad to see another living soul but not sure whether she should approach him since his behavior seems erratic. Whereas Jeffson has grown so accustomed to his solitude—and to his sole "ownership" of the world, of which he fancies himself the king—he actually tries to run the girl off and even toys with the idea of killing her, Ralph refuses to let Sarah live in the same building with him: "People might talk," he explains. It may be a grim joke, but she's not laughing. As for Michael and Roseanne, both starved for company in an isolated place, there's no question of either of them going anywhere.

Inventing the Familiar

Both *Five* and *World* use a few similar motifs that have become staples, even clichés, of end-of-the-world movies. Because *Five* is the first of its kind, it apparently pioneered them. Roseanne and Ralph wander through the depopulated world, searching and calling out for others. Both come across newspapers with dire headlines: WORLD ANNIHILATION FEARED BY SCIENTIST, Roseanne reads (on a paper soon spattered by "soft rains" evocative of Sara Teasdale's 1920 poem, written, as was Shiel's novel, prior to the invention of atomic weapons). For Ralph, it's WORLD DOOMED, SAYS DYING PRESIDENT. Shiel's hero Jeffson finds a copy of the *Kent Express* in which an article (whose lurid headline, if any, isn't revealed) helpfully relates how long ago the march of the purple cloud began and how fast it's moving. The piece expresses diehard skepticism that this is the end, yet notes that civilization is breaking down among the hordes fleeing the cloud's advance. The article ends with a prayer: "[L]ook down, O Lord, and spare." Roseanne and Ralph each visit a church, only to find that God has moved out. The silence in the midtown Gothic venue reduces Ralph to tears, but the lingering message on the signboard at the small-town church Roseanne visits is clear enough, even with missing letters: REPENT YE SINNERS.

Radio writer-producer Arch Oboler came to films with a powerfully developed story sense and a strong feel for parable. In *Five* (1951), just five people survive an atomic war; the Red menace is an irrelevancy. When actress Susan Douglas finally embraces William Phipps, the moment is neither political nor even overtly sexual, but something holy: a chance that the human race might go on, and with decency.

The obligatory journey to the dead city receives strikingly different handling in the two films. *Five* takes place almost entirely in a hilly rural area, mostly at the house. Roseanne wants to return to the (unnamed) city to see if she can learn what became of her husband. Michael strongly discourages her, since the cities, "where the bombs fell," still seethe with radiation. He says he came from New York, and has been to Cleveland and Chicago, and found them all dead. When Roseanne and Eric finally make the trip, late in the story, it's an eerie, surreal, dialogue-free episode: the city, or what we see of it, is intact (the movie no doubt lacked the budget for ruined cityscapes), and the population has been reduced to a few skeletons (always seen one at a time, possibly the same skeleton repeatedly, again due to budget constraints). The air-raid sirens still ceaselessly howl, and radiation still takes its toll.

By way of contrast, *World*'s Ralph, upon digging his way out of the mine in which he was trapped as civilization ended, soon hotwires a '58 Chrysler 300 off the showroom floor and drives straight from central Pennsylvania to New York City. Since the destructive agent was a sweeping cloud of radiation, and not a rain of bombs or missiles, that doomed the world, New York's skyscrapers are intact. Nor is lingering radiation an issue, since an eleventh-hour recording Ralph discovers at a radio station says the isotope has a half-life of fifty-three hours and is deadly for only five days. MILLIONS FLEE FROM CITIES!, another headline had screamed, and indeed, Ralph finds the bridges of Manhattan so choked with abandoned cars that he finally has to get to Manhattan by boat. But there's not a dead body in sight, nor does a single one turn up in the course of the movie. Historian Kim Newman remarks that "people are instantly vaporised" by the cloud, but nobody in the movie says so, seeming to take it for granted that everybody is simply dead *and* gone. MGM may have prissily balked at the idea of releasing a movie with such macabre horror-thriller imagery as piles of human bones, but in any case, it seems an odd omission.

In contrast to both films, Shiel's novel describes cities thickly carpeted with the bodies of throngs that fell as they fled: Jeffson enters "houses in every room of which, and on the stairs, the dead overlay each other, and in the streets points where only on bodies was it possible to step." The dead are unnaturally well preserved for a long time, because "the cloud-poison [had] embalming effects upon the bodies which it saturated."

Clash of Perspectives

Once in New York, Ralph sets up housekeeping in a high-rise apartment, quickly hooking up a generator to provide himself and his entire empty block with electricity. He later does the same for Sarah, and also wires a telephone between their homes; in the novel, Jeffson, too, rigs a phone for himself and the girl. By contrast, Michael, in *Five*, prefers to live a neo–Luddite life of hunting, hardscrabble farming, and household repairs executed with traditional tools. He does not set up a generator until long after the arrival of a couple of other survivors, elderly Oliver Barnstaple (Earl Lee) and Charles (Charles Lampkin). After Barnstaple takes himself to the beach to die of radiation sickness, Charles helps Michael with the household projects, so it's entirely possible Michael didn't know how to do it himself. In any case, Eric, an arrogant Eurotrash snob who disdains the American canned food the others have salvaged, inexplicably sneers at Michael's efforts at farming, deriding it as "this return to nature of yours." He ultimately, and gratuitously, destroys the crop.

Eric also clamors to return to the city. "Everything in the world is there for us," he declares, "everything for the taking." Yet when he finally makes the trip, he loots useless items of jewelry. Most troubling, Eric also shows an immediate dislike, even hatred, for Charles, who is black.

It's in their respective handlings of race that *Five* and *World* appear to differ the most. In *Five*, until Eric shows up, Charles's race is an issue for absolutely nobody. Charles and Oliver, former co-workers and traveling companions in the post-nuclear wasteland, are equally welcome at the house Michael and Roseanne share. Michael and Charles work side-by-side, whether turning on the lights, tilling the field, or mending the roof. They yuk it up like buddies, and Michael asks Charles what he thinks about things. But Eric crassly refers to Charles as "a shuffling black doorman"; the black man may or may not have been the doorman at the bank where he and Barnstaple worked, but let the record show that at no time does Charles "shuffle." And yet there is, arguably, a touch of "minstrel" about him: as soon as the power is turned on, a record player is fired up, and when Roseanne wishes aloud that she knew how to dance, Charles dances for her. Later, as Roseanne's baby (who makes Six) arrives in an off-screen delivery, Charles recites portions of James Weldon Johnson's beautiful poem "The Creation," though at one point substituting the word "mother" for "mammy." (This "minstrel" tendency is more than matched in *World*: since Harry Belafonte is, after all, a famed singer, he's given several contrived opportunities to sing in the course of the story that border on embarrassing.)

The racial harmony existing at the house of survival is destroyed by Eric. He clearly doesn't like or respect anyone, but he particularly unloads on Charles, and makes it plain what his problem is: "Your very presence is distasteful to me. That I must eat with you, sleep under the same roof with you." His reflexive bigotry, his short temper, his take-charge presumption, and his toting of weapons can only add up to trouble, and when trouble comes, it's fatal.

It is noteworthy that *Five*, made just a handful of years after the defeat of the Nazis, depicts race prejudice as distinctly un–American, as literally foreign. It's an unaccustomed notion today, when professional race-baiters make good livings claiming the United States is the most genetically compromised nation the world has ever known. There are those who maintained this belief, or pretended to, even when a black man was in the White House—a man whose first triumph on the presidential campaign trail was the Iowa caucuses, in a state whose population is 96 percent white.

Racial Politics

Whereas *Five* treats race prejudice as it treats the dead city—as a lethal place to which there's no reasonable need to go—*World* makes a beeline for it, just as Ralph does to the vacant Manhattan. From the moment they meet, Ralph and Sarah awkwardly avoid mentioning the matter of their respective ethnicities. Finally, about an hour into the film, the subject is broached when they argue. "If you're squeamish about words," he tells her, "I'm colored. And if you face facts, I'm a Negro. And if you're a polite Southerner, I'm a nigra. And I'm a nigger if you're not."

World, at this point, is no longer a post-nuclear thriller, having become instead a message movie. The Cold War and its dangers, and even postwar survival issues, are forgotten in favor of America's undeniable racial problems of the day—real enough, for all of *Five*'s well-intentioned efforts to disown them. The 1955 murder of fourteen-year-old Emmett Till by impolite Southerners, and the outrageous acquittal of his killers, had energized the nascent Civil Rights movement. In 1957, a young Dr. Martin Luther King, Jr., met with Vice President Richard Nixon to discuss pending civil rights legislation. The efforts of Dr. King and many others activists would culminate in the Civil Rights Act of 1964 and the Voting Rights Act of 1965. As a black man in America, Harry Belafonte could hardly fail to notice and take interest in these developments (the singer was, in fact, a visible civil rights activist). *World*, co-produced by his HarBel Productions, plays out America's racial tensions in microcosm. As a result, the movie has a dated feel that hasn't attached itself to, say, *On the Beach* or to post-apocalyptic movies with "mixed" casts; certainly Robert Neville (Will Smith), the hero of the 2007 film adaptation of Richard Matheson's *I Am Legend*, upon encountering Anna (Brazilian actress Alice Braga) in another spectacularly empty Manhattan, never entertains the thought, "Oh, good, a survivor. Pity I'm a black guy." His race is irrelevant, not an unfortunate fact to be "faced."

That Old Devil, Sex

For its July 1970 issue, *MAD* magazine created a two-page photographic pictorial titled "If There Were Only Two Survivors of World War III Left on Earth." Spinning off the words of a Georgia senator who said, "If World War III leaves only one couple alive on Earth, I want that couple to be American," the first photo shows the senator's presumed vision of a white-suited Southern colonel relaxing in front of the plantation house, sipping

The World, the Flesh and the Devil (1959) is almost pure symbol, reducing post-nuclear American society to two men and one woman adrift in Manhattan. That Ralph (Harry Belafonte, center) is black creates a situation designed to exploit audience tensions and enmities. Ralph and Ben (Mel Ferrer) inevitably fall out over Sarah (Inger Stevens). Significantly, though, Ben doesn't resent Ralph because of his race, but because of his maleness.

a mint julep and attended by a Southern belle in an antebellum dress. The second photo presents an alternate vision of the surviving American couple: against a backdrop of rubble, the same belle is accompanied by an armed black urban guerrilla. Interestingly, this pair seems to have come to grips with their situation better than Ralph and Sarah do: the *MAD* woman smiles fetchingly at the man, and though his rifle is carelessly pointed at her head, he isn't aiming it at her, nor is his finger on the trigger. Indeed, his free arm is draped across the back of her wicker chair in a familiar, even protective gesture. *MAD* may be poking fun at race prejudice rather unfairly projected onto the senator; regardless, the pictorial depicts two people who realize that they *are* both Americans (for whatever that's worth in a post-apocalyptic world), and that now more than ever, they have more in common than they have separating them.

In *World*, Ralph has particular trouble reaching the conclusion arrived at in the pictorial. We aren't told what experiences in his life may have made him so nervous about getting too close to a white woman, even when she may be the last woman on Earth. But the arrival of another man, Ben—a heterosexual white man, no less, of about the same age, and therefore a sexual rival—doesn't help matters. Critic Kim Newman dismisses Ben as "a bigot who thinks he should claim Sarah as his woman and Ralph should shine their shoes." This goes beyond hyperbole into falsehood: although Ben is naturally interested in Sarah, he harbors no grossly prejudiced attitude toward Ralph. Still, one is tempted to conclude that Ben may never have had black friends (as opposed to acquaintances or co-workers); Ben's conversations with Ralph soon become stilted. "I have nothing against Negroes, Ralph," he says, in that patronizing, self-congratulatory way of mid-century white people eager to prove their enlightenment. It may be a full step beyond, "Your very presence is distasteful to me," but it still ranks alongside other gems of the day, such as "He's a credit to his race." Ralph gives Ben the only possible retort: "That's white of you."

The dialogue exchange is tense, but the fact is that race is ultimately incidental here. Ben states it plainly to Ralph: "We have only one problem: there are two of us and one of her. What are we going to do about it?" If all three of these characters were white, or all three black, or if Sarah were Chinese, the situation would be the same: the world's last love triangle. Having abandoned its interest in postwar survival, *World* now leaves behind its message-movie phase as well, and veers into romantic melodrama. Ben says to Sarah, "One of the very few advantages of narrowing down the world in this way is that it reduces the topics of conversation." He's talking about sex, not race. A classic sexual-pressure line during the Cold War was that since this is such a crazy world and it may blow up tomorrow, baby, you may as well give it up tonight. In *World*, the worst has already happened, and the end of the world is still pressed into service as part of Ben's mating call. There is, literally, nothing else to do but each other.

But there's still the matter of a sexual rivalry to take care of. Sarah can't decide between the two men—more proof that race isn't the issue here, or at least not with her, since she doesn't default to the white guy. Ben decides to force the issue the old-fashioned way—with guns—and a most dangerous game ensues. Fortunately for Ralph, Ben is a lousy shot, as survivors go; and fortunately for Ben, Ralph has pangs of conscience as he passes in front of the United Nations building and its inscription of the words of Isaiah: THEY SHALL BEAT THEIR SWORDS INTO PLOWSHARES, and so on. Ralph doesn't want to play anymore, and Ben finds he can't shoot an unarmed, fearless man.

Ralph makes to leave, but Sarah calls him back. The close-up shot of her pale extended hand being taken in Ralph's dark, strong one may have been intended by director

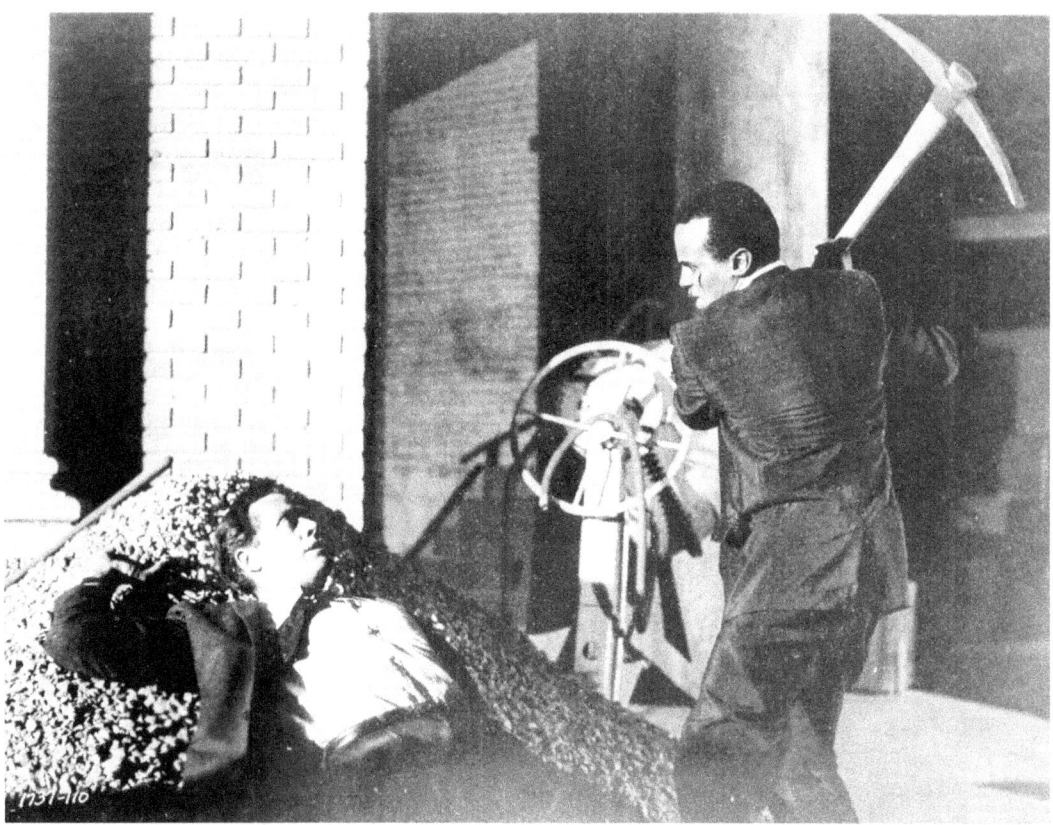

For a while, *The World, the Flesh and the Devil* suggests that the macro war responsible for the annihilation of humankind will continue in micro fashion, as the two remaining men quarrel over the lone woman. Here, Ralph readies himself to hit Ben with a pickaxe. Forged in extremis, neither man's point of view is completely unreasonable, but the question remains: Which man will claim the woman?

MacDougall to be as iconic as Michelangelo's finger of God reaching out to touch Adam's hand. But as the gesture pulls the story away from its brief foray into romantic melodrama back to being a message movie, the image is just as likely to bring to mind the hilariously earnest parade float seen toward the end of *Animal House* (1978), with its gigantic handshake between a black and a white hand. The can't-we-all-just-get-along preachiness is palpable and annoying.

Sarah invites Ben to join them, and the three of them stroll hand in hand in hand up a Manhattan street to live happily ever after, the perfect post-nuclear family. In this brave new empty world, what used to be called "miscegenation"—still illegal in many states at the time of *World*'s release—is no longer taboo. Neither, apparently, are threesomes. If Sarah has some other solution in mind, it'd be interesting to know what it is.

The Allure of Optimism

Back at Arch Oboler's house, Michael and Roseanne face no such quandaries, but entirely different ones. The narrative has progressed, and now the known population of the world has been reduced from five to two. Roseanne's baby, among others, is not a survivor. The man and woman, farm implements in hand, the house looming on the hill behind them, form a picture of pioneer domesticity as they prepare to scratch out a living for as long and as well as they can. Another Biblical quote—not from Isaiah, but from one of the rare non-terrifying parts of Revelation—provides an imprimatur. Michael and Roseanne face the same prospect as Shiel's hero and the woman at the end of *The Purple Cloud*: there's a world literally waiting to be born. Adam Jeffson—who, considering his first name, refuses to allow his companion to call herself Eve—closes out with a little Job: "Though He slay me, yet will I trust in Him."

Though it has the virtue of apparent low-budget sincerity, *Five*'s conclusion may strike some viewers as no less hokey wishful thinking than the conclusion of *World*. Kim Newman quotes a particularly brutal contemporaneous review of *Five* by Robert Hatch of *The New Republic*, who lambasted the picture for its supposition "that the atom will bring quick death for millions and a bright, clean world for a bright, clean boy and girl to repopulate." Nonsense. *Five*'s ruined world—as opposed to the well-lit, corpse-free Manhattan of *The World, the Flesh, and the Devil*—still suggests poisoned cities littered with skeletons and slow death by radiation sickness. The supposedly "bright, clean" heirs, Michael and Roseanne, are in fact bereft and traumatized. It's a world where crops can grow, and be destroyed; where babies can be born, and die; where race prejudice can be banished by the death of the racist, and by the death of the racially different. It's a world of optimism in the midst of pessimism, of making the best of things while knowing that none of us will make it out of here alive.

If, in some distant future, Michael and Roseanne's children do inherit the Earth, they'll build a world much like the one we know. Human nature is imperfect and unchangingly incorrigible. Both *Five* and *World* feature micro populations of world war survivors, some of whom still insist on fighting over something. In the fullness of time, the descendants of Michael and Roseanne will likely create a world in which something very much like the Cold War, with its clashing ideologies, puppet regimes, regional skirmishes, covert agents, and threat of mutual global annihilation, may well roll around again at last.

Filmographies

Five—Arch Oboler Productions/ Columbia; Released April 25, 1951; Black and white; 93 min.

Credits: Producer: Arch Oboler; Director: Arch Oboler; Screenplay: Arch Oboler; Directors of photography: Sid Lubow, Louis Clyde Stouman; Editors: Arthur Swerdloff, John Hoffman, Ed Spiegel; Music: Henry Russell; Art director: Arch Oboler

Cast: William Phipps: Michael; Susan Douglas: Roseanne Rogers; James Anderson: Eric; Charles Lampkin: Charles; Earl Lee: Oliver Barnstaple

The World, the Flesh, and the Devil—HarBel Productions/MGM; Released May 20, 1959; Black and white; 95 min.

Credits: Producers: George Englund, Sol C. Siegel, Harry Belafonte; Director: Ranald Mac-Dougall; Screenplay: Ranald MacDougall; Cinematographer: Harold J. Marzorati; Editor: Harold F. Kress; Music: Miklos Rozsa; Art directors: Paul Groesse, William A. Horning

Cast: Harry Belafonte: Ralph Burton; Inger Stevens: Sarah Crandall; Mel Ferrer: Benson Thacker

Works Cited

Books

Newman, Kim. *Apocalypse Movies: End of the World Cinema.* New York: St. Martin's Press, 1999.
Shiel, M.P. *The Purple Cloud.* New York: Warner Paperback Library, 1973 (1901).

Periodicals

Silverstone, Lou, and Irving Schild. "If There Were Only Two Survivors of World War III." *MAD* No. 136. July 1970.

DVD

Five. Sony. 2009.
The World, the Flesh and the Devil. Warner Archive. 2010.

Dream of Tyranny
Invasion USA

BRUCE DETTMAN

It is a decade still wistfully referenced as carefree and uncomplicated, a cultural and economic nirvana of festive backyard barbeques, cheap gas, and little crime. (Murderers, rapists, and other malcontents of the period, such as Charles Starkweather and Caryl Chessman, remain comfortably pigeonholed as nature's anomalies, along the lines of two-headed calves and feathered salmon.) In truth, the 1950s exhibited contradictory stews of social uncertainty and political paranoia. Selective memory can work just as effectively on mass canvases of recollection as on those reflecting one's personal universe. It is comforting to believe that those ten years of economic prosperity—and the kitchen appliances, wall-to-wall-carpeting, and sitcoms that came with them—were unspoiled bliss wedged between the sacrifices of World War II and the turbulent 1960s. But that later decade and the racial unrest, assassinations, and political chicanery that characterized it, did not spring from the ether, or exist as isolated phenomena connected to no other time or place. Rather, those fractious elements evolved from much that had occurred previously. The 1960s might have been an explosion, but the 1950s were surely the burning fuse that ignited them.

Despite the presumed joy of Hula Hoops and *The Adventures of Ozzie and Harriet* (where an entire episode might revolve around the flavor of ice cream Ozzie has been instructed to buy), the "real" '50s encompassed violent tensions in Korea, Africa, and the Middle East, as well as a domestic arena sullied not just by Jim Crow but by the cynical and opportunistic machinations of the House Un-American Activities Committee (HUAC) and Wisconsin's vindictive, alcoholic junior senator, Joseph McCarthy.

We also must not forget that while the Beaver and Wally, Kitten and Princess, and Dennis the Menace lived bright, inconsequential lives on our televisions, real-life American children of the decade endured continual reminders that even as they enjoyed the latest issue of *Betty and Veronica*, they could—and very well might be—reduced in a microsecond to radioactive silt. Lacking the army of pop psychologists that emerged to comfort a later generation of children following the *Challenger* disaster and 9/11, the kids of the 1950s had to grin and bear it. The Russians were akin to algebra, acne, and household chores—you didn't like the fact that they existed but you lived with it.

Well, you lived with it if you were lucky, because maybe you wouldn't get to live at all. Teachers told you to "duck and cover," to drop beneath your little desk and ram your head between your legs as part of something my school district called a "disaster drill"—but, of course, we knew better. We knew about the flash that could instantly blind you, and the melting waves of heat and the deadly fallout. We grasped that atomic bomb protection gained from ducking beneath our desks was about as likely as getting a date with Annette Funicello or Ricky Nelson. But at least the drills brought relief from arithmetic and the War of 1812. We went along with the joke.

Personally, I don't recall being unduly concerned about nuclear annihilation until the Cuban Missile Crisis in the early autumn of 1962. I came to the realization then that life involved things more pressing than perfecting my hook shot, or mixing just the right shade of green paint for my plastic model of the Creature from the Black Lagoon. I devoured articles on bomb shelters in *Mechanix Illustrated* and similar magazines, and eventually tried to persuade my father to build one in our backyard, but logic (his, not mine) won out. "You and your brother are in school all day," he explained. "I'm at work. That leaves only your mother and she wouldn't want to go on living without us, would she?"

At the time, it made a crazy sort of sense, not that we consulted Mom about it. (For the record, my mother's big concern during the '50s didn't seem to be Khrushchev or the bomb, but my disastrous spill of Welch's Grape Juice on the beige living room carpet. Next to that, all else paled.)

So our family did without a bomb shelter, though the folks finally stockpiled two rows of canned goods—mostly Campbell's Tomato Soup—on shelves in the garage. As a consequence, I experienced more than my share of nightmares about being roasted in a nuclear war. Outside of newspapers, my main reference sources for things atomic came from TV (*The Twilight Zone* was good for at least one atomic-themed episode per season), and the double features I caught each Saturday at the downtown movie house. Serious films about nuclear Armageddon didn't seem to interest the general public or the major studios. Perhaps grownups reasoned that by avoiding such grim subject matter, it might magically go away. (Such pictures as *On the Beach* [1959], *Dr. Strangelove* [1964], and *Fail-Safe* [1964] came much later.) It was therefore left to bargain-basement film producers and quick-buck artists to explore atomic disaster via "sci-fi." What these pictures lacked in quality, they made up for with variety and quirkiness. We got Kurt Neumann's *Rocketship X-M* (1950), which reveals how atomic war on Mars reduced the survivors to vicious mutants; and Ed Bernds's *World Without End* (1956), about spacemen who inadvertently smash the time barrier and land on a future Earth terrorized by hideous, atomic mutants. *Day the World Ended* (1955), an eerily effective Roger Corman cheapie about a clutch of post-nuke survivors sheltering in a mountain valley, also played on the mutant trope, with the fillip that the scaly creature is the heroine's lost brother. Another Corman effort, *The Last Woman on Earth* (1960), looks at a post-atomic love triangle. Atomic touches also figured in *Terror from the Year 5000* (1958), *Beyond the Time Barrier* (1960), and George Pal's *The Time Machine* (1960). There was even a comedy of sorts called *The Atomic Kid* (1954), but as gullible as I might have been at age five, I still couldn't buy Mickey Rooney (at his spunkiest) as the survivor of a direct test-fire hit at ground zero.[1]

Atomic testing didn't have physical consequences just for humans. It set *The Beast from 20,000 Fathoms* (1953) free from its Arctic confines, and drove the giant octopus of *It Came from Beneath the Sea* (1955) onto the docks of San Francisco and all over the Golden Gate Bridge. Radiation also jump-started the careers of the giant ants of *Them!* (1954), the oversized locusts from *Beginning of the End* (1957), the blood-sucking annelids

Terror and sexual frenzy dominate the one-sheet poster for the Italian release of *Invasion USA* (1952). A strident film, hysterical and crammed with grainy stock footage, this nightmare of Communist conquest is nevertheless eventful and frequently startling.

of *Attack of the Giant Leeches* (1959), and the irradiated dinosaur known as *The Giant Behemoth* (1959).

* * *

Despite the fast-and-loose science of the A-bomb mutant thrillers—and the undeniable appeal of these films—perhaps the oddest atomic-war melodrama of the period is Alfred E. Green's hysterically manipulative *Invasion USA* (1952).[2] Independently produced, yet sufficiently timely to move Columbia to pick it up for distribution, this mad melodrama is time-capsule stuff, a crazy-quilt tale reflecting fringe political thought of the period. Its plot is as simple and direct as its message.

A small group of strangers gathers to kill an afternoon in a Manhattan bar. We meet an out-of-town factory owner (Robert Bice) and his beautiful, directionless cousin (Peggie Castle); an Arizona cattleman (Erik Blythe); a bombastic politician (Wade Crosby); a television newsman (Gerald Mohr); and a strange fellow who identifies himself as Mr. Ohman (Dan O'Herlihy).The reporter conducts an on-the-scene interview, asking the others for their opinions about the controversial issue of a universal draft. The reaction across the board is selfish, each person feeling that government already encroaches too heavily into Americans' lives. The factory owner protests that Washington is pressuring him to turn from tractor production to tanks—a switch that promises to reduce his profits. The politician explains that the public only wants peace. (The implication here is that although peace is desired, the public has no interest in working to ensure it.)

Soon, the bar patrons' attention is captured by TV news reports of growing international tension. The enemy—unidentified but clearly Soviet—makes its move. In short order, planes are sighted above Alaska, and a "Red Alert" is on. Bombs and enemy troops begin to rain across America. Losses mount. Although the president assures citizens that the USA has retaliated, newscasters report the fall of the Pacific Coast.

As the narrative moves beyond the bar, the industrialist is shot down by foreign soldiers inside his factory. The rancher and his family are swept away and drowned after Hoover Dam is destroyed. When enemy planes reach New York and drop an atomic bomb on the city, a citizen laments, "We did not provide a strong-enough army to protect ourselves."

The Pentagon ignores pleas from governors, and when Washington, D.C., falls, members of Congress (including the blowhard who had been in the bar) are gunned down in the Capitol halls.

(The sequence is achieved via static photographs of those halls, against which three or four game actors race to and fro.) Back in Manhattan, loutish enemy troops shoot the television reporter and prepare to rape the woman. But in a burst of defiance, the beauty hurls herself from a high window, to her death.

Suddenly, we are back in the bar where all of this started. As it turns out, the whole thing, the entire nightmare of war, has been hypnotic suggestion engineered by the enigmatic Mr. Ohman (omen, get it?). One of the group asks whether the events were a dream. Ohman answers, "It is unless you do something to stop it."

Invasion USA is not so much a feature film stuffed with stock military footage as it is stock military footage affixed to a mere suggestion of a feature film. For each scene shot in service of the story, there are interminable stretches of dark, grainy historical film, most of it culled from World War II sea battles, bomb runs, and dogfights. The viewers' patience is further tried by dull stock shots of U.S. soldiers walking around, doing nothing in particular. The stock stuff is poorly integrated into the narrative, with little thought given to continuity or flow. A frantic call for pilots to intercept incoming enemy aircraft, for example, is set against stock stuff of airmen and crew leisurely strolling around their base, (naturally) unaware of the nuclear catastrophe they're supposed to avert. Albert Glasser's brassy, martial score makes a stab at linking all this old and new footage together, but the continuity is strictly sonic rather than narrative.

Director Alfred E. Green began his career before 1920, and ultimately helmed more than sixty features. His credits are a mixed bag. Early success with *Disraeli* (1929) and *Baby Face* (1933) could not be capitalized on, and Green spent most of the 1930s doing adventures and light mysteries the likes of *The League of Frightened Men* and *The Gracie Allen Murder Case*. The forties treated Green better (*The Jolson Story* and *The Fabulous Dorseys*), but he remained an unremarkable journeyman, a professional who found jobs because he worked fast and cheap.

How Green inherited *Invasion USA*, or what he thought about it, is anyone's guess. Could he have intended the picture as parody? Very doubtful, despite that raft of stereotypical, emblematic characters and over-the-top melodrama. The best that can be said for Green's direction here is that somehow, even amidst tired military footage and hackneyed dialogue delivered by actors who probably struggled to care, he did manage to keep things moving. *Invasion USA* may be many things—nonsensical, moronic, hilarious, stunningly stupid—but it does tell a story.

Although never identified by nationality, and decked out in baggy, generic uniforms, the villains of *Invasion USA* nevertheless speak with heavy Slavic accents, leaving little to the imagination as to their origin. The invading troops' high-flown references to "the leader" add to the suggestion of slavish Communists. Even the American president (uncredited actor Joseph Granby, seen only in silhouette) is unable to name the enemy, referring to the aggressor as "He," as with, "What do you think He is up to?" and "Where do you think He will strike next?" One might expect this sort of contrived silliness in a movie serial of the 1930s or '40s, but by the Cold War era, the device just adds more hokeyness to a movie already drowning in the stuff.

In another serial-like twist, a lowly window washer (Aram Katcher) employed by the industrialist turns out to be not merely a spy for the enemy but one of the leaders, as well! (Wild revelations of identity are another serial staple.) Katcher mugs, screams, and shouts cliché-ridden monologues about "the peoples' army." He's loud and unintentionally endearing.

The enemy makes hash of American defenses—a fact that's never more apparent than during the climactic attack on the Capitol, where the grounds are patrolled by a single, lonesome-looking sentry. (As we see later, the Lincoln Memorial, too, is protected by a single G.I.) Are the other Capitol sentries out to lunch, or did the Pentagon, naturally antipathetic to politicians anyway, decide than one was quite enough? Regardless, the lone sentry attempts to do his duty, growing suspicious at the approach of G.I.s he hasn't seen before. The dialogue that follows cries out to be enjoyed here:

SENTRY: Halt! Who goes there?
ENEMY SOLDIER: Company B, 183rd Infantry.
SENTRY: 183rd, that, that's an Illinois outfit, ain't it?
ENEMY SOLDIER: Yes, *yes*, Chicago Illinois.
SENTRY (after suspicious pause): You ever go see the Cubs play?
ENEMY SOLDIER (clearly off-balance): Cubs? A cub is a young animal, a bear.
SENTRY (swinging his rifle toward the newcomers): Sergeant of the guard! Sergeant of the guard!

Invasion USA is among the most emblematic anti–Communist thrillers of the early Cold War era. After New York is seized, two of the loutish invaders (sneakily tricked out as G.I.s) prepare to liquidate newsman Vince Potter (Gerald Mohr) and have their way with party girl Carla Sanford (Peggie Castle). Exploiting not just the fear of bodily harm and death, but the dread of rape, the movie is almost purely visceral.

The sentry takes out one enemy soldier before he's shot dead, murdered by Communists that neither understand nor deserve America's pastime. Nor are they fit to sample young American womanhood, which fares badly in this adventure, with young beauties either gunned down or carried off as spoils of war. This enemy, the movie makes clear, is sneaky, savage, and depraved. And if they seem to lack nuance, it's because, in this childlike universe, they haven't any.

Much like the narrative, the performances are erratic and inconsistent. Radio and film actor Gerald Mohr, the silky throated Bogart lookalike of numberless Bs, is cocky, even breezy, as the newsman. The intensity one might expect (the reporter is, after all, chronicling the downfall of America) just isn't there. Blonde, feline Peggie Castle, a good actress who seldom found material worthy of her gifts, seems only mildly interested in a world crumbling around her. Only when her virtue is at risk does she come alive, and then—poof!—she's killed herself.

Others, particularly Robert Bice as the hardnosed business executive, are competent, though rubber-faced Wade Crosby, who typically played comic thugs and dopes, is a little hard to swallow as a big-shot politico.

Trivia buffs will inform you that *Invasion USA* gives small roles to the first two actresses to play *Daily Planet* reporter Lois Lane in live-action adaptations of *Superman*, Noel Neill and Phyllis Coates. (So that men had something to look at before *Invasion USA* opened, the Columbia publicity department put Neill and Peggie Castle in swimsuits and heels, and assigned them to stroke the human-sized miniature skyscrapers built for the film's atom-bomb climax.)

Third-billed Dan O'Herlihy had the best career of anyone here (recall him as the tormented pilot at the climax of another Cold War tale, *Fail-Safe*). He was a penetrating and invariably interesting actor, yet *Invasion USA* gives him very little screen time, and uses him as a contrived sort of narrative bookend, a quasi-mystical figure who represents—what? Peace? Common sense? Vigilance? The destiny of Man? The role must not have been satisfying for him.

Special effects are inconsistent and only fitfully successful, and one can sympathize with effects supervisor Jack Rabin about the meager funds he was given. Most of the explosions are simple flashes printed over old footage, and the terrible flood is created mainly with back projection and quick cuts to frothy water that looks like summer wavelets. The A-bombing of New York City, though, is handled with some effectiveness, and accounts for the picture's best sixty seconds. Enemy planes fly high above the city (stock footage), a bombardier announces "Bombs away!" (new footage) and there is a pregnant pause as we cut to brief, silent views of isolated skyscrapers (Rabin miniatures), and then to an obliquely angled overhead photograph of the entirety of Manhattan, which is suddenly enveloped by a giant animated burst and mushroom cloud. The burst is undeniably startling, and the miniature 'scrapers catch fire and tumble rather nicely, adding to the shock effect. However, the scripters seem not to have grasped the particular power of the bomb, because huddled only one building removed from ground zero are citizens killed by falling rubble rather than by the lethal heat flash.

Invasion USA was the first film produced by an attorney named Albert Zugsmith. In subsequent years his career took him into directing, as well, and was defined by wild swings of subject matter and quality: *Written on the Wind* (directed by Douglas Sirk) and *High School Confidential!* (Jack Arnold); *The Incredible Shrinking Man* (Arnold) and *Sex Kittens Go to College* (Zugsmith); *Touch of Evil* (Orson Welles) and *Fanny Hill* (Russ Meyer). Although Zugsmith later lamented *Invasion*'s $127,000 budget and seven-day shooting schedule, he described the film to latter-day interviewers as "a good job."[3]

The patched-together footage and a generally jerry-rigged construction are enough to sink most any movie; add the halfhearted performances and enervating, static nature of the bar sequences, and you have the ingredients for disaster. Yet all of that, while painfully embarrassing, simply pales next to the manipulative script, which is as subtle as, well, an atomic bomb. Few will argue against the need for military preparedness and appeals for public vigilance. But this sort of ham-handed propaganda, coming in the midst of a reactionary period that destroyed lives and careers, is insulting and even dangerous. Right-wing troll Hedda Hopper, an industry gossip columnist who happily ratted out "Reds" to HUAC and ruined many lives, raved about the picture. Her remark—"It will scare the pants off you!"—is prominently featured on the picture's one-sheet, half-sheet, and other promotional material.

In a 1973 interview, Albert Zugsmith claimed that *Invasion USA* showed a million-dollar profit. That figure jibes with information on the Internet Movie Data Base, which shows a box-office gross of $1.2 million.

Did audiences take the film seriously? Undoubtedly, many did. But as unintended parody, *Invasion USA* may never have been equaled.

Filmography

Invasion USA—Mutual Productions of the West/Columbia; Released December 10, 1952; Black and white; 73 min.

Credits: Producers: Joseph Justman, Albert Zugsmith, Robert Smith; Director: Alfred E. Green; Screenplay: Robert Smith, from a story by Smith and Franz Spencer (Schulz); Director of photography: John L. Russell; Editor: W. Donn Hayes; Music: Albert Glasser; Art director: James Sullivan; Special effects: Jack Rabin, Rocky (Roscoe) Cline

Cast: Gerald Mohr: Vince Potter; Peggie Castle: Carla Sanford; Dan O'Herlihy: Mr. Ohman; Robert Bice: George Sylvester; Tom Kennedy: Tim the bartender; Wade Crosby: Cong. Arthur V. Harroway; Erik Blythe: Ed Mulfory

Notes

1. For more about *The Atomic Kid*, see Ted Okuda's essay, "*The Atomic Kid*: Radioactivity Finds Andy Hardy," in *Science Fiction America* (Jefferson, NC: McFarland, 2006).
2. Although the original trailer presents the film's title as *Invasion U.S.A.* (with periods), and poster art says *Invasion, U.S.A.* (with comma and periods), the title card of release prints reads *Invasion USA*.
3. McCarthy and Flynn, *Kings of the Bs*.

Works Cited

Books

Marling, Karal Ann. *As Seen on TV: The Visual Culture of Everyday Life in the 1950s*. Cambridge, MA: Harvard University Press, 1994.
McCarthy, Todd and Charles Flynn, eds. *Kings of the Bs. Working within the Hollywood System: An Anthology of Film History and Criticism*. New York: Dutton, 1975.
Zugsmith, Albert. *How to Break Into the Movies*. New York: Macfadden Books, 1963.

DVD

Invasion USA. Synapse Films. 2002.

The author and editor wish to thank Gary Svehla and Susan Svehla for generous help with this essay.

PART 5

Rot and Response

"[T]here are two irreconcilable enemies in the depth of every soul: good and evil, sin and love. And what use are the victories on the battlefield if we ourselves are defeated in our innermost personal selves?"
—St. Maximilian Kolbe

"When civilization gets civilized again, I'll rejoin it."
—Harry Baldwin (Ray Milland), *Panic in Year Zero!* (1962)

God vs. the Commies
Red Planet Mars

BRYAN SENN

"There it is, the red planet Mars—for 2000 years the symbol of war."

God lives on Mars. Communists are Evil. Science is Bad and religion is Good. Separation of church and state? Not on your life. This is what the *Red Planet Mars* (1952) has to tell us ... literally, as these sentiments come in the form of radio broadcasts from Mars itself!

Over a star-filled backdrop of space, a narrator solemnly intones: "This is a story not yet told. It begins on a warm evening some years hence, when high on a mountain top in Southern California, a giant telescope searches the heavens for the secrets there contained." (Several references in the film place the year at 1957, making "some years hence" a mere half-decade into the future.) Peter Graves plays independent electronics scientist Chris Cronyn, who, assisted by his wife Linda (Andrea King), utilizes a hydrogen valve invented by ex–Nazi scientist Franz Calder (Herbert Berghof) to boost his experimental radio transmitter and send messages to Mars. (Note: The story's premise mirrors a similar endeavor that actually occurred prior to the film's making, in which scientists tried bouncing a series of radio signals off the moon with the hope that someone—or something—might respond.)

When Mars answers, Cronyn (using a system he's based on pi) deciphers the messages, learning of the Martians' advanced society, and inadvertently sending the Western world's terrified economies into a tailspin. Martians live three hundred years, so insurance companies stop writing policies; Martians use "cosmic energy" rather than coal or oil, so mining and steel industries shut down. As the Soviets chortle over the West's imminent demise ("We will build our new world on the ruins of the West"), a "spiritual note" from Mars's "Supreme Being" comes through, intimating that Jesus himself lives on Mars! Suddenly, the whole world starts going to church, the Soviet people revolt, and the atheistic Soviet Union collapses.

Then events *really* get interesting, as the missing radio scientist Franz Calder shows up on the Cronyns' doorstep to explain that all those supposed Martian messages were secretly sent by *him*. Financed by the Soviets, Calder had built his own hydrogen valve-boosted super-transmitter for the Communists' radio and space race with the West. Although Calder failed to contact anyone (or anything) in space, he did begin receiving

226 Part 5: Rot and Response

This half-sheet poster from *Red Planet Mars* (1952) suggests a traditional sort of science fiction thriller, with a strong pictorial emphasis on science, and printed chatter about "oblivion" and "unspeakable terror." But the film is simultaneously far more—and less—than any of that.

Cronyn's missives, and decided to play a little joke on the whole world. His reason, he explains, was "amusement." Now the bitter misanthrope intends to expose the hoax and throw the newly religiously united planet back into chaos and strife—"Paradise Lost, that's my present to the world," he gloats. Chris and Linda must decide whether to make the ultimate sacrifice by blowing up the whistleblower, along with the lab and themselves, to preserve humanity's newfound utopia.

The whole scenario is more than a little silly, but had scripters Anthony Vellier and John L. Balderston[1] stopped there—as the original play upon which the film was based did—*Red Planet Mars* might have retained a shred of dignity, and even expressed something resembling a profound statement. As Linda puts it, "What have [the messages] given us? Nothing we couldn't have had all along." But it turns out that Calder sent only those messages dealing with the scientific and economic issues of Mars; *he had nothing to do with the religious missives*, and assumed that either Chris or the U.S. government (which had taken on the job of translating the messages) had fabricated them. As Chris wonders whether Washington had duped everybody, one final message is received while Calder is present, proving that the religious missives are indeed authentic—while wiping out what remains of the movie's verisimilitude.

The nature of *Red Planet Mars* mandates a script with plenty of palaver. "Boy, it sure

From a lab in the frigid Andes, fugitive Nazi scientist Franz Calder (Herbert Berghof) secretly monitors radio messages sent to Mars by an idealistic American scientist, and responds to them—as God. The ramifications of this politically motivated ploy will be more violently existential than Calder or his Soviet keepers can imagine.

was talky, wasn't it?" admitted star Peter Graves to interviewer Tom Weaver.[2] And no wonder, since *Red Planet Mars* was based on a failed 1932 play called *Red Planet* that John L. Balderston wrote with J.E. Hoare. (The play lasted a mere seven performances at New York's Cort Theatre before closing, and starred Bramwell Fletcher—who made such a memorable appearance in *The Mummy* that same year—as the scientist later played by Graves in the movie version.)

Famous Broadway critic Brooks Atkinson, in his December 17, 1932, *New York Times* review, said, "No one will accuse John L. Balderston and J.E. Hoare of ignoring ideas in *Red Planet*, which opened at the Cort on Saturday evening. In this Jules Verne fabrication, they introduced more ideas than they can finish coherently, and they abandon the whole project to an abortive ending.... *Red Planet* drifts off into a muddle of scrappy notions."

The play was written when the key world crisis was an economic rather than ideological/political one, with the Great Depression in full, ruinous swing. But in Eisenhower-era America business was booming, and the Depression was merely a bad memory; so Balderston and his *Red Planet Mars* co-screenwriter Anthony Veiller simply updated Balderston's old stage play to focus on the preeminent concern of the early 1950s—

communism. In this respect, they succeeded admirably, at least from the standpoint of capitalist ideology/propaganda.

Although looking backwards two decades for their film's source material, Balderston and Vellier were far ahead of their time in one respect: their profound dedication to going green (i.e. recycling). Numerous lengthy dialogue passages are cribbed nearly word-for-word from the twenty-year-old play, making for many protracted scenes of talk, talk, and more talk. Admittedly, some of the chatter incorporates enough Big Ideas to hold one's interest. For example:

> SECRETARY OF DEFENSE (to Cronyn): You've shattered the economy of the civilized world.
> CRONYN: I'm not interested in economics. Who makes or who loses money doesn't seem as important to me as the chance to advance civilization 1,000 years in one jump!
> SECRETARY: Our job isn't the advancement of civilization, it's to preserve the country handed down to us.
> CRONYN: If we believed that, every scientist from Franklin to Edison would have been suppressed.

Food for thought, anyway—on *both* sides.

Another big issue brought up by *Red Planet Mars* (and again cribbed from the play) is the notion of the misuse of science, with an update that invokes the splitting of the atom. Surprisingly, this comes from one of the scientist protagonists herself. Early in the film, when several messages have been received but not yet deciphered, Linda, Chris's wife and scientific partner, suddenly grows fearful of sending another communication. When Chris (reasonably) asks, "What's got into you, Linda?" she launches into the following diatribe:

> Fear, Chris, always eating fear. The whole world's scared. Why shouldn't I be? Every woman in the world—we all live in fear; it's, it's become our natural state. Fear our sons will have to fight another war—or fear they'll face worse. We've lived on the edge of a volcano all our lives. One day it has to boil over.

But Chris sees it differently.

> CHRIS: Me talking to Mars won't affect Vesuvius, Lin.
> LINDA: Chris, how can you be so sure? Don't you understand—*science* has made the volcano we're sitting on. Nobel invented dynamite to ease Man's life. [slight snort] It's eased a good many into annihilation. Einstein split the atom to create energy. Is *terror* energy?
> CHRIS: Why, that's rubbish, Linda. Scientifically, we've advanced further in the past sixty years than we have in the previous two thousand. Radio, television, automobiles, airplanes, atomic fission, jet propulsion—and, and now … if we can once talk to Mars we may be talking to brains as far ahead of ours as ours are ahead of monkeys. In one moment we may be able to leap ahead another two thousand years.
> LINDA: And *you'll* have done it. You'll be the next to advance science—and maybe us—*right into oblivion*!

One suspects that science is not to be trusted, and Chris appears to stand alone in his belief that science will advance rather than destroy civilization. Not only does his own scientist wife balk at the notion, even Calder, the movie's third scientist, surmises that "the Americans also want the secrets of a wiser civilization so that they can turn them into new methods of destruction." Some fifteen years later, the artists who were Buffalo Springfield reminded us that "paranoia strikes deep"—even among scientists on both sides.

Fortunately, religion is waiting just around the corner to save us from the evils of science (or so posits the film)—and, more importantly, the Red Menace, which has denied God and embraced science for its own nefarious ends. *Red Planet Mars* goes out of its way to show the insurmountable differences, both ideologically and materialistically, between capitalism and communism (as personified by the Soviet Union, at any rate). The first scenes set in Communist Russia reveal an impoverished dwelling in which a handful of shabbily dressed peasants illegally listen to a radio broadcast, only to be invaded by a group of jackbooted soldiers who rudely and roughly search for just such contraband. (Fortunately, the good people had some advance warning and hid the radio just in time.) Juxtaposed with scenes of Chris and his family watching their wall-mounted flat-screen television (in this respect, the film proves absolutely prescient) in their modern, comfortable home, the message couldn't be clearer: communism means poverty and secrecy; capitalism brings prosperity and openness. And how is communism to be defeated? By God, of course, as once it appears that the Supreme Being is speaking directly to the world from Mars, the people of Russia (and all the Communist states) rise up to overthrow their atheist overlords.

At one point, after the religious messages begin coming from Mars, the president of the United States (played by Willis Bouchey, purposely suggestive of Dwight D. Eisenhower) broadcasts a speech:

> All over the world, regardless of their religious beliefs, men have found a new faith by which to live. No, not a new faith, but an old one many of us had allowed ourselves to lose. A faith that is universal to men of all faiths. For while to us the words from Mars seem the very essence of Christian doctrine, let us not forget that they are also the essence of all other religions—Christian, Mohammedan, Jewish, Buddhist. All are heeding the call to prayer, kneeling humbly in search of divine guidance. I pray particularly that behind the Iron Curtain, where our eyes are not permitted to see, men will open their hearts to the message of peace and the promise that their rulers have for so long denied them.

Cut to a scene of the Russian peasants listening to the broadcast, and then going forth to dig up their hidden religious vestments and then kneel in prayer. Of course, they're almost immediately gunned down by soldiers, but the revolt is on.

Oscar-winning production designer turned first-time-director Harry Horner, aided by veteran art director Charles D. Hall (who designed the sets for *Frankenstein* and another half dozen of Universal's splendid horror thrillers of the 1930s), makes sure to contrast capitalism and communism *visually* as well ideologically. From what we see, American families live in modern yet comfortable houses accented by cozy furnishings and large glass doors, where they stay informed by watching those luxurious, remote-controlled televisions. The Average Ivan in Russia, however, lives in what literally looks like a converted barn with no electricity, receiving news of the world only over an antiquated—and forbidden—wireless set.

The disparity extends to the environs inhabited by national leaders, as well. While American leaders, both military and civilian, conduct their affairs in modern and efficient offices, the Soviet heads of state meet in an almost medieval-looking hall, conjuring up Old World decadence to complement their totalitarian, godless vision. And the American president couldn't be more different from the Russian premier—the first a calm, confident man who gives reasoned answers to difficult questions; the other a barking, angry despot who instills fear in his underlings and literally chortles as he watches his soldiers shoot down civilians. It's a cartoon-level compare-and-contrast show-and-tell that, while not necessarily reflective of reality, nonetheless hammers home two of the movie's main themes: one, the capitalist lifestyle leads to prosperity, while the Communist system brings only dire poverty; and two, leaders of the United States are reasonable and fair, while the Soviet rulers practice pure, unadulterated evil. Although these cartoonish extremes may appear today more as high camp than sober reality, in 1952, when Red Scare fever was running high, they were portrayals that the film's intended audience absorbed with due solemnity.

Miracle from Mars (the film's shooting title) was Peter Graves's first lead role (he'd played secondary characters up to this point in his film career). Under contract to Ventura Pictures at the time, Graves was loaned out to make *Red Planet Mars* ... but he received a mere 150 dollars a week for his work on *Red Planet Mars*. "I was supposed to have been a little older character than my actual age at the time [twenty-five]," remarked Graves, "so they grayed my temples a little [*laughs*]—even in black-and-white, you *knew* it! *Red Planet Mars* had some pretty good people in it: Andrea King was the leading lady, she played my wife; Herbert Berghof, who played the mad scientist, went on to become a well-known character actor in the film business, and became even better known for being an acting teacher."[3]

Film critic A.W. Weiler, writing in the June 16, 1952, edition of the *New York Times*, was rather too generous when he noted, "Peter Graves and Andrea King are serious and competent if slightly callow in appearance as the indomitable scientists." Time has revealed that Graves gives a likable, if not altogether convincing, performance, bringing an earnest conviction that *almost* overcomes his character's occasional melodramatic outburst. Unfortunately, his partner Andrea King offers no such believability and quickly becomes a major annoyance as she regularly barks out negative comments—almost non sequiturs—throughout the film. King's strident, sour delivery only adds to the grating effect. The script asks us to believe that this woman scientist, who's been working arm-in-arm with her husband for years, has experienced an abrupt change of heart just as they're on the verge of a breakthrough. Well, maybe ... but her bitter harangues ring hollow and sound out of place, and viewers can only scratch their heads when Linda spits out, "There it is—the red planet Mars, for over two thousand years the symbol of war. And we dare to fly in the face of providence and bring it closer to us!" Thanks to Ms. King, there's nothing "melo" about this melodrama.

According to a November 1951, *Los Angeles Times* item, Andrea King left the lead role in an American Pictures film, *Sword of Venus*[4] (a low-budget, black-and-white swashbuckler), to co-star in *Red Planet Mars*. *Sword of Venus*'s loss was *Red Planet Mars*'s ... further loss.

The *New York Times* aside, contemporary reviewers were not particularly kind to this SF-tinged slice of Red Scare cheese. The May 14, 1952, *Hollywood Reporter*, for instance, labeled *Red Planet Mars* a "dull hodge-podge.... This AV production has nothing to recommend it except its misleading title. The story is confused and rambling, lacking any central theme. Its pseudo-science is ludicrous, [and its] pretentious attempt to put over a religious-philosophic message is infantile." The May 14, 1952, edition of *Variety* was more concerned that the story's contemplated attack on Russia could be used as "propaganda fodder for the Reds."

With historical hindsight, more recent assessments have tended to the favorable. In 1974, *Castle of Frankenstein* magazine #24 called the picture "a fascinating document for students of the 1950s.... Thematically continually astounding, certainly higher-class than outright propaganda pieces like *Invasion USA*, but ingenuous to a point beyond absurdity. Could only have been conceived, let alone released, in the McCarthy era." Filmmaker Joe Dante (*The Howling, Gremlins, Matinee*), in an e-mail to interviewer Tom Weaver, noted that "its view of the future was far more sophisticated than most pics of the period, and director Harry Horner brought a nice visual style to the project.... Overall, a much more intelligent pic than the general overview has labeled it over lo these many years."

"I thought it was a wonderful script, and I adored Peter Graves," enthused Andrea King to interviewer Daniel Bubbeo. "The problem was that the studio didn't publicize it. So it didn't really go anywhere. Once it was shown on television, people began to see it and they loved it, and now it's become a cult movie."[5]

But has it? No, *Red Planet Mars* has become more of a bizarre footnote in the Red Scare subgenre than a movie people "love." With characters painted in stark black and white (the Soviets are simply monsters, and the American politicians wear halos), a deficit of action, and some atrocious overacting, *Red Planet Mars* survives as a preposterous (if unique) artifact of the Cold War rather than an effective piece of dramatic filmmaking.

Of course, in the end, all of this encourages the question: If communism is so evil, why does God choose to live on the (ahem) RED planet?

FILMOGRAPHY

Red Planet Mars—United Artists; Released May 15, 1952; Black and white; 87 min.

Credits: Producer: Anthony Veiller; Director: Harry Horner; Screenplay: John L. Balderston, Anthony Veiller, b/o the play *Red Planet* by Balderston and John Hoare; Director of photography: Joseph Biroc; Editor: Francis D. Lyon; Music: Mahlon Merrick; Art director: Charles D. Hall

Cast: Peter Graves: Chris Cronyn; Andrea King: Linda Cronyn; Herbert Berghof: Franz Calder; Walter Sande: Adm. Bill Carey; Marvin Miller: Arjenian; Willis Bouchey: President of the United States; Morris Ankrum: Secretary of Defense Sparks

NOTES

    1. Yes, *that* John L. Balderston, noted for his contributions to *Frankenstein* (1931), *Dracula* (1931), and *The Mummy* (1932).
    2. Tom Weaver, *Earth vs. the Sci-Fi Filmmakers*.
    3. *Ibid.*
    4. tcm.com (Turner Classic Movies blog); "Notes": *Red Planet Mars*.
    5. Daniel Bubbeo, *The Women of Warner Brothers*.

WORKS CITED

Books

Bubbeo, Daniel. *The Women of Warner Brothers: The Lives and Careers of 15 Leading Ladies, with Filmographies for Each*. Jefferson, NC: McFarland, 2002.
Weaver, Tom. *Earth vs. the Sci-Fi Filmmakers: Twenty Interviews*. Jefferson, NC: McFarland, 2005.

Newspapers and Periodicals

Atkinson, Brooks. "At the Theatre." *The New York Times*. December 17, 1932.
A.W. (abbreviated form of A.W. Weiler). "The Screen; Science-Fiction Again" (review of *Red Planet Mars*). *The New York Times*. June 16, 1952.
Dante, Joe, ed. "Frankenstein TV Guide: *Red Planet Mars*." *Castle of Frankenstein* No. 24. 1974.

Holl. (reviewer pseudonym) "Red Planet Mars." *Variety*. May 14, 1952.
"Red Planet Mars." *The Hollywood Reporter*. May 14, 1952.

Web

tcm.com (Turner Classic Movies)

DVD

Red Planet Mars. Cheezy Flicks. 2006.

Special thanks to Tom Weaver and Arthur Lundquist for research assistance.

Violent Saturday
The Danger Within Us

DAVID J. HOGAN

America felt itself destined to win the war on communism because America was virtuous ... wasn't it?

Sydney Boehm and Richard Fleischer's *Violent Saturday* (1955) is ostensibly about the robbery of a prosperous small-town bank by a trio of chillingly professional, quasi-military criminals who quietly enter town to finalize their strategy and tactics. Although the planning, execution, and aftermath of the robbery are satisfyingly—even shockingly—developed, the entire bank robbery plot is an enormous MacGuffin, a device that propels the narrative but that has very little to do with what *Violent Saturday* is really about.

Boehm's script follows closely to major events W.L. Heath's linear novel, suggesting not simply that our undoing may come from insidious outside agents, but that the seeds of destruction may lie within us, dissipating our energies and killing our alertness because of morally reprehensible personal flaws: theft, self-pity, drunkenness, infidelity, satyriasis—even window peeping. Fleischer's direction is remorseless, even pitiless, laying bare the failings of the players in this little drama. And in a perverse twist, personal qualities that are commonly lauded—non-violence, compassion, patience—are shown to be 1) in short supply and 2) ill-suited to deal with the external threat.

Violent Saturday warns us about our lack of virtue as it builds to its ultimate message: In times of dire threat, counter-violence is the best and most admirable virtue. Because we are American, we don't perpetrate preemptive violence, but once attacked, we react with resolute murderousness. The man who is free of self-doubt, and who risks sacrificing himself in order to stand up for others, is the man who is "better" than his neighbors. He is the person best suited to annihilate an outside menace.

Family Man

Shel Martin (Victor Mature) is the competent superintendent at the main economic engine in the sunbaked town of Bradenton, a massive copper mine. He not only supervises day-to-day operations (controlled explosions of the sort that open the film; trucking operations; harangues with customers and suppliers), but also relieves the drunken owner, Boyd Fairchild (Richard Egan), of work-related responsibility. It's not that Shel sets out

Sexual violence, robbery, passionate romance—the *Violent Saturday* (1955) one-sheet promises all of that, and the movie delivers, though with more subtlety and thoughtfulness than these lively graphics suggest. The real threat does not come at the protagonists from the outside, but from within, manifested as a moral lack that defines many of the town's "good citizens."

to be an enabler, just that his efficiencies have the side effect of allowing Boyd to spend his time boozing and feeling sorry for himself because his wife, Emily (Maggie Hayes), is a serial adulteress.

Shel stands in marked contrast: He's happily married, with three lively boys, a loyal, interested wife, and a stable home. At a glance, he represents much of what is best about America.

His neighbors encapsulate much of the worst. Boyd, as we've seen, is sunk in alcoholism. Young, handsome, and wealthy because he inherited the mine from family, he loves his wife but hasn't the guts to confront her about her unfaithfulness with a local wolf (Brad Dexter) and others. In a believable twist, Emily loves her husband but uses his alcoholism as an excuse to ignore her vows.

The Peeper and the Thief

In a clever moment, our first glimpse of timid bank manager Harry Reeves (Tommy Noonan) catches him as he gazes from the bank's front window onto the sidewalk outside. It's clever because, more typically in this story, he gazes *into* a window, specifically, one belonging to local nurse Linda (Virginia Leith). Harry follows after her as she does errands in town, sidles close to her at the perfume counter at the drugstore, and gets a vicarious thrill as she dances with Boyd Fairchild. Harry is obsessed and infatuated with her—or maybe he just likes to watch at night as she undresses.

The middle-aged librarian, Elsie (Sylvia Sidney), has fallen behind on loan payments, so when an opportunity to steal a purse from a library table presents itself, she takes it. Harry Reeves is present later that night when Elsie drops the emptied purse into a curbside trashcan, and confronts her. Well, the librarian has only to slide her gaze upward to Linda's window to see what Harry has been up to, and now the two are locked in a miserable stalemate, each aware of the other's peccadillo, and each obligated to keep quiet about it.

The Professionals

By way of contrast to the unfocused, discombobulated townies, the three bank robbers are models of efficiency, led by their boss, Harper (Stephen McNally), with martial precision. Harper comes to town before the other two and chats up the hotel desk clerk and other locals, gathering information while passing himself off as a traveling seller of costume jewelry. He can pass for a "normal" person, just as the quasi-mythic Communist agents propounded by fiction and agitated politicians had the ability to blend into the larger society without encouraging suspicion.

McNally's confederates, Dill (Lee Marvin) and Chapman (J. Carrol Naish), are similarly professional, if vaguely eccentric. Attired, like McNally, in sober suits, they also could be salesmen or other business people. The two are lightly sketched but compelling, Chapman with his pocketful of hard candy and blunt curiosity about Amish he encounters on a train; and Dill, with his self-confessed predilection for "skinny broads" and his habitual use of a menthol nasal inhaler. Chapman is cold and unflappable, and Dill, like a smart soldier, goes into battle with plenty of extra ammunition for his revolver. He's a bit comic, but he's dangerously prepared, too.

The Nature of Heroism

As the bank robbery plan swings into action, Shel finds himself an unwilling central figure. He's carjacked on the street and forced to drive to an Amish farm, where a fourth confederate, Slick (Red Morgan), has stashed a truck and a shotgun. Slick helps blindfold, gag, and tie Shel and the family and sit them against a wall in the hayloft. Slick stays with the truck as the other three take Shel's car back to town.

The Amish, pacifists by virtue of their faith, are content to see how "God's will" plays out, so it falls to Shel to take action. Early in the film it's established that his oldest boy, Stevie (Billy Chapin), is embarrassed because Shel stayed home and mined copper during the war rather than see combat and return home with a medal, like the father of one of Stevie's playmates. Shel explains to the boy that copper was vital to the war effort and that he did his part for victory, but even though Shel's manner is low-key and reasonable, it's obvious that he's bothered because his boy feels he's inadequate.

Shel's opportunity comes in the hayloft, when a precisely pushed barrel knocks Slick from the ladder, killing him and liberating the shotgun. Shel plans to load himself and the family into the truck and escape, but the robbers return, having shot the bank manager and Emily Fairchild in the course of an otherwise successful job. Shel is trapped but he has the shotgun and the keys to the getaway truck.

The ever-composed Harper, shouting from outside the barn, offers a deal: the keys for the captives' freedom. Well, that's a non-starter, so during the tense and kinetic minutes that follow, Shel beats back the gang's arson fire and kills two of the robbers. But the third drops Shel with a revolver shot and then slowly reloads, intending to kill Shel at his leisure. But inside the barn minutes before, a criminal's bullet has hit one of the Amish children, an affront that causes the Amish father (Ernest Borgnine) to plunge a pitchfork into the last robber's back.

Later, in the hospital, Shel's son brings a posse of his pals to witness the wounded hero. As Shel and his boy embrace and smile, the other youngsters are awestruck. Here is the man who met violence with greater violence, and won.

Aggressive Virtue Trumps Corruption

A virtuous man of action has defeated the invaders, but with no help from the dissolute people in town. Mrs. Fairchild has been killed. Bank manager Harry Reeves will be sent home from the hospital in a couple days but first he must confess his window peeping to Linda, "before I don't have the courage anymore to tell you." Scripter Boehm and director Fleischer are clearly drawing a contrast between types of courage: the ashamed, little-boy variety offered by Reeves, and the aggressively resourceful kind practiced in the barnyard by Shel.

We can assume that Boyd has been at home, quietly plastered, during the robbery, and that the local lothario has been chatting up women at the country club. In a word: useless.

Although Shel's wife (Dorothy Patrick) is inside the bank during the robbery, she's unharmed, apparently protected by her husband's force field of courage and virtue.

In an apparent mismatch not designed to work in his favor, Shel is the man who ultimately walks away, and his innate virtue is an unspoken reason why. The robbers

In *Violent Saturday*, a quiet weekend in the sunbaked town of Bradenton takes a bad turn when a trio of professional criminals holds up the local bank. J. Carroll Naish (from left), Stephen McNally, and Lee Marvin are the holdup men; Sylvia Sidney (far right) is the town librarian—and just one of many citizens holding a dark secret. **Frozen between Marvin and Sidney is Dorothy Patrick (in white blouse) and (face hidden) little Donald Gamble.**

aren't simply professional but eagerly sadistic, too. Lee Marvin's Dill happily pins a boy's hand to the sidewalk with his shoe, and Naish's dour Chapman goes about his assigned chores with quiet resolution, whether shooting Reeves or tricking up a flaming car so that it crashes through the barn door.

Key to the plan is that the town of Bradenton has only two police officers, who are easily lured from town when Naish makes a phony call about a highway accident twenty miles down the highway. Bradenton is unprepared, and the locals have been too preoccupied with their vices to notice. If *Violent Saturday* isn't a symbolic call for a large and alert standing army, nothing is.

The Talent

Violent Saturday was produced for 20th Century-Fox by Buddy Adler. It's a moderate-level "A" picture with an effective blend of established stars, familiar character players, and newcomers. Location shooting in Bisbee, Arizona, adds a lot, and Sydney Boehm and Richard Fleischer were congenial collaborators. Boehm had already carved a niche as a scripter of tough, intelligent thrillers, ranging from Joseph H. Lewis's understated *Undercover Man* (1949) to the conflagration that is Fritz Lang's *The Big Heat* (1953). Boehm had a flair for stripping narrative to its essence, and for establishing characterization via startling set pieces. In *The Big Heat* that moment comes when hoodlum Lee Marvin throws boiling coffee into the face of girlfriend Gloria Grahame; in *Violent Saturday* it's in the barn, when Shel and the Amish farmer discover they can kill. It comes also during the bank robbery, when Marvin's Dill barks at the bank manager, "Siddown, mister, I'll kill you quick!" and when the enigmatic brown eminence that is J. Carrol Naish's Chapman orders a fretful small boy to come to him—so that he can give the child a fistful of hard candy: "Here, kid, put these in your kisser and suck on 'em."

By 1955, Richard Fleischer was quickly becoming one of the most efficient and versatile directors in Hollywood. In the year before *Violent Saturday* he directed *20,000 Leagues Under the Sea* for Disney, and had earlier established his crime-movie credentials with a pair of gems, *Armored Car Robbery* (1950) and *The Narrow Margin* (1953). The last was shot almost entirely on a confining passenger-train set; with *Violent Saturday*, Fleischer was able to work with big-sky landscapes, long winding roads, and a genuine small town that seems alternately spacious and intimate.

Fleischer developed into one of Hollywood's most respected craftsmen, and the reasons are apparent in *Violent Saturday*. The film makes splendid use of the entire repertoire of visual devices: tracking shots, pans, dolly-ins, encompassing establishing shots, and pore-revealing close-ups (as when Mature's Shel crawls beneath a car with the shotgun, hoping to get a bead on one of the robbers). Fleischer provides viewers with a lesson in terse, concise direction, in which every setup and shot seems "right." Crisp editing by Louis Loeffler is a major plus.

The location shooting is emphasized not just visually but on the soundtrack, which buzzes with ambient street noise, background chatter, and other "real" elements.

Hugo Friedhofer's sweeping, ominous music makes effective use of disconcerting minor keys. Although the score is a dominant element, it's never intrusive.

Because of his physique, stolid manner, and sensual features, Victor Mature became a well-intentioned Hollywood in-joke that he willingly perpetuated, but the fact is that he was a judicious actor whose skill at understatement was stupidly mistaken for inadequacy. His emotional moments ring true because of that understatement, and because of a quiet, resolute intelligence he brought to his roles. Mature is *Violent Saturday*'s essential core of conviction.

Richard Egan was a similar physical type (and here, an ironic mirror image) who was given even less credit for acting ability than Mature. He lacked Mature's subtlety but he had a similar gift of understatement mated to a forceful, stoic personality. Egan is effective during a couple of protracted drunk sequences, and is touching late in the film, when he wonders aloud about the final fate of his wife, with whom he had been on the verge of reconciliation. "Alive in the morning and dead in the afternoon," he says sadly. "All those loose ends, left hanging."

Stephen McNally's big breakthrough had come in 1950 in *Winchester '73*, in which he played Jimmy Stewart's no-good brother. Confident of manner and handsome in a slightly feral way, McNally (earlier known as Horace McNally) was well suited to play gang bosses and other independent thinkers. In *Split Second* (1953) he's a smart-cookie crook who outsmarts himself when he inadvertently maneuvers himself and hostages onto an atomic-testing ground. He's similarly clever in *Violent Saturday* as Harper, who plans like a military man but who cannot anticipate that a hostage might be his undoing.

Lee Marvin came to *Violent Saturday* from the aforementioned *The Big Heat* and from *Bad Day at Black Rock* (1954). *Violent Saturday* allowed him to cement his status as one of Hollywood's best and most intimidating young character actors. So skilled is he at base villainy that his later stardom is at once unlikely and logical.

Longtime character actor and radio star (*Life with Luigi*) J. Carrol Naish has relatively few lines as Chapman, but is one of the film's most intriguing characters, a man who speaks only when necessary, and who is completely untroubled by the prospect or actuality of violence. The night before the heist he sleeps like a baby when Harper and Dill cannot, and as the group sets out in the morning he takes a moment to rub a cloth over his shoes. Bloodless and experienced, he's a professional who reveals nothing of himself to the others.

For Virginia Leith, a contract with 20th Century–Fox brought second-tier stardom. Brunette, tall, and willowy, Leith had a sharply beautiful face and an intriguingly assertive voice. Fox dropped her option after a strong featured role in *A Kiss Before Dying* (1956). Just three years later Leith found herself playing a disembodied but very talkative head in *The Brain That Wouldn't Die*, a Z-level independent thriller shot mainly in the redressed basement of an East Coast department store. Fox had discarded a strong and unusual talent; *Violent Saturday* is a particularly good showcase for Leith, whose take on Linda is honest, outspoken, and unsentimental. The role is an unusually strong female part for the period.

Adapting the Novel

As noted, *Violent Saturday* follows the outline of W.L. Heath's very popular 1955 novel. In many particularities, though, Boehm and Fleischer freely invented incidents and bits of characterization that support the film's theme.

The Shel Martin of the novel is a foreman in, of all things, a rug factory—an occupation that is neither cinematic nor compelling. In one sequence designed to suggest his competence, Shel deduces that part of a large order went missing because it was incorrectly dyed. That's clever if you're in the rug business, but rather lackluster for the rest of us.

In the novel, Shel's sons exist only so that we can see that Shel is a family man. The individual boys are not delineated, and there is no conflict about the fact that Shel stayed home during the war, and won no medals. Because of this, the book has no central subtext about the nature of heroism (despite the fact that Shel acts heroically).

Failings of the townspeople are generally more pointed in the film than in the book, and for reasons that we'll see shortly. A propensity to cheerful drunkenness, gossip, and dirty jokes characterizes many of Shel's neighbors. Harry Reeves is still a peeping tom but he's not in direct conflict with Elsie the librarian, as in Boehm's screenplay. And although Elsie takes another person's fifty dollars, it's not quite as premeditated as in the movie, and it causes Elsie considerably more internal grief.

In one respect only does the theme of internal, community divisiveness ring more strongly in the book than on screen: The Shel of the novel is a racist—an essentially un–American failing—with a private antipathy for blacks and Jews. (His wife shares his feelings.) A central deficiency of America is thus summed up in a single character, and disturbingly so.

Readers of novels were prepared to ponder a racist protagonist in 1955, but movie audiences were not. Because Shel's racism, even privately expressed in conversations with his wife, would have made him unpalatable to filmgoers and almost certainly unacceptable to the Motion Picture Production Code, Boehm and Fleischer were obliged to pump up the failings of secondary characters.

The book has no black or Jewish characters of any consequence, and it's obvious that Bradenton is a heterogeneous place—which makes Shel's racism all the more mystifying. There are no Amish in or near the town either, so the issues of religious conviction and passivity aren't explored in the book. In the novel, Shel is imprisoned in the barn by himself, with only Slick outside to keep him company. Shel rather perfunctorily disposes of Slick, Dill, and Chapman (the very cinematic flaming car never appears in the book). The fourth criminal, the leader Harper, flees into nearby woods, where he'll inevitably be captured by the authorities.

The unfaithful Emily Fairchild is killed in book and movie, but in the book, Boyd delivers his "alive this morning" rumination to a pair of male friends, which hasn't nearly the dramatic impact of the same sequence in the film, in which Boyd speaks to a single person, Linda, the nurse. She has a clearheaded but sincere romantic affection for Boyd, but because nothing has gone on between them, Boyd finishes his thoughts and tearfully asks Linda to leave.

In novel and film, Boyd has no illusions about himself, and has no feelings of superiority to anybody. The racist Shel does have such feelings, and is less than appealing. But at the conclusion of the film, as Stevie Martin hugs his hero-dad before the approving gazes of his playmates, we have a violent, unsoiled protagonist dropped into a thoroughly boiled ending that is as easy and as pat as J. Edgar Hoover could have wished. It's the only lapse in an otherwise superior film.

Filmography

Violent Saturday—20th Century-Fox; Released April 20, 1955; DeLuxe color; 91 min.

Credits: Producer: Buddy Adler; Director: Richard Fleischer; Screenplay: Sydney Boehm, b/o the novel *Violent Saturday* by William L. Heath; Director of photography: Charles G. Clarke; Editor: Louis Loeffler; Music: Hugo Friedhofer; Art directors: George W. Davis, Lyle Wheeler

Cast: Victor Mature: Shelley Martin; Richard Egan: Boyd Fairchild; Stephen McNally: Harper; Virginia Leith: Linda Sherman; Tommy Noonan: Harry Reeves; Lee Marvin: Dill; J. Carrol Naish: Chapman; Margaret Hayes: Emily Fairchild; Sylvia Sydney: Elsie; Ernest Borgnine: Amish farmer; Brad Dexter: Gil Clayton

Works Cited

Books

Fleischer, Richard. *Just Tell Me When to Cry*. New York: Carroll & Graf, 1993.
Heath, W.L. *Violent Saturday*. New York: Harper & Brothers, 1955.

DVD

Violent Saturday. Eureka. 2014.

Panic in Year Zero!
It's the End of the World as We Know It (And I Feel Fine)

MARK CLARK

Science fiction author Brian Aldiss once dismissed the work of John Wyndham as "cozy catastrophes," but *The Day of the Triffids* and Wyndham's other post-apocalyptic novels are grim and gritty contrasted to *Panic in Year Zero!*, which makes World War III seem like a week at 4-H camp. *Panic*, a peppy relic of Cold War boosterism, brims with can-do spirit, reflecting a degree of optimism that would soon dissipate in light of world events. It's also one of the liveliest and most entertaining of all movie apocalypses.

Panic in Year Zero! is a picture of its moment, released Thursday, July 5, 1962, a day after the flag-waving pomp of Independence Day and three months prior to the real-life terror of the Cuban Missile Crisis, when the world teetered on the brink of nuclear Armageddon from October 17 through 29. It's a film that almost certainly wouldn't have been made *after* those events, and it reflects the self-assurance felt by conservative Americans during the early 1960s. *Panic* presupposes that a nuclear war can be won, if only pantywaist liberals would get out of the way and hand things over to no-nonsense, gun-toting Real Americans. This approach must have galled author Ward Moore, whose work inspired the movie.

"Somebody dropped a bomb ... crazy kick."

Panic in Year Zero! was based loosely (and without credit) on Moore's short stories "Lot" and "Lot's Daughter." "Lot," first published in *The Magazine of Fantasy and Science Fiction* in 1953, follows a man named Mr. Jimmon as he drives his family away from Los Angeles amid the traffic-choked chaos precipitated by nuclear attack. His wife and son seem unable to grasp the magnitude of the situation, asking to stop for a movie and to spend the night in a hotel. Even more vexingly, they cling to concepts of fairness and decency that Jimmon dismisses as irrelevant, even a nuisance, to the family's desperate flight to safety. The Crisis, as he refers to the attack, gives Jimmon license to reveal the contempt he has secretly harbored for other people—coworkers, neighbors, even his wife and son. Only his beloved daughter Erika seems immune from his merciless misanthropy. At the conclusion of the story, after stopping at a gas station, Jimmon drives away with

The mushroom cloud, an iconic image no less suggestive of the Cold War than the Rutherford-Bohrs atom diagram, dominates this ad mat for Ray Milland's apocalyptic *Panic in Year Zero!* (1962). The ad reflects the blunt power of the film, in which every nicety of 20th century life is reduced to folly, and every action made meaningless unless it contributes directly to survival.

Erika, abandoning his nagging wife and whining son, along with any remaining pangs of conscience.

"Lot" was intended to serve as an indictment of the sort of survival-at-any-cost thinking exhibited by Mr. Jimmon. Ward Moore hoped readers would draw parallels with Cold War hardliners like Edward Teller, a former Manhattan Project scientist best remembered as "the Father of the H-bomb," and Curtis LeMay, the iron-fisted leader of the U.S. Strategic Air Command, both of whom advocated a preemptive nuclear strike against the Soviet Union. (Teller and LeMay were reportedly the basis for the characters of Dr. Strangelove and General Jack Ripper in Stanley Kubrick's classic 1964 satire *Dr. Strangelove, or How I Learned to Stop Worrying and Love the Bomb*.)

However, some critics misinterpreted Moore's message, and read "Lot" as an *endorsement* rather than a rebuttal of Jimmon's attitude. As Michael Stanwick explains in his foreword for a 1996 book collecting both "Lot" stories, these readers pointed out that Mr. Jimmon did, in fact, survive, and that "morality is a luxury that depends first of all on survival."[1] Ward may have confused the issue by naming the story "Lot," invoking the

Old Testament tale of a man and his family whisked away from the doomed city of Sodom by angels. Lot's wife is turned into a pillar of salt when, against the angels' instructions, she casts a backward glance at her former home. Most Jewish and Christian scholars consider Lot, the nephew of Jewish patriarch Abraham, to be a righteous figure.

To answer the critics and clarify his point of view, Moore penned a sequel, "Lot's Daughter," which appeared in *F&SF* in 1954. Set six years after the original story, it excoriates Jimmon's worldview in even more uncompromising terms, demonstrating more clearly than the first story, as Stanwick puts it, "how perfectly unfit such a man would be for rebuilding a culture." "Lot's Daughter" focuses on the relationship between Mr. Jimmon and Erika, who has grown into a reflection of her father's me-first values and "ruthlessness-unsentimentality." In the end, after finding a younger, stronger and more able provider, she abandons her father the same way Jimmon ditched his wife and son, leaving a toothless, enfeebled old man to scrape out a meager existence, living in a makeshift hut, catching scrawny fish, and gathering wild berries.

The *Panic in Year Zero!* screenplay by Jay Simms and John Morton retains the setting of Moore's first story for the film's opening scenes and jettisons everything else. In the process, it stands Moore's moral on its head, siding with the father, here named Harry Baldwin (and played by Ray Milland), who is portrayed as a tough-minded realist rather than as a vindictive misanthrope. Instead of abandoning his family, he's bent on preserving it at any cost. This makes him a far more sympathetic figure than the father of "Lot." The screenwriters also soften other elements of the story to make the father—and his point of view—more appealing.

The Baldwin family—Harry, wife Ann, son Rick, and daughter Karen—is leaving for a fishing trip to bucolic Shibe's Meadow, pulling a camper trailer behind their station wagon. Then, in the rear view mirror, the world comes to an end. Harry pulls to the side of the road and watches as mushroom clouds swell up from what used to be Los Angeles. At first he's unsure what to do, and tries to drive back to the city and rescue his mother-in-law. But as he encounters panicked Angelinos fleeing the city, Harry quickly realizes the folly of that impulse and devises a new plan: He will, by any means necessary, acquire everything needed to secure his family's well-being—food, tools, and, most importantly, guns—and hole up in the family's remote vacation spot. "When civilization gets civilized again, I'll rejoin," Harry says. Like Jimmon, he turns his back on other people. But unlike Jimmon, his decision doesn't include his own wife or children. Rather, he sees this course of action as the only way to safeguard them. "We're fighting for our lives, Ann," Harry explains to his wife (Jean Hagen). "My family *must* survive."

The Baldwins, in effect, emerge as stand-ins for opposing political views, with Harry representing the tough, conservative uber-daddy, and wife Ann the sentimental, liberal mommy figure. Throughout the film, Harry's instincts—while sometimes harsh—are validated as the correct response to the family's plight. However, Ann seems unable to accept the scale of the disaster or its ramifications; like her counterpart in the short story, she seems handicapped by her suddenly inconvenient moral compass. She's appalled when Harry asks their son Rick to point a gun at a hardware store owner (Richard Garland) when the merchant refuses to break state law and sell weapons without a background check. (Scenes like this one inspired critic Glenn Erickson to quip that *Panic* "could have been made as a sales booster for the gun industry.") Rick takes up arms again when, farther on up the road, Harry is threatened by three beatniks-turned-highwaymen. "We're the new highway patrol, dad. Somebody dropped a bomb … crazy kick," says one. Carl

(Richard Bakalyan), the leader of the hoodlums, grabs Harry's gun from the seat of the car and prepares to shoot him, only to be winged by buckshot from a shotgun leveled by Rick. Carl isn't seriously injured because Ann interferes, grabbing the weapon as Rick fires. Her misguided act of mercy allows Carl to survive and become an even greater menace later in the story.

In many respects, the film's most interesting character is Rick (played by teen idol Frankie Avalon), who enjoys this sudden catapult out of adolescence and into manhood. His father begins treating him like an equal, and he gets to do manly things like chop firewood, clean a deer, and (of course) carry a firearm. At times Rick seems like Pinocchio turned loose on Pleasure Island. After wounding Carl, he says, wonderingly, "I could have blown that guy's head off!"

"You liked it, didn't you?" Harry replies. "Then you're as wrong as they are. This is no deer hunt. I want you to use that gun if you have to, but I want you to hate it."

Despite Harry's admonitions, a major component in the film's appeal is the vicarious thrill of watching the Baldwin men simply take what they need and mete out vigilante justice when wronged. Harry, for instance, punches out a venal, opportunistic gas station

Panic in Year Zero! proposes that the consequences of limited atomic war will be a devolution of morality rather than an ascension to altruism. It's the sort of message Americans have never liked, but that has an unmistakable ring of truth. Throughout, much is made of demands placed on teenage Rick Baldwin (Frankie Avalon, right) by his father, Harry (Ray Milland), and Harry's insistence that Rick make the leap from boy to man—that is, to become a male able and willing to kill.

attendant who tries to overcharge for fuel. American International Pictures counted on the allure of these sequences, marketing the movie as a middlebrow think piece designed to leave viewers asking each other, "What would *you* do if the Bomb fell?" (Other than be vaporized or die of radiation sickness, that is.) AIP's brazenly exploitative trailer billed *Panic* as "the most shocking experience of your life! Doubly shocking because it *can* happen to you!" Print ads described the movie as the point "Where Science Fiction Ends and Fact Begins!!" and promised "An Orgy of Looting and Lust!" The back cover copy of Dean Owen's novelization of the film (published under the movie's alternate title, *End of the World*) promised "strange prey" for Rick's new rifle, rape for Karen, and "the beginning of an open season on plunder, murder and assault" for the world at large.

"Everything's gone, everything's changed, including me."

After an eventful trip into the California hills, the Baldwins finally arrive at Shibe's Meadow, where they promptly ditch the camper (which is too conspicuous a target and difficult to defend), hide the station wagon, and take up residence in a cave. Symbolically, at least, Harry has led his family back to the Stone Age. But it's an All-American, upper middle class Stone Age with all the comforts of home, including a picnic table for dining and cots for sleeping. (Harry is clearly a man who likes to be prepared. Who brings cots *and* a camper on vacation?) Ann prepares dinner by lantern-light. Harry prays over the meal, and a family discussion follows. "Maybe we can cope with this by maintaining our sense of values," Harry says. But his idea of values is "carrying on our daily routine as we always have," including continuing to shave every morning. "For the next few days we're going to have the kind of togetherness you never dreamed of," Harry says.

Despite their "togetherness," the rift between the (conservative) Baldwin men and (liberal) Baldwin women continues to widen. Harry and Rick seem in their element—hunting, tying fancy knots, and doing other merit badge-worthy Eagle Scout stuff. "Nothing like eating under an open sky, even if it is radioactive," Rick merrily opines. Yet the womenfolk remain sullen. Ann wants to band together with other survivors, but Harry is against it. He prizes self-reliance and eschews collaboration. Karen grows restive. "This whole thing is a bore," she whines. "It's such a drag!"

At Shibe's Meadow, the Baldwins are reunited with former adversaries—the hardware store owner, Ed Johnson (Richard Garland), who, along with Mrs. Johnson, has moved into Harry's abandoned camper; as well as Carl and the two other hepcat ruffians, who have taken up residence in a nearby farmhouse. At Ann's insistence, Harry makes an uneasy peace with Ed, but soon afterward discovers the Johnsons shot to death. The position of Mrs. Johnson's body suggests she was raped before being murdered. Harry and Rick immediately assume the three young hoodlums are the culprits but refrain from taking any action until two of the gang, Mickey (Rex Holman) and Andy (Neil Nephew), assault Karen. When they learn of Karen's rape, Harry and Rick track down the young perpetrators, and Harry summarily executes them with a shotgun. Although Harry later expresses regret ("I look for the worst in others and find it in myself," he laments), the film never seriously questions the righteousness of his actions.

Indeed, this incident proves to be a turning point in the attitude of the women, who suddenly come around to Harry's point of view. Perhaps the Baldwin gals realize that

Karen's rape, as well as multiple murders, might have been prevented if Ann had allowed Rick to gun down Carl a few reels earlier. Ann—heretofore the picture's personification of compassion and restraint—grabs a rifle and shoots at (but, being a woman, misses) the two young men who have just violated her daughter. Karen is toughened by the ordeal, as well. "Everything's gone," she says, "everything's changed, including me," she says. In the novelization, this transformation is even more overt: Prior to her rape Harry muses that Karen "looked grown up but maybe was still a child." Afterward he decides, "She was a woman now."

Harry and Rick also rescue teenage Marilyn (Joan Freeman) from the farmhouse, where she's been held captive and raped repeatedly, adding a third hardened, battle-ready female to the party. (Harry approves her as a potential mate for Rick in part because she knows how to handle a rifle.) Eventually, Carl comes looking for Marilyn, setting the film's final act in motion.

Panic in Year Zero!'s male leads are better sketched and more active than its docile female characters, who seem more like possessions than people. The women in this film exist solely to be protected or victimized by men. This may be chalked up to the generally patriarchal attitudes of the early 1960s, but in this context it plays like a further elaboration of the underlying political message, with the strong conservative men watching over the weak-kneed, liberal women. Through Harry's grave determination to keep his family together, *Panic* presents the family as the basic building block of civilization—a belief that still resonates. Harry also evidences unwavering faith in the government and the military, which are portrayed as all-wise and incorruptible, even though, presumably, their policies somehow led to the raging nuclear conflict. Early on, the voice of a radio announcer assures the Baldwins that "the organization of military and law enforcement is underway but will take time." No one expresses regret, or even ambivalence, over the idea that the U.S. responds to the attack with retaliatory strikes against "European and Asian targets," virtually assuring the destruction of human civilization as we have known it.

This is just one of many major issues that the film sidesteps. Unlike later post-apocalyptic thrillers, *Panic* depicts a relatively mild social upheaval. Film historian Bill Warren, in his seminal study of the genre, *Keep Watching the Skies!*, notes that *Panic in Year Zero!* is "played seriously, but also dodges many of the issues implied by the subject matter and ends on a highly inappropriate optimistic note.... By completely avoiding certain questions that would seem to arise—radiation sickness, decent folks gone bad, encounters with looting—the film almost makes it seem as though the nuclear war was a good thing." Warren could safely have removed the word "almost" from that analysis.

The movie also operates under the conviction that, even in a global nuclear war, the Forces of Freedom will inevitably triumph. The lone skeptical voice belongs to Dr. Strong (Willis Bouchey), a physician who attends to Rick toward the conclusion of the story.

"The war's over," Harry reports, adding enthusiastically. "We won!"

"Well, ding, ding for our side," Strong sneers in response.

"You have a twisted sense of humor," Harry sniffs, offended.

Later, the doctor warns the Baldwins to be careful. "Our country is still full of thieving, murdering ... *patriots*."

It's revealing that Dr. Strong is the only professional seen in this mildly anti-intellectual film, the only character whose attitudes were shaped by years of higher education. Perhaps not coincidentally, the Baldwins don't bring any books with them, and the only family member seen reading is Karen, who flips idly through a magazine shortly before being assaulted.

In the final scene, an American soldier—the film's unwavering symbol for the Powers of Good—offers a sort of benediction for the Baldwins as they pass by, on the way to a "relocation center." The soldier refers to the group as "five good ones." Although ostensibly he refers to the fact that the Baldwins show no signs of radiation sickness, the double meaning is clear: Here are five solid, red-blooded Americans. The picture concludes with a windy valedictory: "There must be no end, only a new beginning."

This can only be considered a happy ending. All the delinquents, pinkos, and sissies have been eliminated, either vaporized by the bombs, doomed by radiation poisoning, or shot like vermin by paragons the likes of Harry Baldwin. Not only has the war delivered victory to America, it has delivered America back to Real Americans. All of which makes *Panic in Year Zero!* the closest thing to a *pro*-nuclear war movie ever made in Hollywood. In Bob Dylan's chilling protest song "Masters of War," a vitriolic attack on the military-industrial complex written during the winter of 1962–63, he compares institutions to Judas, and takes exception to their contention that world war is winnable. Dylan could be singing about *Panic in Year Zero!*, which wants viewers to believe that not only can World War III be won, but that America would undoubtedly be the victor. Of course, it's harder to avoid a conflict once you convince yourself you have nothing to fear. If triumph is inevitable, why not fight?

"Frightened is a safe way to be."

Panic in Year Zero! was the penultimate directorial assignment for multitalented star Ray Milland. His previous efforts included three undistinguished features, a western and two low-rent crime dramas, all starring himself, and nine TV episodes, including the exceptional "Yours Truly, Jack the Ripper" installment of Boris Karloff's *Thriller*. He went on to direct the tepid thriller *Hostile Witness,* again starring himself, in 1968. Milland's direction of *Panic* is clean and punchy. He traffics in straightforward, unadorned storytelling, more in the style of a western than science fiction, but it serves the film effectively. The picture's B budget and compact shooting schedule didn't afford Milland or cinematographer Gilbert Warrenton the luxury of elaborate camera set-ups or other niceties. Les Baxter's brassy, jazzy score reinforces the film's essentially positive mindset.

Milland's work in front of the camera is similarly direct. His clipped, often exasperated delivery seems appropriate for the tightly wound Harry. The actor's performance is a little one-note, especially after his brilliant work in *The Uninvited* (1944), *The Lost Weekend* (1945), *The Big Clock* (1948), or even *X, the Man with the X-Ray Eyes* (1963)—but Harry Baldwin is a character practically devoid of nuance.

Avalon contributes the single best performance of his screen career, especially in contrast to his interchangeable beach party movie roles and irrelevant, do-nothing appearances in pictures like *The Alamo* (1960) and *Voyage to the Bottom of the Sea* (1961). Jean Hagen, who was so delightful as the tone-deaf Lina Lamont in *Singin' in the Rain* (1952), frowns a lot but has little else to do as Ann. Mary Mitchel, who would later appear in *Dementia 13* (1963) and *Spider Baby* (1968), leaves no impression whatsoever as Karen. Joan Freeman, a former child star whose lengthy career included projects with Vincent

Price, Elvis Presley, and the Three Stooges, mishandles the meaty role of Marilyn, but at least radiates some sex appeal.

The tone of *Panic in Year Zero!* is only slightly less feverish than that of *We'll Bury You!*, a Commie-bashing documentary released by Columbia Pictures later in 1962. Written by Jack W. Thomas, *We'll Bury You!* is a narrated collage of cleverly assembled film clips. Red-baiting advertisements claimed the film starred "the most infamous cast of characters ever assembled in one film," including Nikita Khrushchev ("World Enemy #1"), Fidel Castro ("Bearded Betrayer"), Josef Stalin ("Mass Murderer"), and Mao Tse-Tung ("Red China's Tyrant"). "Red ... or dead! The master plan of Communist terror that brought half the world to its knees," posters screamed. The picture's title, of course, was a reference to Soviet premier Nikita Khrushchev's famous, shoe-pounding United Nations diatribe. *We'll Bury You* was intended to frighten viewers—for their own good. As Harry tells Ann in *Panic*, "Frightened is a safe way to be."

For the most part, however, *Panic in Year Zero!* was an outlier in its tone and approach to the topic of nuclear war. It was markedly different in both content and form from the three other movie apocalypses released in 1962: the antiauthoritarian *This Is Not a Test*, an even lower-budget independent feature; *The Creation of the Humanoids*, an offbeat tale with post-apocalyptic scheming by evil robots; and French filmmaker Chris Marker's dystopian short film *La Jetee*. Previous Hollywood treatments of the subject—such as Columbia's *Five* (1951), MGM's *The World, the Flesh and the Devil* and especially United Artists's *On the Beach* (both 1959)—had been preachy and fatalistic. Foreign films such as the Yugoslavian *Atomic War Bride* (1960), the Japanese *The Last War* (1961), and the British *The Day the Earth Caught Fire* (1961), were equally downbeat. Only independently produced American exploitation pictures such as *Captive Women* (1952), *Day the World Ended* (1955), and *Last Woman on Earth* (1960) seemed to hold out any ray of hope for mankind's possible post-nuclear future. Only the much earlier *Invasion USA* (1952) could match *Panic* for unadulterated, Commie-loathing, pro-war zeal.

The era in which such belligerent, jingoistic films could find a sympathetic audience was fleeting. In the years ahead, movies about nuclear war became even darker and more cynical about human motivations, more pessimistic about the prospects for averting doomsday, and more horrific in their depictions of a post-nuclear landscape. *Ladybug Ladybug* (1963), *These Are the Damned* (1963/65), *Dr. Strangelove* (1964), *Fail-Safe* (1964), *In the Year 2889* (1967), and *Planet of the Apes* (1968) exhibit some or all of these qualities, as do later pictures such as *A Boy and His Dog* (1975), *Damnation Alley* (1977), and the Mad Max series. Even the gruesome *Night of the Living Dead* (1968) and the resulting zombie apocalypse genre could (at least initially) be read as a horrific metaphor for a post-nuclear age.

This shift in tone among apocalyptic movies reflected changes in the geopolitical landscape later in 1962 and '63. First-strike proponents such as Edward Teller and Curtis LeMay lost a great deal of support following the Cuban Missile Crisis, a white-knuckle fortnight of military and political brinksmanship that many feared would end in a nuclear conflagration. The crisis forced millions of Americans to seriously contemplate their potential annihilation. In the months following the crisis, U.S. Secretary of Defense Robert McNamara introduced the doctrine of Mutual Assured Destruction (often referred to by the eerily appropriate acronym MAD). This strategy deterred a first strike against the U.S. by deploying an array of virtually untouchable nuclear weapons potent enough to completely obliterate the Soviet Union and its satellite states. In the event of a nuclear attack and counterattack, nearly all human life on the planet would be obliterated. MAD was a logical, albeit horrifying, extension of the policy of "massive retaliation," a term coined by John Foster Dulles, President Dwight D. Eisenhower's secretary of state, in the 1940s. Ike vowed to nuke the Soviets if they invaded or launched rockets at America's European allies, including West Germany. In 1959, when the U.S. began to equip submarines with ballistic missiles, a second-strike nuclear force became practical. Previously, second-strike capability was limited to long-range bombers armed with nuclear warheads. A fixed number of such planes were kept constantly in the air so they would survive any first strike. (This tactic is depicted in both *Dr. Strangelove* and *Fail-Safe*.) However, submarine-based missiles represented a more credible threat, since they were both more powerful and harder to shoot down. Americans assumed that the Soviets would deploy an equivalent nuclear submarine force, all but assuring that any attack by *either* nation would result in the extinction of the human race. As a result, MAD deterred not only the Soviets but also conservative hardliners in the U.S. For Teller, LeMay, and the other Harry Baldwins of the world, the end was near.

Filmography

Panic in Year Zero!—American International Pictures; Released July 5, 1962; Black and white; 93 min.

   Credits: Producers: Arnold Houghland, Lou Rusoff; Director: Ray Milland; Screenplay: Jay Simms, John Morton; Director of photography: Gil Warrenton; Editor: William Austin; Music: Les Baxter; Art director: Daniel Haller

   Cast: Ray Milland: Harry Baldwin; Jean Hagen: Ann Baldwin; Frankie Avalon: Rick Baldwin; Mary Mitchel: Karen Baldwin; Joan Freeman: Marilyn Hayes; Richard Bakalyan: Carl; Rex Holman: Mickey; Richard Garland: Ed Johnson; Willis Bouchey: Dr. Powell Strong

Note

   1. Moore, *Lot & Lot's Daughter*.

Works Cited

Books

Clark, Mark, and Bryan Senn. *Sixties Shockers: A Critical Filmography of Horror Cinema, 1960–1969*. Jefferson, NC: McFarland, 2011.
Dobbs, Michael. *One Minute to Midnight: Kennedy, Khrushchev and Castro on the Brink of Nuclear War*. New York: Knopf, 2008.
Goodchild, Peter. *Edward Teller: The Real Dr. Strangelove*. Cambridge, MA: Harvard University Press, 2004.
Hardy, Phil, ed. *The Overlook Film Encyclopedia: Science Fiction*. Woodstock, NY: Overlook, 1991.
Moore, Ward. *Lot & Lot's Daughter*. San Francisco: Tachyon, 1996.
Sokolski, Henry D., ed. *Getting MAD: Nuclear Mutual Assured Destruction, Its Origins and Practice*. Carlisle Barracks, PA: Strategic Studies Institute, 2004.
Warren, Bill. *Keep Watching the Skies! American Science Fiction Movies of the Fifties, Volume II*. Jefferson, NC: McFarland, 1986.

Web

atomicarchive.com/Bios/Teller.shtml
dvdtalk.com/dvdsavant/s1571pani.html
imdb.com/title/tt0056331/
pbs.org/wgbh/amex/bomb/peopleevents/pandeAMEX61.html\

DVD

Midnite Movies Double Feature: Panic in Year Zero!/The Last Man on Earth. MGM. 2004

Video

We'll Bury You! Private collection.

About the Contributors

Anthony **Ambrogio** has written extensively for film magazines (*Video Watchdog, Midnight Marquee, Monsters from the Vault*) and film anthologies (*Eros in the Mind's Eye, We Belong Dead, Peter Lorre*). He edited and contributed to the books *Peter Cushing* and *You're Next! Loss of Identity in the Horror Film*.

Zsófia **Bodnár-Hamilton** (a pseudonym) is the daughter of Hungarian immigrants, and volunteers as a long-distance political advocate for Hungary and other nations in Central and Eastern Europe. Cinema studies at CUNY led her, circuitously, to audio-visual education and a Ph.D. in library science.

Mark **Clark** has been writing about classic movies and television programs the past twenty-five years. He is the author of numerous books, and has contributed reviews and essays to many books and magazines. In 2015, his reviews won a Rondo Hatton Award. Previously, he worked as a film critic at the *Louisville Courier-Journal*, and taught film history and genre theory.

Ermine **DeGraffenried** works at a Durham public relations firm focused on municipal budgeting and urban-education issues. She studied political science at Davidson College and Wake Forest University, and is doing graduate work in public policy at the University of North Carolina at Chapel Hill. She regularly programs screenings for clubs, groups, and public libraries across central North Carolina.

Bruce **Dettman** is a freelance writer whose film-related articles have appeared in *Fangoria, Scarlet: The Film Magazine, The Monster Times*, and *Filmfax*, among others. He has contributed essays on Lon Chaney, Jr., Vincent Price, and Peter Lorre to Midnight Marquee's *Acting Series* books. He also is the author of *Hoagy*, a play about the life of composer Hoagy Carmichael, and is editing an essay collection about Jekyll and Hyde.

David J. **Hogan** followed a stint as an entertainment journalist, magazine writer, and book editor in Los Angeles by settling in Chicago and working for nearly thirty years as an executive editor in book publishing. He has written half a dozen books about horror, film noir, and comedy films, and contributed essays to a variety of cinema titles.

Reynold **Humphries** is a former professor of film studies at the University of Lille 3, France, and the author of books about Fritz Lang, horror films, and the Hollywood blacklist, among other subjects. He has contributed essays on aspects of film noir and other topics to various edited collections and has been a member of the editorial board of *Horror Studies* since the journal's inception.

Lyndon W. **Joslin** is a thirty-year veteran of radio in Houston, Texas. He has done traffic, news, and conservative political commentary. He has also been a reporter and weekend news anchor for KTRH AM-740. His published film commentary includes *Count Dracula Goes to the Movies* and a pair of essays in *Science Fiction America*.

About the Contributors

Gaye Winston **Lardner** is a native Hawaiian and U.S. Army Captain (Ret.) who is pursuing a second career in music publishing and film studies. She is working on a book about the intersection of popular music and Hawaii in movies set on the islands.

Arthur Joseph **Lundquist** is an actor and playwright living in New York City. He portrayed a slasher in the 1990 horror film *Pledge Night*; the title scientist/monster in *The Regenerated Man* (1994); and a scientist abducted by aliens in *The Alien Agenda II: Under the Skin* (1997). He has contributed articles and essays to a number of publications about horror movies.

The late Mark A. **Miller** was the author of *Christopher Lee and Peter Cushing and Horror Cinema* and the coauthor (with Tom Johnson) of *The Christopher Lee Filmography*. He contributed essays to five Midnight Marquee Press anthologies and wrote for *Filmfax*, *Outré*, *Monsters from the Vault*, and *Shivers* magazines.

Ted **Okuda** is a Chicago-based film historian who has written and cowritten numerous books on film history. His articles, reviews, and interviews have appeared in *Filmfax*, *Nostalgia Digest*, *Cult Movies*, *Classic Images*, and *Classic Film Collector*. He has also appeared on *Chicago Tonight*, *The Today Show*, *The Three Stooges Stooge-A-Palooza*, and *Your Chicago Show*, and in *Jerry Lewis*.

Bryan **Senn** writes about cinema for such magazines as *Filmfax*, *Shivers*, and *Monsters from the Vault*. He is the author a number of books about film, including *The Werewolf Filmography*, *The Most Dangerous Cinema*, and *Sixties Shockers*. He has also contributed essays to myriad collections, including *Science Fiction America*.

John T. **Soister** has been writing about science fiction and horror films since the heyday of fanzines in the 1960s. Over the past couple of decades, he has written or cowritten numerous books about film history and contributed to edited collections. He is a retired teacher of modern and classical languages.

Steven **Thornton** is a writer and musician. His work has appeared in *Midnight Marquee*, *Monsters from the Vault*, and *Little Shoppe of Horrors*. When not writing about film or playing music, he works as an IT analyst for a major automotive firm.

Chase **Winstead** holds a master's degree in film studies from Texas State University at Dallas. He writes for film journals and was a contributor to *Science Fiction America*. When not writing or lecturing about genre movies, he runs Winstead Wrecking, a sixty-year-old family business that operates forty-five tow trucks from various locations around Dallas.

Index

Numbers in *bold italics* indicate pages with illustrations

Aaker, Lee 110
Above and Beyond (1952 film) 106
Addams, Dawn 181, *183*
Addy, Wesley *116*
Adler, Buddy 237
Adventure Road (TV series) 72
Agar, John 7, 55
Alaska 72, 74, 75, 196, 217
Albania 29
Albert in Blunderland (1950 animated cartoon) 122
Albritton, Louise 147
Aldiss, Brian 241
Aldrich, Robert 7, 115, 116, 133, 198
Alfred Sloan Foundation 119, 122
Allen, Lewis 133
Allied Artists 14, 52, 113, 197
American International Pictures 45, 245
American Releasing Corporation 45
Anderson, James 205
Andes, Keith 112
Andrews, Dana 155, 187, *188*, *191*, 199n5
Ankrum, Morris 48
Apocalypse Movies (book) 204
Arctic Manhunt (1949 film) 72, 75
USS *Arizona* Memorial 165
Arness, James 157, 160
Arnold, Kenneth 48
Artists and Models (1955 film) 89–*90*, 91–*92*, 93–98; comic book controversy 94–94; filmography 97
Artists and Models Ball 97
atomic bomb 2, 43, 63,70, 77, 106, 108, 122, 124, 198, 215, 217, 220
The Atomic City (1952 film) 110–11; filmography 111
The Atomic Kid (1954 film) 215
Atomic War Bride (1960 film) 248
Attack of the Giant Leeches (1959 film) 217
Autry, Gene 61–62
Avalon, Frankie *244*, 247

Bakalyan, Richard 244
Baker, Art 147
Balderston, John L. 226, 227, 228, 231n1
Balenda, Carla 81, 188
Barbera, Joe 120
Barker, Lex 100, 102, *103*
Barrier, Edgar 81, 188
Barry, Gene *44*, 45, 110
Barry, Joan 179
Bates, Harry 43
Bavier, Frances 41
Baxter, Les 247
Baylor, Hal 162
Beason, George Stewart 119–20
The Beast from 20,000 Fathoms (1953 film) 215
Beginning of the End (1957 film) 215
The Beginning or the End (1947 film) 106
Belafonte, Harry 204, 205, 207, 208, *209*, *211*
Belli, Melvin 125
Bells of Coronado (1950 film) 63–65, 66, 67, 70; filmography 70–71
Beneath the Planet of the Apes (1970 film) 108
Berghof, Herbert 225, *227*, 230
Berlin Express (1948 film) 195
Berlin Wall 2
Bernds, Edward 122, 215
Bernstein, Leonard 78
Bessie, Alvah 78
Beyond the Time Barrier (1960 film) 215
Bezzerides, A.I. 116, 133
Biberman, Herbert 78, 87n11
Bice, Robert 65, 217, 219
The Big Heat (1953 film) 238
Big Jim McLain (1952 film) 6, 111, 141, 150, 157–*59*, 160–*61*, 162–66; filmography 166; tokenistic casting 165
Bikini Atoll Baker test 203, 205
Birch, Paul 22, *24*, 26, *31*, 46
Birdwell, Russell 102, 105n4

Bisbee, Arizona 237
Bissell, Whit 113, 133
Black Dahlia murder case 131–32
Blaisdell, Jackie 46
Blaisdell, Paul 46
The Blob (1958 film) 30
Blythe, Erik 217
Boehm, Sydney 110, 233, 236, 237–38, 239
Bond, Ward 85
Bonestell, Chesley 40
Borg, Veda Ann 161, 166n4, 190
Borgnine, Ernest 153, 176, 236
Bouchey, Willis 229, 246
Bovee, Christian Nestell 141
Bowie, Stephen W. 168, 169
A Boy and His Dog (1975 film) 248
Bradley, Omar 201
Brady, Pat 64
The Brain Eaters (1958 film) 194, 196
The Brain from Planet Arous (1957 film) 30, 86
The Brain That Wouldn't Die (1959 film) 239
brainwashing 30, 31–32, 49, 54, 193
Brand, Neville 138
Breakston, George 125, 126, 127
The Bridge at Andau (book) 100
Bristol, Howard 144
Brocco, Peter 81
Brookings Institution 193
Bruce, George 147
Bryant, Bill 130, 132
Bubbeo, Daniel 231
Budapest, Hungary 25–26, 49, 99, 100
Bulganin, Nikolay (Nikolai) 104
Bulgaria 25, 29
A Bullet for Joey (1955 film) 130–31, 132–33; filmography 133
Bullet the Wonder Dog 67, 69, 70
The Bullwinkle Show (TV series) 5
Burr, Raymond 81, 83,147, 189

Cahn, Edward L. 55
Campos, Rafael *169*, 173

253

Canada 118
Canutt, Yakima 70
Captive Women (1952 film) 248
Carey, Olive 83
Carey, Phil 154
Carradine, John 55, 56
Carroll, Anne *31*
Castle, Peggie *v*, 7, 217, *219*, 220
Castle of Frankenstein (magazine) 230
Castro, Fidel 248
Ceausescu, Nicolae 25
Chapin, Billy 236
Chaplin, Charles 7, 178–*81*, 182, *183*–84, 185; FBI file 179; HUAC 179
Chaplin, Michael 181, 184
Chaplin, Oona O'Neill 180
Chaplin: Genius of the Cinema (book) 179
Chaplin Studios 180
Chasing Spies (book) 198
China 7, 29, 77, 120
China Gate (1957 film) 129
Chou En-lai 180
Chrysler Corporation 119
Churchill, Winston 2
CIA (Central Intelligence Agency) 3, 124
Cicero, Marcus Tullius 59
Clarke, Lydia 110
Clavell, James 137, 139
Cleary, Leo 64
Cliff, John *131*
Coates, Phyllis 220
Cohen, Herman 14, 16,18
Cold War, background 1–6, 8
Cole, Lester 78
Columbia Pictures 48, 108, 109, 122, 124, 143, 153, 204, 217, 220, 248
Comintern (Communist International) 164
Communist Party USA (CPUSA) 5, 8, 34, 128, 158, 163, 164, 194, 196
Condon, Edward U. 147
Condon, Richard 134
Connors, Mike "Touch" 46
Conrad, Mikel 72, *74*, 75
Conried, Hans 162, 166n6
Conroy, Frank 41
Coon, Gene L. 102
Cooper, Maxine 115, *116*
Corman, Roger 7, 25, 26, 27, 31, 35, 47, 204, 215
covert political activity by America 3
"The Creation" (poem) 207
Creation of the Humanoids (1962 film) 248
Creature with the Atom Brain (1955 film) 55
Crosby, Floyd 134
Crosby, Wade 217, 219
Crowley, Kathleen 15, *18*, *19*
Crowther, Bosley 147
The Crucible (play) 13, 14, 19
Cuban Missile Crisis 4, 203, 215, 241, 248

Cvetic, Matt 150, 151, 153, 196
Czechoslovakia 25; 1956 student revolt 25

Daily Express (London newspaper) 182
Daily Herald (London newspaper) 182
Daily Mail (London newspaper) 182
Daily Variety (Hollywood trade paper) 85
Damnation Alley (1977 film) 248
Dante, Joe 231
Darien, Frank 81, *84*, 189
Darvi, Bella 129
Daryll, Natalia *103*, 104
Da Silva, Howard 78
Dassin, Jules 185
Da Vinci, Elena 100
Davis, Joseph E. 179
The Day of the Triffids (novel) 241
The Day the Earth Caught Fire (1961 film) 248
The Day the Earth Stood Still (1951 film) 41–*42*, 43; filmography 43
Day the World Ended (1955 film) 3, 45–47, 204, 215, 248; filmography 47
"Deadly City" (short story) 13–14
Dein, Edward 113, 134, 135, 136
Dekker, Albert 116
de Kova, Frank, *112*, 134
Democratic Party 163, 164, 168–69
Denning, Richard 7, 15, *17*, *18*, 46
Dent, Vernon 122, *123*
Depar, Edwin 155
Derr, Richard 39
Desmonde, Jerry 181
Dexter, Brad 235
Dimitrov, Georgi 29
disaster drills 215
Dmytryk, Edward 6, 78, 190
Dr. Strangelove (1964 film) 215, 242, 248, 249
Dolenz, George 130
Doney, Jim 72
Donovan, King 50
Douglas, Gordon 143, 144,147, 155
Douglas, Susan 205, *206*
Driscoll, Luma 138
Dubov, Paul 46
Dulles, John Foster 249
Dylan, Bob 247
Dzhugashvili, Yakov 105n3

Earth vs. the Flying Saucers (1956 film) 48–49, 50, 55, 109; filmography 50
East Berlin 2, 3, 105n2
East Germany 2, 3, 77, 105n2
Edwards, Penny 59, 67, *68*
Egan, Richard 233, 238
Einstein, Albert 41, 122, 190
Eisenhower, Dwight D. 99, 190, 193, 227, 229, 249
Ekberg, Anita 91
Elam, Jack 198
Eldredge, John 54

End of the World (novel) 245, 246
England 106, 180, 181
Erickson, Glenn 243
Esmond, Carl 147
Essex, Harry 109
Evans, Charles 147
Evans, Dale 63, 64, *65*
Evening Standard (London newspaper) 183
Eyman, Scott 160

Fail-Safe (1964 film) 109, 215, 220, 248, 249
Fairman, Paul W. 13
Fapp, Daniel L. 89
FBI (Federal Bureau of Investigation) 5, 78, 146, 147, 149–50, 153, 179, 196, 197, 198
The Fearmakers (1958 film) 187–*88*, 189–*91*, 192–94, 197–200; filmography 199
Ferguson, Frank 147
Ferrer, Mel 205, *209*, *211*
Fine, Larry 122, *123*, 124
The First Yank in Tokyo (1945 film) 106
Five (1951 film) 108, 204, 205–*6*, 207–8, 211–12, 248; filmography 212
Five Gates to Hell (1959 film) 137–39; filmography 139
Fixed Bayonets! (1951 film) 129
Fleischer, Richard 233, 236, 238, 239
Fletcher, Bramwell 227
The Flying Missile (1950 film) 106
The Flying Saucer (1950 film) 72–*74*, 75; filmography 75; 1953 re-release campaign 75
Foran, Dick 187, *188*
Ford, Glenn 7, 168, *169*, *170*, 173
Ford, Henry 119
Ford Motor Company 119
Forrest, William 67
The 49th Man (1953 film) 108–10, 111; filmography 110
Fowler, Gene, Jr. 53
Fox, Michael 100
Fox theater chain 180
Francen, Victor 129
Freeman, Joan 246, 247–48
French Indochina 129, 134, 138
Friedhofer, Hugo 238
The Front (1976 film) 176
Fryer, Peter 26, 35, 36
Fuchs, Klaus 2, 77, 146
Fuelin' Around (1949 film) 122–23, 124; filmography 124
Fuller, Sam 126, 128, 129, 130, 200n18

Gabor, Eva 91
Gabor, Zsa Zsa 99, 100, *101*, 102, *103*
Gamble, Donald *237*
Garfield, John 78
Garland, Beverly 23, *24*
Garland, Richard 243, 245
Gates, Larry 52

Gaylor, Gerry 138
General Motors 118–19
Geray, Steven 130
German-American Bund 196
Gero, Erno 26
Gerry, Toni 131, 132
The Giant Behemoth (1959 film) 217
Gilmore, Art 137
Gilmore, Lowell 147
The Girl in the Kremlin (1957 film) 99–*101*, 102–*3*, 104–5; filmography 104
Glasser, Albert 128, 218
God 2, 34, 35, 38, 45, 206, 211, 225, 227, 229, 231
Gold, Harry 2
The Gold Rush (1925 film) 178
Goldfinger (1964 film) 108
Gomery, Donald 182
Gomulka, Wladyslaw 25, 29
Gordon, Roy 187, 191
Grahame, Gloria 238
Granby, Joseph 218
Graves, Peter 225, *226*, 227, 230, 231
Great Britain 3
The Great Dictator (1940 film) 178, 179
Greece 3
Green, Alfred E. 218
The Green Berets (1968 film) 165
Greenglass, David 2, 69–70, 77, 111
Grey, Virginia 15, *17*
Griffith, Charles B. 25, 26, 27, 35
Guilfoyle, Paul 173
Guilty by Suspicion (1991 film) 176
Guthrie, Carl 102

Hadley, Reed 144, 148n2
Hagen, Jean 243, 247
Haggerty, Don 67
Haida, Katsuhiko 126
Hall, Charles D. 229
Hall, Jack 158
Hall, Leonard 193
Hammett, Dashiell 78
Hanna, Mark 25, 26, 27, 35
Hanna, William 120
Hansen, Peter 39
Harbin, Vernon 78
Harding, James 119
Harding College (Arkansas) 119, 120, 122
Hardwicke, Sir Cedric 45
Harryhausen, Ray 48
Hart, Dorothy 150, 153–54, 155
Harvey, Laurence 193
Hatch, Robert 212
Hatton, Raymond 46
the Hawaii Seven (targets of federal probe of Hawaiian Communist activity) 158
Hawks, Howard 196
Hayes, Maggie 235
Hayward, Louis 143, *144*, 145, *146*, 147
Haze, Jonathan 23

Heath, W.L. 233, 239
Hell and High Water (1954 film) 128–30; filmography 130
Hernandez, Juano 173
The Hidden Persuaders (book) 192–93
High Noon (1952 film) 185
Himmler, Heinrich 104
Hiroshima, Japan 106, 203
Hiss, Alger 2, 48, 77, 185
Hitler, Adolf 1, 76, 83, 85, 86, 104, 105n2, 143, 179, 189, 194, 196
Hitler-Stalin Pact 169
Hoare, J.E. 227
Hoberman, J. 147
Hogan, David J. 122
Hollywood Anti-Nazi League 169
Hollywood Canteen (1944 film) 61
Hollywood Reporter (trade magazine) 230
the Hollywood Ten 78, 80, 170, 185, 190
Holman, Rex 245
Hoover, J. Edgar 5, 144, 146, 147, 148n3, 149–50, 179, 198
Hopper, Hedda 85, 180, 220
Hopper, Jerry 110
Horner, Harry 229, 231
House Committee on Internal Security 185
The House on 92nd Street (1945 film) 144–45
House Un-American Activities Committee (HUAC) 2, 5–6, 77, 78, 80, 87n11, 128, 143–44, 147, 150, 153, 157–58, 163, 176, 179, 181, 183, 184, 185, 192, 198, 214, 220
How to Survive an Atomic Bomb (book) 3, 5
Howard, Moe 122, *123*, 124
Howard, Shemp 122, *123*, 124
Hoxha, Enver 29
Hoyt, John 39, 173
Hughes, Howard 78, 79–80, 82, 84–85, 86, 87n7, n11, 185, 189, 197
Hungarian Tragedy (book) 26
Hungary 25–26, 29, 34, 35, 49, 99–100; 1956 Hungarian Revolution 25–26, 49, 99–100
hydrogen bomb 43–44, 110, 147, 150, 194

I Am Legend (novel) 208
I Am Legend (2007 film) 208
I Married a Communist (aka *The Woman on Pier 13*, 1949) 80
I Married a Monster from Outer Space (1958 film) 6, *53*–55, 86; filmography 55
"I Was a Communist for the F.B.I." (magazine series) 153
I Was a Communist for the F.B.I. (1951 film) 6, 85, 149–*51*, 152–*54*, 155–56, 196; filmography 155
I Was a Communist for the F.B.I. (radio series) 155
"If There Were Only Two Sur-

vivors of World War III Left on Earth" (magazine article) 208, 210
In Dubious Battle (novel) 170–71
In Like Flint (1967 film) 155
In the Year 2889 (1967 film) 248
Inouye, Daniel 163–64
International Longshore and Warehouse Union (ILWU) 158, 163
Internet Movie Data Base (imdb.com) 195, 204, 220
Invaders from Mars (1953 film) 196
Invasion of the Body Snatchers (1956 film) 11, 50–*51*, 52, 54, 86, 109, 133, 185, 196, 197, 198; filmography 52
Invasion USA (1952 film) *v*, 3, 109, 201, *216*, 217–*19*, 220–21, 248; filmography 221; stock footage 217–18
Invisible Invaders (1959 film) 55–*56*, 57; filmography 57
It Came from Beneath the Sea (1955 film) 215
It Came from Outer Space (1953 film) 196
Italy 3
Ives, Burl 78
Izuka, Ichiro 158

James, Sidney 184
Japan 13, 30, 124–25, 126, 127, 128; Communist Party 127, 128; domino effect 125; labor unions 125, 127; Occupation government 124, 125, 127; Tokyo 126–27
Jarrico, Paul 78, 80, 87n11
Jergens, Adele 46
Jet Pilot (1957 film) 165
La Jetee (1962 film) 113, 248
Jewell, Richard B. 78
John Sutherland Productions 120
Johnson, James Weldon 207
Johnston, Oliver 181, 184
Jones, Barry *107*
Jones, Carolyn 50
Jones, Gordon 67, 166n8
Jones, Morgan 24
Jurado, Katy *170*, 173

Kádár, János 100
Kallis, Al *47*
Kanawo, Jack 158
Katcher, Aram *101*, 218
Katzman, Sam 108, 109
Kazakhstan 124
Keep Watching the Skies! (book) 246
Kefauver, Estes 95
Kelley, Stanley, Jr. 193
Kelly, Paul *112*
Kendall, Kay 181
Kennedy, Arthur 168, *170*, 171, 173
KGB (Komitet Gosudarstvennoy Bezopasnosti) 8, 146

256 Index

Khrushchev, Nikita 3, *4*, 8*n*1, 25, 36*n*2, 48, 99–100, 104, 180, 248; Secret Speech 25, 36*n*2, 105*n*7
Kim il-Sung 29
King, Andrea 225, *226*, 230, 231
A King in New York (1957 film) 178, 180–*81*, 182–*83*, 186, 188; filmography 186
King of the Cowboys (1943 film) 62
Kiss Me Deadly (1955 film) 115–*16*, 117, 198; filmography 117
Kiss Me, Deadly (novel) 115
Knight, Shirley 138
Korean War 30, 49, 77, 124–25, 129, 134, 187, 188, 189, 194, 214
Kramer, Stanley 185
Kubrick, Stanley 242
Kulp, Nancy 138

Ladybug Ladybug (1963 film) 248
Lambert, Jack 198
Lampkin, Charles 207
Lardner, Ring, Jr. 78
The Last War (1961 film) 248
The Last Woman on Earth (1960 film) 215, 248
Lawson, John Howard 78, 190
Leachman, Cloris 115
Lee, Ann 173
Lee, Earl 207
Leigh, Janet 165
Leith, Virginia 235, 239
LeMay, Curtis 242, 248, 249
Lenin, Vladimir 29
Lewis, Jerry 6, *90*, 91, *92*, 93, 95
Lewis and Martin 6, *90*, *91*, *93*
Lifton, Robert Jay 30; *see also* brainwashing
Limelight (1952 film) 178–79, 180
Lincoln Memorial 218
Liu, Dan 164
Loeffler, Louis 238
Loews theater chain 180
Lords, Traci 35
Los Angeles Times (newspaper) 230
Losey, Joseph 78
"Lot" (short story) 241–43
"Lot's Daughter" (short story) 241–43
Lovejoy, Frank 7, *114*, 134, *151*, 153, *154*, 155
Low, David 108
Low, Jack 63
Ludwig, Edward 160, 165
Lydecker, Howard 62
Lydecker, Theodore 62

MacArthur, Douglas 127
MacDougall, Ranald 204, 211
MacLaine, Shirley *90*, 91, *92*
MAD (magazine) 208, 210
Mad Max film series 248
The Magazine of Fantasy and Science Fiction (*F&SF*; magazine) 241, 243
Mahoney, Jock 124
Mainwaring, Daniel 133, 197
The Majestic (2001 film) 176
Make Mine Freedom (1948 animated cartoon) 120–22; filmography 122
Malone, Dorothy 90
Maltz, Albert 78
The Man He Found (1951 lost film) 76, 80, 81, 84, 86
The Man He Found (script) 80
Man on a Tightrope (1953 film) 150
The Manchurian Candidate (1962 film) 193
The Manchurian Candidate (novel) 134
Manhattan Project 147, 242
Mankiewicz, Don M. 168, 169, 170, 171, 172, 175
Mankiewicz, Frank 168–69
Mankiewicz, Herman 168
Mankiewicz, Joseph 168
Manson, Maurice 100, *101*, 105*n*5
The Many Loves of Dobie Gillis (TV series) 5
Mao Zedong (Mao Tse-tung) 29, 77, 120, 248
Marijuana (1952 film, aka *La Droga Infernale*, Italian-release title of *Big Jim McLain*) *159*
Marker, Chris 248
Marlowe, Hugh 48
Marly, Florence *125*, 126
Marshall, George 93
Marshall, Mort 15, *17*
Martin, Dean 6, 89, *90*, 91, 92–93, 97
Martin, Lewis 44, 81
Martin, Pete 153
Martin and Lewis 6, *90*, 91, 93
Marvin, Lee 113, 134, *135*, 136, 235, *237*, 238, 239
"Masters of War" (song) 247
Matheson, Richard 208
Mature, Victor 7, 233, 238
Mayehoff, Eddie 94
Mazzei, Joseph 196–97
McCain, John 8
McCarthy, Joseph 2, 13, 16, 19, 77–78, 177, 185, 198, 214,
McCarthy, Kevin 11, 50
McCarthy, Nobu 138
McCarthyism 13, 184, 185, 194, 198
McGowan, Dorrell 125, 127
McGowan, Stuart 127
McGuire, Dorothy 168, 173
McIntyre, Christine *123*, 124
McMahon, David *154*
McNally, Stephen *112*, 235, *237*, 238
McNamara, Robert 248
Meeker, Ralph 115, *116*
Meet King Joe (1950 animated cartoon) 122
Menzies, William Cameron 80, 83–84, 85, 86, 187, 194
Metamorphosis (book) 28
Michaels, Dolores 138
Michener, James 100
Middleton, Robert *170*, 173
Milland, Ray 176, 223, 242, 243, *244*, 247

Miller, Arthur 13,14, 19, 78
Miller, Dick 26
Millican, James 152, *154*
Miracle from Mars (shooting title, *Red Planet Mars*) 230
Mission to Moscow (1943 film) 5
Mitchel, Mary 247
Mitchell, Cameron 129
Modern Times (1936 film) 178
Mohr, Gerald 109, 217, *219*
Molotov, Vyacheslav 104
Monsieur Verdoux (1947 film) 178, 179
Moore, Terry 113, *114*, 133, *135*, 136
Moore, Ward 241, 242
Morgan, Harry 157
Morgan, Red 236
Morris, Seymour, Jr. 127
Morton, John 243
Mostel, Zero 78
Motion Picture Production Code 92, 95, 240
Murrow, Edward R. 177
Musuraca, Nicholas 80, 83, 84, 85
Mutual Assured Destruction (MAD) 203, 204, 248–49

Nagasaki, Japan 203
Nagy, Imre 26, 99
Naish, J. Carrol 235, *237*, 238, 239
Nakamura, Tetsu 126
Napier, Alan 162
The Narrow Margin (1953 film) 238
NATO (North Atlantic Treaty Organization) 2, 134
Nazi Party (National Socialist German Workers' Party; NSDAP) 196
Nazis 83, 84, 86, 129, 143, 145, 169, 196, 197, 198, 208
Neal, Patricia *42*, 43
Neill, Noel 220
Nelson, Lori 7, 46
Nephew, Neil 245
The New Republic (magazine) 212
The New York Times (newspaper) 146, 147, 227, 230
Newcom, James 147
Newman, Kim 204, 206, 210, 212
Nibley, Sloan 66, 69
Night of the Living Dead (1968 film) 55, 248
Nineteen Eighty-Four (novel) 29, 107
Nixon, Richard 2, 169, 208
Nolan, Lloyd 149
Noonan, Tommy 235
Norris, Eddie *154*
North, Edmund H. 43
North Korea 29
Not of This Earth (1957 film) 21–*24*, 25–*31*, 32–37, 86; augmented TV prints 23; filmography 36; myth and folklore 28–29
Not of This Earth (1988 film) 35
Not of This Earth (1995 film) 35

Oboler, Arch 7, 204, 206, 211
O'Herlihy, Dan 217, 220
O'Keefe, Dennis 143, **144**, 145, **146**, 147, 155
Olson, Nancy 161, 166*n*3
O'Mahoney, Jacques *see* Mahoney, Jock
On the Beach (1959 film) 108, 109, 204, 208, 215, 248
On the Beach (novel) 204
Operation Paperclip 147
Operation Washtub 75
Oppenheimer, Robert 147, 190
Ornitz, Samuel 78
Orwell, George 29, 107
Otani, Reiko 126
Owen, Dean 245
Owens, Patricia 138

Packard, Vance 192–93
Pal, George 40, 43, 45, 215
Panic in Year Zero! (1962 film) 241–**42**, 243–**44**, 245–49; filmography 249
Paramount Pictures 40, 43, 53, 78, 93, 111, 129
Parker, Dorothy 78
Parker, Thomas A. 33–34; LAPD corruption 33
Patrick, Dorothy 236, **237**
Pauling, Linus 190
Pelly, Dudley 169
Perinal, Georges 184
Permanent Subcommittee on Investigations 185
Peyton, Robert 126
Phipps, William 205, **206**
Photographers Ball 97
Picerni, Paul 150
Pickup on South Street (1953 film) 129, 200*n*18
Planet of the Apes (1968 film) 248
Poland 25, 29; 1956 national strike 25
Polonsky, Abraham 78
Priestley, J.B. 182
The Purple Cloud (novel) 204–5, 206, 207, 212
Putin, Vladimir 8

Rabin, Jack 220
Raft, George 7, 130, **131**, 132, 133
Rákosi, Matyas 29
Raynor, William 14, 19
Reagan, Ronald 11
Realart Pictures 75
realpolitik 27–28
Red Channels (pamphlet) 6, 78
The Red Menace (1949 film) 190
Red Planet Mars (1952 film) 225–**26**, **227**–32; filmography 231
Reeves, Richard 15
Reid, Elliott 79, 80–81, 82, 83–**84**, 85, **195**
the Reluctant 39 (HUAC targets in Hawaii) 158
Rennie, Michael 41, **42**, 43
Republic Pictures 61, 62

Republican Party (aka GOP) 193, 198
Reuther, Walter 119
Reyher, Ferdinand 204
Riders of the Purple Sage (singing group) 64
RKO Radio Pictures 76, 78–79, 80, 82, 87*n*7, 147, 180, 189 *see also* Hughes, Howard
The RKO Story (book) 78
RKO theater chain 180
Roan Group 14
Roark, Robert 15
Roberts, Arthur 35
Roberts, Roy 150
Robeson, Paul 185
Robinson, Ann 44
Robinson, Edward G. 78, **131**, 132
Robinson, George 144
Robson, Mark 168, 172
Rocketship X-M (1950 film) 218
Roerick, William 23
Rogers, Roy 6, 59, 61–**65**, 66–**68**, 69–71
Romania 25, 29, 99
Rosenberg, Ethel 2, 34, 48, 69, 77, 164
Rosenberg, Julius 2, 34, 48, 69, 70, 77, 146, 164
Rubin, Stanley 76, 80–81, 83, 84–85, 86, 87*n*20, *n*25
Russia, post-USSR 7, 8, 34, 58

St. Maximilian Kolbe 223
Saitô, Tatsuo 126
Salt of the Earth (1954 film) 185
Sarris, Andrew 182
Sartre, Jean-Paul 26
The Saturday Evening Post (magazine) 153
Schallert, William 100, 102
Schary, Dore 79
Schneer, Charles H. 109
Sears, Fred F. 109
Seduction of the Innocent (book) 94–95
Semipalatinsk test site, Kazakh SSR (now Kazakhstan) 124
Seven Days to Noon (1950 film) 106–**7**, 108, 111, 112; filmography 108
Shack Out on 101 (1955 film) 113–**14**, 115, 133–**35**, 136–37, 153; filmography 115, 137
Shayne, Konstantin 152
Shayne, Tamara 145
Shiel, M.P. 204, 205, 207, 212
Short, Elizabeth 131
Shute, Nevil 204
Sidney, Sylvia 235, **237**
Siegel, Don 50, 51, 52, 185, 194, 197, 198
Silver Legion (aka Silver Shirts) 169
Silvermaster spy ring 48
Simms, Jay 243
Sinclair, Upton 179
Sloan, Alfred P. 118
Small, Edward 143, 146
Smith, Will 208

Smith Act 158
Sons of the Pioneers 61, 63
South Korea 3, 8, 77
Soviet satellite states *see* Albania; Bulgaria; Cuba; Czechoslovakia; East Germany; Hungary; Kazakhstan; Poland; Romania; Warsaw Pact
Soviet Union 1, 2, 3, 7, 8, 16, 29, 35, 56, 57, 70, 73, 75, 77, 96, 99, 100, 104, 124, 134, 164, 179, 188, 194, 197, 199*n*8, 225, 229, 230, 242, 248; breakup 7, 29, 57, 96; 1949 A-bomb test 77, 124
Spillane, Mickey 115, 133
Spionaggio atomico (1955 film, Atomic Espionage; Italian-release title of *A Bullet for Joey*) 133
Split Second (1953 film) 111–**12**, 113, 238–39; filmography 113
Spoilers of the Plains (1951 film) 59, 67–**68**, 69–71; filmography 71
Sputnik 199*n*8
Stainback, Ingram 157
Stalin, Josef 1, 2, 25, 29, 36*n*2, 44, 100, 101, 102–4, 105*n*2, 105*n*3, 105*n*6, 194, 248
Stalin Archives 34
Stalinism 34, 35
Stanwick, Michael 242, 243
The Steel Helmet (1951 film) 129
Steinbeck, John 170
Sterling, Jan 112
Stevens, Inger 205, **209**
Stevens, Onslow 147
Stone, Jeffrey 100
The Stooge (1952 film) 93
Storm Center (1956 film) 185
Stout, Archie 165
Studebaker 119
Suez Crisis of 1956 100
Sunday Times (London) 182
Sutherland, John 120, 122

Talbott, Gloria 54
Tarantino, Quentin 61, 66
Target Earth (1954 film) 6, 13–**17**, **18**, 19–20, 86; filmography 19–20
Tashlin, Frank 7, 89–90, 91, 93, 94, 95, 96, 97; animation career 93; censorship 95
Taurog, Norman 93
Taylor, Joan 48
Teasdale, Sara 205
Technical University of Budapest 100
Technicolor 89, 120, 126
Télérama (magazine, Paris) 197
Teller, Edward 242, 248, 249
Territory of Hawaii 157–58, 163–64; Communist labor agitation 157–58; federal raids 158; Molokai leper colony 163
Terror from the Year 5000 (1958 film) 215
Them! (1954 film) 147, 155, 215
Theoharis, Athan 198

258 Index

These Are the Damned (1963 film) 113, 248
The Thing from Another World (1951 film) 80, 109, 196
This Is Not a Test (1962 film) 248
Thomas, Jack W. 248
Thordsen, Kelly 190
Three Brave Men (1957 film) 153, 176
The Three Stooges 6, 122–*23*, 124
Time (magazine) 158
The Time Machine (1960 film) 215
Tokyo, Japan 126–27
Tokyo File 212 (1951 film) *125*–28; filmography 128
Tokyo Metropolitan Police 125
Tonge, Philip 55
Torey, Hal *56*
Torme, Mel *188*, 192
Tors, Ivan 109
Totter, Audrey 131
Tourneur, Jacques 187, 188, 194, 195
Treaty of Versailles 124, 196
Trial (1955 film) 6, 149, 150, 168–*69*, *170*–77; filmography 177
Trial (novel) 168, 170–73, 174, 175, 176; 1955 Harper prize 168
Trigger, the Smartest Horse in the Movies 61, 62, 63, 64, 66, 67, 69, 70
Trucolor (color process) 63
Truman, Harry 77, 78, 124, 127, 165, 194
Trumbo, Dalton 6, 78, 190
The Truth About Communism in Hawaii (pamphlet) 158
Tryon, Tom 53, 54
20th Century-Fox 237
20th Party Congress (Soviet Union) 25, 36n2, 105n7
The Twilight Zone (TV series) 215

Under Nevada Skies (1946 film) 63
United Artists 248
United Nations General Assembly 99
U.S. allies *see* Canada; England; France; Great Britain; Greece; Italy; Japan; NATO; South Korea; West Germany
U.S. Army 125, 129, 146
U.S. Army Far East Command 125
U.S. Capitol (Capitol Building) 48, 109, 217, 218

U.S. Department of Defense 125
U.S. State Department 2, 77
U.S. Strategic Air Command 242
U.S. Supreme Court 6, 78
Universal-International 102
Untamed Women (1952 film) 75
USSR (Union of Soviet Socialist Republics) *see* Soviet Union

Vance, Jeffrey 179
Van Eyck, Peter 131
Van Zandt, Philip 122, *123*, 147
Variety (Hollywood trade magazine) 147, 230
VCI Video 14
Vellier, Anthony 226, 228
Verona project 146
Vietminh 138
Village Voice (New York City newspaper) 182
Violent Saturday (1955 film) 6, 233–*34*, 235–*37*, 238–40; filmography 240
Violent Saturday (novel) 233, 239–40
VistaVision 89
Vitale, Joseph *131*

Walk a Crooked Mile (1948 film) 143–*44*, 145–*46*, 147–48; filmography 148
Walk East on Beacon (1952 film) 190, 197
Wallis, Hal 93
Walt Disney Productions 120
The War of the Worlds (1953 film) 16, 43, *44*,45, 49, 55; filmography 45
The War of the Worlds (novel) 45
Warner, Jack 5
Warner Bros. cartoon unit ("Termite Terrace") 93, 119, 122
Warren, Bill 246
Warren, Earl 197
Warrenton, Gilbert 247
Warsaw Pact 2, 26, 134
Wayne, John 7, 85, 111, 141, 157, *159*, 160, *161*, 163, 164, 165
Wayne-Fellows Productions 157, 166n1
Weaver, Tom 227, 231n2
Webb, Richard 154
Weiler, A.W. 230
We'll Bury You! (1962 film) *4*, 248
Welles, Orson 78, 80, 185

Wells, H.G. 45
Wertham, Fredric 94–95
West Germany 134, 249
When Worlds Collide (1951 film) 39–41; filmography 40–41
The Whip Hand (1951 film) 76–*82*, 83–*84*, 85–88, 150, 187, 188–89, 194–*95*, 196–98; filmography 87, 199
Whitman, Gayne 162
Why Play Leap Frog? (1949 animated cartoon) 122
Widmark, Richard 129
Wiig, Jon 158
Wilbur, Crane 152
Willing, Foy 64
Wilson, Cecil 182
Winslow, George "Foghorn" 96
Wise, Robert 7, 43
Withers, Grant 63, 67, *68*
Witney, William 66, 69
The Woman on Pier 13 (aka *I Married a Communist*, 1950) 80, 150, 190
World Peace Council 180
The World, the Flesh and the Devil (1959 film) 108, 204–*9*, 210–*11*, 212–13, 248; filmography 212; racial theme 208, 210–11
World War III 203, 204, 208, 210, 241, 247
World War II 1, 2, 7, 13, 55, 77, 82, 86, 95, 105n2, n3, 124, 127, 129, 139, 143, 146, 149, 157, 160, 163, 171, 185, 196, 198, 214, 217
World Without End (1956 film) 215
Wright, Richard 78
Writers Guild 80
Wyndham, John 241
Wynn, Keenan 113, 133, 135, 136
Wynorski, Jim 35
Wynter, Dana 50

Yakovlev, Anatoly 70
Yates, Herbert Y. 62
York, Michael 35
Young, Clifton 63

Zhou Enlai *see* Chou En-lai
Zinnemann, Fred 185
Ziv, Frederick 155
Zugsmith, Albert 101–2, 220

www.ingramcontent.com/pod-product-compliance
Lightning Source LLC
Chambersburg PA
CBHW081547300426
44116CB00015B/2789